WENG'S CHOP

Editorials	2
IN MEMORIUM: JESÚS FRANCO 1930-2013	3
BOW YOUR HEADS, Russell S. Doughten Jr Interview	7
RAPTURESPLOITATION: The Quartet of Terror	12
CARDONA-MANIA	16
It Came From MEXPLOITATION	18
Haunting Career of MARY MENDUM	21
MEXICAN MONSTERS ON PARADE, Pt. 1	23
THE INCUBUS	25
POSSESSION: ONE MAN'S THERAPY	27
FROM JAKARTA WITH LOVE	39
The Contributors	42
REVIEWS!	43
SEVEN DEADLY SYNTHS	62
SIMON, KING OF THE WITCHES	63
CULT CINEMA UNDER THE GUN	66
DANCING YETI Interview!	70
SNAKES ALIVE! Indian Films, Part 4	72
The Bookshelf	99
Literary Reprint: MONSTER! INTERNATIONAL	103
Literary Reprint: VIDEO VOICE: Michael Weldon Interview	114
The WC CrossWord	117

Front Cover: Jesús Franco
Back Cover Art: Franco montage

April 2013

Brian Harris, Editor & Publisher
Timothy Paxton, Editor & Design
Tony Strauss, Assistant Editor
Special thanks: Cara Romano

WENG'S CHOP is published quarterly. © 2013 Wildside Publishing / Kronos Productions. All rights reserved. No part of this publication may be reproduced, distributed, or transmitted in any form or by any means, including photocopying, recording, or other electronic or mechanical methods, without the prior written permission of the publisher, except in the case of brief quotations embodied in critical reviews and certain other noncommercial uses permitted by copyright law. For permission requests, write to the publisher, addressed "Attention: Permissions Coordinator," at the address below. 4301 Sioux Lane #1, McHenry, IL 60050, United States

wengschop@comcast.net

Volume #1 / Issue #3 / 1st Printing, Cover C

A WORD FROM THE EDITORS...

THAT'S NOT A UFO, MAN. IT'S A BOOGER ON YOUR GLASSES!

• Brian Harris (Co-Editor)

To start things off right I figured I'd quote a little something from Buddha,"Going bareback seemed like the right thing to do at the time but now I'm feeling a little insecure. Are you absolutely sure you're clean?"

Okay, I lied, that wasn't Buddha. You thought it was going to be some deep shit though, right? It's all about perception and perception is generally subjective. What I see as "good" may be perceived as garbage by others. That's their right, as it is mine, it's how we see the world around us. So when I tell you that this magazine is amazing, I believe with every ounce of my being that it is. Cover to cover, it's filled with passion and sacrifice, it's a living, breathing work of art. You may not see the same thing as you leaf through the pages, quickly glancing at articles, reviews and pictures, but take a moment to truly SEE what has been created here. From nothing, there is something.

Like a phoenix rising from the ashes, both creation and destruction are integral parts of life. From one thing often comes another. This issue marks a bittersweet period in my life in which I bid Wildside Cinema farewell and Weng's Chop welcome. It's sad to see something you've put so much hard work into go but from it something new has emerged. That's how I know this magazine is amazing. I hope you all enjoy issue #3.

P.S. It really was a booger. HAPPY HOLIDAYS!

http://boxsetbeatdown.blogspot.com

ENTHUSIASTIC WANNABE AUTHOR OF OBTUSE BULLSHIT...

"You are no more than an enthusiastic wannabe author of obtuse bullshit" was one remark that has always stuck in my head. That was from a letter I received after publishing MONSTER! INTERNATIONAL #2. I won't tell you who wrote that poison pen, but it was from an editor of a well-known fanzine back in the heydays of the 1990s. I wasn't insulted, and probably chuckled over the comment. Why? Well, because I had hoped than my excitement over discovering weird films would pop out of the pages. Yea, I am not the most amazing writer, but I've never crowed about it either. I suck as a word editor. Give me a 'zine to design or subject to research and I'm happy. Trying to work with words...man, that's tough; Dave Todarello would curse and scribble "rewrite" on many of the article and reviews I would pen for VIDEO VOICE, MONSTER! or MONSTER! INTERNATIONAL. Dave was a damn good editor, as is Tony Strauss who stepped up to the plate to help out with this issue.

The best thing about Weng's Chop is that our authors can write on just any genre. I really don't care if it's as broad as "The History of Zombies in World Cinema" or as esoteric as the "The Psychological Impact of Shirley Temple on the Rights of Redheaded Childhood Stars"—if it sounds like it'll be a fun read, well then go ahead and write it. I am very guilty of forcing articles on readers that feature movies that I know a lot of folks just don't give a shit about. They are usually rare or obscure gems that I had to dig deep into The Cloud to find, or happened to come across it on sale at an "ethnic" grocery store in their gift isle. I mean, how many of you really want a 25-page spread on Indian Cobra Lady films? But again, that's why Brian and I work hard to get this zine out four times a year. We love the stuff most snotty cinema buffs would normally poo-poo.

• Tim Paxton (Co-Editor)

This issue is a fine example of what I like in a fan-based film 'zine: diversity. WC has a lot to offer these days: film reviews, to informative articles, book, zine, and music coverage, classic reprints, and even a crossword puzzle. Sure, the majority of the magazine wallows in murky waters of "Psychotronic" cinema, but, heck, that's just who we are.

Weng's Chop is all about discovering film. And writing about it. More to come!

Over 3,000 of the wildest movies ever made!! Hundreds of rare illustrations!!

My worn, torn and taped up copy of the 1983 original edition.

IT'S BEEN 30 YEARS OF PSYCHOTRONIC CINEMA!

Check out the 1988 interview with Michael J. Weldon on page 114 of this issue of Weng's Chop!

If you're in the Auguata area why not patronize Weldon's store:

**Psychotronic Retail Store
859 1/2 Broad St.
Augusta, Georgia 30901**

The 1996 edition

IN MEMORIUM:
JESÚS FRANCO 1930-2013

"Two years before Jack Hill ventured into the Philippines for Roger Corman, Spanish director Jesús Franco transformed the Hollywood Women-in-Prison melodramas into an exploitation gold mine of sleaze and brutality with **99 WOMEN** (1969). Jesús would return to the genre often directing **LOVERS OF DEVIL'S ISLAND** (1974), **BARBED WIRE DOLLS** (1975), **WOMEN BEHIND BARS** (1975), **WOMEN IN CELL BLOCK 9** (1977), **ILSA, THE WICKED WARDEN** (1977), **LOVE CAMP** (1977) and **SADOMANIA** (1980). These are the Franco films that have inspired me. Not just for their creative depictions of physical tortures but the deep levels of psychological cruelty; a recurring Sadean theme that runs throughout his entire body of work. I have cursed and cheered more Jess Franco films than all other directors combined. He's a genre unto himself and I will remain not only a fan but a Jesús Franco fanatic." - *James Bickert (dir. DEAR GOD NO!)*

"With the passing of his flesh into the smoke and ash he loved so much, Jess Franco has moved beyond being a filmmaker and takes his place as a legend. His name is now a genre, because no matter who takes pulp, porn, phantasms and flesh and mixes them into one short sharp shot of cinema, they will never be able to do it the way Jess Franco did. I'll bet Lina was waiting with her wigs, a camera, a pack of cigarettes and that one script they never got to film. It's going to be a wild afterlife and I hope I get to see it with them." - *David Zuzelo (Tomb It May Concern)*

"Jess Franco, you certainly were loved. But then, all of the truly unique filmmakers of our time are to some degree—it just usually takes awhile for them to be recognized. Your work in cinema, as expansive as it was, proved at times to be outrageous and breathtaking, especially when it combined sex and death in such an artistic and compelling way. You influenced an entire generation of genre filmmakers, and ended up as perhaps the ultimate example of a filmmaker who proved that using words like "good" or "bad" to talk about movies is totally irrelevant and nothing but a matter of perception. Thank you for creating a body of work that I will enjoy unearthing and pouring through for decades to come after your passing." - *Robin Bougie (Cinema Sewer Magazine)*

"Miss Muerte has claimed her final victim, but the legacy will forever live on. R.I.P. Mr. Franco." - *Jeff Goodhartz (Far Reaching Films)*

"Have a drink on you, Jess." - *François Gaillard (dir. LAST CARESS)*

"Thank you for creating on screen some of very taboos that come to reveal the curious nature of the human mind. Your films always challenge the audience to think outside and beyond. Your work lives on." - *David 'DB3' Barnes*

"They tell me Jess Franco's dead. Don't believe it for a minute. Go on. Rifle through your DVD collection and pop in **VENUS IN FURS**. Or **A VIRGIN AMONG THE LIVING DEAD**. Or **VAMPYROS LESBOS**. Or **BLOODY MOON**. Go on, even throw **DEVIL HUNTER** in and give it a watch. Then tell me that Jess Franco's dead." - *Ryan Carey (Trash Film Guru)*

"One of my favorite Spanish madmen died today and a era in Spanish cinema has ended. I hope he's joined his muse and lover, Lina, and the stunning Soledad Miranda in Heaven so they can all meet Howard Vernon for drinks and to catch up on old times." - *Steven Ronquillo*

"From the grand masterpieces to the really cheap ones, they all have that one moment of brilliance. That unique fragment of Franco magic that makes it all worthwhile. The films of Jess Franco have always been there, and they always will be. The visionary, the artist, the auteur, the jazz musician, the prankster, the lover, the victim, the storyteller, the jester, the writer, the director, the editor, the filmmaker, the master. This is the only Jesus I will ever believe in." - *Jason Meredith (Cinezilla)*

"Goodbye, Jess. Although I didn't know it at the time, Jess Franco was one of the first directors whose films I sought out. The lurid box art caught my eye much quicker than many of the other more familiar film titles I saw on the shelves during my trips to the many video rental stores I lurked about at as a teen. Titles like **A VIRGIN AMONG THE LIVING DEAD, DEVIL HUNTER, THE DEMONS** and **BARBED WIRE DOLLS** were some of the first films I rented as a young impressionable boy let loose on his own. When I was older and more well-read, I learned who was behind these dreamlike collections of sex, violence, and zoom lenses, and I would continue to seek out his work. While I would never say Jess was one of my favorite directors I have always been fond of him and his cinematic cocktails of smut, and am sad that his journey has ended." - *Mike Haushalter*

"As much as Jesús 'Jess' Franco gained notoriety throughout circles for creating films that scraped the bottom of the barrel, his name held meaning for a greater reason. It was almost impossible to avoid the influence that Jess cultivated, not only in regards to Spanish film, but throughout the realms of exploitation cinema itself. Jess Franco was one of the principal key figures in the development of the Spanish horror genre in the 1960s, in the face of absolute resistance from a conservative restrictive government. Regardless of political restraints Jess stuck to his guns, and followed through with his convictions, government opinion be damned.

"Going back from his *Fu Manchu* films (**THE BLOOD OF FU MANCHU, THE CASTLE OF FU MANCHU**) through his take on *Dracula* with Christopher Lee, and Klaus Kinski, Franco showed that he was capable of expressing more than just his infatuation with sexual perversity. He was also a horror director that not only made his indelible mark in the industry, but also indirectly kicked countless numbers of metaphoric asses, compelling many to go forward to create their own films. Even without knowing his name, Franco's style and form was unmistakable, and his work was like liver and onions—in the sense that you could either take it or leave it. Fans of Franco's work were rewarded with a rich filmography that spanned several decades, and he worked practically right up until his passing. While pegged by some as 'the king of the crap', Jess Franco was first and foremost a filmmaker, and someone with a true passion for cinema. Jess was also one of us, and paved the perverted path for all of us to follow. Cheers to you Maestro, may you rest in Peace with Lina." - *Tim Merrill*

"With nearly two hundred films tackling virtually every genre, the legendary Jess Franco has left us with countless fond movie memories, and his distinct style will never be duplicated. May you rest in peace and work that zoom lense in the great beyond, reunited with your muses." - *Daniel Schein (Creep Show Radio)*

"Dear Jess Franco, Thank you for making **A VIRGIN AMONG THE LIVING DEAD** for me. It is my favorite movie. Say hello to Lina for me. I miss you both." - *Douglas Waltz*

"In 1972, I was fortunate enough to "work" at a drive-in with Howard, the projectionist. He was an avid fan of Eurotrash, and would fill the drive-in screens with Jess' films. That's where I first saw the triple-feature of **THE DIABOLICAL DOCTOR Z**, **99 WOMEN**, and **VENUS IN FURS** in all their glory. Howard also had a theater in his home, so I also got to see **EUGENIE**, **COUNT DRACULA** and **VAMPYROS LESBOS**...Did I mention all these films were seen in a marijuana haze??...I didn't think so. I am so proud of the fact that Jess Franco was one of the people who forever warped the mind of an impressionable 14-year old. I am blessed that he came into my life....I'm still not normal after over 40 years. RIP Jess." - *Karl Kaefer*

"Goodbye to Jess Franco. We will miss him." - *Sci-Fi Ninja Theater*

"Jess Franco will most definitely be remembered...how he is to be remembered is up to the individual. Many people did not "get" the kinds of films he made...but that matters little with his career of almost 160 films! He contributed so much to countless exploitation film variations. And yes, he as well as his many other male counterparts made violent, perverse, graphic, sexual & sadomasochistic films featuring women...but Franco's films always stood out because unlike other filmmakers who depicted the women in their pictures to be weak, he depicted them to be strong-willed, powerful & yes even beautiful...a triple-threat if you will; It was the man who was often the weaker sex. The female characters were the *foundation of* the film, not simply to be *used for* the film. I guess it is fitting in a way that he suffered his stroke the day after his last film premiere...At least he did get to see it. And at least now he will be with his long-time partner & muse of many of his films, Lina. This particular woman writing this will remember him as being a true one-of-a-kind artist who respected the women in his films. Yes, I did enjoy them immensely—in a Franco film the woman could do & be it all while the men tended to be the submissives. Most would say "Rest in Peace" but I say "Rock On, Jess Franco!" - *Rebecca Long*

"My familiarity with Mr. Franco is a little lacking when compared to others, but that doesn't mean he wasn't of great interest to me. I had (and still have) tons of respect for the man. How many people get to direct far over 100 films in their lives? My first encounter with his work was with **OASIS OF THE ZOMBIES**. I (obviously) didn't care much for it and I was ready to write off Jess Franco as another two-bit hack. Then, I saw his wonderful adaptation of Bram Stoker's *Dracula* with Christopher Lee and Herbert Lom and started to feel that there was a lot more to this guy. I soon afterwards purchased **DRACULA, PRISONER OF FRANKENSTEIN** and had a total blast with it. I even really enjoy **DEVIL HUNTER** and **MANSION OF THE LIVING DEAD**. Franco was able to mix horror with soft core pornography and somehow make it seem less sleazy than most directors would make it look (I'm looking at you, D'Amato...). You can trash him all you want, but the man was a true artist and a true film maker. I'm sorry for ever having any doubts about your work, Mr. Franco. You were one of the good ones. R.I.P. (P.S. I must sadly say that I have never seen **FEMALE VAMPIRE** or **THE AWFUL DR. ORLOFF**, but they are on my to-buy list and I shall be seeing them soon.)" - *Seb Godin*

"For more than six decades Jess Franco provided audiences with some of the most original and startling images ever committed to film. Despite this Franco was a classic case of an artist who faced more ridicule than acclaim in his lifetime, due to his uncompromising and unbelievably unique visions. My early memories of discovering Jess Franco in the 'Nineties, via Tim Lucas' *Video Watchdog* and the Tohill and Tombs book *Immoral Tales*, are a blur of trading fuzzy grey market VHS copies with friends of his then-hard-to-find films that we had gotten from companies like Midnight Video, European Trash Cinema, Video Search of Miami and Luminous Film and Video Werks. The highlight of my experience of discovering and falling in love with Franco's world in my twenties was getting to actually meet Jess and Lina at a Chiller Theater Convention in New Jersey in the mid-'Nineties. I still remember the long drive up from Kentucky fuelled by narcotics, Elvis Costello and the realization that I would soon be shaking hands with one of the most important artists cinema had ever known. The line to meet Jess and Lina was long but nobody minded waiting. Ironically, I ended up standing next to Craig Ledbetter, the man who had shipped me so many tapes from his European Trash Cinema. Lina was charming, sweet, kind…a real ray of light that made everyone feel instantly welcome. Jess was a bit gruff, seeming simultaneously confused and intrigued by the attention being showered on him. With Lina I shared conversation, with Jess just a handshake but I saw a hint of a smile that I will never forget. It was a wonderful, wonderful day. The loss of Jess Franco is heartbreaking but the thought of him back together with his two greatest muses, Lina and Soledad, in a sweet, distant otherworld should bring us all comfort. We love and miss you Jess and thank you for your great mad genius and spirit." - *Jeremy Richey*

"I'm terrible at eulogies. I'm never quite sure what to say—how do you sum up a life in a few sentences? Especially one as full and colorful as Franco's. But my friend Jonathan D. Cox said the following over at the A/V Maniacs forum, and I can think of no better way to put it: "He lived life doing what he loved alongside the woman he loved. That, my friends, is the very definition of a successful life." We should all be so lucky! Adios, Jesús!" - *Jared Auner*
"R.I.P. director, producer, writer, composer Jess Franco (1930-2013), who just passed from a stroke on April 2nd. Although I have not seen many of his nearly 200 directed films, I have been a fan of the noted films he made with actor Christopher Lee: **THE CASTLE OF FU MANCHU, THE BLOOD OF FU MANCHU**, and **THE BLOODY JUDGE**. Your memory will live on in celluloid for decades to come." - *Chris Broadstone (Black CAB Productions)*
"We are very sad at the passing of Jess Franco." - *Obulious Toobach & The Staff of Unwatched, Unboxed and Reviewed*

"A PENIS FOR THREE, A BUTTCRACK FOR TWO and nearly 200 films for you and me. If there were a lesson to learn from Jess Franco's film it would be to ALWAYS keep it pervy! RIP Jess Franco" - *Gigantor*

"You shot some of the most beautiful women against the backdrop of just-as-beautiful landscapes. I am still deep, deep underground, nowhere near scratching the surface of your impressive filmography, but it's a journey I have loved and will continue to love. Thank you for entertaining and inspiring." - *Peter Davies (Mondo Squallido)*

"Jess, your world was wild and wonderful, peopled by magical characters that enriched my viewing experience. Live forever!" - *Steve Langton*
"You were a pioneer and visionary. Never before was the language of cinema spoken with such poetry. I'd say goodbye but, for me, you will forever live on in your films."
- *Nigel Maskell (Aenigma Magazine)*

"Jess Franco is dead. LONG LIVE JESS FRANCO!" – *Tony Strauss*

"PLEASE BOW YOUR HEADS FOR PRAYER."

by Andrew Leavold

"When will the Lord return? Anybody could put a date on it, but it could be (clicks fingers) the next second. Because there's nothing that has to be perceived as coming, and when He comes, then the world will be totally changed. And it could happen now, today, this moment."

So says the father of the Rapture Thriller genre, Russell S. Doughten Jr, on the phone from his Des Moines, Ohio film ministry. Since forming his own Christian film missionary in the 1960s, Doughten has witnessed firsthand the rise of the industry from its humble beginnings. "When Ken Anderson began in 1949, there wasn't really a Christian film industry. The Gospel films that he created pretty much created that. Friedrich in the 30s made films based on the Bible—they were the first, made for churches. Derwin Bloom started making films in the mid-forties. They were very helpful, they were scientifically based, and he created several techniques—stop motion pictures, things like that. Those were some of the precursors, the real pioneers of the Christian industry. Ken Anderson began Gospel Films in '49, which is now GospelCommunication.com (*no longer a valid website, and its domain name is now up for grabs -Editor*). And then of course Ken Anderson Films was founded about ten years later. Those were the premiere filmmakers at the beginning, in the history of the industry."

Christian "films", as you can loosely term them, were often little more than filmed sermons with very little flair or flash, lest they incur the wrath of a disapproving, deeply conservative and circumspect congregation. Austere and formal by their very nature, they served as permanent record of a famous sermon by a noted preacher, and could travel many more miles than the most mobile of prognosticators. One of the most prolific Christian film companies, Evangel Films, made Poverty Row a place to aim for; their stories were simple but concise, and their clunky, endearing stock of regular players, short of a 300-pound transvestite and performing asshole, give the films an early John Waters-esque charm.

In their 1955 cold war paranoia short **SECONDS TO MIDNIGHT**, Evangel resident theologian Pastor Ted Anderson invites his friends over for burgers and to watch a few 8mm training films, one a black and white government issue training film called "One World Or None". Amidst animated footage of neutrons and Hiroshima bomb victims, New York is shown disappearing into a puff of smoke, to be transformed into a circle of crosses with a skull in the middle. Pastor Ted coolly puts on the second film, this time colour footage punctuated with shots of nuclear blasts. Once the film show is over, the gathering begins to sing, before Pastor Ted contemplates the spread of Communism. "We can't trust the Commies," he muses. "Communism is a religion that is anti-God," and is therefore "Satan inspired". We are definitely in the End Times, he concludes, and if the history of the world was a 24 hour clock, we are only seconds to midnight. "We're sitting on a powderkeg!" he exclaims to the general agreement of the room. The good news, he says, is that Jesus will come "like a thief in the night", thus anticipating the title of the most famous of all Rapture thrillers. Scores of anti-Communist Christian films dotted the landscape like mushroom clouds over the South Pacific throughout the '50s and '60s, all with the fervent biblical "duck and cover" message of Seconds To Midnight, but the ever-enterprising Evangel beat them to the bell.

It is generally agreed in the Christian film community that the first depiction of the Rapture was in the earlier Evangel two-reeler **THE MISSING CHRISTIANS** (1952), one of the most widely seen devotional films throughout the 'Fifties. As frugal as ever with their production values but with an ambition that transcends its modest trappings, The Missing Christians opens with a pious churchgoing family returning to their two-dimensional stage set (ostensibly a lounge room) and heading straight to the couch to pray for their wayward daughter Norma. Norma returns home with her boyfriend from a night in his rumble seat looking like a cat that swallowed the whole bowl of cream, but the audience can tell deep down she senses something's missing. Her mother tells Norma it breaks her heart that she's tainted with "modernism" and "worldly pleasures". Unrepentant, Norma takes to her bed where, we presume, she slides off to sleep thinking of Charlie Parker and heavy petting.

That night Norma has a dream where Jesus (or what appears to be an actress in a fake beard) appears in her room bathed in a blinding spotlight and, dressed in a white bathrobe, descends from the ceiling in horribly white pancake makeup and a golden dime-store wig. The scene jumps to her family on the couch, the church, flashbacks to her dead father, and a flock of sheep. Jesus invites her to "meet the Lord in the air". She resists, but the rest of the family, asleep on the lounge and at the piano, suddenly find themselves dressed in sheets and, in what seems like the twinkling of an eye but is in fact a ragged jump cut, are launched into the air. Before the collective gasp of the congregation leaves their mouths, the reel ends.

In the second reel, Norma wakes and finds her entire family gone. Meanwhile at the local Church (a similarly two-dimensional plywood set), the Reverend, a fallen preacher who had not preached the Gospel, discovers his own wife and daughter have disappeared as well. With a frozen face and deadpan delivery, he declares, "That certainly is mysterious." As news slowly comes through of the rest of the town's missing ones, Norma turns up to the Church and berates the Reverend for not preaching the True Word of God. True to form, he registers this information without a trace of emotion.

7

Jesus of Nazareth and John Carradine in **THE HOSTAGE**.

Norma suddenly wakes up: the Rapture was all a dream, but she warns herself, "It will come true...if I'm truly converted!" In a tearful finale she accepts Jesus into her heart while her mother beams with happiness. The music swells, and an announcement for the congregation reads, "Please bow your heads for prayer."

1972 would prove to be a watershed year for Rapture films and Christian cinema in general, when Mark IV Productions released the seminal Apocalypse thriller **A THIEF IN THE NIGHT**. Still based in Des Moines, Ohio, producer Russell S. Doughten had previously formed Heartland Productions in 1965 to make low-budget devotional films; on his first production with Heartland, **THE HOSTAGE** (1967), the cinematographer was none other than Ted V. Mikels (director of such incredible shockers as **THE CORPSE GRINDERS**, **ASTRO ZOMBIES** and **BLOOD ORGY OF THE SHE-DEVILS!**)

"My first film was in 1954," says Russell, "working for Good News Productions in Pennsylvania. Jordy (Irvin) Yeaworth was the pioneer in Christian film-making. I worked with him there for about four and a half years, making many Christian films…I made most of them before **THE HOSTAGE**. I made television films, several of them; I did a whole series there, producer, director, of children's gospel hours, we did 26 of them. And we did films for people like Percy Crawford, an evangelist with a school, Kings College; we did some of his television programs. We had a whole bunch of others, missionaries, churches… In 1957, we produced a secular film called **THE BLOB**."

You were involved with **THE BLOB***?!*

"I was the producer of it. Jordy was the director. He shot it there in Chester Springs, Pennsylvania and in the surrounding areas. It became a science fiction classic!"

50s classic SF Flick **THE BLOB**: Russell S. Doughten Jr., associate producer and (uncredited) director.

It seemed like he was destined to make films in the service of God. "Well, I always wanted to do that. But for a little while in my career I was thinking that I needed to make secular films in order to master the technique, the nature of film. And also, you know, to make money and so on. Later, the Lord convinced me that was not His message, not what He wanted.

"In 1967 I made a film called **FEVER HEAT**, which was a racing story, with Nick Adams. And while that was being premiered, my company Heartlands also participated in managing theatres and building theatres, motion picture theatres - the Spectre Theatres. And we were premiering **FEVER HEAT** in the Spectre Theatre that I had my office in, called River Hills, a Panorama Theatre here in Iowa. And during the premiere of it, the Lord reconvicted me into telling these, you know, 'This is a nice film, people are enjoying it and all, but it doesn't lift up Jesus Christ, and what you're supposed to do is that.' So that was the last secular film I worked on."

"Then the Lord brought this young man into my office one day, saying 'I've got a book here that I'd like to make into a film, and would you produce it for me, I would direct it.' And I asked him, 'Well, why do you want to make a film on that kind of a story, because it's a Christian story.' And he said, 'Well, I'm a Christian! And I think the Lord wants me to make Christian films for Him.' That happened to be Donald Thompson."

The two men formed a partnership in 1972. Russell: "It was actually more of a corporation company, of Mark IV Pictures. And after a lot of prayer, we met together several times and prayed and asked the Lord what He wanted, and Donald already had a company."

Donald Thompson: "Russ and I had a tremendous time; Russ has a real knack for knowing what really should be in the scripts. And he knows to tell - although I was a writer of sorts, I didn't write a film until after I'd spent twelve years with Russ - he would teach me a lot of things about it, and the Holy Spirit helped us with that script. We had a lot of fun. Because he was down here at this end of the building at Heartlands, and I was at the other end of the building, although we worked together he was still making movies and I was also making TV shows, syndicated coast-to-coast TV specials for Walter Kennedy and Message for America. So we had a busy time here, and couldn't get over the fact that the Lord helped us with films, to help make them right. We felt honoured, we felt like we were totally going to get anybody, if we ever wanted them."

Russell: "I have a script now called *The Battle For Armageddon*, which we hope to film when we've raised the $35 million it takes, which we've had in the works here for seven years. This is the fifth of our Prophecy films, and Lord willing, there would be two more beyond that; we would have a total of seven.

A THIEF IN THE NIGHT was written by Donald and Russell. Says Russell: "We didn't have elaborate discussions about this, but I think we were both of the same mind that we wanted to present the story that ordinary people would easily identify with. So we tried to use characters that were somewhat like the ordinary person in the audience might consider themselves being. But we wanted to also show that even ordinary people are very diverse in the way they respond to the Lord. So like in **A THIEF IN THE NIGHT**, we chose six young people that were the central part of the story, each one of them had a different kind of characteristic in terms of how they responded to the Godly revelation of the scripture. And to show because of their choices that they made, how that led to their eventual final relationship with the Lord. And to show how... everyone in the audience could identify with one of these characters, would be facing similar kinds of choices and therefore similar kinds of destinies, if they make those kinds of choices."

The snowballing evil characters of Jerry and Diane span all four Mark IV Apocalypse films, as does Reverend Turner, a fallen preacher played by Russell S. Doughten Jr. who in **THIEF**... preaches the rationalist, humanist approach to Christianity, and sees the Bible as nothing more than a metaphor. When Patty discovers Reverend Turner in his empty church just after the Rapture, the agony on the face of a man who has condemned his flock to damnation is palpable. Although he appears on an ambulance stretcher beaten to a pulp towards the end of **A THIEF**..., he returns to the same empty church in **A DISTANT THUNDER** (1978), before heading for an underground bunker in the hills, born again and fighting fit for the rest of the Tribulation period.

Dramatic moments from **A THIEF IN THE NIGHT**

A THIEF IN THE NIGHT was a truly groundbreaking film: an effective B-grade supernatural thriller which also happens to be a Christian film. While a little rough around the edges, particularly with the location sound editing, it introduces the quartet of Mark IV Rapture films nicely and sets the general boundaries for all future Rapture thrillers. For a low-budget series, the Rapture Quartet is an incredibly ambitious exercise; it manages to convey global chaos on a micro-scale, using radio broadcasts and newspaper headlines to cut corners, while utilizing tanks and helicopters to maximize production values.

"The most expensive one I think we made was **THE PRODIGAL PLANET** [1983]," says Russell. "And that was just under a million dollars. The other ones were made somewhat over five hundred thousand." "**A THIEF IN THE NIGHT** was for 68 thousand," adds Donald. "The next one was made for less than two hundred thousand, I know that." Russell: "But of course we didn't make all those films at the same time. In '72, the prices of things were different then, from '84 when we made the last one. There was quite a change in costs in all kinds of things. And of course with **A THIEF IN THE NIGHT**, we had all kinds of things in the film that would have cost a lot more if we had to pay for them. For instance, my three sons worked on the crew and got virtually no pay at all, and I worked somewhat on it, and as an actor I think I got a hundred dollars..."

"And he hasn't gotten that yet!" laughs Donald. "We had a lot of people from California that were friends, that worked for us and didn't charge us. They always used to say, 'Whatever you want to pay us, when you want it.' And then they would come to help us. The picture's going to cost a lot more if—we had one film, we had a tiger. The tiger cost $17,000 to rent for two days. We had a dog; we had to pay five thousand dollars. We had Eddie Dayno, one of the top stunt drivers in the world, working—we figured what it would cost to have four major stunts in the film—it would come to probably eight or nine hundred thousand dollars. He charged us five thousand dollars!

"The stunt people who did **TORA! TORA! TORA!** and **FIRST BLOOD**, we got a trailer truck full of stuff—charge: "whatever". But that all came from Monty Cox, who'd then handle it because Monty was one of the largest animal holders in Hollywood. He and I became friends after we did a movie in Arizona. And Monty wanted to do stunts and asked me if I would write stunts into a movie. I said they were too expensive. He became a stunt man, we kind of traded off, and he now is the President of the International Stunt Association in Hollywood, and so we kind of helped each other. He provided all the animals and stunts! It was a 'scratch my back, I'll scratch yours' kind of thing."

I asked Russell if he was influenced to make **A THIEF IN THE NIGHT** after the popularity of "The Late Great Planet Earth"—how much of an impact did the Hal Lindsey book, coming out in 1970, affected his decision to make a Tribulation movie in 1972? "Well, I knew that book, and I had read it. And so I can't say it had no impact. Although the idea, from my point of view, of making a film on the End Time had been on my mind for a long time, but I ignored it because I figured it was going to cost me too much money. But somehow the Lord swept those things away when Don and I got together and it became clear after we discussed several possibilities of what to write. We started with the realization that the Lord wanted us to work together. That's what I perceived. And then we examined several ideas, and the idea that I had had for a long time, of making a film on the End Times, I put it on the table, and after discussing it, thinking about it and praying about it, we decided to go with that. The influence on me, on the End Times, came through the book called 'Dispensational Truth' by Clarence Larkin. He wrote that book in the early 1900s. And a copy of it was given to me in 1955, I think it was. Before that, my attitude towards prophecy was...I was a Christian then, but my attitude was: it's too deep, too much symbolism, too much intrigue. I didn't understand it. Although I read it, occasionally, and took a study class on scripture, I originally felt, that nobody can really KNOW this. Until I got Larkin's book, where he charted out the prophecies on several charts. And as I read that book, and studied the scripture, it suddenly, gradually revealed to me that these are very profound truths in the prophecy that mankind is supposed to know about, because God, He put it there in the book for people to study. And that gift brought to me fuel for presentation to the world, to the average person in some manner that he can begin to understand it and not worry about all the symbolism and things that appear to be there. I had thought about it for a long time, but I had put aside for me making this into a film until Don and I got together and we started discussing it, and saw that the Lord could lead us through a way of doing it."

I asked Russell if he had seen the other films that came in the wake of **A THIEF IN THE NIGHT**. "Since we're working on Prophecy films, I made a vow that I would not watch other people's prophetic films. So I have not seen any of them, except one. Tim LaHaye asked me one time to view *Left Behind*. He wanted me to look at it for him. I did that because we had a lawsuit that came up over our third film, **IMAGE OF THE BEAST** [1980]. A company had come to our offices and seen scenes from another prophecy film, the first, and we had a long lengthy talk with them about it, how they were done and so on. And then we were making **IMAGE OF THE BEAST**—at the time we called it **YEARS OF THE BEAST**, it was our working title—starting to do advertising for it. And lo and behold, they took us to court saying that we had stolen their story—which was quite the reverse! And they were going to try to sue us and prevent us

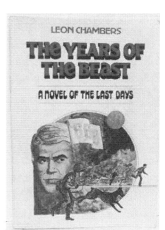

9

from releasing the film. But anyway, having gone to court over it, when we were the innocent party, I decided that I was not going to put myself in that kind of position by watching everybody else's work. So, for better or for worse, I have not seen any of these, except for one film."

To be fair to the producers of **YEARS OF THE BEAST** (1981), their film was based on a book by Leon Chambers called *Years of the Beast: A Novel*, published by Beacon Hill Press in 1979. Chambers had already published a number of prophecy books: *Interpreting End Time Events* and *Interpreting Satan-Antichrist: His World Empire*, both written with Mildred Chambers in 1973. It is also fair to say that Chambers' novel borrows liberally from **A THIEF IN THE NIGHT** and **A DISTANT THUNDER**, and that Thompson and Doughten Jr. have every reason to feel slighted. I suggest dueling pistols at sparrow's fart, if Mr. Chambers is still *compus mentis*.

Thompson and Doughten Jr. returned to the fold in 1983 with **THE PRODIGAL PLANET**. A good two years into the *Road Warrior* post-apocalypse genre and sporting a John Carpenter-sounding synth score straight out of **ESCAPE FROM NEW YORK, THE PRODIGAL PLANET** pours the Seven Bowls of Revelation onto humanity—a plague of boils, seas and rivers turning to blood, intense heat and darkness—as Mark IV takes the series conclusion deep into Tribulation territory. David (again played by William Wellman Jr.) stands at the guillotine just moments before a stock-footage montage of missiles and mushroom clouds turns most of the United States into a smoking Ground Zero.

Even after 22 years, Mark IV (now Russell Doughten Films) still have the fifth film on the drawing board, *The Battle of Armageddon*, at a proposed cost of a staggering $35 million. "Filming in Jerusalem, in and around and on the Temple mount," says Russell. "Half of that budget would be for the production, the other half would be for the world-wide release." Does it really cost that much for prints of films to be struck now? "I don't know, maybe by the time we get it made, maybe they'll be showing them by digital measures. Which would be a lot cheaper. But you have to buy up to three or four thousand prints, so you're big budget already." I mentioned seeing **MEGIDDO: THE OMEGA CODE 2** (2001) which staged an impressive-looking Armageddon at the $20 million mark. "Oh yeah, we're going to have to do that too. Our budget was for the actual filming, so it might have to be upgraded - we set the budget about three or four years ago. It includes about five million dollars' worth of effects."

Donald adds, "The thing is, you have to have one wrangler for every three horses. Russ can get to two hundred million horses but can't afford the wranglers!" And all the union fees for the rioters. Russell says, "We wouldn't even attempt *The Battle of Armageddon* if it weren't for the computerization possibilities. But to stage that kind of effects, the end of the world, the final appearance of Christ and His destruction of all His enemies...half of the world's population will have already been destroyed through the Tribulation period, but still, we're talking about probably four or five billion people, of whom a huge portion of them will be destroyed in the coming wars. And that's a horrendous thing, how can you show that on film? And our approach to *The Battle of Armageddon* will also be the human approach; our main characters will be relatively simple people, facing life under the circumstances of the battle of Armageddon."

Even without the ambitious Battle of Armageddon or further proposed sequels, **THE PRODIGAL PLANET** is a partially satisfying bookend to the series. Of course there's no final battle between God and Satan, but we do witness the destruction of the UNITE computer headquarters and Mike and his companions safe (for now) with the Believers Underground. The final image of Prodigal Planet is of Jerry, covered with sores and pinned under the collapsing UNITE building, screaming in agony and getting just a taste of his eternal damnation.

Russell: "I feel that it's particularly important for prophetic scripture to be represented properly in a prophetic film. Because, as we say in one of our films..."

Donald: "The story is fiction, the prophecy is not."

Russell: "This is a story, a *true* story, that is yet to happen, is our approach to it. And since it is a true story, the truth of it comes from the scripture. And what comes from the scripture can't be something that a fiction writer makes up. And so that's the approach that we have tried to take. It's very easy for the Hollywood imagination to go off on forty tangents from the scripture, and something that seems like a great dramatic idea. But we didn't allow ourselves that privilege. We tried to only illustrate what could be, based upon the scripture itself, and tried not to imagine other things. Tried to picture, as best we could, and in the simplest manner possible, through ordinary characters—people like those watching the films—what might happen, when these events that are chronicled in this prophecy actually do happen, and what these people might be experiencing when that happens. We put quite a few limitations on ourselves so that we do not go off into our own imaginations about it."

On recent events: "One of the things that intrigued me when I started writing **A THIEF IN THE NIGHT** was that the scriptures about the two witnesses of Revelations, who are like Elijah and Moses, who are slain by the Antichrist and left on the steps of the temple for all the world to see that he has met with God's messengers. And then the whole world sees them resurrected, and taken up to Heaven. That stimulated my thinking a lot, and I came to realize that John wrote those things back in probably 96 AD. Who could know that the world would see a man like that? Everybody in the world could see it? That would be impossible to imagine. But today, we have a soccer game played in Italy a few years back where over two billion people watched the same program at the same time. And there have been some events since then that have had even more people than that. The whole world today through technology can see an event like that. They can actually see it while it's happening.

"How many people saw the Trade Center?" Probably billions. "So therefore what would have been amazing and improbable, two thousand years ago, today is easy to accept. And that's one of the things that causes me to feel that we are in End Times. As far as the prophetic things are necessary: nothing, there are no prophecies left to be revealed before the Rapture occurs. So that means that the idea of immanency prevails now. When will the Lord return? Anybody could put a date on it, but it could be (clicks fingers) the next second. Because there's nothing that has to be perceived as coming, and when He comes, then the world will be totally changed. And it could happen now, today, this moment. And I've felt conscious about that many times, thought about it, and prayed about it. And I believe that the reason why God put it that way in the scriptures, and that even Paul was saying that we who are still alive will meet the Lord in the air. He was thinking about himself, at that point. So the immanency being of Christ's return, of the Rapture of the

Church, is something that God wanted us to know about and to incorporate into our lives. If you think that the Lord could come today, how are you going to behave today? Are you going to continue with sin and say, well, some day I'll take care of this, some time before death, but for now, it's a lot of fun. That doesn't make sense. If the immanency of the return of the Lord is true, He could come today. And I think God wants us, and wants the whole world to think He could come today so that we'll behave like He's coming. And to behave like He's coming, what do you do? Well, you honour Him. One of the things you do is you try to obey Him. What did He say to do? He said, love another, as I have loved you, so love one another. And He said to look up, so your redemption comes high. He wants us to go into all the world and tell every creature—these are things that we are supposed to be doing—now. And if we aren't doing these things, we're not paying attention to His command, or to the idea that He could come and call us to account at any moment."

Would you say that a large percentage of Christians don't subscribe to the idea of the Rapture, or would you say they're not exactly Christians?

Russell: "Well... a Christian is someone who has faith in the Lord Jesus Christ and has confessed their sins and been forgiven. Everybody who has not done that is not a Christian. And it doesn't matter whether they go to a church or proscribe, or boast—nothing! It doesn't have anything to do with whether they're Christian or not. I think that many people who have received Christ and have been forgiven, when they look at the scriptures seriously, and really pray for the Spirit to enlighten them, they will come to that position. Because I think the scriptures are quite clear when you take them all together.

"Unfortunately many denominations not only don't believe in it, but preach against it. The average Christian does not read the Bible sufficiently to inform himself, and he therefore gets pulled into one camp or another by some leader, who may or may not also believe in scripture and take it seriously as historical data. To me, I, by my own studies of scripture and reading things like Larkin's books, came to believe that the scripture was God's word. Every word of it is intended to be a communication to us. Intended to reveal true history of the world, from the Creation on through the appendices and the historical books, so that we would know, from God's perspective, what actually happened in the formation of the world, in the fall of Man, and in the redemption of Man. And that therefore, it has been my position, to me, that the scripture is true. So I believe what it says and that it is historically accurate. I think anybody who studies the scripture openly and with the idea that God is trying to talk to him personally, is likely to come to that same conclusion. And those who do not may not study the scriptures sufficiently. I think the average Christian doesn't, and therefore is subject to being influenced by one theory or another without discovering it for themselves. And unfortunately, some leaders—I wouldn't say they're NOT Christians—but through some misreading have taken on some of these other positions and have either distorted the scripture themselves or left some parts of it out, coming to their conclusions."

And so at some point in the mid-eighties you stop - was that because of the rising budgets?

Russell: "No, there were a lot of factors involved." (long pause) "You don't have to go into them. There were various things. The 16mm film industry started to wane in the early eighties, and churches went away from showing films in churches. Today, there is no 16mm film church circuit today. Except overseas, because a lot of missionaries are using them. But by 1979 there were no national stores for video in the United States. By 1982, they were starting to be there, and video stores and other stores were starting to make videos very prominent. And in 1982, we experienced a Satanic attack of major public proportions, through the IRS. The IRS came and started to audit us. They camped on our doorstep for about four months. And then came up with a totally new approach to auditing our kind of situation and told us we owed several hundred thousand dollars in back taxes."

Oww...

"By 1984, when we had finished our **PRODIGAL PLANET** and **THE SHEPHERDS**, they were our last productions as Mark IV. The IRS now had taken it to a point where they were saying, you must pay this tax bill, which would have put us out of business. And we contested it. It took us fourteen years to contest the IRS tax levy. And we lost. We took it to an Appeals court. It went to the Tax Court—we lost. We took it to the Appeals Court—we lost.

YouTube grab: "Russ Doughten, Jr. renowned Christian film maker shares his understanding of How motion pictures catch and hold their audiences."

The result was the dissolution of Mark IV Pictures. It doesn't exist now. And also, to save time, it was an attack on Heartland, and *it* was dissolved. Both of those companies had been destroyed by the IRS. So although I was able to raise funds on an offsite basis and buy our films, I now, through Russell Doughten Films, own all the films we produced, both as Heartland and Mark IV. But we had a struggle, a fourteen year struggle, during which we could not raise money to make a film, because we had to acknowledge to any investor that we were being stymied by the IRS, and then why their investment would also be stolen for tax. We were not able to raise money during that period of time. That is why there were no films made during that period."

And so through Russell Doughten Films and Mustard Seed International, you are now able to distribute the back catalogue of Mark IV and Heartland?
Russell: "That's correct. So we still have international distribution for those films. We have produced several scripts, including *The Battle of Armageddon*, and Donald and I and another gentleman here wrote a script called *Harking From Hell* which is waiting for production. We wrote another script for a children's series called *Angel Gang*, and we have several other scripts in various stages of production. We have many possibilities for future filming, but the IRS, I believe, was a real hand of the Devil, working hard on a very successful film evangelist. And some reason the Lord allowed that to happen. And we have never fully recovered from it."

•••

OIIOIIO OIIOIIO OIIOIIO
MEMORIES OF A THIEF, THE THUNDER, A BEAST & A PLANET
by Brian Harris

Just for a second, imagine tucking your children in for a bedtime story. Their eager eyes shine with the spark of imagination and their excitable little hands wring in anticipation, hoping to be delighted with beautiful princesses and devoted princes. This is no Disney though, there are no talking fish or beasts with hearts of gold, instead you spin a yarn...so malicious...so abusive that their night terrors are guaranteed to extend well into their teen years. Forget Grimm's Fairy Tales, the author of this nightmare is believed to have been a mystic in exile, possibly influenced by psychoactive drugs. The book is Revelation. The setting...The Great Tribulation!

Be sure to double-up on the rubber sheets.

According to Christian tradition, The Tribulation will be a time of terror and torment, filled with multi-headed monsters rising from the depths of the ocean, the dead leaving their coffins, ferocious flying beasts with the stingers of scorpions, politicians possessed by demonic entities, gory public executions, blood as deep as rivers, plagues and starvation on a level unseen in human history. Top all of that off with a battle between the combined armed forces of the world and a supernatural, sword-wielding warrior legion. It may all sound like the stuff of exhilarating horror cinema or the work of a fantasy novelist but the Evangelical Christian movement believes every single word of it. 100% fact. Not only do they believe it, they actively teach children as young as three and four years old that it's not a matter of if it will happen...but when. Naturally, for the Christians that believe this malarkey, there's a way out, a Get Out of Jail Free card called, "The Holy Ghost." Choose Jesus or burn for eternity. Free will is starting to sound like a raw deal, ain't it?

As a youngster attending a Pentecostal church, I was taught this insidious doctrine and, being the rabid horror fan that I was, hung on each and every word. How could it not be true, it was The Holy Bible! It wasn't until years later that I came to see the teaching of this doctrine—to children especially—as a form of abuse by organized religion, a means of controlling minds through fear, the Boogeyman for a tongue-talkin' crowd. Reject the world and its wicked ways or you'll be...DUM DUM DUMMMMM...LEFT...BEHIND. Those "wicked ways" included watching television, listening to music, wearing jewelry, growing facial hair, attending sporting events, going to theater and countless other activities considered to be normal by...well, normal people. If you did it, chances are I wasn't allowed to. There were exceptions, though—films that God had given his holy high-five to, his spiritual stamp of approval if you will, were allowed to be played for revivals and youth meetings.

Donald W. Thompson's Rapture film series (I prefer Raptuersploitation), beginning with 1972's **A THIEF IN THE NIGHT**, is a great example of the rules not applying to all films. Not only was the film series deemed acceptable to watch, they were shown to many church members on VCRs...in their own churches! *gasp* That's how important these films were and how powerful fear as a motivational tool was (and still is) to Evangelicals. Bringing a VCR into a Pentecostal church was like the Amish listening to hymns on a radio.

Keep a sharp lookout! For you do not know when I will come, at evening, at midnight, early dawn or late daybreak. Don't let me find you sleeping! - Jesus Christ

Thus begins Thompson's **A THIEF IN THE NIGHT**. The groovy (and paraphrased) words of Christ himself set up an unthinkable scenario for our heroine Patty (Patty Dunning) when she awakens to an emergency broadcast over her radio announcing that, while she slept of course, thousands (PERHAPS MILLIONS!) mysteriously disappeared from around the globe without a trace and with no reasonable explanation. Stunned and in disbelief, she calls out for her husband Jim (Mike Niday) and receives no reply. Rushing to the bathroom she discovers Jim's electric razor still running, with no husband in sight! It quickly becomes clear to poor Patty that all the jive being preached about by the youth ranch Christians was true, the Rapture had come and she was unprepared! She's been...LEFT...BEHIND!

Collapsing on the floor next to her bed she takes a trip down memory lane, recounting the sermons, how she met her husband and all the missed opportunities to find true salvation and accept Jesus Christ as her Lord and personal Savior. Each time, convincing herself that she was a good enough person and didn't need to "get saved" in order to go to Heaven. Boy was she wrong! Unwilling to make that leap of faith, even when Jim is bitten by a deadly cobra and survives due to the prayers of friends and family, Patty simply refuses to believe in the possibility that the Rapture might actually happen. If all of that was true, why hadn't her minister been preaching about it and why wasn't she taught about it in Sunday School? How could she have been so stupid?

Thankfully she'll not have to face the horror alone, as her friends Diane (Maryann Rachford) and Jerry (Thom Rachford) have both been stranded as well, and it's business as usual around the world. Or is it? When governments across the globe are disbanded by the United Nations and replaced by a large committee under the U.N.I.T.E. (United Nations Imperium of Total Emergency) banner, what initially looks like a light at the end of the tunnel takes a dark turn. Promising to relinquish control once civilization is no longer showing sign of collapse, the one-world government known as U.N.I.T.E. wastes no time imposing questionable laws in the name of order. When citizens are asked to voluntarily accept an identification mark on their hands or foreheads as a symbol of their patriotism, Patty's concern grows. Signs begin popping up in the windows of businesses all over the city stating that only tagged citizens

will be welcome, and U.N.I.T.E. decides to make the I.D. mandatory, insisting those without a mark will be subject to arrest and incarceration!

Hopeless and without a mark, Patty is forced to flee her home when U.N.I.T.E. forces end up on her doorstep! On the run and with nowhere to turn she makes her way to her old church for comfort, finding her pastor Rev. Turner (Russell S. Doughten Jr.) there, still distraught over his failure to teach the true word of God and lead his flock to Heaven. Before their conversation can go any further though, a U.N.I.T.E. guard ambushes them and they're both put under arrest. Despite assurances by her captors that there's nothing remotely satanic about the mark, she witnesses the executed corpse of her minister being loaded into a truck during her incarceration and immediately realizes what lies in store for her. Her only option is to make a break for it, and escape she does, running and running...and running...and *sigh* running until she stops at a pay phone to make a call. Turning to the only friends she has left, she agrees to meet with Diane and Jerry under the assumption that they'll help her. Instead she's greeted by U.N.I.T.E. soldiers and her best friends...sporting the mark! Truly alone, Patty climbs over the railing of the bridge she's on to avoid capture and she's pushed to her watery death.

The end?!! NOT ON YOUR LIFE! Instead of meeting her maker, she's back in the comfort of her home and it was all a dream. Before relief sets in though, an emergency broadcast over the radio explains that thousands (PERHAPS MILLIONS!) mysteriously disappeared from around the globe without a trace and with no reasonable explanation. Stunned and in disbelief, she calls out for her husband Jim and receives no reply. Rushing to the bathroom she discovers Jim's electric razor still running, with no husband in sight! Her scream says it all, it may have started out a dream but it is now reality and her worst nightmare has come true!

But of that day and that hour knoweth no man, no not the angels which are in Heaven neither the Son but the Father. Take heed, watch out and pray for ye know not when the time is...

So ending **A THIEF IN THE NIGHT**, director Thompson and his partner Russell S. Doughten Jr. joined a very small group of elite filmmakers specializing in the production of Christian exploitation cinema, or Rapturesploitation. Some may take exception to my labeling this film exploitation, but when you accept the historical facts that point to religion being a man-made control device, it's easier to see **A THIEF IN THE NIGHT** for what it is—a big, fat "we told ya so!" It's not about the love and forgiveness but the regret and punishment, it's about showing believers what can happen should they backslide and the non-believers exactly what they can expect to experience if they do not accept Jesus as their Lord and personal Savior. In my opinion it is akin to the Klan making a film that shows the aftermath of a race war in which whites end up on the receiving end of a cracking whip (read: you should have listened to us!). Now if shameless propaganda and scare tactics cannot be considered exploitation, I don't know what can be.

Though lacking in the sleaze department—it was made by Christians after all—it's just as effective as anything the likes of which legendary exploitationeer Kroger Babb was likely to have put out in the early days of the drive-in exploitation circuit. The only difference is, Thompson's film was fully backed by a producer more powerful than Hollywood had ever known. Yeah, you guessed it...Jesus Christ.

I can probably go on all day about the questionable nature of the content but the production itself was really quite impressive for the $60,000 it was made for, and there's no denying that. It was likely no easy task financing and shooting considering it was made outside of the mainstream studio system for a niche market. Production company Mark IV Pictures made great use of the budget and it shows in the breathtaking locations, foreboding (and catchy) score, intricate costume design and, what seemed to be a cast of hundreds. Today this very same production would have run, at the very least, between $2-4 million to make, easily.

The only things, I believe, that kept **A THIEF IN THE NIGHT** from achieving the same level of recognition received by secular pre/post-apocalyptic B-movies was the stilted dialogue and amateur acting. Poor delivery can often be tolerated so long as there's solid writing to back the actors up, but in this case, Thompson and Doughten Jr. wrote a script filled with incessant preaching, slang that was bound to be dated in just a few short years and very little characterization. The cast of characters were cliché, predictable and, outside of lead

actress Patty Dunning's character, expendable. It's obvious that Patty is meant to represent the non-believing audience; she's the "devil's advocate," so to speak. She's a good person but ultimately damned for remaining on the fence with too many questions about the strict rules regarding salvation outlined in the Bible. Through Patty's tragedy we see the error of our own ways regarding salvation and come to the realization that we're either not doing it or not doing it right. In the end, despite all of its flaws, **A THIEF IN THE NIGHT** is an interesting landmark in Christian cinema and a passable attempt at a tense sci-fi thriller.

The motion picture you are about to experience is fiction. The prophecy is not. The producers of this film are not prophets. They are drawing to your attention what God has said in his own Word.

This film is based upon many references in the books of Daniel and Revelation and upon the following prophecy: "For the Lord himself shall descend from Heaven with a shout, with the voice of the Archangel, and the dead in Christ shall rise first: then we which are alive and remain shall be caught up together with them in the clouds to meet the Lord in the air." - 1 Thessalonians 4:16,17

And from Matthew 24:21: "For then shall be great tribulation, such as was not since the beginning of the world to this time, no, nor ever shall be."

While I have no way of knowing just how well the film did upon its release in '72 or subsequent screenings throughout the Seventies, it must have done well enough to warrant spending a $200,000 budget six years later. Thompson and Russell S. Doughten Jr. (executive producer and co-writer) introduced **A DISTANT THUNDER** (1978) to viewers hungry for more Tribulation and boy did they get just that! No longer a bad dream, Patty is now in the hands of U.N.I.T.E., incarcerated in a housing unit with others, facing possible execution for her refusal to take the mark. We're treated to a series of flashbacks, re-telling Patty's story and the many opportunities she'd had to accept Christ and avoid her current dilemma. This time around she won't be going it alone: accompanying her are sisters Wenda and Sandy, both good women who, like Patty, refused to believe.

During their attempts to remain off the grid and off U.N.I.T.E. radar, Patty and the girls meet a stranger wandering about the wilderness preaching salvation, an opportunity that this time around Wenda gladly accepts, putting her in even more jeopardy. When reports begin filtering back to them that missionaries are being put to death and clinics are being set up to administer the mark to citizens, the three decide it's time to go underground with the help of Patty's old friends Diane and Jerry. Unfortunately the girls don't maintain their anonymity for long as the sisters are arrested seeking medical attention and Patty is captured by soldiers after Diane and Jerry report her.

Now in the clutches of the nefarious U.N.I.T.E. and local overseer Kent Onan—as in the Sin of Onan—they all face the unthinkable: execution by guillotine! Did Diane and Jerry really turn all of them in or was the traitor with

Patty all along? Well, let's just say things don't end well for Wenda, and yet another films ends on Patty screaming in terror.

"For God so loved the world that he gave His only begotten son, that whosoever believeth in Him should not perish but have everlasting life." - John 3:16

If you'll remember, **A THIEF IN THE NIGHT** didn't actually happen; it was all part of Patty's elaborate nightmare, one that in the last few moments of the film appears to come true. **A DISTANT THUNDER** takes place shortly after and this time the nightmare is real. While Thompson and Doughten Jr. do their best to throw in a few twists and turns in to keep the sequel from feeling like we've "been here, done this," it all still feels far too familiar. And like the first film, we're subjected to sermon after sermon, missed opportunity after missed opportunity in this as well. Very little of the story actually takes place in the present as most of the production is comprised of flashbacks. One begins to wonder whether there was a script at all as the entire affair feels padded to the Nth degree. Thankfully a brief beheading ratchets the tension back up and reminds viewers that the shit has indeed hit the fan for those that waited too long to accept salvation.

Those of you that have never seen these films in a church setting, amongst other Christians, probably can't imagine the impact they had but, trust me, they ignited quite the firestorm of revival (read: weeping and wailing). I often wonder though how many were truly "saved" after watching these films. I can't imagine that the constant preaching was embraced by the unsaved, it seems far more likely to me that these films preached more to the choir (pun intended) and those that already laid some claim to salvation. As a witnessing tool, I just can't see the Rapture films being very effective.

Whether or not the Rapture films truly reached the heathen it was intended for is moot, they made enough money and garnered enough support from the first two installments to return three years later with a third, **IMAGE OF THE BEAST** (1980). By this time the world has gone computer-crazy with home computer sales skyrocketing, giving Thompson and Doughten Jr. the perfect opportunity to flex Christianity's cyberphobia and make connections between the Antichrist, his reign of terror and the rapid growth of technology.

The book of Revelation reveals a time to come, of great tribulation. A time of such great catastrophe, that no film could portray its reality. It is the belief of many bible scholars, that the facts presented in this film story, could become a reality in your lifetime. After viewing this film, we hope you will take seriously what God says in His word about these prophecies, and turn to Jesus Christ-- and avoid the events you are about to experience in this motion picture.

"And when they said unto you, seek unto them that have familiar spirits, and unto wizards that peep and mutter, should not a people seek unto their God?" - Isaiah 8:19

The film picks up exactly where the last left off, with Patty and fellow prisoners awaiting their grisly fates in front of the guillotine. Our reluctant heroine is finally given the chance to do the "right" thing by taking the mark and returning to society, a decision we're pretty sure she plans to reject, that is until she's loaded into the contraption—the sky goes black and the ground begins to quake. There, beneath the blade, Patty begs for the mark and, as if by divine intervention, the guillotine's latch gives way and she's sent to her eternal damnation...headless.

Now a new set of characters emerge: Leslie (an escaped prisoner), David Michaels (posing as a U.N.I.T.E. Soldier), Kathy and her young son Billy. Despite valiant efforts to avoid detection, poor Leslie is shot and separated from the others during an ambush, leaving David, Kathy and the boy to seek out a new place to lay low. Luckily for them, Rev. Matthew Turner (Doughten Jr. reprising his role from the first two films) finds them and offers them food and shelter. With a base of operations situated, David lets Kathy in on a major development in the war against U.N.I.T.E that he's been working on...A PHONY MARK! Which comes just in the nick of time as the heat is on and two familiar faces return: Diane and Jerry. Seems they're special agents now, out to eradicate fanatics by any means necessary, and they're hoping to enlist David in their cause and expose undercover believers working against U.N.I.T.E....a lapse in judgment they may later regret.

With the world falling apart, and the U.N.I.T.E. leader Brother Christopher being inhabited by the Devil himself and David in the clutches of the enemy, Kathy must replicate the code behind the mark and find a way to help David or all hope is lost.

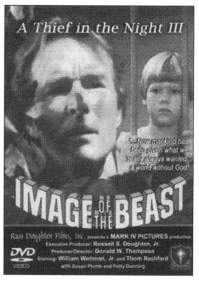

IMAGE OF THE BEAST definitely steps up the Tribulation terror by offering viewers all the horror the previous installments weren't able to show, including the Antichrist himself, monsters and rivers of blood. In my opinion, while the first two films may have generated a considerable amount of tension, this film delivers on many of the most memorably outlandish scenarios from The Book of Revelation, a few to great effect, as well. A sequence showing Bro. Christoper (the Antichrist) sitting on a throne resembling the Ark of the Covenant, speaking in a voice that had an almost alien quality, was definitely chilling. Throw in the galloping hooves of the Four Horsemen of the Apocalypse, some mushroom clouds and random screams of agony and you've got a film that leans a bit more toward the horror genre than sci-fi in its execution. I must admit, this was one of my favorites in the series. Still is.

On the technical front, **IMAGE OF THE BEAST** is clearly an improvement over the last two, as Thompson and Doughten Jr. wisely focus the story on the characters and the present rather than the countless flashbacks that bogged down the first two installments. While we do get quite a few long, uneventful sequences of nothing but preaching and gabbing, things get pretty heavy toward the finale as the fate of an innocent prisoner is marked by a red, runaway balloon. All of the drama and emotion the series had lacked was here, even with the presence of a few flat comedic bits, **IMAGE OF THE BEAST** is, I feel, the most powerful in the franchise.

It should be noted that the presence of William Wellman Jr. (**BORN LOSERS** & **BLACK CAESAR**) as David almost certainly lent this production a bit o' acting class, finally giving the series a strong actor capable of emoting real emotion. He's no Heston in **PLANET OF THE APES** but he gets the job done. Much respect should also be shown to Patty Dunning for giving it her all in three films but the character of Patty seemed to exist for the sole purpose of punishing, nothing more than a whipping post. With Wellman Jr. now the focus of the final half of the series, things begin kicking into high gear and the Rapture films take on a more accessible vibe—not quite secular, mind you—but still veering into what feels like real cinema.

A fire devoureth before them; and behind them a flame burneth: the land is as the garden of Eden before them, and behind them a desolate wilderness; yea, and nothing shall escape them." - Joel 2:3

This is the story of a few people in that wilderness.

Last in the series, **THE PRODIGAL PLANET** (1983) sees David rescued before his execution by a group dedicated to constructing a transmitter capable of broadcasting to all Christians in hiding. They need David's help in deciphering a cryptic map obtained by a spy that will lead them to the secret location of U.N.I.T.E.'s transmitter. He's convinced the only person that can help them break the code is good old Rev. Matthew Turner. Luckily for them the disgraced preacher is still alive and well, hiding in the woods from U.N.I.T.E. forces.

Along the way, David and his double-agent companion happen upon some fellow mark-less travelers, marauding bands of mutants, soldiers afflicted with a strange illness, ghost towns, paranoia, double-crosses, soaring helicopters, weather gone wild and an underground resistance preparing the way for the return of Jesus Christ!

"The rain came down, the streams rose, and the winds blew and beat against that house; yet it did not fall, because it had its foundation on the rock." - Matthew 7:25

Of the entire series, **THE PRODIGAL PLANET** seems to be more in line with what post-apocalyptic cinema should be, with harsh, arid terrain, an incurable disease and futuristic tank-style vehicles. Don't expect **MAD MAX** though; where expositional chit chat between characters would normally go, Thompson and Doughten Jr. fill large chunks of the film with constant preaching and religious reflection. Lapses in action become nothing more than clunky opportunities for non-stop blah-blah-blah and it really got my eyes rolling. I know, it's a Christian film—what the hell was I expecting, right? It just got to the point where I felt my finger itching to hit fast forward the minute the heart-to-hearts began. That said though, yeah this film was filled with *CRAZY* action. Definitely more action in this film than damn near all of them combined. Like I said, this felt like a real post-apocalyptic sci-fi flick.

So, there you have it, Rapturesploitation at its best and worst, all in one series. Here's the kicker, I love it despite the twinge of animosity I feel each time I consider putting them in. If they'd been shown to me for entertainment, I might feel differently today, but these weren't "entertainment," they were true stories, just waiting to happen. New converts, like I was, were led to believe that this would be hell on earth and I would experience every excruciating moment if I didn't "get right" with God. These weren't supposed to be fun, that's for sure; their true intention was to bring bawling viewers to their knees, begging for forgiveness and a place in Heaven. There are no lessons to be learned in the Rapture series except,"We're right and you're wrong." Thompson and Doughten Jr. want viewers to know that the here and now is their last chance because in the blink of an eye, they'll end up being fed into The Beast's guillotines. Salvation may have been first and foremost on their minds, but their salvation comes at a price: the relinquishing of your free will and skeptical thought. Just ask Patty.

While this article may feel as though I hated **A THIEF IN THE NIGHT** and its sequels, that's the furthest thing from the truth; I love them for the exploitation cinema they are. They're poorly written, poorly acted and outrageously expensive to purchase on DVD, but they hold a lot of memories for me.

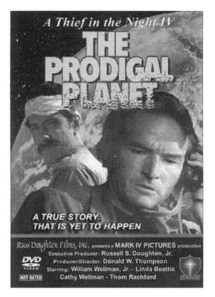

Some good, others not-so-good. When I talk with others about this series, I do so with a half-cocked smile. They're not high art, they're propaganda, but they do hold an important place in Christian cinema and exploitation cinema as well. When you have the time, you should give them a look-see. Just be sure to keep in mind that the unsaved will sell you out, computers are the Antichrist's tools, barcodes are the Mark of the Beast and ministers like Rev. Matthew Turner, who lead their flock astray, shouldn't bother to ask for forgiveness from God. Ouch.

There are still stores, including Christian book stores, that sell the Rapture series in a box set but prepare yourself for major case of wallet rape, as new sets will run you anywhere from $75-100. Just imagine how much they'd cost if they had special features! I should also mention that the transfers I've seen are watchable but not great-- details are soft, colors are muted in some places and audio is a bit tinny. No biggie...as cult cinema fans, we deal with stuff like this on the daily. Grab the collection, crack you a beer and kiss your sinning ass goodbye for four of the most excruciatingly entertaining Christian fun you never thought you'd have!

The Rapture films are by no means the only Rapturesploitation/Godsploitation (props Andrew!) cinema you should check out; classic examples worth looking into include **THE LATE GREAT PLANET EARTH, EARLY WARNING, IF FOOTMEN TIRE YOU, WHAT WILL HORSES DO?, THE APOCALYPSE** series, Michael Tolkin's big-budget Hollywood production **THE RAPTURE** and who can forget Cloud Ten's *Left Behind* films. At some point in the future I'll write a bunch up in another article for those interested in furthering their collection of religious propaganda films. In the spirit of fairness I may throw in a few Islamic entries as well. Naturally this is all dependent on whether or not The Rapture does actually occur and I've been caught up to meet Him or I'm...LEFT...BEHIND! Yeah, so, keep an eye out for my next article.

•••

STEVE'S VIDEO STORE VOL.1:
CARDONA-MANIA

by Steven Ronquillo

René Cardona Sr. (born René Cardona Andre on October 8, 1906 in Havana, Cuba, and died April 25, 1988 in Mexico City, Mexico at age 81) and René Cardona Jr. (born May 11, 1939 in Mexico City, Mexico and died in the same city on February 5, 2003 at age 63) were the First Family of Mexploitation. Both did many fun and just plain wacky movies during their filmmaking careers. In this article I am going to talk about a few of my Cardona faves, so let's go south of the border, Mexico-way, for gorillas, luchadores and tabloid filmmaking!

The first film I will be talking about is 1963's **DOCTOR OF DOOM** (Las luchadoras contra el médico asesino), the first film in the "Wrestling Women" series. As you get started in Mexploitation you'll find out that they love their luchadores with a passion, and this wacky sub-genre mixes them with mad scientists, half-men/half-gorillas and half-luchadora/half-gorillas for a very fun mix…if you're into that kind of insanity.

A mad scientist and his man-ape creation Gomar kidnap women to conduct illegal—and highly unsuccessful—brain transplants, but the failures happen far too often for his liking, so he listens to his assistant who says maybe they need smarter women. They kidnap our heroine's sister but fail again. That makes her so upset that she and five other luchadoras beat the crap out of a guy who comes into the gym, an amazing scene which really looks like they're beating his ass, badly.

Gloria Venus and Golden Rubi, our two heroines (don't get used to their names because they change from film to film), go after the madman in what plays like a series of short half-hour movies, until the doctor gets pissed and creates a half-luchadora/half-gorilla, and she kicks their asses until the movie is long enough, then they get shot off of a water tower.

Our heroines return in 1964's **WRESTLING WOMEN VS. THE AZTEC MUMMY** (Las luchadoras contra la momia), no relation to the other Aztec mummy film series. This is about a group of five archaeologists who find a book that will lead to the titular mummy's treasure, so they decide to hide it. Then a Mexican Fu Manchu-wannabe goes after it (because that's pretty much what bad guys do) and the last one who lives is the wrestling woman from the first film. Someone has the bright idea of splitting the book into four parts but having all four of them stay in the same fugging house!

So with logic like that, and the fact they're damn sure not going to show the title monster, the Fu Manchu-wannabe gets to the tomb and from there it goes on with the standard silliness…'Til they tie the mummy to a pole and the movie ends. The Wrassling Women vs. the Kung Fu Bimbos fight is awesome, though!

1959's **SANTA CLAUS** is a masterpiece of kiddy-film weirdness with Santa holding little racist caricatures as slaves to make his toys while Pitch, a minion of the Devil, tries to stop him from giving toys to all the good little boys and girls. This is pure fugging insanity, as we see Lupita Quezadas get tortured by the scariest damn dolls ever, as they call her a punk-ass for not stealing a doll, and three little asshole kids who try to tie up Santa and steal his toys. This is pure Christmas fun of the highest standard, and I watch it every Christmas so I can enjoy the Christmassy weirdness.

1969's **NIGHT OF THE BLOODY APES** (La horripilante bestia humana) is a remake of Cardona's earlier **DOCTOR OF DOOM**, only with tits and gore and bald men getting scalped and actual medical stock footage of a heart transplant! Instead of a mad doctor doing a brain transplant we have a sweet old man doing a monkey heart transplant into his son's body so he won't die, but, in accordance with bad movie logic, the heart is too powerful—sort of like putting a Harley engine into a lawn mower—so it makes him into a raping, scalping, murdering machine (or me, that one weekend in Tijuana)! This movie is special to me, because my mom saw it the year I was in her belly, so it might be one of the reasons I am so warped today!

1977's **¡TINTORERA!** is about two guys who like to fuck Susan George, but have to stop to kill a shark. This movie I have labeled The Duel of the Bulging Crotches because of the way Hugo Stiglitz and Andres Garcia stuff their pants…it seems Andres likes overinflated footballs and Hugo likes pythons as pants stuffer. This may be the goofiest **JAWS** cash-in ever, with more about fucking Susan George than shark hunting, and it's like a live-action "this is how a stud lives in the 70s" pictorial from Playboy. Another goofy Cardona classic!

And now for the two pulp journalism classics from Cardona, Jr., and 2 of my fave sleaze films of all time…

1976's **SURVIVE!** (Supervivientes de los Andes) was based on the plane crash with the rugby team that led to them having to eat the flesh of some of their fellow teammates to make it until help came. This was big news when it happened but the Cardonas were the first ones to snap up the movie rights to it. This was taken from interviews with the survivors, so even though it was done on the cheap it doesn't have the goofiness you usually expect with a Cardona film. The only really bad thing about this movie is when they leave the mountain to show the search for them. It has always been my experience that if you're making a movie where isolation is a main part of the mood and character, then leaving the isolation and terror kills the mood and all it does is remind you that it's just a movie. But besides that this is a scary and very intense movie that doesn't shy away from some aspects that the 1993 version called **ALIVE** gloss over, and is worth a watch.

1979's **GUYANA: CULT OF THE DAMNED** was rushed out about 7 to 8 months after the Jonestown Massacre to capitalize on what was the most shocking story of the year. The reverend Jim Jones took his followers/cult members down to Guyana to escape the harassment by the IRS and it ended about 7 months later with murder and mass suicide. So Cardona, after hearing CBS was gearing up its own movie, rushed this out to theaters, and, good god, is it sleazy.

It doesn't waste any time wallowing in the muck, since you see someone blow his brains out and someone lain across the train tracks and ran over as soon as the credits roll, as if to say, "Yes, this is going to be a sleazy, nasty ride". I like it when a film is like that, because if you know how sleazy a film is from the start, you can stay or run away like a chicken within minutes. This covers all the sleazy bases, from murder to forced white-on-black sex as the guy from **KENTUCKY FRIED MOVIE** (1977) comes out and fucks a couple for the crime of being a couple.

And then there's the scene where three kids steal some food. They make one of them stand in a water pit for two days, then another a snake pit naked, and the third they show him hanging nude and then they get out battery cables and *holy shit they're hooking up his balls to a car battery!* That scene is cut from most prints because 1) a naked under-aged boy is frowned on, and 2) hooking his damn nuts up to a car battery is damn sure frowned on!

This goes on until the climactic Jonestown Massacre which, because they had video from it to go with the end, is a nasty, ugly thing to see. This is a sleazy masterpiece and god, do I love it to death! Yes, they changed all the names and pull a "This is inspired by" card so they wouldn't get sued by the survivors, and yes, the TV movie with Powers Boothe is better, but damn, is this a bucket of ice water thrown in your face!

1978's **CYCLONE** has it all: a plane crash, a boat lost at sea, and sharks. So why in the name of hell is it so damn boring? This movie actually captures the experience of being trapped on a boat at sea with all the tedium and graphic animal abuse that entails. Yes, you read that right, there is a scene where they actually kill a dog with a knife, and, is it nasty as hell. But it doesn't save the movie from being a boring-boring-boring waste of time.

1979's **CARLOS THE TERRORIST** (Carlos el terrorista) is boring shit and the only thing that saves it is how Andres Garcia getting shot in the side at the end causes a bunch of cars to explode. I hope if I am shot it cause cars to explode.

And now for the last film I'd like to talk about, and proof there is a hell for movie watchers, is 1972's **THE NIGHT OF A THOUSAND CATS** (La noche de los mil gatos). There is bad, there is horrid, and there is **THE NIGHT OF A THOUSAND CATS**. This movie about how Hugo, played by Hugo Stiglitz, can make any woman wet by annoying the fuck out of her with his helicopter (since it is a fact that bad Mexican actors landing on your lawn will make any woman wet). But he has a secret: he kills the women and puts their heads in a jar and feeds the rest to a bunch of cats that could give a fuck that they're in a movie; you see them wander off camera, bat at the lens… they are in all honesty the cutest cannibalistic killer bloodthirsty cats you will ever see.

They keep repeating the Hugo-meets-girl, Hugo-kills-girl for about an hour, then his butler beats him at chess, and, because Hugo is an asshole, he kills him. Then, because thank god the movie's time is up, the cats kill Hugo and his last girl gets away. There is reportedly a longer cut out there, but in the name of all that is sacred, please god do not let it turn up!

To sum up, they may be silly, goofy, and sometimes downright horrible, but the films by the Cardonas are all loveable and they need to be seen by Mexploitation buffs. I haven't even scratched the surface of what the Cardonas did, so go out and find some more for yourself, because half of the fun of being a Cult Film fan is the search.

•••

For more additional information on the films of René Cardona Sr. check out page 104!

IT CAME FROM MEXPLOITATION!
Post-Apocalyptic Mexican Cinema
by Aaron Soto

*Mexican Cinema has its own amount of good genre films, but aside from the masked Luchadore (wrestler) movies most of the stuff is pretty obscure and almost unknown by international fans and film critics alike. You all know Mexican genre masters like Guillermo Del Toro (**CRONOS**) and Alfonso Cuaron (**CHILDREN OF MEN**), but have you heard about Mexploitation kings director Christian Gonzalez and actor Mario Almada? If you put their body of work together you'll get close to 500 films! And most of them are genre related, from Horror Slashers like the atmospheric **LA TRAILA ASESINA** (aka **THE KILLER TRAILER**, 1986) to intense Thrillers like **38. EXPANSIVA** (1996), Gonzalez and Almada own the Mexican genre cinema like no one else and they both managed to maintain a nihilistic and decadent quality of the third world society that shows a very strong apocalyptic and post-apocalyptic vibe in their films, an aesthetic and concept relegated to Mexican Exploitation Cinema, or like I love to say: Mexploitation Cinema.*

INTREPIDOS PUNKS

If you look at modern movies made by foreign genre directors inside Mexico, you will discover an eclectic group of movies that could be a copycat of Mexploitation Cinema, like Alex Cox's **EL PATRULLERO** (UK, 1991), Robert Rodriguez's **EL MARIACHI** (USA,1992) and Alex de la Iglesia's **PERDITA DURANGO** (Spain, 1996), three films that feel or suggest that they happen in a wasted Mexican land, but even far away from the Exploitation circuit, it seems that you can't make a genre film that takes place in Mexico without evoking some kind of a apocalyptic feel, just take a look at Buñuel's bizarre mex-trio, **VIRIDIANA** (1961), **SIMON DEL DESIERTO** (*Simon of the Desert*, 1965) and **EL ANGEL EXTERMINADOR** (*The Exterminating Angel*, 1962)—an isolated town full of freaks, a mystical journey in the desert and a middle-class nightmare of biblical proportions.

Officially, Apocalyptic Cinema in Mexico started with Julian Soler's **PLATILLOS VOLADORES** (1955) and Rogelio A. Gonzalez's **LA NAVE DE LOS MONSTRUOS** (1959) both fun science fiction films about alien invasion, but the sub-genre went over the top with the Luchadores film craze, like **NEUTRÓN: EL ENMASCARADOS NEGRO** (1960), **LAS ARAÑAS INFERNALES** (1966), **SANTO VS LA INVASION DE LOS MARCIANOS** (1966) and Rene Cardona's **LA INVASION DE LOS MUERTOS** (1971), all of them in the tradition of the most successful American B-movies from the '50s and '60s, and all of them fulfilled the cliché of the masked wrestler films: low budget commercial films based around one of Mexico's favorite sports.

But during this period a couple of Mexican filmmakers glimpsed that the sub-genre could lead to somewhere else, with a diverse group of films that weren't straight Sci-fi films but indeed suggested a parallel Mexico, examples are Fernando Duran Rojas's **ALERTA ALTA TENSION** (1969) and **VIBORA CALIENTE** (1978), Juan Lopez Moctezuma's **LA MANSION DE LA LOCURA** (1973), Rafale Corkidi's **DESEOS** (1977) and Alberto Mariscal's **BRAZO DE ORO** (1977), a mix of Westerns, Dramas, Musicals and Action films so strange and bizarre that it was hard to label them, but obviously they were a serious attempt to create something unique out of the Mexican magic realism mystique.

In this period there were some Post-Apocalyptic co-productions shot in Spanish and English language with Mexican actors mixed with an international crew, like Jack Hill's **ALIEN TERROR** (1971), Alejandro Jodorowsky's **THE HOLY MOUNTAIN** (1973), Sutton Roley's **CHOSEN SURVIVORS** (1974) and Umberto Lenzi's **NIGHTMARE CITY** (1980), very interesting Apocalyptic films, but too foreign to be considered Mexican.

From the late '90s to the new millennium Mexican Cinema got a few Post-apocalyptic films from the New Wave of Mexican independent cinema out of film schools, like the shot-on-video **UTOPIA-7** (1995) and the CGI extravaganzas **DEPOSITARIOS** (2010) and **SERES GENESIS** (2010), but it was Peruvian filmmaker Alex Rivera who stole the show with **SLEEP DEALER** (2008), a Mexican-American co-production inspired by the Tijuana short-film sci-fi scene. Still most of the best Mexican Post-apocalyptic films came from the '80s, a decade were Mexico saw the rise of B-movies and the birth of the so called "Videohome producciones", a very successful straight-to-video circuit created by the private sector that ignored the term jumping the shark, but that maintained a better degree of imagination and passion for the genre than the so-called "art films".

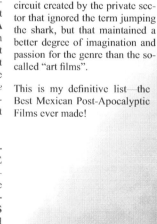

This is my definitive list—the Best Mexican Post-Apocalyptic Films ever made!

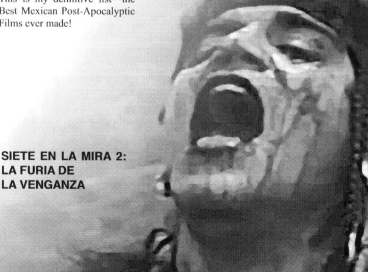

SIETE EN LA MIRA 2: LA FURIA DE LA VENGANZA

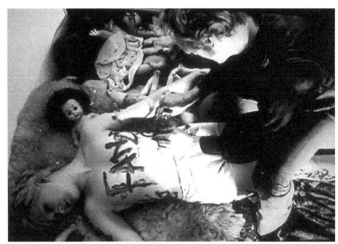

FANDOS Y LIS

INTREPIDOS PUNKS
(Dir. Francisco Guerrero, 1980)
If you are a hardcore genre fan you might already know this legendary piece of Mexploitation Cinema that has become one of the biggest cult films of the last couple years, a lightly third-world ode to **MAD MAX** (1979). It is Francisco Guerrero's first film, but he really knew his Exploitations—the film touches almost every single sub-genre of the Grindhouse circuit, from Nunsploitations to Rape/Revenge films, from Biker films to Punks films, to even Mexicao's own sub-genres like the Luchadores films and Vedettes movies. Imagine Roger Corman producing **THE WILD ANGELS** (1966) written by Salvador Dali, directed by early John Waters, with the hairstylist and make up director of **LIQUID SKY** (1982) and the costume designer of **THE WARRIORS** (1979) down in the Mexican 80's Narco world! Insane and fascinating at the same time.

Ironically the film plot does not mention anything related to a devastated wasteland, but the bizarre occurrences, nihilistic characters, over-the-top vehicles, and badass futuristic-looking clothes makes this one a top contender for pure 80's sci-fi madness. Plus, it's got the baddest, toughest and sexiest lead actress in the Grace Jones side of the universe: Princesa Lea. A cult classic that really deserves its status.

FANDO Y LIS
(Dir. Alejandro Jodorowsky, 1967)
Before **EL TOPO** (1970), Jodorowsky experimented with a B&W surreal film about a couple of hippies' road trip through a post-apocalyptic wasteland in search of the mythical city of Tar. It might be the first openly Mexican post-apocalyptic film and one of the first films to combine metaphysics and the wasteland. Imagine **THE WIZARD OF OZ** (1939) written by Richard Matheson as directed by Fellini. The film plays like absurd performance art pieces, in fact it's too artsy to be consider pure sci-fi entertainment, but the wonderful post-apocalyptic visuals and innovative ideas make this one a must in the history of Post-apocalyptic films.

To this day I can't help to think that it might have had some influence on future sci-fi/post apocalyptic/wasteland films, like the sand segments of **STAR WARS** (1977), the spiritual quest of **MAD MAX BEYOND THUNDERDOME** (1985), David Lynch's **DUNE** (1984), and could those hippie rebels trashing Yank cars in an isolated town and singing and dancing around a abandoned cemetery have been the prototype of those **INTREPIDOS PUNKS**? No doubt Jodorowsky was ahead of his time.

SIETE EN LA MIRA
(Dir. Pedro Galindo III, 1984).
INTREPIDOS PUNKS might be the film that started the Mexican futuristic Punk sub-genre, but **SIETE EN LA MIRA** is the one that popularized it. Right out of the enormous success of their late '70's and early '80's films, the Almada brothers (Mario and Fernando) and genre vet writer Gilberto de Anda reunited to make the ultimate Punk box office hit; Almadas and de Anda realized that what **INTREPIDOS** was missing was a great hero for their awesome villains, so they give us a badass Mexican sheriff living in a Texas border town that would rather use his whip than his own pistol to kick the shit out of cool villain Jorge Reynoso.

SIETE EN LA MIRA took the bizarre formula of **INTREPIDOS PUNKS** and made it accessible, turning into the most famous B-movie that ever played Mexican cinemas, still considered by many a Post-Apocalyptic wasteland film a la *Mad Max*, even though there is no mention about this concept in the plot.

HISTORIAS VIOLENTAS
(Dir. Daniel González Dueñas, Diego López Rivera, Carlos García Agraz, 1985)
The best Mexican anthology film ever made—five directors, five segments: including an alien invasion segment and a tale that suggests that the end of the world could happen in a second grade Cinema; very Lynchian film, with some strange twists in the simplest segments, like the bizarre Halloween party piece and the brutal neighborhood killing that involves a noisy car alarm that just won't shut down.

The whole movie had a very disturbing feeling of the end of the world, like an old school Twilight Zone as directed by Luis Buñuel.

LA VENGANZA DE LOS PUNKS
(Dir. Damián Acosta Esparza,1987)
This is part of the "Post-Apocalyptic vibe" trio of films from superb Exploitation director Damián Acosta Esparza, the other two films are the sick and nasty **EL VIOLADOR INFERNAL** (*The Infernal Rapist*, 1988) and the action-packed **YO SOY LA LEY** (aka **SIETE EN LA MIRA 3**, 1991), but no other Esparza film feels like the end of the world like this sequel to **INTREPIDOS PUNKS**. Another over-the-top rape/revenge story with crazy glam custom designs and the same nihilistic atmosphere of the first movie, but **LA VENGANZA DE LOS PUNKS** goes way beyond just horny Punks killing and raping housewives; this film puts the Punks as Satanic evil entities that live in caves full of non-stop ritualistic ceremonies that include some gross activities, but it is the hero side of the story that really steals the show with some brutal and bloody killings that turn the story into a Slasher type of tale. No Princesa Lea here, but still feels decadent as hell!

SIETE EN LA MIRA stole **INTREPIDOS PUNKS** formula, but it is fair to say that **VENGANZA DE LOS PUNKS** stole **SIETE EN LA MIRA 2**'s satanic concept.

EL AÑO DE LA PESTE
(Dir. Felipe Cazals,1977)
Written by legendary author Gabriel Garcia Marquez and directed by the undisputed king of '70's independent cinema Felipe Cazals, the story of **EL**

SIETE EN LA MIRA

AÑO DE LA PESTE is a straight-up Post-Apocalyptic scenario were the Mexican government deal with the crisis of a horrible Virus, a big drama of talking-heads characters that works as a very pretentious version of George Romero's THE CRAZIES (1973).

Both used to critical acclamations and winning awards, Cazals and Marquez work hard to make an "important" social/political film about the horrible state of the country under the PRI party with a intriguing sci-fi plot, but the movie fails because it's boring and tries to be so intellectual. Still, **EL AÑO DE LA PESTE** is very-well crafted and takes the Outbreak sub-genre very, very seriously. It might be the best-made Post-apocalyptic Mexican film ever produced.

RETEN
(Dir. Sergio Goyri, 1989)

The best thing that Mexican actor Sergio Goyri ever did was to take the director's chair on B-movies during the late '80s and early '90s, because he was as good as Mexploitation director Christian Gonzalez and, may I say, even better in the Fantasy/sci-fi circuit. Most of Goyri productions were done inside the Baja Films Studios, a Videohome production company from Tijuana, but Goyri films weren't like their typical shot-on-video quickies; he turned Baja Films into the Mexican version of Full Moon productions, with well-crafted films with beautiful cinematography and very elaborate special effects for Mexican B-movie standards.

Just when everybody thought that Alex Cox's **DEATH AND THE COMPASS** (1992) was the only film turning Mexico City buildings and abandoned warehouses into a futuristic outland, Goyri creates a B-movie masterpiece out of the architecture in an action-packed film with plenty of explosions, plenty of bullets and Jorge Luke as the ultimate sci-fi rebel! Imagine an Albert Pyun film down in Mexico!

SIETE EN LA MIRA 2: LA FURIA DE LA VENGANZA
(Dir. Pedro Galindo III, 1986)

Pedro Galindo III managed to make a decent sequel without the Almada brothers, assuring that the *Mad Max* suggestion of the original get the point across, with a hero attacking with bow and arrows, bloody chainsaws killings, Punks exploding (!), scissors cutting noses and a town full of witches.

The *Siete En la Mira* films have no nudity or sex as the *Intrepidos Punks* films did but they are stronger in brutal violence, and in this case, in the Witchcraft department, the devil rules the future.

EL VIRUS DEL PODER
(Dir. Jorge Noble, 1988)

Obviously, Videohome expert Jorge Noble wanted to make an important film a la **EL AÑO DE LA PESTE**; he even tried to sell this film as a Drama, but how can you turn a shot-on-video film about a gang of Punk Bikers raping everyone and everything in sight under a virus outbreak in Mexico City into a serious art film? His answer is with lots of talking heads, and in the same vein of **EL AÑO DE LA PESTE**, there are lots of government and health institution characters unnecessarily talking about the cause and effects of the virus. But keeping the ridiculous dialogs aside, **EL VIRUS DEL PODER** is a fun and nasty little film; there is no gore, but you get plenty of sleaze and cheese, enough to make you wanna take a shower after watching it.

For me the charm of a shot-on-video production lies in the non-professional qualities arising from an attempt to make something that works under their limitations—like watching a bunch of people not knowing what they are doing but still trying hard, and in this case the whole cast is overacting like there is no tomorrow, including over-the-top scenes like the raping of a entire aerobics class by the Punk Bikers and some terrible infected characters dying. The Mexican Post-apocalyptic film has never been as trashy and fun as **EL VIRUS DEL PODER**.

RATA MALDITA
(Dir. Ruben Galindo Jr. 1992)

We gotta be grateful for the Videohome circuit that give us some of the most imaginative Mexican films ever made; they are responsible for 99% of sci-fi Mexican cinema between the middle '80s and late '90s, and during this period it was the only film scene that was proudly part of the Mexican Fantastic genre before Guillermo del Toro arrived.

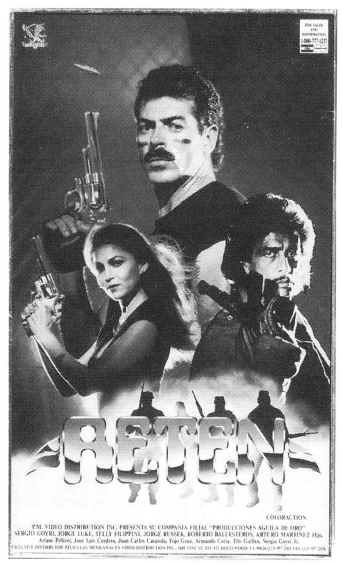

RATA MALDITA is one of those few Mexican modern films that are a straight-up Monster film, a Videohome shot on film about a Post-Apocalyptic society living under those creepy gas masks, with ambitious ideas that are rare for a straight-to-video film, like the special alarms that keep the contamination out of Mexican homes and those kitschy giant rats attacking the innocent citizens, all rendered in a atmospheric sepia tone.

RATA MALDITA could work well as a Troma movie, but missed the sarcasm; director Ruben Galindo Jr. had what it takes but he needed a better budget to go from Z film to B film.

•••

VENGANZA DE LOS PUNKS

DISTANT DREAMS

The Haunting Career of Mary Mendum

by Jeremy Richey

On the morning of July 17th 2012 a sixty year old woman named Mary Mendum accidentally drowned near her home in Boca Raton, Florida. Her passing went all but unnoticed, and few people in the area knew of Mary Mendum's past as one of the most distinctive and memorable actresses of the seventies. While the media ignored it, the news of Mendum's untimely demise filtered through to her adoring fans via message boards and social media outlets like a tragic whisper in the months following her death. For most film fans the name Mary Mendum—or her more famous pseudonym Rebecca Brooke—won't register at all, but for the cinema connoisseurs moved by her work in the seventies for the likes of Chuck Vincent, Radley Metzger and especially Joseph H. Sarno her memory has lingered long past her last moment on celluloid flickered more than three decades ago.

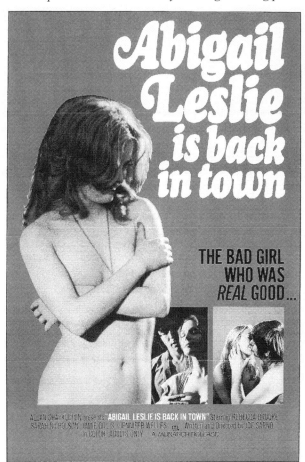

Speaking to noted film historian and Sarno biographer Michael Bowen in her final interview, Mendum reminisced on her career as an actress and noted, "Sometimes I feel I missed the mark; there just wasn't time to form the character", but for her many fans moved by her work it was precisely her great abilities as an actor that separated her from the many other beauties that were known for their work in erotic cinema. There was something remarkable about Mendum, something both grounded and haunting—as Bowen would write in the liner notes of her finest film, **ABIGAIL LESLEY IS BACK IN TOWN** (1975), she had "a profound composure and a deep vulnerability that appears to transcend theatrical training."

The future erotic star of such works as **THE IMAGE** (1975) and **FELICIA** (1975) was born into a relatively poor environment outside of Chicago during the late winter of 1952. Like many of her contemporaries who would find a home at the center of the Sexual Revolution of the 'Seventies, Mendum came from one of most conservative eras in American history and would experience the sudden rise of rock and roll, Playboy and increasing sexual permissiveness as she matured. By the time the sexual revolution kicked into high gear in the late sixties, Mendum had blossomed into a stunning looking young woman with an adventurous and open sexual attitude and an interest in the arts—especially acting.

Mendum's acting career began on the stage and she found her footing quickly as a performer in a variety of shows, including a role on Broadway in *Lenny* during the summer season of 1971. Blessed with a striking face and luscious body, Mendum also began modeling as the 'Sixties gave way to the 'Seventies, and she soon came to the attention of blossoming adult auteur Chuck Vincent, who cast her in her first role in the largely forgotten 1973 feature **GRACE'S PLACE**, one of the first of many hardcore sex comedies that Vincent directed throughout the 'Seventies.

After a brief bit in Ken Shapiro's silly-but-fun satire **THE GROOVE TUBE** in 1974, Mary was billed for the first time as Rebecca Brooke in Chuck Vincent's **MRS. BARRINGTON**, a 1974 sex farce that would team Mary up for the first time with her future roommate and Sarno co-star Jennifer Welles. Indeed, it was around this time that Sarno became aware of Mary Mendum, and the two were introduced in 1974 in Sarno's Manhattan apartment where they discussed the possibility of working together.

Mendum recalled to Michael Bowen, "she liked (Sarno) immediately, and the feeling

21

was mutual." The feeling was indeed shared although neither could have known at the time that they were getting ready to embark on one of the most fascinating and noteworthy collaborative cinematic paths of the seventies. Starting with 1974's **CONFESSIONS OF A YOUNG AMERICAN HOUSEWIFE** and ending with **MISTY** (1976) just two years later Mendum and Sarno shot 5 films together and they all stand with the great erotic works of the seventies, with **ABIGAIL LESLEY IS BACK IN TOWN** in particular standing as one of the most resonate works of the period. Bowen would call Mendum perhaps "Sarno's quintessential siren," and her most alchemical moments on-screen come in these films with the legendary and influential American independent icon.

It was immediately apparent with **CONFESSIONS OF A YOUNG AMERICAN HOUSEWIFE** that Sarno had found someone special in Mary Mendum. An actress who would have been at home in the fifties melodramas of Sirk, the sixties therapeutic works of Bergman (or even the later works of Almodovar), Mendum radiated a fierce intelligence and instantly showed herself as the perfect actress for Sarno's particular vision which melded melodrama, satire and sex, often in the same scene. Sarno would tell Bowen on the **ABIGAIL LESLEY** disc that, "She was a very good actress to begin with, she took direction very well", and that "she was able to get across the small moods of a character. " From the swinging young wife in **CONFESSIONS OF A YOUNG AMERICAN HOUSEWIFE** to the lost title character in **MISTY**, Mary Mendum as Rebecca Brooke brought an almost mystical power to Joseph W. Sarno's films in the mid-seventies, a power that transcended the low-budgets and quick shooting schedule each film was subject to.

Mendum's second film with Sarno was the ferociously funny 1974 sex comedy **THE SWITCH OR HOW TO ALTER YOUR EGO**, a film which would give Mendum the chance to flex her considerable comedic chops in a duel role as Dr. Shirley Jekyll / Sherry Hyde. Billed this time as Veronica Parrish, Mendum tears through **THE SWITCH OR HOW TO ALTER YOUR EGO** with a wild abandon and go-for-broke attitude that would make most 'mainstream' actresses blush with envy. The perfect introductory film to Mary Mendum's charms, **THE SWITCH OR HOW TO ALTER YOUR EGO** stands as one of the funniest, and sexiest, films of the seventies.

While she was essentially a Sarno stock-player in this period, Mendum did appear in a few other films here and there including 1975's **THE BLAZER GIRLS**, a forgettable Jean-Paul Scardino sex comedy that is also known as **NAUGHTY SCHOOL GIRLS**. A much more notable step-away from the world of Joe Sarno was Mendum's legendary appearance in Radley Metzger's haunting art-house masterpiece **THE IMAGE**, a startling S&M themed hit that stands as probably the most well-known film Mary Mendum ever appeared in.

As the beautiful young Anne, Mendum (again billed as Rebecca Brooke) gives a staggering performance for Metzger in **THE IMAGE** and it is a shame that the two would never work together again. **THE IMAGE** is a pulverizing film powered by Metzger's sure-handed direction and Mendum's incredibly brave and touching performance that is both savage and tender.

While in Europe filming **THE IMAGE**, Mary was sought out by Metzger's friend and peer, the extremely talented Max Pécas, who offered Mendum a starring role in his sophisticated hardcore film **LES MILLE ET UNE PERVERSIONS DE FELICIA**. Released in the States as **FELICIA**, Pecas' film would find Mendum participating in some of the most explicit hardcore footage of her career but it is far more than just another sex film from the period. Nicely directed, beautifully shot and well-acted by all, **FELICIA** is a rewarding work and Mary is both beautiful and winning in the film.

The incredibly prolific year of 1975 would also find Mendum working again with Sarno, in probably the weakest film of their collaboration (**LAURA'S TOYS**) and the best (**ABIGAIL LESLEY IS BACK IN TOWN**). Shot outside of Stockholm, **LAURA'S TOYS** is actually quite a satisfying work, but it ultimately doesn't have the mesmerizing power of the other Mendum-Sarno films. The film would give Mendum the opportunity to bond even further with Sarno and his wife Peggy behind the scenes though. Peggy would tell Bowen that Mendum would prepare meals for the cast and crew of **LAURA'S TOYS** (Peggy would call her a,"Master chef") and that she even pitched in with the costume designs, as she could "sew any costume, any dress." When Bowen asked Mendum what her memories were of her years with Sarno she would admit that she felt, "a great fondness." The feeling was also shared by Sarno who told Bowen before he passed away that Mendum, "was so great to work with."

If **LAURA'S TOYS** turned out to be a disappointment, the opposite can be said for the astonishing **ABIGAIL LESLEY IS BACK IN TOWN**, Sarno's delicious and moving 1975 melodrama that stands as one of the truly great works of his iconic career. With its pitch-perfect 'Fifties-melodrama-inspired dialogue (which Mendum recalled that Sarno amazingly, " would literally write the day's pages the night before"), inventive direction and great performances (a dream team featuring Mendum, Jamie Gillis, Eric Edwards, Jennifer Jordan and Jennifer Welles), **ABIGAIL LESLEY IS BACK IN TOWN** is quite unlike any other film ever made, a work that perfectly melded Sarno's own erotic visions with the over-the-top emotion of Douglas Sirk and the under-the-table intensity of Ingmar Bergman.

Mary Mendum is truly remarkable as the damaged Priscilla Howe in **ABIGAIL LESLEY IS BACK IN TOWN**. While some might argue for **THE IMAGE**, I believe **ABIGAIL** is Mendum's greatest role and it is rare to find a performance of this depth in low-budget erotica of this or any other period. Mendum was hard on herself as an actor but Sarno wasn't. She would tell Bowen that, "I pressured myself...Joe Sarno never pressured me", and "He would ask me for something exact and be very specific about it but there was no yelling or screaming or criticism." Whatever working chemistry the two had on set together translated beautifully to the screen and their special connection shines through in **ABIGAIL LESLEY IS BACK IN TOWN**.

Mary Mendum would find great support on and off the set during her years working with Joe Sarno. The great Jamie Gillis would tell Bowen that she was "a great favorite of mine as a person and beauty" while Peggy Sarno would emotionally say, "She was such a real person as well as an actress. It was so wonderful just to be with her", but by 1976 Mary Mendum was growing more and more exhausted and unhappy with the direction her career was going. That weariness was still apparent more than thirty years later when she told Bowen, ""I left acting because the market started to dry up in the mid-to-later 'Seventies for the low budget films I was doing. Everything pretty much became hardcore by that time."

Mary would only have a few films left in her by the time of **ABIGAIL LESLEY IS BACK IN TOWN**'s release in 1975. She would reunite for a bit with Chuck Vincent in 1976's hardcore offering **BANG BANG YOU GOT IT**, but the fire and commitment was disappearing. The fizzle was also apparent in director Roberto Mitrotti's **LITTLE GIRL...BIG TEASE**, a limp 1976 rape drama that stands as probably Mendum's weakest work.

Thankfully before retiring completely from acting, Mary Mendum worked with Joe Sarno one more time, in 1976's **MISTY**, one of Sarno's hardest to come by films. Perhaps sensing that it was her final hoorah on screen, Mendum again gives Sarno an accomplished and complicated performance that has lingered in the memories of those lucky enough to have gray market copies of this criminally obscure Sarno treasure.

After a brief appearance in the forgettable 1977 teen comedy **CHERRY HILL HIGH**, Mary Mendum vanished and would drop out of the public eye until her surprise appearance on the supplemental material gathered together by Michael Bowen for the **ABIGAIL LESLEY IS BACK IN TOWN** special edition DVD. All but unrecognizable from the searing and free beauty who made such an impression during the seventies as Rebecca Brooke, Mary Mendum seemed both proud of her work and regretful. It is doubtful that she truly grasped the impression she made on many of us at the time and since. Peggy Sarno would remember that "She had piercing eyes. Her face would glow and not many actresses had that." Viewing her greatest works today, all these decades later, it is now more apparent than ever that there was something really special about Mary Mendum. A great beauty with talent to burn, it is tragic that her career and life were both cut short but her story is ultimately a triumphant reminder of a time in American cinema when openness and freedom counted for more than critical kudos and box-office success.

...

Reference source:
Retro Seduction Cinema's **ABIGAIL LESLEY IS BACK IN TOWN/LAURA'S TOYS** DVD set featuring Michael Bowens' liner notes and video interviews with Mary Mendum, Joe and Peggy Sarno and Jamie Gillis.
IMDB Bio and filmography

MEXICAN MONSTERS ON PARADE
Part Uno

by Douglas Waltz

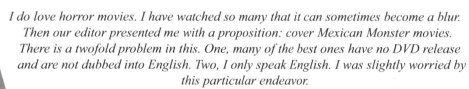

I do love horror movies. I have watched so many that it can sometimes become a blur. Then our editor presented me with a proposition: cover Mexican Monster movies. There is a twofold problem in this. One, many of the best ones have no DVD release and are not dubbed into English. Two, I only speak English. I was slightly worried by this particular endeavor.
In the end, I'm glad I did this. There are some things that are universal.

Monster movies are one of those.

My plan is to cover a set of films each issue of the magazine. Some are good. Some are horrid. Kind of a mixed bag.

Before we get into the reviews of the film, I would like to mention that Mexican movies are not Spanish movies. They might share a language, sort of, but they couldn't be more different. I look at the Mexican horror film as the working man's horror movie. Spanish horror tends to have loftier goals.

First up is **LA DINASTÍA DE DRACULA** (*The Dynasty of Dracula*, 1980, D: Alfredo B. Crevenna). Luckily, this one is subtitled. At first I thought I had stumbled into a long lost Jess Franco film. A warlock is dragged before the villagers. Sometimes he is a dog, sometimes a man. His name is Orloff and they are getting ready to execute him for his heinous crimes. His mistress is along for the ride and she swears that she will return in three hundred years to resurrect him.

Cut to modern day with a lengthy shot of huge ships on the ocean and you know why I thought I was in Franco territory. Maybe director Alfredo B. Crevanna was inspired. He was responsible for 151 of his own films so anything is possible.

So, the mistress returns—she can also turn into a dog, by the way—and she has brought some muscle in the form of Dracula. This Dracula with huge mutton chops and fangs so large he can't close his mouth is a sight to behold. At first he is just a force of evil, killing everyone in sight. But, then he becomes sophisticated and tries to seduce the local wealthy family's daughter, killing her mother in the process and turning her into a vampire. It is up to Dr. Fuentes, fiancée of the daughter, to convince the local priest that they are up against a vampire and need to act accordingly.

This was such a fun take on the Dracula mythos. The scene where he slaughtered an entire family, including the little boy was unnerving. No slick swoop in and cloak to hide the effect. He picks the kid up screaming and the blood flows as he slakes his thirst. I liked how they used various alternate methods against the vampire like communion. Mexico being predominantly Catholic, that didn't surprise me too much. The credits said Fabian was in it, but after a little research I found out that actor Fabian Aranza who plays the hero used to refer to himself as Fabian. Oh well, still a great effort.

The next film steers to comedy with **CAPULINA CONTRA LAS MOMIAS** (*Capulina Versus the Mummies*, 1973, D: Alfredo Zacarías). Capulina is actually a beloved Mexican comedy character performed by Gaspar Henaine who appeared in over thirty films as a bumbling goof. Think Ernest for this guy, but more popular. At least in Mexico.

Capulina plays a taxi driver who is taking a man to visit his scientist friend out in the country at his huge villa. Unbeknownst to them, the scientist friend is experimenting with bringing mummies back to life. Hijinks ensue as they try to keep away from the mummies. The scientist friend appears to have a heart attack every few minutes and they have to revive him. A lot of slapstick becomes predictable after a while; when Capulina walks out to the side of the

pool where a beautiful woman is sunbathing you know it isn't going to be long before he falls in the pool. He does.

The mummies become more human when they are processed properly and soon they are up to their ears in mummies. Like I said, silly, but a fun kind of silly that reminded me of watching movies when I was a kid.

But that is nothing compared to our next comedy/horror fusion.

CHABELO Y PEPITO CONTRA LOS MONSTRUOS (*Chabelo and Pepito Versus the Monsters*, 1973, D: José Estrada) is an all-out monster fest! We get Dracula, Frankenstein, Werewolf, Mummy, A Creature from the Black Lagoon knock-off along with evil men trying to do brain transplants and robots! In 90 minutes!

The scene in the cave where Chabelo and Pepito are trying to keep The Mummy in his sarcophagus while the Creature knock-off fights Frankenstein is cinematic gold! The actor in the Creature suit takes flying leaps and tries to beat the crap out of Frankenstein to no avail. It felt like a surreal Lucha Libre match.

After watching this I was curious about the character Chabelo. Here is a full grown man hanging out with a little kid and appears to be a kid as far as the movie is concerned. More research revealed that Chabelo makes Capulina look like an amateur.

When Chabelo (Xavier Lopez Rodriguez) was a boy he got laryngitis and his voice never matured. Turning this into a bit, he became the most beloved actor in all of Mexico. Don't believe me? His television show En Familia con Chabelo has been on the air every Sunday since 1968! Take that!

When you accept Chabelo at face value in the movie it works. My only regret is that there were no subtitles. There is some dialogue I would really like to understand. Probably time to dust off my Spanish language program I got for Christmas a few years back.

Finally, we have **EL BESO DE ULTRATUMBA** (*The Kiss from Beyond the Grave*, 1963, D: Carlos Toussaint). The basic plot is this jackass thinks he will be the next big writer and needs a rich wife. He finds an heir to a huge dynasty and whisks her off her feet. Then the other shoe drops when her father kills himself and it comes to light that he was bankrupt. The only thing he left his daughter was a half million in life insurance. The jackass is so disgusted that he forces her to move to his boyhood home and work herself to the bone. He is trying to scare her to death so he can collect the money and become a writer.

I did find it interesting that this jackass never once wrote anything in the movie. A typical writer that you can find at any Starbucks.

He tells her of the legend that the villa is haunted and strange things begin happening.

I'm going to leave this one right here. The movie is slow, creaky and the lead male character is so unlikable that anything that happens to him is nothing more than well deserved. Nothing happens for the entirety of the film. The end is supposed to be the big shocker, but I was just happy it was over. I can't blame the language barrier because it had subtitles. THIS had subtitles. I had to suffer through not knowing every detail of Chabelo, but THIS had subtitles.

I tell you folks, the world is unfair.

●●●

My first foray into the world of Mexican cinema had its highs and lows and I discovered so many interesting characters along the way. Next time? Well, you'll have to wait and see.

THE INCUBUS: CASSAVETES AND HOUGH CHART THE KRUEGER FAMILY TREE

by Ryan Carey

When it comes to the twisted and complex family tree grown out of Wes Craven's classic A NIGHTMARE ON ELM STREET, it's a safe bet to say that most here are no doubt well familiar with its branches—there's the progenitor of the clan itself, dating back to 1985, followed by five direct descendants (those being the "official" sequels), two let's-call-them-cousins (in the form of the meta-fictional Wes Craven's NEW NIGHTMARE and the franchise mash-up/cash-in FREDDY VS. JASON), and a bastard offspring no one likes to talk much about (the 2010 Michael Bay-air-quote-produced remake). But what about its roots?

John Cassavetes as Dr. Sam Cordell seen here with a doppelgänger of Henry Fuseli Füssli's 1781 painting "The Nightmare".

To explore those, my friend, we have to go back to medieval folklore, specifically the legends surrounding a creature known as an incubus. Evidently, this homicidally-inclined, violently horny variety of demon would first appear in some unlucky pubescent male's head in the form of a recurring dream, then somehow find its way out into the real world and wreak a fairly astronomical amount of havoc, raping any and every human female it could gets its hairy, scaly hands on (and presumably equally scaly-and-hairy schlong into) in a desperate desire to procreate like crazy in the short time it was able to take physical form before the virile lad from whose nightmares it escaped woke up again. There was just one flaw in the logic of yer average incubus, though—since it invariably went on to kill whoever it forced itself upon, those offspring it was after would never come to be, and alas, the sound of tiny hoof-steps was never to be heard in any family home.

Alternately, though, if you don't feel like rifling through a bunch of dusty old tomes in the cavernous sub-basement of some European castle-converted-into-a-library to learn about these things, you can just watch the decidedly gothically-tinged 1982 Canadian tax shelter production THE INCUBUS and be done with it.

Starring the obviously-awesome John Cassavetes (who you most likely know as an actor thanks to ROSEMARY'S BABY or THE DIRTY DOZEN, or as a director thanks to his groundbreaking, highly personal films like FACES, HUSBANDS, THE KILLING OF A CHINESE BOOKIE and A WOMAN UNDER THE INFLUENCE) and directed by the less-obvious-but-no-less-awesome John Hough (a household name only in the abodes of the most seasoned exploitation fans despite a stellar track record that includes DIRTY MARY CRAZY LARRY, THE LEGEND OF HELL HOUSE, and such fondly-remembered Disney fare as THE WATCHER IN THE WOODS, ESCAPE TO WITCH MOUNTAIN and RETURN FROM WITCH MOUNTAIN), our story here centers around the supposed New England (even though it was filmed in and around the Toronto area and the license plates on the cars read, for some reason, Wisconsin) town of Galen, where local pathologist/medical examiner Dr. Sam Cordell (Cassavetes) and police chief Hank Walden (the always-great John Ireland) are investigating a non-stop series of brutal rapes/murders that leave many of the victims so pumped full o' spunk that the initial investigative hunch both men play is that there absolutely must be more than one perpetrator—in fact, they feel it's quite likely that a whole gang of wild n' reckless youths are behind this sordid spree.

Maureen Sweeney's creature for John Hough's **THE INCUBUS**. Sweeney was also responsible for the monster in the 1982 film **HUMONGOUS**.

There's just one wrinkle—all the semen still scurrying about in the dead victims matches, and it's all red. Complicating matters even further is the fact the a local newspaper reporter named Laura Kincaid (Kerrie Keane), who's covering the developing story, just so happens to be a dead ringer for Cordell's deceased wife, and that his ethereally-beautiful teenage daughter, Jenny (Erin Noble, billed here as Erin Flannery) is dating a kid named Tim (Duncan McIntosh) who the good doctor is, shall we say, decidedly less-than-impressed with. Tim's got a less obvious problem than his choosing to get overly-familiar with Sam's precious little angel, though; he's been plagued with horrible, vivid nightmares lately—nightmares invariably revolving around the brutal, ritualistic rape and murder of young women. Oh, and our young would-be-Romeo's last name? It's Galen. Somehow, of course, it's all connected: the dreams, the rapes/murders, the intrepid doppelganger lady reporter, even the secret lineage of the family the town is named after—but how?

Don't let the admittedly salacious nature of the plot fool you, though—for a flick that drops the word "sperm" more often than your average gang-bang porn loop and revolves around an unending string of what are, we're told, the most violent killings the cops have ever seen, almost all the truly horrific stuff happens off-screen. A supernatural I SPIT ON YOUR GRAVE this ain't. Hough instead relies on a constant, oppressive atmosphere of Gothic foreboding—for a Canadian movie purportedly playing out in New England it sure does feel like we're moving between one ancient, dank, stone hall of records here and another—and serious-minded, thoroughly professional performances from his uniformly fine actors to bring the horror home in this one. The script

has some serious flaws and gaping holes, but Hough knows that flawed source material will, when left in good hands, be elevated to a level it may not, technically speaking, even deserve. Just because it doesn't read terribly well on paper or make a tremendous amount of sense in retrospect doesn't mean that John Fucking Cassavetes can't do something good with it, after all.

I guess if I were more inclined to brevity (I'm trying!) I'd sum this one up by saying, "Don't expect a horror classic here, but something of a largely-forgotten, hidden gem—albeit one of more ornamental than actual value." Sound about right?

Fortunately, the "largely forgotten" part of the previous verbal equation is no longer necessarily the case, as Scorpion Releasing has recently seen fit to offer up **THE INCUBUS** as part of its "Katarina's Nightmare Theater" DVD series hosted by former/supposed WWE "diva" Katarina Leigh Watters (apparently when you're a female ex-pro wrestler your two career options are either to start dating George Clooney or become a horror host). The film is presented in a good-looking, remastered 1.85:1 widescreen transfer with pretty decent, also-remastered mono sound. "Extras," such as they are, consist of Watters' semi-informative intro and outro bits, the original theatrical trailer, and a smattering of trailers for other Scorpion titles of semi-recent vintage.

At the end of the day, I have to believe there's just no way Wes Craven didn't see this movie, unless he took up the study of medieval folklore as a hobby there for awhile, because three short years after this was releases he latched onto the core concept of the incubus demon, took its thinly-disguised allegory for the onslaught of male puberty in general down a pedophilic road (oh yeah! remember when Freddy was a child molester who didn't snap off clever one-liners and was actually kinda scary?) and gave it metal claws a la the just-getting-popular-at-the-time X-Men character, Wolverine. The rest, as they say, is history.

•••

One Man's Therapy Is Everyone Else's Horror:
Andrzej Zulawski's POSSESSION

by Tony Strauss

*"The story of **POSSESSION** is the story of my life. This is the only film I've made in my lifetime which is really autobiographic."*
-Andrzej Zulawski

Ukrainian-born Polish expatriate Andrzej Zulawski is a filmmaker whose work has always been synonymous with controversy. And that controversy, for better or worse, has been a primary catalyst in the creation of a diverse, globe-spanning, multilingual body of work for the auteur. His often shockingly violent, political, psychosexual, taboo-shattering films have frequently suffered backlash that has resulted in his need to relocate from country to country in order to find willing homes for his creative output. The 1981 Horror/Drama POSSESSION, while easily his best-known work, remains a divisive film even among its most avid fans. Although the film's basic premise is initially quite straightforward, the narrative eventually gives way to symbolism and allegory as the characters descend into madness, leaving many viewers confounded by the bizarre presentation of what is at its core a deeply intimate retelling of one of the most traumatic periods in the filmmaker's personal life.

Zulawski's debut feature, **THE THIRD PART OF THE NIGHT** (*Trzecia czesc nocy* – 1971), an adaptation of his father's novel of the same name, enjoyed success in Poland despite the film's provocative setting during the country's WWII Nazi occupation. After his second feature, **THE DEVIL** (*Diabel* – 1972), was banned by the Polish government for its blasphemous themes and harsh political allegory, he relocated to France and made **THAT MOST IMPORTANT THING: LOVE** (*L'important c'est d'aimer* – 1975). Following the European success of that third feature, he returned to Poland to direct what was intended to be his fourth film, the ambitious sci-fi epic **ON THE SILVER GLOBE** (*Na srebrnym globie* – 1988). After nearly two full years of development and production, filming was abruptly shut down by the government, who found the political subtext within the story offensive, and the footage was confiscated (he managed to save the negative, thankfully), leaving the film unfinished for over a decade. Disillusioned and defeated, he returned to France with his family. Not long after, his marriage fell apart and ended in a messy divorce, inspiring him to write his most autobiographical film to date: the horrific, psychotically emotional monster movie, **POSSESSION** (1981).

To hear Zulawski tell the story of the film's initial inspiration, and the concept he pitched to financiers—the story of "a woman who fucks an octopus"—one might be inclined to think he was attempting to adapt Japanese artist Hokusai's

Hokusai's *The Dream of the Fisherman's Wife*, an 1814 erotic woodcut in the ukiyo-e genre, was the artist's most famous work, and would appear to be part of the thematic inspiration behind **POSSESSION**.

famous woodcut, *The Dream of the Fisherman's Wife*, into a narrative film. One can easily see how that thematic connection can be made, for **POSSESSION** does involve the horrific coupling of a woman and a hideous creature in one of its key sequences. However, viewing the film, it becomes clear that Zulawski's pitch of the film was a bit on the glib and sensationalistic side, because what he ultimately delivered was a dark and personal examination of loyalty and betrayal in a crumbling relationship, and the powerful emotions and pain experienced in its destruction…with a monster thrown in the mix, for good measure.

To play out his autobiographical monster drama, adept casting was essential, as the script required performances of a vast range of aggressive emotions displayed in methods not commonly called for from actors (outside of a Zulawski film, that is). Working within his casting budget, Zulawski cast then-relatively-unknown Australian actor Sam Neill to play Mark, the onscreen representation of Zulawski himself, and young French superstar Isabelle Adjani—whose much-publicized diva behavior had recently made her a less-desirable, hence less expensive, casting choice—as Anna, the surrogate for his ex-wife. Budget restraints or not, it's hard to imagine how he could have chosen better, for their performances in this film remain among the most powerful in either actors' careers.

Zulawski chose West Berlin for the film's location, feeling the then-divided city to be the perfect setting for a pitch-black family drama tackling the themes of duality, deception and doppelgangers. The stark and ominous ambiance of the locations adds tremendously to the film's sense of claustrophobia and captivity, and furthermore, Zulawski shot the exteriors completely devoid of background action. The streets are always deserted of cars and people, save for the primary characters involved in any given scene. This gives the overall atmosphere a sense of being apart from society and the world, existing on its own isolated plane of lonely existence. This desolate atmosphere, combined with the deeply personal and honest story, and the aggressively manic, externalized emotions (a Zulawski trademark, for which he was famously accused by Adjani of making "psychological pornography") of the characters that inhabit it, delivers a truly uncomfortable and fascinating cinematic experience that has both captivated and confounded audiences for over three decades.

The film received wildly mixed reviews when it was initially released; it was a minor success in France, but after a limited theatrical release in the UK, it was banned as a Video Nasty until 1999. For American distribution, the film was cut by some 43 minutes, with scene order being completely rearranged to emphasize the horror elements of the story, and released unceremoniously on home video by Wynmore Films. Despite the near-incomprehensibility of the butchered cut, the film acquired a cult following due to the unsettling atmosphere, the shocking violence and the surreal nature of the story and imagery. In May of 2000, Anchor Bay released the 123-minute director's cut on DVD, allowing many to see the film as intended for the first time.

In the intervening years, **POSSESSION** has gained significant cult status among both horror and art-house fans, as well as hateful backlash from many who consider the film too uncomfortable, too violent, too boring, or too deliberately obtuse. However, viewing the film within the right context—as the autobiographical catharsis of an artist whose identity has been viciously torn away, first by loss of country and then by the dissolution of his own family—enables a deeper understanding of the film's esoteric and often psychedelic proceedings.

Readers should be warned that, as this is a scene-by-scene analysis of the film, it is necessary for the discussion at hand to include flagrant plot spoilers. Every attempt has been made to organize this article in chronological order within the film's plot, so those who have not seen the film have the option of reading as much or as little of the narrative's contents as they choose. Readers who wish to avoid the details of the film's conclusion should skip sections 5 and 6 until they have viewed the film in its entirety.

1 – Possessions Now Lost

"This film comes from a very simple vision: We are all unhappy, and we don't deserve it. We would love to see things around us—in us—otherwise than they are, and we don't know how to deal with that, how to do it."
- Andrzej Zulawski

The dissolution of a long-standing relationship can bring about some of the most painful and traumatic experiences of a person's life, not only from having the security of an established stasis and lifestyle broken down and torn away, but a loss of one's own sense of identity and place in the world. Regardless of the pains that come from continuing to live in an unhealthy relationship, the thought of admitting defeat and actually ending things to start one's life anew—even when it is obviously for the better—can be terrifying. The hurt, mistrust, and sense of betrayal involved in a bad breakup can bring about the absolute worst in people's behavior, causing those who once bonded in love and trust to lash out at each other in utter loathing and contempt. The emotional shockwaves emitted are far-reaching and manifold, affecting not only the couple, but family and friends, as well. If there are children, the pain just grows all the more.

But the devastation of a breakup is a Universal Truth. It is something almost all of us will have to go through at least once in our lives—for most people, multiple times—and it never gets any easier or less painful. The relationships we have are some of the most significant milestones in our lives, and many a story has been told on the subject of breaking up and starting over; it is the topic of countless novels and films, and has, over time, developed its own narrative formula, wherein the involved parties suffer the loss of what they once knew and loved, only to be reborn stronger and wiser having lived through the hardships, and having presumably gained a greater insight to themselves and life in general from the experience. This formula is a staple of the Family Drama and Romantic Comedy genres, and a very successful one due to its universal relatability, and the catharsis of experiencing this familiar process with likeable characters, resulting in a comfortable and uplifting ending.

That Zulawski chose to exorcise his own relationship-based demons by

Anna and Mark discuss the emotional void within their marriage.

making a movie is hardly innovative—stories about relationships would ring completely false without the author's interjection of personal experience. But where Zulawski's film breaks away from form is in his method of telling, by turning his own deeply personal experiences of a Universal Truth into a surreal, allegorical tale that, while superficially following the standard formula of loss and emotional rebirth, metamorphoses from Family Drama into outright Horror, while never flinching away from depicting the most intimate emotions and behaviors involved—it actually assaults the audience with them—and comes out in the end more honest and truthful than most other stories within the genre.

As the film opens, we find Mark on the curb with his luggage in front of the couple's apartment building, having returned from an extended business trip. Anna has just informed him of her desire to separate, and Mark is completely taken aback by the news. Anna can't give a reason for her feelings, nor does she have a plan or endgame in mind, but she's clearly unhappy. The scene is an immediately familiar one in a breakup scenario: Mark wants to know reasons, to discuss possible courses of action, but he's up against a blank wall with Anna, who is either uncertain or unwilling to admit what she wants. Frustrated and apparently uninterested in further discussion, Anna goes inside, and Mark follows.

While Mark gives their son Bob (Michael Hogben) a bath, he calls Anna into the bathroom to admire him. They share a genuine laugh for a brief moment over their mutual love for their son, but any hope gleaned from the moment would be false. Later, lying in bed together—naked, but clearly without passion, and emotionally separated by leagues—Anna speculates, "Maybe all couples go through this...Maybe I was asking too much." Mark blames himself for being away for so long, and not being more attentive to his family's needs. They both claim to have been completely faithful to one another, but feelings have clearly changed. Mark claims that without her, he wouldn't feel anything at all. She asks him what he feels now, and when he asks her if she's really interested, she shakes her head and sadly replies, "No." Mark has come home to find he has no home.

At a mysterious work-related meeting, in which he is questioned by a panel of men in a large, sparsely-furnished room, Mark is revealed to be a spy, having just returned from a successful surveillance mission. The men ask him questions regarding some transaction with the subject to whom he has been assigned. There's no exposition in the conversation, so there's very little context given as to the nature of the mission, other than the fact that the transaction involved two vials, and that the subject has a penchant for wearing pink socks. Mark turns in his report, "To fill in my successor...I've completed my job." He refuses an offer for rehire, declaring family matters as his reason for doing so. His employers strongly imply that it may not be in his best interests to refuse the job, but he stands firm and informs them that he'll be unavailable for the foreseeable future, but he hopes that it won't be

Mark arrives home from a business trip to find his marriage in shambles.

for too long. He walks away from the meeting and stops outside to open his briefcase and quickly examine the huge stack of money inside. He returns to the apartment to find Anna and Bob are not at home. He stares out the window at the Berlin Wall, where two guards seem to be watching him.

It may seem a bit cliché to have made the protagonist a spy, but when you consider that this is an autobiographical work, the choice is hardly arbitrary. Mark, as the surrogate for Zulawski himself, has, by walking away from his top-secret government job, essentially rendered himself without a country as well as an occupation. Zulawski's career has been fraught with political censorship and controversy, ultimately resulting in the filmmaker also becoming a man without a country—a major layer of his identity stripped away—so this parallel only adds weight to the autobiographical aspects of the story.

After country, the two most powerful sources of an adult's identity come from one's family and profession. They are how we define much of who we are, and the two biggest areas by which we measure our own worth. Mark is faced with the danger of losing his family, and in an effort to save it, he is abandoning his work, immediately propelling his primary sources of identity and self-worth into a state of limbo. At a time where his greatest inner strength and resolve are desperately needed, he is crippled from the onset, greatly from his own willingness to sacrifice his own (obviously highly important) job in an effort to focus on his family. With adept shorthand, Zulawski displays the disarming helplessness that can so easily come about from simply attempting to do the right thing, and the immediate repercussions that so easily add to the damage already accrued. No good deed goes un-punished, as they say.

2 – *Empty Spaces Filled*

"For me, it's the story of a very sweet guy who goes into the woman's folly, the woman's craziness, and he follows. He goes down with her."
- Andrzej Zulawski

What makes "moving on" so difficult in the aftermath of a breakup are the constant reminders of what we once had that remain all around us when the other person is gone. Every facet of our lives suddenly becomes tied to our time with the person we've lost, and subsequently the absence of that person makes all those reminders so much more noticeable to us. Our own identity, once inexorably tied to our significant other, is suddenly halved, making the act of simply getting up and going on with our lives a herculean task, for the vacant hole left in our world is all-consuming. Mark, suffering this sudden loss, cannot even entertain the possibility of moving on without Anna. He can only think to do everything within his power to find answers and fix things, for the alternative is too bleak to even consider.

Having fallen asleep at the apartment, Mark is awakened by a phone call from Anna. She tells him she needs time to think. When he asks what she needs to think about, she angrily replies, "To think about me," and hangs up. Enraged, Mark begins frantically searching through Anna's belongings for some insight into what's going on with her. Tucked into a book on Tantra,

Mark suffers a total breakdown facing the loss of his family, his job and his very identity.

he finds a postcard from the Taj Mahal reading, "I've seen half of God's face here. The other half is you... -Heinrich".

From a pleading phone call with Anna's best friend, Margie (Margit Carstensen), Mark finally gets confirmation that there is definitely another man in Anna's life. Anna phones again, and when he confronts her with his new knowledge, she admits that she's calling from her lover's place. He interrogates her, demanding specific information, getting her to admit that she's been seeing him for a long time, that they are indeed sleeping together, and that it's better with him than it is with Mark.

Anna seems to be in the midst of her own identity crisis, fleeing from her responsibilities of family in favor of something/someone new, regardless of the repercussions. She is aloof, angry and deceptive in the face of Mark's pained pleadings. She denied that there was another man, yet when confronted with it, she touts it coldly, caring only about herself. This is clear representation of Mark's (and therefore, Zulawski's) point-of-view in this situation of loss. We see her as her abandoned husband sees her: as a cruel, heartless, selfish person who seems to have no remorse for the hurt that she is causing. This (initially) one-sided perspective is ironic, because by viewing her only from Mark's point-of-view, we are effectively guilty of the same selfish perspective, and not considering what her feelings might be. But this, of course, will change somewhat when more is revealed, for this is much more than merely a personal domestic revenge piece.

Completely alone and stripped of identity, Mark here officially begins his personal downward spiral, forcefully asking all the questions that no one in his position would never want the honest answers to. He is desperate for answers that he can address, understand and control, but in a vulnerable place of loss and hurt, he is, in a seemingly deliberate act of self-abuse, opening the doors to even more sorrow. Anyone in his situation always thinks they want to know those very answers, but would be woefully unprepared for the pain that the truly honest answers would bring. At that moment, there is nothing more painful than to hear one's worst fears so coldly and casually confirmed.

Mark and Anna meet at a café to work out a course of action. Although seated next to each other, they face in opposite directions while they talk. Mark agrees to give the apartment and a monthly stipend to her and Bob, but has decided not to see Bob, feeling he will "fuck him up even more by playing Sunday Daddy". Anna calls him inhuman, to which he replies, "Then what you're doing must be human...How do you dispose of ideas like loyalty and honesty?" Mark becomes twitchy and erratic as she admits that she was in her lover's bed the first night she met him. She tells him, "No one is good or bad, but if you want, I am the bad one, and if I knew he existed in this world, I would have never had Bob with you!" Mark blows up, shouting and throwing chairs, and chases her out of the café.

This is yet another familiar scenario in the course of a bad breakup. No matter how civilly the two parties attempt to act toward one another, something

Even when meeting together, Mark and Anna are far apart.

always gives way to argument and reactive biting, exacerbating the situation. There is so much hurt and anger in the air that proper communication becomes impossible, for both parties so badly wish to voice their grievances that civil discussion falls by the wayside. Here, even a simple attempt at arranging lodgings and visitation plans immediately erupts into spiteful conflict. Though he is powerless to stop himself, Mark is causing himself ever more sorrow with his desperate idea that this can somehow be fixed, that if they establish some kind of plan, things can begin moving toward reparations. His desperation is understandable; he has returned from an extended absence to find that his place within Anna's life (an important station of his identity) has been replaced by some stranger. He doesn't yet understand that Anna has already moved on in her mind, that she is already establishing a new identity for herself, and any pleading attempts on his part will only drive her away further, as is quite obviously happening.

Mark takes a hotel room, where, alone in his misery, he falls completely apart, drinking, becoming filthy and unshaven, and suffering from spasms and seizures. He attempts to make a phone call, but can only utter guttural, choking sounds. He staggers around the trash-littered room in a sweaty blazer like a dazed lunatic, pale and sickly-looking. The maid arrives to clean his room, and he asks her how long he's been there. She informs him, "Three weeks, Sir."

By bringing us so subjectively into Mark's sudden loss of family and self, and then forcefully dragging us to bear intimate witness to his personal breakdown, Zulawski is cementing our identification with Mark as the victim in this situation. We are intended to experience this emptiness alongside both the storyteller and his character, to feel as disoriented, isolated and alone as they do. And as we discover the ever-more painful truths that are to come, we will all suffer together, as well.

3 – Control Taken

"The clash of the characters in this film is between people pushing behaviors and values forward, because this is their only shield."
- Andrzej Zulawski

Mark confronts Anna about her responsibility to her family.

Invariably, in situations of intense personal loss, when the rug has been pulled completely out from under us, our first instinct is to desperately attempt to seize control of any facets of our life that we can. Unfortunately, when we are so psychologically disoriented and damaged, any such attempts are usually misdirected or misprioritized, and at best result in wasted time and effort or embarrassment, but usually end up causing more damage and hurt. But from the bottom looking up, any desperate attempts to climb upward seem appealing, even when we're in no condition to do so. Despite the fact that Mark is in the midst of a personal breakdown, his reaction to what he perceives as rock-bottom is to stubbornly attempt that climb.

Having showered and shaven, but still looking sickly and pale in his still-sweaty and stained suit, Mark visits the apartment to find that Anna has left Bob home alone, for apparently quite a long time. Both Bob and the apartment are a mess. As Mark helps his son undress to get cleaned up, he tenderly grasps the boy's body while his arms are raised, and gazes upon him lovingly. This is a significant gesture that recurs multiple times in the film, to different effect; it is a simple, tactile symbolization of loving appreciation for the physical presence of those closest to us, and for the bodies they inhabit, the space they occupy in our lives. Here, he is looking upon this innocent child—his child—who is caught in the middle of all this family pain, pain for which Mark, himself, is partially responsible.

Anna returns home, flustered and embarrassed and full of excuses. Mark assures that he's not taking Bob away from her, but sternly announces, "I'm taking over here." He demands that she call her lover and break it off, but she insists that she can't do it over the phone, promising to do so in-person. Just like he's done with Bob, he helps her get undressed to clean up, and he repeats the gesture of gently grasping her body in his hands, gazing upon the familiar flesh of the one who is at this moment slipping from his very grasp.

Mark puts Anna to bed, and they hold hands. Shed of her ubiquitous blue dress and in the soft light of the room, Anna looks for the first time vulnerable, relaxed, almost tender, once again luring Mark (and the viewer) into a sense of eager hope that somehow the two might work this out and reconcile their situation.

But as Mark is awakened in the harsh light of day by the blaring of the telephone, he realizes he is once again alone. He answers the phone, and a man's voice informs him, "Anna is with me, and she'll stay with me," before abruptly hanging up. He falls back on the bed next to a note from Anna reading, "My love, I had to go to talk to Margie, so I would never hurt you again." He calls Margie, and finding that Anna is not with her, demands Heinrich's phone number. But when he phones, Heinrich's mother (Johanna Hofer) answers the phone and tells Mark, "Anna's not here...haven't seen her for weeks. I miss her so much." Mark hangs up, confused.

The next day, Mark brings Bob to school and meets Bob's teacher, Helen (also played by Adjani), who, aside from different hair and eye color, is identical in appearance to Anna. At first, Mark thinks it's a joke—that it's Anna in a wig—but Helen is obviously a very different person; she's vivacious, friendly and relaxed...the polar opposite of Anna. Mark asks her if she's ever seen his wife. Laughing, she replies, "Naturally, every day of the school year." Mark is baffled.

With a one-two punch, Mark's perception of his entire situation is challenged. First, believing Anna to be with her lover, having just received a threatening phone call from him, Mark is told that she has not been at Heinrich's flat for weeks. Then, as soon as his wife goes missing, he meets her exact double. For someone so desperate for answers and understanding, what little he thought he did understand is being shattered, replaced with even more questions. His attempts to control the situation in any straightforward manner are continuously being thwarted; if anything, he knows even less than before. Completely heartbroken, afraid, and utterly confused, he is at his weakest and most vulnerable at the moment he's attempting to restore order.

Mark holds his son (above, top) and his wife (above, bottom) in the same loving grasp, as he contemplates the loss of the things that are most important to him.

With Bob safely at school, Mark shows up at the apartment of Anna's lover, Heinrich (Heinz Bennent), demanding to see her. Heinrich, a suave, confident, immediately irritating new-age guru-type, invites Mark in to prove that Anna is not there. Where Mark is tense and angry, Heinrich is relaxed and calm, telling Mark that they don't have to be hostile with one another, and quipping prophetic nonsense like, "Our situation is like a mountain lake we are trying to swim in, starting from different shores." Heinrich arrogantly claims to have opened Anna up sexually in ways that benefit all three parties, and that he wanted the affair—which has been going on for a year—to be out in the open, but Anna refused, and he always accepts Anna's ways. When Mark demands why, then, Heinrich felt the need to phone him up and speak for Anna, Heinrich is confused; he's just arrived back in town from Hamburg—he'd left town the day Mark got back to give Anna a chance to decide for herself.

Played with annoying perfection by Bennent, Heinrich is immediately loathed by both Mark and the viewer alike. He's the kind of person who lives a charmed life with no real problems who claim to "know the answers",

Mark is shocked to learn that his son's teacher, Helen, is his wife's perfect double.

Mark meets self-styled guru Heinrich, the man for whom he has been rejected.

31

obnoxiously touting themselves as having reached inner peace with all of existence, and gazing upon everyone around them as unenlightened fools to be pitied and shepherded. He is a character obviously very important to Zulawski's autobiographical tale; Zulawski himself says of Heinrich, "I hate him. As simple as that. I hate the guy. And he comes from true life…This guy is dangerous like poison."

We don't know who the Heinrich in Zulawski's personal life was, nor how true-to-life the screen representation of him is, but the character is an astute representation of the kind of image a rejected husband might form about his rival: "Whoever she left me for must *seem* superior in every way, but is really a complete scumbag who's somehow pulled the wool over her eyes." Heinrich, with his shirt always obnoxiously unbuttoned to show his chest, seems like just the kind of scumbag who would prey on unhappy wives, and expect to be thanked by the cuckolded husbands.

When the two men are interrupted by the arrival of Heinrich's mother, Mark asks if she was always there, even when Heinrich and Anna were fucking. Heinrich quips, "But of course," and Mark gives in to his seething rage and lashes out at Heinrich. Naturally, a smug lothario like Heinrich who preaches spirituality and gives women books on Tantra would also be a martial artist, which Heinrich turns out to be. He easily deflects Mark's blind-rage attack and viciously counterattacks, beating Mark to a pulp while pausing for ridiculous meditative poses between blows. He picks the bloodied Mark up off the floor and holds him close, seeming to admire and pity him while displaying an air of having both physically and sexually conquered him. Mark makes a strained attempt to choke Heinrich, and gets kidney-chopped for his effort. Heinrich effortlessly heaves Mark across his shoulders and carries him out like a sack of garbage. So much for Mark's desperate and ill-advised attempts to regain control. He has now been robbed of any understanding of his situation, and has been physically bested—effectively, controlled—by his sexual rival.

4 – Doppelgangers Encountered

"The ultimate thing for me was to take a soap opera…and pull it into a dimension which doesn't exist."
- Andrzej Zulawski

Fantasizing scenarios where our problems are non-existent is a trait that all of us share, no matter who we are or what our problems may be. Restructuring our situation in our mind, we imagine how things could be returned to the way we were before our troubles arose; we concoct alternate versions of reality, in which we and those with whom we are in conflict behaved differently. Zulawski, never content with simple dramatics, will take this basic human tendency from the level of soap-operatic fantasy into the realm of horrific literality with Mark and Anna's spiral into misery and madness.

Mark arrives back at the apartment to find Anna home, having lunch with Bob, laughing and singing. The moment she sees Mark, her smile fades to seething hostility. Bob goes to play outside, and the inevitable fight begins. Mark demands to know where she was, since she wasn't with Margie as she claimed in her note. "I was with *him*," she claims. But Mark tells her that he's just come from Heinrich's, and she wasn't there. She attests that she was with "new friends", and claims that she left last night to be alone, but Mark points out that she *just said* she was with friends. Hell-bent on getting some answers, and still struggling for some semblance of control, Mark pushes her into an all-out screaming match. She slaps him, and he tells her to do it again, but she just grins wickedly and bolts for the door. He stops her and begins slapping her repeatedly, "For the lies." Defiantly, she spits back through a mouthful of blood, "Then you'll have to hit much more," and flees the apartment. He follows her outside, and she darts in front of an oncoming truck, causing an accident which she doesn't even notice, for she has suddenly fallen into a trance. She has become fully possessed by whatever force is pulling her farther and farther away from her family and her captive life. She follows that ever-more-powerful call away, down the deserted streets.

It's at this point that we are shown that Anna is more than just an unhappy housewife who's decided to shun her life for more selfish interests. Thus far, we've seen the emotional outbursts and the cold, cruel detachment she displays toward Mark, but this time we see something more. When Mark attempts to stop her from leaving—even to the point of physical attack—the force that has overtaken her is far more powerful than any simple violence inflicted can hope to control. She has left herself completely, and is now obviously being moved by some other sinister control. This is our first glimpse at the fact that Anna is truly a woman divided, two opposing personalities vying for possession of her body. But this is still just the tip of Anna's iceberg, as we are soon to discover.

Walking back to the apartment, Mark is greeted by Margie, who's shown up to babysit Bob. He tells her that he loathes her, and her reaction is nearly sexual in its excitement, cooing back at him, "I love seeing you miserable… it's so reassuring!" According to Zulawski, the character of Margie also comes from his own life, presumably drawn from his ex-wife's close friend who was present during their breakup. She doesn't play a vital part in the film; she's

Drawn away from her family in a trance, Anna is a woman possessed.

primarily used to aid in the depiction of the various stages of Mark's emotional breakdown, and to help show that he is truly alone and without any genuine support from anyone.

Mark goes to a private detective agency and speaks to a man named Zimmerman (Shaun Lawton) about hiring them to follow Anna, to find out where it is she goes but cannot say. In almost any other film about a breakup, this would be a trite and well-worn cliché, but Zulawski uses this tired plot device to further show how desperate Mark's situation is. After all, Mark's profession is in espionage and surveillance, yet he is so defeated and powerless that he is reduced to hiring a shamus to snoop on his own wife. His embarrassment and insecurity are palpable as he provides the necessary information for the investigation to begin.

Back at the apartment, Bob and Margie are both asleep. Mark tucks Bob into bed, loving, fatherly and gentle, then goes into the master bedroom and tucks in the slumbering Margie in the exact loving, father-to-a-child fashion—even muttering to himself the same "beddie-bye" phrases he whispered over Bob—and closes the bedroom door. A moment later, he re-enters the bedroom and wakes her by sitting down on the edge of the bed, now not at all fatherly, but almost childlike, seeking affection, even if it's from a woman he openly detests. He raises his arms, assuming the pose of the receiving end of the loving grasp he placed on his son and wife, but Margie whimpers and wraps her arms around his waist, laying her head submissively in his lap. Mark looks uncomfortable, obviously not having received the kind of affectionate embrace he sought.

Again we see the recurrence of this gesture, and again it is used to convey a slightly different message. The first two occurrences symbolized feelings of loss and a desire to hold onto that which is in danger or has already begun to slip away; here it is used to show Mark's unfathomable loneliness, and his hopeless desire to be loved and needed by someone, anyone. But once again, the gesture of love becomes a sad reminder of the lack of something important to Mark—in this case, actual human connection. The next day, Anna returns home, her blue dress soiled and stained, much like Mark's suit when he came home after his breakdown. She's impatient and hostile, and doesn't want any discussion. Mark pleads with her as she begins cutting and grinding meat for dinner. Echoing the earlier café scene, they face away from each other while attempting to communicate. Mark questions her as she nods yes or shakes her head no in response, all of which is unseen by Mark. She claims to be happy, in love with her new paramour, and denies seeing Bob and Mark as obstacles in her way of finding a new life. Though not afraid of Mark's temper, she is afraid of what he would think of her if she were to open up. Mark breaks down into tears, begging her to just help him understand…just to help him. In response, she cuts herself on the neck with the electric knife, screaming. Mark stops her and wrestles her into the bathroom as she kicks and thrashes in a fit.

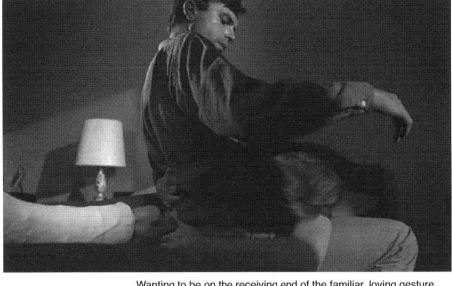
Wanting to be on the receiving end of the familiar, loving gesture, Mark seeks affection from Margie.

During Mark's line of questioning, we are shown rare glimpses of genuine sorrow from the heretofore emotionless Anna, which Mark never sees, always faced away from her when she responds—a depiction of the way we are prone to an inability to listen to or understand others when we are experiencing pain. Her guilt, self-loathing and sadness is clear to us here; she doesn't want to reveal her secrets because not only would she have to face what Mark might think of her, but she might have to come face to face with her own self-judgment. In an act of desperate avoidance of such emotional trauma, she attacks herself physically, diverting the focus to a more tangible, manageable kind of pain, and ending the line of questioning that is penetrating her defenses.

Her divided behavior is becoming more and more typical of traditional "possessed" behavior, erratically veering into spastic fits without notice, in which she becomes completely unaware of her surroundings. When Mark is able to calm down her fit by reminding her of Bob, she is shown to visibly "come to", and seem suddenly disoriented by how or why she got here, having no memory of what was occurring just seconds before. Mark seems to see the return of the Anna he knows; he whispers to her, "You're my whole family." Again we see the tortured, helpless sorrow in Anna's face.

But Mark is starting to at least subconsciously become more aware of the doomed nature of his and Anna's situation. Even after a moment of emotional connection, he knows what's coming next; he knows that Anna will revert to her possessed state at any time, and he knows it will bring more pain. Taking a cue from Anna, he sits down in the kitchen and begins to slowly cut his arm with the electric knife, turning his own focus away from the psychological trauma to something physical and tangible. Confirming what Mark already anticipated, Anna appears in the doorway, her eyes glazed and trance-like, her neck neatly bandaged, announcing that she doesn't have time to wait for Bob; she has to go—now. This time there is no emotion from either of them; she is possessed, and Mark is calm and tranquil and accepting. She follows his gaze to his bleeding arm and observes, "It doesn't hurt." "No," Mark agrees. The act of self-mutilation is preferable to the emotional damage they are causing each other.

Up to this point in the film, it is easy to believe that the soap-operatic-yet-universally-familiar events were probably more or less dramatized directly from Zulawski's own personal life—there has been nothing too out-of-the-ordinary in terms of narrative believability. But beginning with the self-mutilation scene (although we've been given a handful of subtle clues before this moment), and continuing with the events that follow, the film turns to an even darker, more surreal and supernatural realm of storytelling. As an autobiographical piece, it most certainly departs from physical reality at this point, but it does so in order to better reveal the author's own inner feelings of defeat—even madness—at this time in his life. For, as a cathartic piece of art, merely re-telling the sequence of events is a terribly limited and insufficient means of addressing the profound inner suffering that is experienced throughout those events.

The first big mystery is revealed when a detective (Carl Duering) from the agency Mark hired follows Anna to her new flat as she carries groceries. She is clearly entranced as she makes her way there—she doesn't even notice a vagrant on the train steal food from the grocery bag on her lap—nor does she notice the fact that she's quite obviously being followed by the only other person on the deserted streets. The force drawing her becomes more powerful the closer she gets to her destination, and she breaks into a full run for the last stretch of the journey, still not noticing the man desperately sprinting after her.

The apartment building she enters is in a seedy-looking part of town, populated by buildings ranging from the poorly-maintained to the condemned. The detective calls Mark to give him Anna's address, then, urged by Mark to try to find out more, gains entrance to the apartment under subterfuge of investigating some broken glass that has fallen to the sidewalk outside. He ignores her frightened protestations and strolls through the run-down and spartan flat, checking all the windows. Anna's nervous demeanor suddenly segues into an amused acceptance of the inevitability of the situation. Now, instead of protesting, she offers the confused detective a glass of wine, suddenly seeming drunk and sociable, if a bit too aggressively so. He refuses

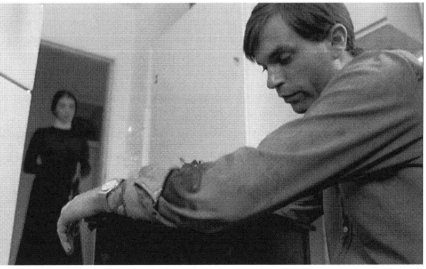
Anna and Mark find that physical pain is better than emotional trauma.

Mark's private detective is the first to discover Anna's terrible secret, and it costs him his life.

and makes his way to check the bathroom, despite her laughing assurance that there are no windows in there. Wild-eyed and grinning, she intentionally drops the wine bottle to the floor, where it shatters.

The detective enters the dark, filthy bathroom and discovers an unrecognizable, tentacled creature, covered in blood and slime, residing in the bathtub. He is dumbfounded, completely unable to comprehend the monstrosity before him as it gazes back at him. Anna suddenly lunges into the bathroom, screaming, and stabs him in the neck with the broken wine bottle, killing him almost instantly. We have now had our first glimpse and the secret Anna has been protecting so fiercely, and it's definitely not human…at least, not yet.

Although there have been hints dropped along the narrative that Anna had already abandoned Heinrich for another, there has been nothing up to this point to prepare us for the introduction of a literal monster into this strange family drama. But now that we've been indoctrinated into the actions and events of Mark and Anna's problems, Zulawski is laying the groundwork for presenting us with his own analysis of the troubled psyches caught in the conflict. To address the issue of Anna's diametrically opposed personalities bringing about the destruction of Mark and the family unit, Zulawski turns to allegory, and introduces actual, physical doppelgangers into the proceedings—the second of which has just been revealed to us as a hideous creature. Without fully realizing it, we have already met the first, who wasn't as easy to recognize, being presented in the laughing, bubbly guise of Anna's lookalike, Helen. Initially, she might have seemed like the embodiment of Mark's search for someone to replace his wife, finding an idealized version of Anna—who always wears a melancholy blue dress, representing despair and loneliness—in her exact double, Helen—who always wears white, the color of purity and new beginnings. But appearances can be deceiving, and new beginnings aren't always for the better.

While Mark watches Bob bathe (playing an "underwater diving world-record" game that will become significant later), Helen shows up to the apartment, ostensibly to speak with Anna about Bob. Mark explains that Anna no longer lives with them, and invites her in to talk. Almost immediately, the doorbell rings again, and Mark leaves Helen to watch Bob while he finishes his bath. Heinrich is at the door, seemingly on hallucinogens and wanting to see Anna. Mark watches smugly as Heinrich, who seems to have been literally knocked off-balance by Anna's lack of contact with him, bounces from wall to wall, explaining in his new-age philosophical jargon his lack of understanding of the situation. Mark is now seeing behind the smoke and mirrors of this charlatan who had previously dominated and conquered him. Heinrich's confident façade has been shattered, and he's rendered to a reeling mess of confusion when he feels that control of the situation has been taken from him. Mark mocks Heinrich's assumption that he was the one in possession of Anna, "You, with your yin-yang balls dangling from your Zen brain…I used to be afraid of you, but I don't think I am anymore." Heinrich spouts that there is nothing to fear, except god. Mark tells him, "For me, god is a disease," rejecting any and all higher-consciousness beliefs that Heinrich espouses as cancerous and foul.

Mark goes back inside to help Helen put Bob to bed. While they clean up the kitchen, he explains to her that he is at war against women, finding them to have no foresight, and to be untrustworthy and dangerous. Helen seems very amused by his point-of-view, and explains to him that she comes from a place "where evil seems to be easier to pinpoint because you can see it in the flesh. It becomes people, so you know exactly the danger of being deformed by it… which doesn't mean I admire your world, but I find pathetic these stories of women contaminating the universe." Of course Mark thinks she's speaking metaphorically, not realizing that she has just directly told him that she is not a human being, but is in fact a monster in the guise of a person. And if what she said of her world is to be believed, the very fact that she *is* in the guise of a person is proof that she is evil.

But Mark is still blinded by his fractured focus on his own problems, and either doesn't hear or completely ignores the implications of Helen's confession. Instead, he coaxes her to spend the night with him, naked, in bed, although they don't make love. The next day when Mark drops Bob off at school, he looks at Helen but doesn't say a word to her. She watches him through the fence as he walks away, and there's something ominous and sinister in her lingering stare.

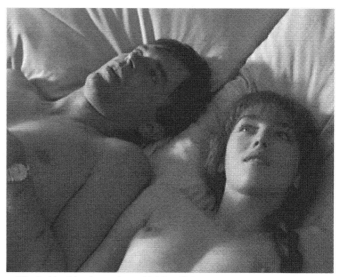

Blinded by his obsession with his wife's monstrous behavior, Mark invites an actual monster into his bed.

Zulawski seems here to be introducing a harsher assessment of Mark's (and by extension, his own) responsibility for his situation. Initially presenting us with the image of Mark as the victim of Anna's actions, he has now placed greater onus on Mark's self-absorbed reaction to his problems. Mark has become responsible for inviting danger in the door to satiate his own selfish needs for affection, and any harmful outcome resulting from it will fall directly on his shoulders, not his wife's. Zulawski is warning us that even in times of duress, we are always in danger of worsening our own predicament, even if it was not initially of our making.

On his way home from the school, Mark is intercepted by Zimmerman, who informs him that the detective following Anna has gone missing. He confesses to Mark that he is particularly concerned, because the detective is his lover. Mark gives him Anna's new address, and Zimmerman promises to be in touch.

When Zimmerman arrives at Anna's apartment to question her, she is again detached and trance-like in her behavior, and she directs him to the bedroom, telling him, "He's in there." He enters the bedroom to find the tentacled creature, now bigger and more humanoid in shape, writhing in the blood-stained bed. Anna explains, "He's very tired. He made love to me all night. He's still unfinished." Zimmerman spots his lover's body behind the door, and screaming, pulls out a revolver and fires at Anna, missing. Paralyzed by grief and terror, Zimmerman watches helplessly as Anna stiffens, then begins to spasm. She savagely attacks him, grabbing the revolver and shooting him dead. We have now been given confirmation of the fact that the creature Anna has been hiding is, in fact, her lover, and that now, both she and her estranged husband are sharing their beds with monsters.

5 – *New Family Born*

"It says something—and this is the reason I wrote it—about my personal problems as a man with a woman I dearly loved. It's a film about breaking up; it's a film about the end of a relationship, of a marriage. And I'm a strong believer in couples, in marriages and children."
- Andrzej Zulawski

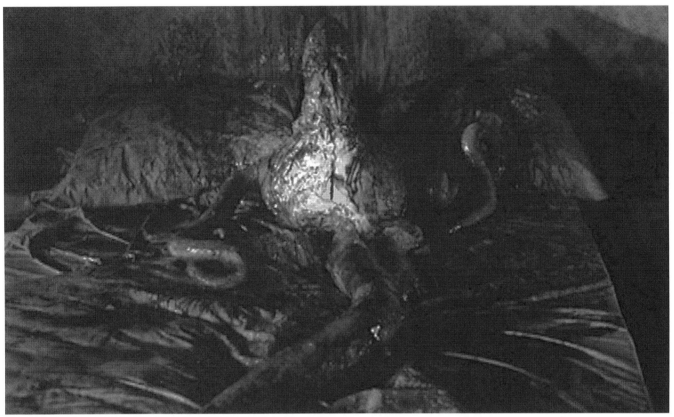

Anna, it seems, has also been bedding down with a monster.

We've so far witnessed the events surrounding and leading up to Mark's loss of identity and subsequent breakdown, thereby maintaining greater sympathy with Mark's (Zulawski's) point-of-view in this drama. But again, Zulawski has more to say here than merely dramatizing his marital grievances from his own perspective; he is examining the far-reaching effects of personal and familial loss from multiple perspectives, and now he begins to broaden his scope to show a bigger picture, to challenge not only Mark's, but also our own suppositions.

Mark arrives home to find a package on his doorstep, containing 8mm footage of Anna, shot by Heinrich, apparently in the early stages of their affair, while she still worked as a ballet instructor. In the footage, she intentionally torments and humiliates one of her young students until the girl runs screaming from the room. She tells Heinrich that nobody had ever taught her how hard she would have to struggle to be a success in the world, and explains that the reason she is with him now is "Because you say 'I' for me." Struggling with her words, she attempts to explain her dual nature to Heinrich, claiming that there are two conflicting personalities inside her—two sisters, whom she calls Faith and Chance—grappling for control. The struggle feels like it's tearing her apart; she is aware of her harmful betrayal of Mark and her family, but admits to achieving some small form of enjoyment from the freedom to harm. "Goodness is only some kind of reflection upon evil; that is all." For the first time, after spending so much time observing from Mark's point-of-view, we are given some insight into Anna's struggle, which reveals itself to be a far more profound, destructive and far-reaching one than Mark's loss of family and identity. She seems to be struggling for her sanity, indeed, for her very soul.

Anna arrives at the apartment, completely frenzied and insane, storming from room-to-room in a psychotic pantomime of domesticity, picking up laundry and putting it into the refrigerator and sweeping food off pantry shelves. She's coming completely unglued from the battle raging inside her. She escalates into hysteria-like fits as she tells Mark that she feels nothing for no one. "It's as if the sisters were too exhausted to fight any more. You know these women wrestling in an arena of mud, with their headlocks on each other's throats, each waiting to see who will die first, and both staring at me." Then, in flashback, we at last witness the moment all of her frustration, feelings of imprisonment, unhappiness and self-loathing physically released themselves from her body (much like the "Psychoplasma" phenomenon featured in David Cronenberg's 1979 film **THE BROOD**—incidentally, a film also inspired by a messy divorce) and became sentient, in perhaps the film's most powerful (and most famous) sequence:

One day on her way home with groceries, she visits a church, and while staring up at a statue of the crucified Christ, she begins to moan in discomfort, as if something is causing pain to her lower abdomen. She walks down into the subway and begins laughing hysterically, giving to fits of screaming rage as she smashes her groceries against the wall, writhes in the filthy mess on the ground, and then sits up to her knees as she vomits, with blood and pus oozing from her ears and out from between her legs. She is giving birth to the creature.

It is interesting that the sequence beings in a church, with Anna seeming to plead to Christ for release, and is then granted it, though probably not in the manner she had wished. It is almost as if Zulawski is implying an immaculate conception here, but he could just as easily be drawing reference to an exorcism, with the offending entity being divinely expelled from her suffering body.

Anna explains to Mark that what she miscarried that day was Sister Faith, and what was left is Sister Chance, and she has to take care of her Faith, to protect it; that's what she has been doing there the whole time. Mark looks at her in amazement and tells her that for the first time, she looks vulgar to him. It seems her fears of Mark's judgment have been realized. He tells her to give him back her ring and the watch he gave her last time he was home. She does so and

Anna's torment and hatred manifests itself physically, causing her to give birth to a monster.

announces that she has to leave, answering the call of her new possessor. In her ongoing struggle to be free, she has first traded one captor, Mark, for another, Heinrich, and her continuing anguish has resulted in the creation of a wholly new and all-encompassing form of captivity. She is now possessed in every sense of the word, and any hopes she ever had of her fugue leading to freedom of any kind have revealed themselves to be nothing but illusion.

Mark seems still to be coming to a greater and greater degree of understanding of Anna's complex struggle—for he is now actively following her into the abyss of madness—and he decides to diabolically use this newfound understanding to his own advantage, as if he has given up on his dreams of restoring his life in favor of harming those who have wronged him. He sets his trap by phoning Heinrich's home and giving Anna's address to Heinrich's mother. Many of the events that follow as a result of this trap show that Zulawski, while still reaching for a higher level of artistic catharsis, isn't above a modicum of revenge fantasy in the process.

Heinrich shows up to Anna's flat on his motorcycle (of course he would ride a motorcycle), and without inquiry as to her well-being or state of mind, immediately starts trying to dominate her sexually, telling her not to resist him, and offering her a packet of hallucinogenic powder. She is vacant, but superficially complacent to his advances, as she lures him into the bedroom. Sitting in the corner is the creature, now much bigger and very human-like in shape. It stares back at the dumbfounded Heinrich, who is struck momentarily blind by his inability to comprehend what he's seen. He stumbles into the kitchen as Anna opens the refrigerator, which is full of human body parts. She taunts the horrified Romeo, poking at him with a kitchen knife, telling him that he's no different from anyone else. "We are all the same, but in different words, with different bodies and different versions, like insects." She stabs him superficially under the arm, and he flees the apartment in horror. Anna enters the bedroom, where the creature has moved onto the bed, and begins to undress.

Heinrich, the self-proclaimed Superior Male, has now been dominated and cast away by the woman he stole, and been replaced sexually by an inhuman creature. Whatever Mark had hoped would arise from sending Heinrich to Anna, it has certainly put in place the beginning of Heinrich's downfall.
Leaving Bob home in care of Margie, Mark meets the injured Heinrich in the lavatory of the corner bar near Anna's. Heinrich babbles like a maniac about monsters, body parts and blood. Mark pretends not to believe Heinrich (although he had visited Anna's now-vacated apartment just before meeting Heinrich, and had seen the blood and body parts himself), and jokes that maybe the monster that Heinrich had witnessed was divine. "Perhaps you met god a moment ago and didn't even realize it." He coaxes Heinrich into a bathroom stall and knocks him out with a toilet tank lid, then pushes Heinrich's face into a stopped up toilet, sprinkles the packet of powder all over him, and leaves him to die. He returns to Anna's apartment long enough to set it on fire, then speeds away on Heinrich's motorcycle. Here, Mark is very much Zulawski himself, playing out his revenge against his own Heinrich, vanquishing his foe, first by figurative castration (dominated and rendered impotent by the woman he believed himself to possess), followed by humiliation (Mark's mockery of his spiritual beliefs while Heinrich bleeds in a public lavatory), and then death. Heinrich is left to be discovered (and remembered) with his head in a toilet, having died of an apparent overdose.

When Mark returns home, he discovers Margie dying in the lobby, her throat slit. Again, we see the destruction of another character drawn directly from

Heinrich attempts to regain sexual control of Anna, at his own peril.

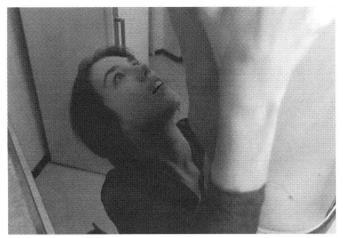

Anna finally returns the loving embrace to Mark, although she is no longer the woman he once knew.

while her eyes show she clearly belongs to another. Afterward, Mark tells her to go wait for him at Margie's house while he cleans up and takes care of everything.

Mark seems to have acquiesced to his fate, recognizing that his family is no more. He, too, has now become possessed, though in a different way from his suffering wife. He is possessed by defeat, hatred, and a burning desire for vengeance. He realizes that he is doomed, and is now only interested in the destruction of those who doomed him, and the eradication of all the hurt and pain that has grown out of his own life. He has lost the family he so cherished (at least, his idealized vision of a family), hence, nothing to lose. With his enemies dead and his family unit destroyed, he now has only one purpose: to stop the evil that has blossomed from his situation from spreading.

After cleaning up and stashing Margie's body in the trunk of her car, Mark drops the sleeping Bob off at Helen's house, telling her that he's going to see his wife. Helen asks him to promise her something, and he replies earnestly, "I promise," before she can ask—perhaps in an understood acceptance of his fate, he is promising to see things through to the end, to his doom. He arrives at Margie's and hears the sound of moaning. He discovers Anna in Margie's bed, fornicating with the grotesque monster. She looks up at Mark and moans, "Almost… almost…" The transformation of Anna's lover/child/sister is nearly complete.

Zulawski's life, but Margie is permitted a less-humiliating demise than the odious Heinrich. Zulawski claims no genuine hatred for the real-life Margie—he refers to her as an "innocent idiot", rather than an actual enemy—so he allows her a somewhat more honorable death: she dies protecting the child.

Mark carries Margie's body upstairs to the apartment, where he finds Anna, there to welcome him. She sinks to her knees and holds him in that familiar, loving grasp, her eyes dazed and wild. Finally, in the fourth and final recurrence of the loving grasp, Mark receives the affectionate embrace he has so desperately sought, but when it finally comes, he and Anna are so far gone that the gesture is profoundly disturbing in its irony. She tells him to take her, and he does, all the

6 – *The World Ended*

"I try to make films about morals, but without morality, because I don't believe in preaching."
- Andrzej Zulawski

The final part of the film quickly becomes extremely hectic, violent and symbolic, as Anna and Mark are now both possessed, and are being driven by forces leading them plummeting to their inevitable demise, and all we

Anna makes love to her nearly fully-formed creation.

Their purposes fulfilled and their fates sealed, Anna and Mark share a last kiss before dying.

are left to do is watch the wake of destruction occur, helpless to stop, only to bear witness. The suffering husband and wife, shed completely of their former identities—in essence, their humanity—have become, in a fashion, apocalyptic horsepersons, Mark representing death and destruction, and Anna representing birth and creation, albeit both in negative ways.

In his final errand as a harbinger of doom, Mark visits Heinrich's mother to confirm her belief that her son is dead and, he believes, to kill her. She lets him in, in full acceptance of her fate, musing that it would be good to think that the soul lives on without the body, but it isn't so. She tells him, "I was wondering which is worse: take away someone's wife, hurt a child, or to kill," displaying her awareness of the entire situation, and of not only Heinrich's, but also Mark's and Anna's place within it. Telling him not to worry about her, she takes a handful of pills and lies down on the bed to die, not wanting to be here if her son is not around anymore. The wind blows the window open, as if to let her soul exit in contradiction to her assessment of the finality of death.

Mark stands near the Berlin Wall, staring at a dog's corpse floating in a canal, He is approached by a sinister, bespectacled man (Maximilian Rüthlein), who informs him that, "Our man won't confide in her successor—he wants you." Obviously, Mark's abandonment of his job has caught up with him. The man insists that Mark's help is needed to save "a drowning world", and is not willing to accept refusal. No longer capable of the kind of free will needed to derail himself from his own path of destruction, even for the supposed greater good of the world, Mark also abandons this opportunity (or threat), and rides away on the motorcycle. His ending has already been written, and he must see it through.

Mark rides up to Margie's house to find the police just arriving. He hijacks a taxi, forcing the driver at gunpoint to ram the cab into the back of the police car. He jumps out just before the collision and flees, but the police manage to shoot him in the back. He returns fire, killing one of the officers and escapes on the motorcycle, speeding through the city, screaming in rage. In a seemingly deliberate move, he crashes the bike, badly injuring himself. He staggers into a nearby building to climb several flights of stairs before collapsing, bleeding and broken, on a landing. From downstairs, Anna calls his name. She has arrived to present to him the fully-formed creature, now an exact replica of Mark himself. "I wanted to show it to you. It is finished now."

Mark, faced with his own doppelganger and suddenly comprehending the horrible ramifications, raises his pistol to shoot, perhaps in a last-minute attempt at redemption, but the police suddenly open-fire on them from below, mortally wounding both Mark and Anna as the Mark-creature calmly stands unharmed in the hail of gunfire. With her last burst of strength, Anna pulls herself on top of Mark and kisses him. She puts his gun to the small of her own back and fires, the bullet penetrating them both. Anna dies instantly, having completed her purpose, her fate fulfilled.

The Mark-creature crouches over them and says to the dying Mark, "So hard to live with it, eh, brother?" then walks up the stairs and mesmerizes a young female onlooker, giving her the gun and instructing her to shoot the police. He escapes to the roof as Mark leaps to his death over the stair railing, having failed to stop this evil from being unleashed on the world.

Below in the lobby, the bespectacled man examines Mark's corpse briefly, then continues up the stairs, stopping momentarily to remove a stone from his shoe. We see he is wearing bright pink socks, alleviating any doubt that the warnings made early on by Mark's superiors were not made lightly. One cannot simply ignore one's responsibilities in favor of others, for they will catch up to us.

Back at Helen's, Bob is eating cereal at the table, surrounded by plastic army men. The doorbell rings, and Helen asks Bob to answer the door. He refuses, obviously afraid. Helen says it could be his father, but Bob begins screaming, "Don't open! Don't open!" as Helen walks to the door with the Mark-Monster waiting on the other side. Still screaming "Don't open!" over and over, Bob runs upstairs, and in an apparently suicidal act, throws himself facedown into the full bathtub, ending the forgotten boy's life in a macabre tableau of the bath-time game he played with his father.

The sounds of air-raid sirens and military planes flying overhead fill the air, and exploding bombs shake the house as Helen stands by the door, the writhing Mark-Monster visible through the door's frosted glass. We close on a close-up of Helen's unreadable face as we listen to the sounds of destruction. The monsters have won, and the world is ended.

Zulawski, always preferring ambiguity and raw emotional response to explanation and treatise, refuses to answer any specific questions about the meaning of his films; he feels it best when the audience brings their own experiences and interpretations to the table when approaching his work, even in such an autobiographical instance as **POSSESSION**. But he obviously has much to say here about ego, self image, sexual insecurity, the concept of freedom (and loss thereof), and the importance of personal responsibility—especially within the family unit. He seems to be warning us of the dangers of self-obsession in times of suffering, and the collateral damage that often goes unconsidered while we are focused too intensely on ourselves. Perhaps as a statement of self-blame on Zulawski's part, he shows us that Mark, so concerned with repairing his broken family, failed to address the individuals involved and the needs they each had, only concentrating on his idea of what his family should be, and as a result, helped destroy it. Both Anna and Mark became so solipsistic in their own desires that their own son—the remaining lynch-pin of their world together—was left forgotten in the hands of monsters, ending as a mere casualty of their selfish war.

As mentioned before, loss of identity is an important theme with Zulawski (few can claim to have suffered as much loss in that arena as he has); the integrity of our identity is what holds us together, both psychologically and socially. But, by focusing too much on attempts to control the individual pieces of what we feel define us, we can lose sight of the greater picture, and become destructive forces unto ourselves. We cannot impose control on such an all-encompassing, abstract schism, but are better served by responding empathetically to the individual crises rather than trying to lasso our world into a definable order. Our ability to reconcile peacefully with the people in our lives is also essential to the integrity of our identity, for an inability to reconcile our connections with those most important to us creates monsters of us all, effectively destroying our world.

•••

The two doppelgangers, triumphant, listen to the sounds of the apocalypse.

FROM JAKARTA WITH LOVE: FEROCIOUS FEMALE FRIGHTMAKERS

A Few Frightening Phantom Female Films from Indonesia

by Larry Conti

Stumbling on Southeast Asian cinema has really changed my perspective. Most film geeks think they've struck gold when they delve into the newest adrenalin-fueled Thai gangster flick, or the recent wave of Korean sci-fi political thrillers. But fear not, we're about to break the international celluloid barrier. Welcome to Indonesia and world's largest Muslim nation, with one heck of a horror film industry. Believe it, or not.

After hunting down Indonesian films over the years—which is not an easy task, mind you—I've accumulated easily over 300 flicks. Them Indonesians seemed to prefer the shoddy VCD format—you know, DVD's illegitimate cousin. I'm happy to report that there are literally tons of fantastic Indonesian horror films. With darkly-lit black magic rituals, powerful shapeshifting dieties, traditional gruesome creatures of yore, and usually some choice flesh on display, these are true gems, despite their obvious shoestring budget. Their ancient culture is so richly drenched in haunted lore, there's plenty of new stories to tell this modern world and then some. What does sting is that they haven't really taken care of what's actually left of their source materials. Many films remain lost, and some are rumored to have never existed at all.

Indonesia's first film was the 1926 silent picture, **LOETOENG KASAROENG.** Dutch directors G. Kruger and L. Heuveldorp created a mythological fantasy story about a young girl who falls in love with a magical monkey, the Lutung. It was made with local actors—actually the children of local noblemen—by the NV Java Film Company in Bandung. To this day it's considered a lost film, with very little promotional material unearthed. The early years also produced Indonesia's most important films, both tales of forlorn lovers battling against all odds. **PAREH** (*Song of Rice*, 1936) follows the forbidden love between a fisherman and a farmer's daughter. **TERANG BOELAN** (*Full Moon*, 1937) weaves a tale of two lovers that elope, after the bride is almost forced to marry a dangerous opium smuggler.

Soon after its promising birth during the Dutch colonial era, the Indonesian film industry was forcefully repurposed by the occupying Japanese during World War II as a propaganda tool. They halted all national film production in Indonesia, and began producing educational films and newsreels for audiences in Japan. Soon after Japanese occupation, both the Koreans and Australians migrated to Java in order to produce documentaries on the struggles of the Indonesian people, but were met with heavy opposition. After Indonesia's independence, the Sukarno government used the film industry for nationalistic, anti-Western purposes. All imported films were seized and banned. After the overthrow of Sukarno by the New Order regime, a censorship code that aimed to maintain the social order was strictly enforced.

By the 1980s, the Indonesian film industry had reached its peak. **NAGA BONAR** (*Dragon of Bonar*, 1987), a scathing political comedy, caused a lot of controversy with the national government. **CATATAN SI BOY** (*Boy Says*, 1989) followed the exploits of a debonair playboy. It was so popular with teens of the day that it managed to spawn five sequels.

Horror films were initially made to react publicly to the political strife most of the country's poor was facing at the time. Witty sarcasm, and political allegory abounded, all thinly disguised by a monster-of-the-week plotline, and some seriously splattery effects.

The *sundel bolong*, one of Indonesia's most famous phantom femmes, showed up on screens across the nation, gripping the audiences' throats and cackling maniacally. The rebirth of popular cinema was now upon them. Films such as **MALAM SATU SURO** (*One Dark Night*, 1980), and **BERANAK DALAM KUBUR 2** (*Birth in the Tomb 2*, 1982), both starring screen goddess Suzzanna, exceeded most foreign import film ticket sales by astronomical numbers. Beware, you just might find yourself hunting down these rare, un-subtitled gems of cinematic glory. Enjoy at your own risk.

The *sundel bolong*, one of Indonesia's most famous phantom femmes.

VCD sleeves

SUNDEL BOLONG (1981)

Let's start off with a personal fave, **SUNDEL BOLONG** (*Hollow-backed Ghost*). Traditionally, the titular creature's transformation hails from a pregnant woman wrongfully killed. The almost fully-developed fetus is expelled post mortem, bursting through her backside, leaving a huge gaping hole, spinal cord exposed, munched by maggots aplenty. Swathed in her *kain kafan* (burial shroud), and streaking through the jungle skies, she vents her wrath. She's basically akin to a Muslim version of Sadako (from the *Ringu* films) or other stereotypical Asian long-haired banshees, but with helluva thirst for some fresh Javanese jugular.

An honest yet naïve woman falls for a model agency scam, where she's expected to pose nude. Being a devout Muslim, she refuses, and is brutally murdered by some mindless thugs. She rises from her crypt to exact vengeance in some creatively gruesome ways.

Starring Indonesian film icon Suzzanna, this flick explodes off the screen like a jet-fueled comic book rocket. It's drenched in creeptastic atmosphere, a haunting score infused with some synth-pop disco, ghoul gore galore, and some truly inventive cinematography. They sure knew how to freak their audience. Not to be outdone, her fiancée, played by action-star hunkaholic, Barry Prima, kicks major ass after finding the thugs' hideout, but is thrashed soundly nonetheless. No creep is left alive. Suzzanna easily slices and dices her way through them, one by one. Some are run over by a possessed bulldozer, others are impaled with pitchforks and other rusty jagged metal objects, leaving Swiss flesh behind.

One spectacular chase-n-kill scene has Suzzanna in the form of a *pocong*. It is basically a corpse trapped in its shroud. The dead body is covered in white fabric, tied over the head, under the feet, and on the neck. Looking rather silly to Western eyes, it's actually quite a formidable creature. The soul will linger on Earth for 40 days after death. Once the 40 days are up, and the knots haven't been untied, the deceased will pop outta the grave to warn people that it needs releasing. As there's a knot binding the feet, the corpse cannot walk. But it sure can hop, just like it's Chinese hopping vampire cousin, the *jiangshi*.

Soaked in grue and about to meet their maker, they realize karma really is a bitch. An elderly cleric is called upon. By simply reading passages from the Quran, he finally soothes the restless spirit of our wronged heroine. An equally fantastic sequel, **TELAGA ANGKER** (*The Haunted Lake*, 1984) followed a few years later.

Suzzanna's prolific career has made her Indonesia's undisputed 'Queen of Horror', due not only to her immense body of work, but also her mystic lifestyle. At 65, she looked younger than most women in their 30s, attributed to her mystical diet of jasmine flowers and rare herbs. She was an avid practitioner of yoga as well. In almost every one of her films, you can see her wearing a snazzy blue sapphire ring, supposedly given to her by a powerful mystic healer. She starred in over 60 films during her career, and *all* of them were Indonesian blockbusters, thanks to her enigmatic screen presence.

She's even starred in several television soaps. *Misteri Sebuah Guci* (*Mystery of the Holy Vase*) saw her as the powerful *dukun* (witch healer), Lady Sparrow. She reappeared in 2007 with **HANTU AMBULANCE** (*Ambulance Ghost*) where she still looks to be in her early 40s! Not such a great film, but I kept my peepers peeled every second she was onscreen. Sadly, she passed away on October 14*, 2008, losing her battle with diabetes.

MISTERI JANDA KEMBANG (1991)

A woman in red rises from the grave, with a faithful hellhound at her side. It seems she's hungry for revenge, as well as some tasty flesh. Tearing out hearts still beating from some unfortunate clowns, she feeds the offal to her dutiful hound. Her name is Asih, and this is her story.

Brutally gang raped by four creeps in a rainstorm, she committed suicide to save her devout Muslim family the humiliation. Back from beyond, poor Asih has a blood mission to fulfill. As if pulled right out of an old pulp comic, she picks off her perps one by one in fantastically gruesome ways. Perpetually bathed in eerie gel lighting, she remains eerily sexy in her red satin slip, as the body count rises.

As in many Indo horror flicks, the sheer amount of wild and innovative effects are plentiful, albeit cheap. They are true artists combining amateur video effects and old-fashioned rubber monster techniques. You can't help but chuckle as Asih launches her head at one creep, and chomps at his privates. In agony—or pure embarrassment—he hops around wildly with a mannequin head stuck to his crotch, as her devil doggie howls.

Asih has many supernatural talents in her arsenal, but best of all she's a *penanggalan*. She has the power to detach her head from her body, which can fly about, chasing her prey, complete with dangling spine and internal organs. Many films were made about this popular creature all over Asia, such as Tjut Djalil's own **MYSTICS IN BALI** (1981), and the more obscure 1977 Hong Kong treat, **WITCH WITH THE FLYING HEAD**.

In another great scene, a mulleted thug watching TV notices Asih on the screen. She taunts him sexily, and then reaches straight outta the boob tube, in a cartoony attempt at **VIDEODROME**, and quite possibly inspiring Hideo Nakata's **RINGU** a bit, too. After some clawing and choking, he's literally pulled inside the television.

It's time to call in the local cleric. He tries to persuade her to leave willingly, but she refuses, and offs a few more lowly punks. He begins a passage from the Quran, and before we can say, "The power of Allah compels you!" Asih wretches wildly, and then vanishes in a poof of smoke.

Softcore starlet Sally Marcellina was a perfect choice as Asih. She dominates every scene, captivating and seducing her prey. In one steamy flashback scene we're even treated to a blindfolded Asih, writhing on the floor, as her boyfriend traces her curves with an ice cube. And yes, said scene is set to a new age sax number by an Indo Kenny G. wannabe. As for Sally, she just might be Indonesia's very own Linnea Quigley.

PEMBALASAN SETAN KARANG BOLONG (1989)
(Vengeance of the Hollow-backed Demoness)

Herman and Mira, two young Muslims deeply in love, are expecting their first child, out of wedlock. His uppercrust parents have another idea: 'kill the slutty bitch'. It's all planned, and during a downpour, Mira is stalked by a group of smarmy thugs. We watch in excruciating detail as she is hunted in a ramshackle stable, in a scene reminiscent of Pauline Wong in **HER VENGEANCE** (1988). Horses neigh and look on as she's brutally attacked, raped, and afterwards hung to make it look like an apparent suicide.

Filled with rage and a lust for revenge, she erupts from her flower-petal-covered grave like a bottle rocket. She looks spectacularly evil with neon facepaint, bathed in black light, cackling maniacally. The flesh melts from her back, exposing her spine and innards, a gooey mess, and also the telltale sign you've got trouble on your hands. She's transformed into one of Indonesian folklore's vilest vixens, the *setan karang bolong*, or 'hollow-backed demoness'. You don't wanna mess with this demoness.

Rapist #1 rolls around in bed with one of his whores; she's possessed by Mira, who messily chews off the tip of his tongue. She exposes her maggot-riddled wound as he wretches in disgust, just before his head is bashed-in with a possessed television.

She finds Rapist #2 steadily grinding his old lady in a junkyard. With one swipe of her finger, the burnt out cars begin revving their engines, and steaming from their hoods. As she reappears, cackling from behind the wheel of a

Toyota 4x4, he's gored by the reanimated wrecks, lotsa the red stuff splashing the pavement.

Herman's mama calls on the aid of a crooked-toothed mystic to rid them of Mira's wrath once and for all. The kooky shaman uses a fire-breathing skull wand to taunt her spirit in the graveyard, but she quickly trumps that with a windstorm. He fires back with some super-imposed cartoon fireballs to no avail. He runs away in fast-forward, pants around his ankles, leaving mama to fend for herself. Face to face with her mortal enemy, Mira exposes her gaping ghostly wound once again, and pins mama with a fallen tree. Straight outta nowhere a gunshot rings out, the bullet lodging its girth into mama's skull. Gushing with gore from every orifice, she croaks. Turns out Rapist #3 had other ideas for our villainess. Mira gestures her palm and he's laughably swallowed up by an enchanted length of astroturf. Desperately pleading for his life, he's pulled down to pay his debts in the underworld. Herman and the local cleric arrive on the scene, reciting the holy Quran. With a smile and a nod, Mira acknowledges her fate and explodes in a shower of sparks.

•••

ABOUT THE CONTRIBUTORS ...

Jared Auner - watches a lot of movies. Sometimes he writes about them. You may remember him from a blog called Worldweird Cinema, but he got lazy and quit a few years ago. Now he's been persuaded to come out of retirement and review obscure foreign genre movies for the periodical you currently hold in your hands. He currently blogs for Mondo Macabro, who pay him in DVDs, which is pretty sweet. He would like to thank Stephen Buck, for his exceedingly helpful suggestions and comments on the reviews in this issue, and Dr. Robert Kiss, for providing him copies of the very rare films he wrote about.

Lucas Balbo - started his own fanzine (Nostalgia) in the early '80s, then collaborated on Shock Xpress and Psychotronic prozines/magazines. Took ten years of his life to write the first directory of Jess Franco's Film (OBSESSION, THE FILMS OF JESS FRANCO). Nowadays, he runs his own photo library and collaborates with various DVD distribution companies (http://artclips.free.fr/archives-english.htm).

David Barnes - has his own line of comics and also creates vintage ''grindhouse '' t-shirts. His work can be seen at zid3ya@yahoo.com and myspace.com@paramere.

Gary Baxter - British born Baxter grew up on a diet of video nasty greats and slasher movie sickness, exploitation excellence and Italian cult gems. When he's not reading about, writing about or watching trash movie madness he volunteers with a group of young wannabe movie makers called Film Junkies. Gary recently got to realize a childhood dream of appearing in a zombie movie, Convention of the Dead and is currently working on his own idea for a short film called Til Death, to be filmed early 2013.

Stephen R. Bissette - a pioneer graduate of the Joe Kubert School, currently teaches at the Center for Cartoon Studies and is renowned for Swamp Thing, Taboo (launching From Hell and Lost Girls), '1963,' Tyrant, co-creating John Constantine, and creating the world's second '24-Hour Comic' (invented by Scott McCloud for Bissette). He writes, illustrates, and has co-authored many books; his latest include Teen Angels & New Mutants (2011), the short story "Copper" in The New Dead (2010), and he illustrated The Vermont Monster Guide (2009). His latest ebooks are Bryan Talbot: Dreams & Dystopias and the Best of Blur duo, Wonders! Millennial Marvel Movies and Horrors! Cults, Crimes, & Creepers.

Lawrence Conti is an established graphic artist and ravenous cinephile based in NYC. He can be found scouring Chinatown's all over the East Coast slaking his thirst for rare Asian films. Follow his rants on weird, wild, foreign films & television here: extralarry. wordpress.com.

Aaron Dilloway is the author of "Andy Milligan's The Weirdo: The Broadway Play" and "The Footloose Companion". He spends most of his time making tape loops from the audio of Tim Paxton's old VHS collection. He lives in Oberlin, OH. He can be contacted at www.hansonrecords.net

Danae Dunning - is a goth/metal/hippie chick from Hobbs, New Mexico, USA. Her other interests besides movies are music (just about anything except rap, big band, and polka), writing poetry, and driving people insane. Her first experience in horror that She remember was somewhere in between the ages of 2 and 4 when she saw Fiend Without A Face on TV. She was scarred for life, but in a good way. Her mainstay is horror, but she loves exploitation, some sci-fi and fantasy, even a few chick flicks. And she is the proud owner of Emmett Otter's Jug band Christmas DVD. She is also working on broadening her horizons by exploring the films of The French New Wave.

Phillip Escott - is a British movie lover with a boner for not just the finest trash, but the best art house. Basically he likes anything that shows boobies. When he's not admiring naked bodies he's attempting to make films. He urges/will blow you if you come and watch his 'films'. You can reach Phill through www.facebook.com/441films

Ron Fiasco - is a rabid horror film fan whose steady diet of Fangoria and Gorezone magazines when he was a kid helped form his slightly askew view of entertainment in general. His preferences are Pastaland Chunkblowers, Anime with Tentacles, J-Horror, Horror Gaming and Abstract Visions in Technicolor. He dabbles in writing fictional nightmares and creating creepy Soundscapes. He can be found on occasion as a Co-Host on Creep Show Radio, and, despite persistent rumors, does not have a "History of Violence."

Kris Gilpin grew up in Florida (hated it), went to L.A. for 22 years (he has an IMDB. Com page), interviewed/wrote for many film zines during the '80s (he's in this year's great Xerox Ferox book) and is now still trying to find personal happiness, this time in the Midwest...

Seb Godin - has been an avid fan of horror, sci-fi and fantasy his entire life and grew up on a steady diet of everything from Universal Horror classics to Godzilla movies to swords & sorcery flicks. He directed his first short ''Eating Out'' when he was 15 years old and has since directed the horror film VOICES FROM THE FOREST and is currently working on his next project THICKER THAN WATER. He hopes to continue advancing his film-making career and do anything he can to help out with others in their efforts.

Travis - was born in Vancouver, BC. He's a movie junkie looking for his next fix with no interest in a cure. He's written/contributed to numerous publications around the world and spent the majority of his adult life overseas. He recently returned from an 8 year stint in China where he tried his best to corner the Chinese DVD market. facebook.com/dvd.ghoul

Greg Goodsell - recently had his interview with the fabulous character actress O-Lan Jones published in Steve Puchalski's indispensable SHOCK CINEMA magazine. Read it today, and let Greg know what you think at gregoodsell@hotmail.com

Brian Harris - can be found skipping the halls of Arborea, pondering the existence of David Lynch and plotting his next foray into the literary world. When he's not dressing up in a cowboy outfit and taping a cut-out of Franco Nero's face to his own, he's furiously masturbating to the sounds of Futurecop. Known for inspiring others, in an almost cult-like manner, Brian marches to the beat of his own drum and prefers the taste of Cherry kool-aid...so will you. You can find four of his books online, if you look hard enough, and he runs a box set blog for his own sadistic amusement.

Mike Howlett - is the author The Weird World of Eerie Publications (Feral House) and recently made The Weird Indexes of Eerie Publications available as a made to order book on Lulu and Amazon. There is clearly no hope for him.

Andrew Leavold – is the founder and co-owner of Trash Video, a writer and film critic, TV presenter, festival programmer, MC, agnostic evangelist and occasional guerrilla filmmaker.

Tim Merrill - is a rabid unrepentant cinephile based out of Seoul, South Korea. He has written for Asian Cult Cinema, and Asian Eye, as well as a number of long lost film rags. When he isn't scouring DVD/VCD shops throughout Asia for out of print treasures, he can be found in his underground bunker hidden deep along the North Korea border watching repeats of Ultraman, and Mario Adorf Euro crime movies.

Tim Paxton - Has been publishing stuff about monsters since 1978, and currently lives to write about fantastic cinema from India. He is even considering publishing a book on the subject. What a knucklehead.

Chaitanya Reddy - Man of letters and master of many tongues; Sanskrit, Abugida, and English included. Chaitanya covers many genres in his blog moviemaniac100.blogspot.in.

Jeremy Richey - is a writer on film and music who created, and runs, the blogs Moon in the Gutter and Fascination: The Jean Rollin Experience. His writing has appeared in numerous spots online and in a number of various publications. He lives in his home state of Kentucky with his wife Kelley, their two dogs Molly and Mazie and their cat Mazzy.

Steven Ronquillo - is a pretentious know-it-all who looks down on his fellow film fans and refuses to reveal his faves to them unless it makes him look good.

Aaron Soto - is an award-winning Mexican horror filmmaker best known for Omega Shell, the first Mexican cyberpunk film. He is curator and programmer of the San Diego Latino Film Festival genre section "UN MUNDO EXTRAÑO" and coordinator of Rue Morgue Magazine Mexican page Rue Morgue Mexico.

Tony Strauss - has been writing about cinema online and in print for nearly two decades. His existence as that rarest of creature—a movie snob who loves trash cinema (yes, it's possible)—often leaves him as the odd man out in both intellectual and low-brow film discussions. Most movies that people describe as "boring" or "confusing" enthrall him, while the kinds of movies that are described as "non-stop action" usually bore him to tears. He once turned down an offer from Disney for one of his screenplays, and never regretted it for a second.

Dan Taylor - has been writing about junk culture and fringe media since his zine Exploitation Retrospect debuted in 1986. 26 years later the publication is still going strong as a website, blog and -- yes -- a resurrected print edition. Check it all out at Dantenet.com, ERonline.blogspot.com or Facebook.com/ExploitationRetrospect.

Douglas Waltz - lives in the wilds of Kalamazoo, MI where he is experimenting with primitive pottery techniques. His zine, Divine Exploitation, has existed in print or online form since 1988 and can be found at divineexploitation.blogspot.com. His recent book, A Democrazy of Braindrained Loons; The Films of Michael Legge can be purchased at https://tsw.createspace.com/title/3814218. Douglas would like you to know that all Jess Franco films are good. ALL OF THEM!

Dave Zuzelo - is a full time HorrorDad, a full time Media Mangler and a full time Trash Cinema Sponge. He is also a sometime blogger at TOMB IT MAY CONCERN (David-Z. blogspot.com) and enjoys spewing words of sleazy musing across every publication that will have him. Check out his book TOUGH TO KILL-THE ITALIAN ACTION EXPLOSION and see just how many exploding huts he can endure, and he'll beg for more!"

reviews

Utagawa Kuniyoshi's portrait of Oiwa. Yotsuya Kaidan (四谷怪談).

A RAG, A BONE, A HANK OF HAIR
— A POST-HIROSHIMA HAUNTING:

四谷怪談

YOTSUYA KAIDAN / *Tôkaidô Yotsuya Kaidan*
(1956)
Review by Stephen R. Bissette
© 2013 Stephen R. Bissette

Director Masaki Mori's version of this venerable kaiden tale—synthesized from two supposedly true 17th Century murders, popularized as a kabuki play credited to Tsuruya Nanboku (first performed in 1825) and filmed over thirty times between 1912 and 1994—effectively dramatizes an age-old tragedy that still resonates in Japanese pop culture. Some modern versions of this kabuki staple eschew its supernatural elements, but Masaki Mori and his creative collaborators embraced them whole-heartedly. It is, for its time, a terrific horror period piece worthy of revival.

The primary interest to most contemporary viewers will without a doubt be actor Tomisaburo Wakayama's turn as the weak-willed samurai Iemon. Wakayama's international reputation rose in the 1970s when he produced and starred in the infamous *Kozure ôkami*/*Lone Wolf & Cub*/*Baby Cart* films, adapted from Kazuo Koike and Goseki Kojima's popular manga series. He'd played plenty of samurai heroes and ronin antiheroes before inhabiting that iconic role, starring in over 130 films before his death in 1992—including another shot at the role of the cowardly haunted samurai Iemon in director Tai Kato's 1961 version for Toei Studios, **KAIDAN OIWA NO BOREI**. Born to a theatrical family and trained as a youth in kabuki performance and judo, Wakayama turned 27 when **YOTSUYA KAIDAN** showcased his second screen role, and it's a hoot to see him playing a samurai at such a young age. He's instantly recognizable, and his dour playing of the luckless, melancholy Iemon anchors the film. By the climax, though, Wakayama sheds his deceptive reserve; as Iemon's plight intensifies, Wakayama's performance dips into an energized fusion of naturalism and kabuki-stylized extremes, literally slashing and gnashing the scenery and shifting the film into maniacal overdrive.

TÔKAIDÔ YOTSUYA KAIDAN essentially presents the archetypal tale of an innocent young woman whose life is destroyed by a samurai who covets her, and her spectral vengeance upon those who plotted to kill her so he might marry the daughter of a rich merchant.

This film version begins peacefully enough with Iemon's evident discomfort with his wooing of his mistress Ume as fireworks explode in the sky overhead. It takes a bit of screen time to detail the reasons for his unease. Dedicated to his impoverished but loving life with Oiwa (Chieko Soma), Iemon initially resists his manipulative mother's schemes to marry her son off to the wealthy Ume Itô. His manner of doing so betrays his weak selfishness: maintaining his devotion to Oiwa, who has long "lived with [him] as if a wife," Iemon proposes to Ume's father that he permit Iemon to keep Ume as his mistress (!). It's a proposition the father angrily spurns as an insult to all. Iemon's Machiavellian mother, intent upon arranging her son's marriage to Ume to lift them both out of poverty, then manipulates Iemon into killing Oiwa, aided by the blackmailer Naosuke.

Swearing to avenge her father's death, Iemon has lived with Oiwa for three years, wearying of their family life (they have a baby son) and resenting his dependence upon her working in a tea shop to make household ends meet. In the film's only flashback, we see that Iemon had in fact slain Oiwa's father after the old man's refusal to give his daughter's hand in marriage to the low-caste Iemon. Furious and humiliated, Iemon slew the man before he was able to draw his sword; the only witness, Naosuki, fled and told no one, preferring to exhort all he can from Iemon over the years to keep their secret.

By now, it's apparent that although he indeed loves Oiwa in his way, Iemon is a lazy, deceitful shit, to put it succinctly. Still, Wakayama conveys the character's struggle to maintain some measure of dignity under increasing pressure from his avaricious mother, and he retains our sympathies. Those sympathies fade as Iemon grows increasingly abusive to Oiwa and their child after Naosuki convinces the ill woman that her two-timing husband is intent upon dumping her for another (all part of the mother's plan, mind you). Oiwa's desperation grows; inevitably, Iemon's craven nature caves to his mother's guile, and the devoted Oiwa is doomed.

The first horrific sequence erupts 45 minutes into the film. In the kabuki tradition, Oiwa was traditionally depicted as a hideously disfigured specter with a distended eye and pale swollen visage topped by a balding forehead, her face partially shrouded by her remaining shock of disheveled hair; she is an obvious precursor to the amphibian-like Sadako in Hideo Nakata's chilling adaptation of Koji Suzuki's now-classic リング/**RINGU**/**RING** (1998). In all versions of the tale, Oiwa's shocking appearance must be established by the terrible manner of her death.

Director Mori doesn't disappoint. Having unknowingly been given a lethal dose of "poison from Holland" in her tea by her deceitful husband Iemon, Oiwa is left alone with the lecherous masseuse Takaetsu. She spurns his aggressive sexual advances; having skirted being raped, seconds later, Oiwa begins to suffer the effects of the toxic mickey. Her forehead and right eye swells, as if ravaged by a terrible burn; when she pathetically combs her infected hairline with a beloved heirloom turtle-shell comb (all she has left from her

43

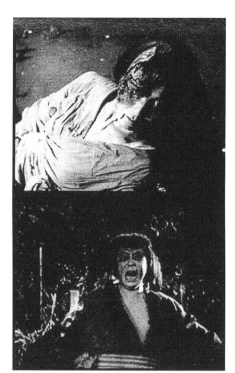

Terror from 四谷怪談 / **YOTSUYA KAIDAN** / *Tôkaidô Yotsuya Kaidan*

Shintoho Studio's modest production remains engaging and convincingly staged. It is undeniably an artifact—the onscreen mayhem seems tame in light of what was to come later in the 1950s (Akira Kurosawa's staging of violence in his samurai dramas irrevocably altered the landscape)—but for its era it was an unabashedly full-blooded horror movie, especially in the wake of the understated stately elegance of Kenji Mizoguchi's internationally-beloved ghost tale 雨月物語/**UGETSU MONOGATARI/UGESTU** (1953), and is well worth revisiting as such. Only the graveyard climax, as Iemon huffs and puffs and lashes out at stick-wielding villagers, seems unfortunately risible, as do some shots of the crude putty-and-buck-teeth spectral faces. In two shots of the disfigured Oiwa rising from the marsh waters, the obvious separation of waterlogged sculpted flesh-putty from the actress's real skin seems dangerously close to complete disintegration. Overall, though, the ghosts are memorably ghoulish and given a dollop of color would have been right at home in any Lucio Fulci 1980s opus.

Adhering to the specifics of its kabuki source, Hideo Oguni and Torao Tanabe's screen adaptation quite effectively establishes the characters and situations and complicates their duplicities with mounting tension. Oguni and Tanabe admirably refuse to flinch from the expected horrors once they arrive, but they leave one dangling narrative thread unanswered: whatever happened to Iemon and Oiwa's infant son? Hiroshi Suzuki's black-and-white fullscreen cinematography remains evocative throughout, making the most of art director Haruyasu Kurosawa's medieval sets; though much of the action is studio-bound, director Mori and cinematographer Suzuki mesh the faux-exteriors with enough true outdoor scenery to work, all paths leading to the claustrophobic artifice of the graveyard finale. Urato Watanabe's orchestral musical score has its dated flourishes, but is for the most part quite effective, occasionally anticipating James Bernard's distinctive Hammer Films scores soon to come.

Just as the Hammer color interpretations of Frankenstein and Dracula left their predecessors in the dust for contemporary audiences, **TÔKAIDÔ YOTSUYA KAIDAN** was quickly eclipsed by more vivid color remakes of the kabuki staple. Kenji Misumi (future director of those same *Kozure ôkami /Lone Wolf & Cub/Baby Cart* films) and popular kaiden director Nobuo Nakagawa made their own adaptations of the tale just three years later. Still, it's a treat to see this monochrome chestnut over half a century later, particularly for Tomisaburo Wakayama's performance and as a harbinger of the more vivid horrors and haunts soon to come (the Japan Horror Classics/New Star Ltd. companion DVD editions provided an immediate context, showcasing eight more films from this era with an emphasis on Nobuo Nakagawa's seminal films which followed). This would make an ideal double-bill with any one of its 1950s contemporaries, one of its 1990s J-horror descendants or the first or second entry in the *Kozure ôkami /Lone Wolf & Cub/ Baby Cart* series. Screened solo or as a companion feature, this is recommended viewing!

JAPAN, 1956. DIRECTOR: MASAKI MORI
CURRENTLY AVAILABLE ONLY AS GREY MARKET 3D DVD-R

mother), her scalp pulls away from her skull. "Is this...my face?" she stammers as she looks in a mirror. Coming as this does midway through one of the most frequently-filmed kaidan, it is a still shocking evocation of the radiation burns suffered at Hiroshima and Nagasaki; the connection with a toxic substance from a foreign land further reinforces that association.

This makes Mori's version of the play particularly of its era, when nuclear horrors were still essentially sublimated in all but the A-bomb shrouded daikaiju-eiga from Toho Studios.

Oiwa's awful end is immediately followed by Iemon's betrayal of Takeutsu, providing two vengeful ghosts to plague Iemon, his mother and Naosuki. To their respective bitter ends, all three conspirators see the gory specters, asserting the supernatural presences are not Banquo's Ghost-like manifestations of Iemon's guilt and mounting insanity (as in other film adaptations); if they are delusions, they are shared by all three culprits. Seeing the ghastly Oiwa and Takeutsu in place of his new bride Ume and Ume's father, Iemon inadvertantly slays his spouse and her proud papa on their wedding night; Naosuki, having married Oiwa's sister, gives away his role in Oiwa's death, and is summarily stabbed to death and pitched down a well (another *Ringu* association). Fleeing the authorities, Iemon's mother hides with her son in a nearby temple, but prayers fail to pacify the angry spirits, culminating in a long overdue settling of accounts between mother and son and bloody matricide before a mob of villagers finally take down the completely unhinged Iemon.

Seen today (thanks to the limited availability of the excellent transfers on the 2001 Japan Horror Classics DVD edition, and the 2003 New Star Ltd. reissue in Greece, both with English subtitle options),

BACKWOODS SUE: THE 'LOST' SUE GRAFTON MOVIE

LOLLY-MADONNA XXX (1973)
aka **THE LOLLY-MADONNA WAR** (UK)

Review by Stephen R. Bissette
© 2013 Stephen R. Bissette

This insular but atmospheric and curiously powerful tale of contemporary Hatfields/McCoys-like backwoods clan rivalry, retribution and self-destruction has virtually disappeared—making it almost as sought-after as its source novel. Based on the second published novel (1969, now an ultra-rare prized collectible) by Louisville, Kentucky native and now-famed and extremely popular mystery novelist Sue Grafton, **LOLLY-MADONNA XXX** was produced and released by MGM at the height of the Vietnam War.

That was the lens through which most critics considered (and dismissed) the film at the time of its theatrical release. Like many westerns of its era, **LOLLY-MADONNA XXX** was considered a metaphor for the War itself: the ongoing conflict between two hillbilly patriarchs vying for a meadow both claim as their own consumes their families, ultimately claiming their wives (one is shot dead, the other disowns her husband when he beats their elder son to death) and killing all but one of their sons. Rod Steiger plays Laban Feather, brooding husband of Chickie (Katherine Squire) living with their moonshiner sons Thrush (Scott Wilson), Skylar (Timothy Scott), Hawk (Ed Lauter), young widower Zack (Jeff Bridges) and backward Finch (Randy Quaid). Their rivals are the Gutshalls, led by Pap (Robert Ryan) and Elspeth (Teresa Hughes) and their offspring Vietnam veteran Villum (Paul Koslo), pacifist Seb (Gary Busey), Sister E. (Joan Goodfellow) and Ludie (Kiel Martin).

The spark of this self-immolation is a false note signed "Lolly-Madonna XXX," claiming that Gutshall sibling bride-to-be is arriving on the local morning bus. Eager to capitalize on fresh opportunity, the intercepted note prompts the Feathers to abandon their corn-liquor still long enough to intercept the bride, kidnap her and hold her hostage for the meadow. However, there is no Lolly-Madonna; she's completely invented, a ruse created by the Gutshalls to distract the Feathers long enough to steal back their pigs and destroy the Feather's still—there is no fiancé, there is no courtship, no pending wedding. Alas, young Roonie Gill (Season Hubley) is unlucky enough to be passing through town en route to the city and waiting at the local bus stop when Thrush and Hawk arrive. They kidnap Roonie, believing she's Lolly-Madonna, and Laban will hear none of it when she claims to have never heard of either Lolly-Madonna or the Gutshall family. Trapped amid the mounting violence within and between the feuding clans, Roonie bonds with Zack and does her best to stay clear of the mayhem.

Shot in Tennessee and boasting stellar technical credits (prominent among those Philip H. Lathrop's cinematography, Tom Rolf's editing and Fred Myrow's excellent score), **LOLLY-MADONNA XXX** also earned Grafton her inroad to screenwriting, co-adapting her novel with producer Rodney Carr-Smith. Grafton needed the venue: with only two of her seven completed novels published with no measurable success, she was eager to pursue scriptwriting for movies and TV. Grafton's **LOLLY-MADONNA XXX** screenwriting credit channeled her into a lucrative 15 year run scripting television movies throughout the TV movie heyday of the '70s (including two Agatha Christie adaptations), culminating in a vitriolic divorce and the urge to return to writing fiction (literally with a vengeance). This led to her launching her popular Kinsey Millhone "alphabet novel" series with *'A' is for Alibi* (1982), and she was able to forever retire from screenwriting after the publication of *'G' is for Gumshoe* (1990). The rest is history—and so is **LOLLY-MADONNA XXX**.

Despite its top-drawer cast and excellent direction from Richard C. Sarafian (still best known for helming **VANISHING POINT**, 1971), this somber, downbeat sleeper with an unusual anticlimax soon sank from sight in second-and-third run drive-in and grindhouse playdates before disappearing into rare late-night TV runs. It was violent enough (including the rape of Sister E) to alienate mainstream audiences and keep it off primetime television, and lacked the literary cache of, say, the studio feature adaptations of Erskine Caldwell's backwater sagas **TOBACCO ROAD** (1941) and **GOD'S LITTLE ACRE** (1958, also starring Robert Ryan as the patriarch of an eccentric mad hillbilly clan). Ironically, despite the 'XXX' in its title—hitting theaters the very year that invented rating would be forever linked with triple-X adult sex films, making the title yet another market liability against the film—**LOLLY-MADONNA XXX** wasn't violent, sexist or exploitative enough to hit grindhouse/drive-in circuit paydirt the way the thematically similar **POOR WHITE TRASH** (the retitled recut version of 1957's **BAYOU**), **SHANTY TRAMP** (1967) or Russ Meyer's **MUDHONEY** (1965) had in the decade before. Neither fish nor fowl and essentially abandoned by MGM, **LOLLY-MADONNA XXX** has become an orphan 'lost' film.

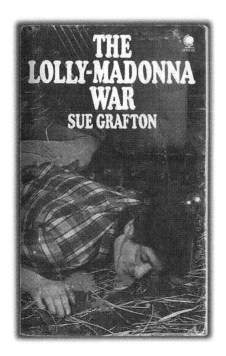

I saw it in its initial theatrical run just before I graduated from high school and never forgot it; judging from the handful of *IMDb.com* comments, it's left quite an impression on those lucky few who caught one of its infrequent screenings since. I also read Grafton's novel in its movie-edition paperback in '73 (damn, I should have held on to that book!), and at the time thought it a stateside kin to British author Gordon M. Williams' *Siege at Trencher's Farm* (1969), which I'd read, like most Americans, in its 1971 **STRAW DOGS** movie paperback edition when Sam Peckinpah's riveting adaptation seared theatrical screens. Grafton's novel and Sarafian's film adaptation came to mind again years later when I first read Ernest Hebert's *The Dogs of March* (1979) and Carolyn Chute's *The Beans of Egypt, Maine* (1986); though both of those were New England-based, their candid portraits of rural poverty, quiet desperation and loss recalled Grafton's book.

Grafton has since dismissed the film as well, saying, "It was a terrible movie but a great cast. I learned a lot. So that's the way life goes…" (Grafton, interviewed by Linda L. Richards, 2008, January Profile: *'G' is for Grafton: Sue Grafton's Murderous Moments*, http://januarymagazine.com/grafton.html). It's not a terrible movie, though—it's actually quite good, executed with considerable skill from stem to stern and magnificently performed. It's indeed a great cast, one of the finest of its year, boasting excellent ensemble playing from veterans like Ryan and Steiger (both dominating the drama without chewing the scenery) to young bucks Bridges (effortlessly convincing and beguiling as Zack), Wilson, Lauter, Busey and Quaid, to the steadfast presence of the relatively unknown Squire and Hughes as the put-upon backwoods matriarchs. Teresa Hughes and Joan Goodfellow bring real gravitas and conviction to their roles, particularly in their mother-daughter intimacy after Sister E's rape, wherein their irrevocable roles in an impoverished male-dominated universe is perversely reinforced by the mother's stoic resignation.

Curiously, Season Hubley's Roonie is the most vaguely-defined of all the characters, an odd oversight given Hubley's central role, fleeting onscreen chemistry with Bridges and her character's dire plight. She should be in almost unbearable jeopardy, the most sympathetic character of all, but the script leaves her merely comfortable throughout and dramatically high and dry, a veritable cipher spared the abuses showered upon Sister E. Perhaps the cacophony of male creative collaborators in the production literally drowned out Grafton's narrative voice: Roonie's brief onscreen narration is never followed up on, eschewing the novel's primary voice. Given the narrative focus on the actions of the male characters, this makes a certain amount of sense, but it doesn't excuse Roonie being so uselessly shunted to the periphery of the narrative. We should empathize with her above all; instead, Zack becomes our primary concern for much of the film, unobtrusively watching over Roonie's safety while quietly mourning his long-lost wife whose death precipitated the disaster now spiraling completely out of control. Roonie's given none of the emotional clarity or potency of Hawk or Thrush (Sister E's attackers), both of whom are economically sketched and given such resonance that we genuinely mourn their tragic deaths despite their transgressions.

The characters are otherwise vividly inhabited and remain the film's front-and-center focus, as they should be. Scott Wilson in particular delivers a memorable performance; having debuted in 1967 in the one-two punches of **IN THE HEAT OF THE NIGHT** and **IN COLD BLOOD** (as Dick Hickok), Wilson's role here as the abused/abusive son Thrush echoed his turn as Slim Grissom in Robert Aldrich's thematically similar **THE GRISSOM GANG** (1971, a box-office casualty in which Wilson raped a youthful kidnap victim played by Kim Darby).

Director Richard C. Sarafian's focus on characters was a virtue of almost all of his work, which included episodes of I Spy and Gunsmoke, the family film sleeper **RUN WILD, RUN FREE** (1969), the cult favorite **VANISHING POINT** as well as unsung but muscular audience-pleasers like the Richard Harris western **MAN IN THE WILDERNESS** (1971—one of the few films I saw in the early 1970s that prompted audience applause as its credits rolled into view). It was a virtue lost to critics and audiences caught in the polar extremes of either rejecting outright, or utterly intoxicated by, the plethora of cinematic violence dominating screens that year.

1973 was a troubling year for mainstream studios and movie-goers: rape was a dominant theme in surprisingly prominent films, and rape and the threat of rape was central to **LOLLY-MADONNA XXX**. This was and remains ugly stuff, and one can see why a film like **LOLLY-MADONNA** didn't fill theater seats despite its quality. Sarafian's next western, the Burt Reynolds vehicle **THE MAN WHO LOVED CAT DANCING** (1973), fed the critical backlash against the role rape was playing in more and more mainstream studio films. This quickly took a toll on Sarafian's career, relegating him to more TV work amid only occasional theatrical features (**THE NEXT MAN**, 1976; the underrated **SUNBURN**, 1979; etc.).

Graphic onscreen violence was also at an alarming peak in '73, and audiences were frankly worn out: a trip to the most star-studded movies was usually an unpleasant wallow in carnage and depravities

45

previously relegated to exploitation fare. This was gravy for adventurous moviegoers, exploitation fans, gorehounds and no-account lowlifes, but wider audiences and mainstream critics were growing increasingly resentful of the trend, making it easy to relegate oddities like **LOLLY-MADONNA XXX** to the pop cultural dumpster, the quicker the better.

As noted, however, despite its narrative hook and high body count, **LOLLY-MADONNA** didn't wallow in its potential mayhem. The violence, when it comes, is vivid but tastefully handled: Sister E's rape (unlike many staged in major studio films in the '70s, beginning with those in 1971's **A CLOCKWORK ORANGE** and **STRAW DOGS** and 1972's **DELIVERANCE**) builds to the assault then cuts away, focusing instead on the after-the-fact paucity of the father's response to the crime and Sister E's subsequent misery and shame and mother Elspeth's caring but confused attempt to comfort her. (An aside: Sister E proves to be the most sensible of the lot, last shown strutting away with her suitcase packed as her father and brothers mobilize for the final showdown.) Most of the bloodshed occurs offscreen, as in Hawk's mortal wounding during the Feathers' ill-fated torching of the meadow, a confrontation again staged with optimum dramatic power but minimal graphic horror (two tied pigs are torched, rousing both Roonie and Elspeth to risk their lives to intercede; the animals are not harmed onscreen, but we hear their piercing cries throughout the sequence, pitching the dread to a feverish level). Even the most shocking onscreen murder was staged with no gore but maximum impact (perfectly timed and framed by Sarafian and Lathrop, the gunshot wound vividly evoked via a jet of air blasting the victim's long hair).

This deference to characterization and dramatic impact over splashy gore cost the film at the boxoffice. On the one hand too despairingly violent, on the other weak tea compared to the stiffer competition, **LOLLY-MADONNA XXX** was fucked coming and going, especially in contrast to the blood-spattered competition like Warner Bros. slick *Dirty Harry* sequel **MAGNUM FORCE** and down-and-dirty exploitation gold like Hallmark's **MARK OF THE DEVIL** and **LAST HOUSE ON THE LEFT**.

Among the reasons for its boxoffice failure and subsequent orphan status was its eleventh-hour refusal to embrace the expected cathartic showdown between the patriarchs. Both fathers lose their families—Laban retreats into childlike madness, banished to his room by Zack amid the final melee, left with the backwards son Finch, while Pap Feather witnesses all three of his sons' death throes—and the momentum ends, sliding into freezing and fading into sepia-toned revery (echoing the opening credits montage of family photos), thus leaving viewers 'on the hook' emotionally. This greatly frustrated audiences at the time, further mirroring the national Vietnam Era zeitgeist with sobering clarity: there is, in fact, no dramatically satisfactory end. One wonders if another ending was shot and previewed; the final theatrical edit left Zack, Roonie, Chickie and Sister E. alive, along with the grieving fathers, frozen in time at the very moment it seemed further bloodshed was inevitable. We never find out what happened to Roonie.

Given Grafton's contemporary celebrity, the astronomical prices the single UK printing and two US printings of Grafton's novel are demanding on the collector's market, and the unfortunate limbo to which the film adaptation has been consigned, rescue of both Grafton's novel and Sarafian's adaptation seems like a no-brainer. There's money to be made, and an audience for Grafton's work that simply didn't exist in 1973. Fox (current proprietors of most of the MGM movie properties) and some enterprising publisher should join forces to get Grafton's source novel back into print and this film into a legit widescreen DVD release—even in the current glutted, cluttered marketplace, "From best-selling novelist Sue Grafton and the director of **VANISHING POINT**" would certainly reel in potential customers and viewers.

USA, 1973. DIRECTOR: RICHARD C. SARAFIAN

MANEATER

Review by Stephen R. Bissette
© 2013 Stephen R. Bissette

TWILIGHT fans, take note: **MANEATER** (2009) from Lightning Media and Entertainment One is a stronger-than-usual cable TV horror effort starring Dean Cain (*Lois & Clark*) playing, essentially, Bella Swan's sheriff Dad Charlie. I kid you not—there's even the Native American tribal monster to further the association—and it's worth a viewing. Cain is Harry Bailey, retired FBI serial-killer profiler, now a sheriff and troubled single father raising his about-to-turn-18 daughter Pearl (lovely Lacy Phillips) in a tougher-than-**TWILIGHT** spin on the venerable Wendigo (here "Windigo") legend effectively plugged into a Northwestern US small town, a-la *Twin Peaks* and **TWILIGHT**. Bailey is plagued by the lingering mystery of his wife's disappearance 15 years ago, a puzzle intensified by the fresh blood spilled in an eruption of inexplicably savage recent murders; Pearl is bedazzled by the attractive new-kid-in-town (Stephen Lunsford, former lead of the TV series **KAMEN RIDER: DRAGON KNIGHT**) and stuck with Dad's old baggage about her missing mom and his resulting over-protective paternalism. The locals want to blame a renegade grizzly bear, but Bailey is certain it's something far, far worse—and fears it might even be himself.

This was the first directorial effort from actor Michael Emanuel, and he does a decent job of it. Cain's investment in his role (he co-produced the feature) is matched by a solid supporting cast; the mystery is compelling, the murders brutal but not overly so, and Phillips and Lunsford and friends generate enough chemistry and heat to keep interest (cineastes take note: one of their pals is played by Maximillian Roeg, son of vet visionary director Nicolas Roeg and actress Theresa Russell, who registered earlier in the gay feature **DREAM BOY**, 2008). Despite the fangs and shape-shifter components, **MANEATER** leaves **TWILIGHT** unchallenged, but makes for a satisfying evening entertainment for horror and mystery *X-Files* and *Fringe* fans.

USA, 2009. DIRECTOR: MICHAEL EMANUEL
AVAILABLE FROM ENTERTAINMENT ONE

SANTA SANGRE

Review by Stephen R. Bissette
© 2013 Stephen R. Bissette

The DVD label Severin Films is making quite a mark for themselves in short order, releasing terrific restored DVDs of venerable 1970s and 1980s cult titles (**THE BABY** [1973], **BLOODY BIRTHDAY** [1981], the Aussie biker classic **STONE** [1974], the original **THE INGLORIOUS BASTARDS** [1978], and—soon!—beloved British 1960s and 1970s Amicus Films titles) while ambitiously rolling out wide cult theatrical releases of genuine curios like James Nguyen's **BIRDEMIC: SHOCK AND TERROR** (2008) to cultivate new **TROLL 2**-like cult status. Key to Severin's strategy is their recent first-ever US DVD release of Alejandro Jodorowsky's cult classic **SANTA SANGRE** (1989), which debuted stateside at the Boston Film Festival. The film also has another New England association, in that previous American distributor Expanded Entertainment hand-picked Northampton MA's Pleasant Street Theater to test-market **SANTA SANGRE** back in 1991. Alas, it was a dumb move: who expected hyper-feminist NoHo to embrace a visionary, violent, semi-surreal sympathetic portrait of a traumatized circus boy (Adan Jodorowksy) who grows up to be a serial killer (Axel Jodorowsky), guided by the madness of his armless mother (an astonishing performance from Blanca Guerra)?

With its confrontational fusion of virgin-rape-victim-as-saint, drunken abusive father (a truly monstrous Guy Stockwell), tattooed temptresses (Thelma Tixou), dominating/demonic mother, and string of bloody murders of exclusively female victims, **SANTA SANGRE** sure wasn't cult fodder for Smith College or the local activist lesbian community, burying any hopes of the film enjoying an American release. Jodorowsky was the Chilean artist who co-founded the Panic Theater movement of the 1960s and who launched the midnight movie phenomenon of the 1970s with the stunning countercultural embrace of his religious

western **EL TOPO** (1970), and **SANTA SANGRE** is his last feature film to date—and like **EL TOPO** and its successor, **THE HOLY MOUNTAIN** (1973), it is bloody, beautiful, bombastic, poetic, ravishing, lunatic, and unforgettable. It is also not for all tastes; that said, it is driven by a compelling story, strong characters, and it's certainly the most accessible of all of Jodorowsky's films, an entry point for the uninitiated. Adding to **SANTA SANGRE**'s international cult status is the fact that it was produced by Dario Argento's brother Claudio Argento, lending the set-in-Mexico epic a distinctively Italian/Fellini flavor that perfectly compliments the Luis Bunuel, **FREAKS**, **INVISIBLE MAN**, and Santo references and flourishes. Severin has done a stellar job with this release (on DVD and Blu-Ray), packed with extras that only intensify this as the ideal introductory package for those curious about Jodorowsky and his extraordinary body of work. This is must-viewing for adventurous viewers seeking truly daring, different fare—casual viewers, though: approach with caution. You've been warned!

MEXICO/ITALY, 1989.
DIRECTOR: ALEJANDRO JODOROWSKY
AVAILABLE FROM SEVERIN FILMS

UROTSUKIDOJI: LEGEND OF THE OVERFIEND

(Chōjin Densetsu Urotsukidōji)

Review by Ron Fiasco

Houston, we have a problem. Every 3000 years the Human world, the Beast world and the Demon world are visited by the OVERFIEND—a messiah with multiple members the size of hospital corridors—who, it is said, will rise and unite the three worlds. Sound like a super shindig of palpable import? Yes, indeed! In this groundbreaking "Hentai" Anime (unless you found this rag under the cool kid's History book, we assume you know what the word "Hentai" means; if not, then it roughly means "pervert"), we see the brave new world of "Tentacle Porn" opened with a vengeance.

The film opens with all manner of Demons and three-boobed concubines getting it on in the flames of the Inferno. (Intrigued yet? I knew you would be!) The scene then shifts to two sibling members of the "Beast" race looking for the "Cho-Jyn" or "Overfiend" to bring on the New Age of supreme sexiness—at a High-school, nonetheless! While the head cheerleader, Akemi, is doing her cheers, Nagumo, the (seminal?) class loser is in the basketball storage container spanking the monkey furiously. Needless to say this pisses off the star basketball player, who flings a basketball directly at Nagumo's noggin, sending him flying. The Beastly siblings comment that there is no way THIS loser could be the Overfiend, and that the star player is more likely the potential fiend.

The scene then shifts to Akemi getting escorted by her teacher into the nurse's office...But guess what? She is no nurse! Her face splits open into rows of teeth, and phalli and tongues fly everywhere, penetrating Akemi's every orifice! Disney this ain't! Afterwards, Nagumo meets Akemi on a park bench with ice cream to help her get over her "experience", which is always the way to go after Demon Rape. The brother and sister Beasts then proceed to follow the star of the basketball team to an orgy in which he is boffing random chicks until a duo of Demons show up and make the women explode all over the place. One Demon wearing a trench coat and having a slit with teeth as a face tells the poor guy to slice off his member and replace it with the Evil Green Phallus, and without hesitating, he proceeds to do so...

I will leave the plot description there, because it gets so convoluted that after repeating viewings, you may still do a facepalm, exclaiming "WTF!"

This movie makes up for lack of cohesive plot with sheer bad-assery. There are scenes with Hell denizens being pleasured by ghosts, crazy martial arts madness with extreme gore, huge werewolf beasts with dicks the size of city buses, etc. I am sure in today's desensitized society you've seen far worse, but in 1987 this was the Bees Knees. There is a "cut" hour-and-a-half version of the flick, but I would suggest going out and getting the "Perfect Collection", which has all of the OVAs' moist and meaty bits. The animation is top-notch for the time, and you can't deny the power of being able to pop this sucker on at any house party and seeing your guests do a double take at what madness you have on the screen. Keep in mind that the dubbing is particularly bad and the music is dated, but for a great time and a wonderful date flick, try **UROTSUKIDOJI: LEGEND OF THE OVERFIEND**—there won't be a dry pair of undies in the house!

JAPAN, 1987-1989.
DIRECTOR: HIDEKI TAKAYAMA
ORIGINAL SERIES RELEASED BY CENTRAL PARK MEDIA [CURRENTLY OOP]
MOVIE VERSION AVAILABLE FROM ALLEGRO CORPORATION

DER KREIG DER INFRAS

(The War of the Infras)

Review by Jeff Goodhartz

What we have here is a German-dubbed version of **SUPER RIDERS WITH THE DEVILS** which in itself was a Taiwan film that utilizes footage from two Japanese *Kamen Rider* featurettes, *Kamen Rider vs. Shocker* and *Kamen Rider vs. Ambassador Hell*. Okay perhaps I should back up just a bit...

In 1971 Japan's Toei studio released *Kamen Rider* (Masked Rider). Created by Shotaro Ishinomori, *Kamen Rider* told of an evil organization called Shocker that was creating cyborg monsters with the intention of (wait for it) ruling the world. Their prize creation, a captured motorcycle racer whom they transformed into a grasshopper-like cyborg, escapes and turns on the organization with the intent of stopping them. The show was a sensation with Toei having created a superhero who's

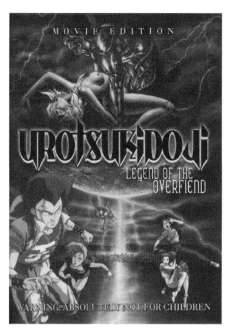

popularity rivaled Toho's *Ultraman*. Follow-up programs were inevitable (and most welcome) with *Kamen Rider V3*, *Kamen Rider X*, *Kamen Rider Amazon*, *Kamen Rider Stronger* and *Kamen Sky Rider* keeping the premise running without a break throughout the decade. Accompanying each series were theatrical shorts, each running roughly thirty minutes. These usually served as stand-alone widescreen episodes that would be shown before whatever feature film they were supporting. And since I'm a huge fan of the early *Kamen Rider* adventures, I found these short features incredibly entertaining. As pure camp goes, it just doesn't get any better.

As the series and short films' popularity spread, some enterprising filmmakers in Taiwan had the idea of doing a local version. The way they went about this was to edit together the original short features into one longer whole. The first example of this was to combine the first two theatrical shorts, *Kamen Rider vs. Shocker* and *Kamen Rider vs. Ambassador Hell* (both coming from the initial series, both 1972 and both directed by Minoru Yamada). In order to give the Japanese features a more familiar Taiwanese look, all scenes of the Japanese actors were removed and look-alike locals were inserted. Taking it one step further, they were apparently able to borrow the original costumes from Toei in order to stage extra fight scenes. On top of that, they even created a brand new costume (a Sphinx-like creation) in order to add plot points and help connect the two separate original shorts. The completed mishmash was titled **SUPER RIDERS WITH THE DEVILS** and released in 1976 with the additional footage directed by Lin Chong-Guang. For those like myself who were already familiar with the original series and films, **SUPER RIDERS WITH THE DEVILS** is a schizophrenic experience; a Bizzaro World of sorts with familiar faces, Hiroshi Fujita, Takeshi Sasaki, Jiro Chiba (younger brother of Sonny Chiba), Akiji Kobayashi (whom most will know as Captain Muramatsu in the original *ULTRAMAN*) and Eisei Amamoto replaced by unknown (to me, anyway) actors who, while good, paled beside the originals.

47

So how do the Germans figure in? Well for that, we must look at **SUPER INFRAMAN**, the 1975 film from Hong Kong's Shaw Bros. studio that was their big budget (relatively speaking) feature film response to the whole Japanese TV superhero craze. It was apparently a huge hit in Germany—so much so that when local audiences screamed for more, the studio happened upon **SUPER RIDERS WITH THE DEVILS** and in 1981, released it under its new moniker, **THE WAR OF THE INFRAS** billing it as a kind of sequel to **SUPER INFRAMAN**, even going so far as to feature the Shaw hero prominently on its poster ads (never mind that the character does not appear in the actual film). Dubbing the Taiwanese product into German (which merely adds another layer of oddness to the proceedings), they have finally released it on DVD, marking the only official home vid version of this oddity that I'm aware of.

So after all of that, is **DER KREIG DER INFRAS** worth seeing? If you are a Kamen Rider fan, then the answer is an emphatic yes. Sure, it's confusing (both in viewing and in description) and no, it isn't quite on the level of the original Japanese short films, but it still supplies many cheesy thrills as only a *Kamen Rider* adventure can.

Incidentally, this wasn't the German's only excursion into *Kamen Rider* territory. They also released edited feature versions of *Kamen Rider V3 vs. Deathtron* and *The Five Riders vs. King Dark*, but that's another story...I think.

JAPAN, 1972.
DIRECTOR: MINORU YAMADA
KAMEN RIDER VS. SHOCKER RELEASED BY TOEI
JAPAN, 1972.
DIRECTOR: MINORU YAMADA
KAMEN RIDER VS. AMBASSADOR HELL RELEASED BY TOEI
TAIWAN, 1976.
DIRECTOR: LIN CHONG-GUANG
SUPER RIDERS WITH THE DEVIL RELEASED ???
GERMANY, 1981. NO DIRECTOR CREDIT
DER KREIG DER INFRAS (The War of the Infras) RELEASED 2006 BY TRASH COLLECTION

GHEYSAR

Review by Jared Auner

GHEYSAR (or **QEYSAR** or **GHEISAR**) is a hard-boiled revenge melodrama from Shah-era Iran. Although it might be surprising to some, Iran at the time had a vibrant and profitable film industry, with domestic productions regularly outgrossing American and European fare at the box office. These days, pre-revolutionary Farsi-language films are very rare, but some have surfaced. **GHEYSAR** is considered one of the best, and I was lucky enough to track down a copy.

A young girl has died by her own hand. A letter posted to her grieving family in the aftermath details why. She had been raped by a local thug named Masoud, and could not live with the shame. Her eldest brother, a hulking ex-con turned butcher, vows bloody revenge, but is stabbed in the back (literally) while confronting the rapist.

The family's youngest son Gheysar (a Farsi transliteration of "Caesar"), played by Behrouz Vossoughi, returns home from working abroad into this atmosphere of grief and hatred, unaware of the tragedy. After he learns of his siblings' fate, Gheysar broods and delays, weeps and fumes, until he comes to the conclusion his own life means nothing in the face of this affront to his family's honor. Despite pleas from his beloved uncle, Gheysar vows revenge, both on the rapist himself and his two mobbed-up brothers, who have shielded their sibling from prosecution.

This is where the meat of the film's drama occurs. It's a rather talky movie, with lots of crying and emotive gesticulating. But the scenes where Gheysar hunts down his prey are well-filmed, suspenseful, and contain a gritty lyricism that imbues the scenes with real tension and verve. They are also fairly violent, but without the cartoonish aspect you might expect from a Third World thriller.

The first of these scenes is set in a public bath, with the camera prowling behind and around actor Behrouz Vossoughi as he wanders the marble labyrinth, capturing his character's crushing mix of dread and determination. He puts his doubts behind him, spots his target, and closes in. He catches the man unawares in the shower and the two grapple realistically. Gheysar finally gets his lucky stab in, washes away the blood, and slinks out before anyone is the wiser.

The next encounter takes place in a slaughterhouse, with the track-and-kill interspersed with footage of a cow being slaughtered. It's surprisingly poetic, predicting a similar scene a decade later in a far more famous film, Coppola's **APOCALYPSE NOW**. These scenes are great, and make up for the excessively talky bits (a problem if you don't speak the language, since there aren't any subtitles!) which do tend to bog the movie down.

Gheysar's ultimate quarry, his sister's rapist, has gone into deep cover. Gheysar, too, has to make himself sparse, hiding out from the cops as well as his grieving and disapproving loved ones. A lucky break sends him to a nightclub where the

headlining act is a sexy scantily-clad singer-dancer who happens to be Masoud's moll.

I'm always fond of the nightclub scene in movies like this, as they often prove a welcome relief to the tension or the suffocating, doomy mood of the film. It's a nice one too, the girl wiggles her bum seductively and the song is a great swingin' '60s Farsipop number. Gheysar catches her eye and she takes him home, disrobing in front of him. But he doesn't have hanky-panky in mind, only vengeance. His forlorn charms are such that she willingly spills the beans on Masoud's location, setting up the final confrontation. I won't spoil it for you in case you ever get a chance to see this film. But as you might guess, things don't end happily.

GHEYSAR was a landmark production that inspired countless imitations of its gritty, brooding style. The film could be considered an example of the Iranian "New Wave" of the 1960s, along with films like Farokh Ghafari's **NIGHT OF THE HUNCHBACK** (1965) or Dariush Mehrjui's **THE COW** (1969), as well as a departure point for the usual characterization of heroes in Iranian cinema. After **GHEYSAR** came a deluge of noir-inspired antihero movies. The film's director, Masoud Kimiai, was a trailblazer of Iranian cinema himself. Only 28 when he directed this, his second feature, his success opened the door to a new, young generation of filmmakers, who revitalized the industry only a decade before the Islamic revolution put a serious damper on all things fun and exciting.

What might be surprising to those unfamiliar with pre-revolutionary Iranian cinema is the level of sex and violence depicted. While nothing compared to what was going on in the US or Europe at the same time, it's still a shock to see such potentially scandalous material from a country most in the West assume to be rife with religious prudery. Although the film contains no full frontal nudity, there are a few quick tit-flashes in a couple of scenes, including a flashback depicting the rape that set the plot in motion. This scene may have been cut down in the version I saw; the editing gets rather choppy at the moment the victim is unsheathed. At one time, it may have been even stronger. But this is pure speculation on my part.

Iran under the Shah was a very Western-oriented country, and so the introduction of prurient images and subject matter in films would seem to be a key aspect of the "modernization" which accompanied close political, economic, and cultural ties with the 'States and Western Europe during this era. And while Iran never went as far as the "anything goes" impulse found in neighboring Turkey during the '60s and '70s, things got much wilder there than in the much more conservative Egypt, home to the Middle East's largest and most robust film industry at that time.

Iranian films were never widely exported, and after the revolution in '79, movies such as this were never made again. In fact, many films were destroyed in typical revolutionary fervor, though some were smuggled out of the country. The copy of **GHEYSAR** I viewed seems to have been taken from a US-made VHS tape (it's introduced with an FBI warning), probably marketed solely to Persian immigrant communities.

More and more Iranian movies made during the Shah's reign are surfacing in bootlegs and online, though they remain mostly very scarce. When copies of these movies are found, they often feature terrible, almost unwatchable audio & video and never, ever have subtitles. But interesting pictures like this one or the violent 1975 film **MARG DAR BARAN**, directed by the "Iranian Hitchcock" Samouel Khachikian, expose an area of world cinema that deserves wider recognition and analysis. You just have to know where to look!

IRAN, 1969. DIRECTOR: MASOUD KIMIAI
AVAILABLE FROM *iranianmovies.com* [GREY-MARKET]

DEVIATION

Review by Brian Harris

Lovers Paul (veteran actor Malcolm Terris) and Olivia (Lisbet Lundquist), on their way back to the big city after a randy tryst in the countryside, wind up stranded on the side of the road, their car unresponsive after hitting something running across the road, shrouded by the fog. A concerned couple passing by offers the shaken lovers a place to stay for the night and a ride to town in the morning to hire a tow and a mechanic. They gratefully accept the strangers' kindness, but not all is well as Paul becomes convinced the shape he struck was a person that had purposefully thrown himself in front of the vehicle. His odd hosts Julian (Karl Lanchbury of **VAMPYRES**) and Rebecca (Sibyla Grey) assure Paul that nobody has been hit and that it may well have been his eyes playing tricks on him, perhaps even a dream he may have experienced after falling asleep behind the wheel. Adamant that he'd run somebody down, Paul begrudgingly accepts warm milk for he and Olivia and they all retire.

Later that night, Paul finds the sleeping Olivia unresponsive and suspects their drinks have been drugged so he slips out into the night to inspect the car, hoping to get it up and running. Instead of minor repairs though, he finds some unauthorized "work" has been done to the engine, rendering it inoperable. Why would somebody want to keep them from leaving? The answer quickly becomes clear when Julian, his creepy sister Olivia and a small entourage of hippies catch Paul unawares and drag him off to a dingy basement to play cruel games. The frivolity is short-lived when Olivia loses her cool and stabs poor Paul to death while nympho Vivian attempts to seduce him. The group have skeletons—and illegal substances—in their closet and cannot afford to have law enforcement poking about, so the corpse is rolled into an open sub-cellar used as Julian's taxidermy workshop.

The next day Olivia joins Rebecca and her Auntie (Shelagh Wilcocks of **THE VAMPIRE LOVERS**) downstairs for breakfast, there she's told that Julian and Paul have gone to town and should be back later. Afterward in the sitting room, a startlingly lucid Auntie shoves a gun into Olivia's hand and tells her to leave before "they" kill her. Before the flustered and confused girl can get more information from the old woman though, Rebecca and the hippies arrive at the house and Olivia is forced to quickly cram the gun into the couch and follow them into the basement. What goes on below the house and what esoteric rites do the group partake in?

The late Spanish filmmaker José Ramón Larraz may be better known by genre fans for his sexploitation horror classic **VAMPYRES** (1974) and **LOS RITOS SEXUALES DEL DIABLO** (a.k.a. **BLACK CANDLES**, 1982)—the latter he hated—but he had quite a few accomplished works under his belt, some sadly under-appreciated and many rarely seen. **DEVIATION** would certainly fall into both categories, in my opinion. Written and directed under the pseudonym J.R. Larrath, **DEVIATION** is a tense, psychosexual thriller that had absolutely zero to do with the artwork that adorned the cover of the VHS. By the way, that would be Jo-Ann Robinson from Fred Olen Ray's **SCALPS** (1983). Naturally with an *Evil Dead*-esque cover viewers might of been inclined to believe that this film was horror, and it certainly does have horrific moments, but this really focused more on the claustrophobic manor and the taboo subjects that take place within its walls, such as incest, lesbianism and interracial sex. Oh, and murder too! One thing I immediately took notice of was the menacing Manson Family vibe that permeated throughout as Julian, his sister and their followers raised all kinds of hell. Sexual slavery, drug orgies, murder, hippies, taxidermy? There's no doubt this film probably raised some eyebrows considering the gruesome Tate-LaBianca murders were still fresh in the minds of those living in 1971.

Of course, none of this means anything if it's not a "good" film, right? I mean, nobody is going to watch this just for drug-fueled hippie orgies featuring massive breasts, right? Yeah that's not how Weng's Chop readers roll! As the occult/supernatural angle is never fleshed-out we're left to wonder whether spirits really do haunt the boarded up rooms of the manor or they're just the guilt-induced byproducts of our antagonists' chemical-soaked brains. And that probably was Larraz's intention from the start. Truth be told, the

sexual tension that builds between siblings as this film progresses was far scarier than any wandering spirits or hippie cult's witchcraft. One particular sequence during an orgy, in which Julian and Rebecca stare at one another as they each make love to different people, was positively chilling. Even with a low budget the solid English actors and outstanding locations combined with Larraz's disturbing tale of sex and murder make this film well worth hunting down, whether the original VHS release or a DVD bootleg, especially if you're a dedicated José Ramón Larraz fan. I've been on a quest to hunt down all of his work, even the later comedies he directed, and this is definitely a keeper for me.

UK, 1971. DIRECTOR: JOSÉ RAMÓN LARRAZ

MONKEY KING WITH 72 MAGIC

Review by Seb Godin

MONKEY KING WITH 72 MAGIC: What is one supposed to expect when they hear that title? Well, after having watched the film, I can tell you that I'm still not too sure...

This is one of many films based on the classic epic Chinese novel *Journey to the West* by Wu Cheng'en which tells the story of the pilgrimage of a Buddhist monk and his many bizarre adventures along the way, which includes an encounter with a strange creature known as the Monkey King. This obscure little slice of cinema serves as a prequel, relaying the origins of the Monkey King.

It tells the bizarre story of a monkey-like creature (played with over-the-top enthusiasm by Hwa Chung Ting) who hatches from an egg in Heaven.

Before long, he finds himself the king of a race of hyperactive monkey children whom he protects from all manner of evil. He fights monkey-eating demons, gods and all other types of baddies using his 72 forms of magic.

Now, reading that little plot synopsis alone should be enough to tell you if you would enjoy this flick. What did I think about it? Well, it's...entertaining.

This movie is quite the mixed bag. On the good side of things, it's really a ton of fun to watch. If I had to compare it to anything, it would be if **FLASH GORDON** (1980) was directed by Godfrey Ho while on an acid trip. It's bright and colorful with some rather impressive set design and some really entertaining action sequences. It offers up a virtually unlimited amount of strange characters and is certainly never a boring film. However, it does have quite a few major flaws to it. The biggest one is the fact that it never really has an actual story arc that it follows. There is never a real main villain and our protagonist is pretty much just fighting a plethora of villainous foes over the course of the movie. Because of this, it feels very episodic and, while never really becoming boring, it does get pretty damn tedious after the first forty minutes or so.

MONKEY KING WITH 72 MAGIC ends with the Monkey King becoming imprisoned in the mountain where he is found in Cheng'en's novel, making this a prequel to the original source material. I'll say this much, it's a better prequel than most I have seen...

This film is easy enough to find. It is available on the "Super Kung-Fu Box Set" and is also available as a double feature with the Godfrey Ho-scribed/Phillip Ko-directed **NINJA UNTOUCHABLES** (1988, which stars Pierre Kirby and that should be all you need to know about it). The latter is the version that I own and I can't say I fully recommend this release. The subtitles are often cut off and it switches from widescreen to full screen at least twice over the course of the movie. I would, however, recommend picking it up for **NINJA UNTOUCHABLES**.

TAIWAN, 1976. DIRECTOR: FU CHING-WA
AVAILABLE FROM FORTUNE 5

THE WAILER
(LA LLORONA)

Review by Brian Harris

A group of twenty-somethings visiting Mexico is looking to get their party on after finding themselves stranded in a small village, so they eagerly take a local up on his unbelievable offer to put them up in a super cheap cabin with a beautiful view. The catch? Outside of his request that nothing be destroyed or removed from the cabin, there is none and they immediately get busy smoking, snorting and screwing. Things take a dark turn though when a few items in the house are broken during one couple's amorous encounter, unleashing the angry spirit of a mother tortured by the unforgivable act of killing her own children. The partiers attempt to escape the cabin but it has been plunged into a spiritual dimension, trapping them inside with the vengeful apparition with no way out. Could this ghost and the tragic circumstances that damned her be the inspiration for the Mexican legend of *La Llorona*?

Andrés Navia's **THE WAILER** is a pretty by-the-numbers affair to be sure, but as generic as it is, the film still succeeds in entertaining. The combination of bare skin and a visually striking antagonist, reminiscent of Sadako from **RINGU** (1998) or Kayako from **JU-ON: THE GRUDGE** (2002), was definitely a plus because it was nearly impossible to find any redeeming qualities in the characters. In my experience it's hard to connect with rude, selfish characters only interested in sex, drugs and alcohol. Then again, maybe that was the point as they seemed to serve no other purpose in this film other than to keep things moving by making the "Final Girl" seem even more angelic by comparison and providing La Llorona with victims. You could easily replace the supernatural elements in this film with a run-of-the-mill masked slasher without skipping a beat.

Sounds like I hated **THE WAILER**, right? Well, don't be so sure.

We all know low budget productions are usually plagued by weak writing, direction, acting, lighting, sound and editing but today those things are almost par for the course. Often times—for me, anyhow—you can look beyond the negatives and find a film as a whole entertaining, warts and all. As I mentioned above, beautiful women in very little clothing and J-Horror influences gave this film the boost it needed to go from being "Just okay" to "Hey, that wasn't bad." Isn't it amazing how just a little nipple and a cool monster can enhance a mediocre viewing experience? Seriously, despite the lackluster writing that director Navia and the cast had to work with, performances were tolerable and characters were believable (enough).

Videography was static and uninspired but it was clean and the locations kept things interesting. The lighting during interior shots was sketchy but that probably ended up helping the gory FX, which was pretty cool, more than hindering it. Did I mention the conclusion wasn't half bad either? So there you have it! Does all of this mean it's entertaining enough to watch again, perhaps even purchase for your collection? If I were to happen upon a double feature of **THE WAILER** & **THE WAILER 2** sitting in the $5 bin at Walmart, I might grab it but I won't be going out of my way to hunt it down. If you're able to give this a spin on Netflix, do so.

USA, 2006. DIRECTOR: ANDRÉS NAVIA
AVAILABLE FROM LAGUNA PRODUCTIONS

THE WAILER 2
(LA LLORONA II)

Review by Brian Harris

Dios mio! *The Wailer* film series continues with this adventurous sequel that attempts to continue the story laid out in the first while also expanding upon the mythology of the original *La Llorona* folk tale. This time around we're treated to likable characters—which, when combined with a better story, actually succeeds in entertaining a bit more than the first film.

Seems the tragic events of **THE WAILER** (2006) don't go unnoticed when the headlines of the murders end up splashed all over the front pages of Mexican newspapers. Professor Tomas McBride sets out in search of the only person not found in the massacre, his daughter Julie. How does he know she's even alive? Well, he's been having some pretty vivid dreams featuring strange symbols that have some connection to Julie, which in his mind, confirms that she is alive and well. Hopefully. Maybe.
His dedication to the search pays off as he earns himself a nickname given to him by the locals (they think he's crazy) and the attention of the local police who find him to be a royal pain in their asses. It also attracts the guide services of an anthropology student moonlighting as local taxi driver. Together they set about decoding the arcane symbols that keep appearing to McBride, leading them to the legend of La Llorona and the possibility that Julie is not only alive but she's being used by the ghost as a means to continue killing. If they don't find her in time, La Llorona may swallow her soul, extinguishing any goodness that remains within Julie McBride.

Director Paul Miller, new to the series, tackles a relatively inventive script by returning writer

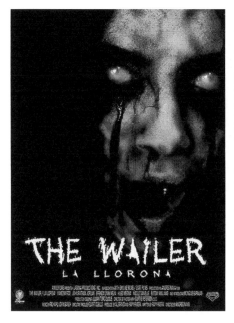

LA LLORONA III
THE WAILER III

Rafy Rivera, utilizing some outstanding locations, including real deal *Dia De Los Muertos* festivities, to great effect. The final product opens the affair up a bit and actually feels more like something one might see on late-night Telemundo, versus the made-for-DVD horror cash-in vibe of the first installment. Everything from the look, feel and dialogue of this film is a step forward, giving **THE WAILER** series a much-needed kick in the pants. Not many low budget endeavors get the opportunity to continue on with a sequel, let alone a third film, and **THE WAILER 2** certainly makes good on that by giving viewers a bit more of what made the first so much fun, and thankfully a whole lot less of what made the first such a tedious viewing experience.

Sticklers for cinematic authenticity (read: whiners) may want to take note that Miller and Rivera veer way off course from the original tale of La Llorona so expect to see the wailing woman doing things that just don't seem to jibe with what you expect. Tradition be damned. This time around she seems interested in taking out her unearthly anguish specifically on men, attracting them with her innocence and nudity and then handing them their bloody asses. Not quite the baby-stealing specter most might expect, but then again she didn't seem all that interested in that in the first film either. I think Rivera figured the concept could have grown stale quickly had La Llorona kept doing the same shit over and over with each successive sequel so by giving her more motivations to murder, he gave her a wider base of operations and more victims to choose from. The whole magical symbol mumbo jumbo may lose a few folks but in my opinion it did indeed spice things up, adding a bit o' the mystical to the mix.

No doubt about it, **THE WAILER 2** is a better film all the way around so if you're like me, and you found the first film entertaining, you're going to really enjoy watching the sequel. The two leads, played by Seth Michaels and Roger Cudney, were easy to connect with, production values were definitely better and there were some impressive gore set-pieces. I'm still not sure this can be considered a keeper but there's a double-feature release of this floating around that should be considered if it can be had for a few bucks. After I finished this flick the first thing that came to mind for me was, "I should definitely check out part three when I get the chance." Yeah, there is a third. Laguna Productions should pat themselves on the back for a low budget job well done.

MEXICO/USA, 2007.
DIRECTOR: PAUL MILLER
AVAILABLE FROM LAGUNA PRODUCTIONS

THE WAILER 3
(LA LLORONA III)

Review by Brian Harris

Whoa, déjà vu! Six years after the last installment in **THE WAILER** series (2007), Laguna Productions returns with another sequel that improves upon the last in terms of quality. Instead of continuing the story started in the first and second though, **THE WAILER 3** marks a new direction for the legendary she-specter, taking her out of her native stomping grounds and relocating her to, what appeared to be, a small suburb of Los Angeles. I can only assume their decision to move *La Llorona* from Mexico to the 'States was an attempt to broaden the franchise's appeal by giving it a familiar American setting with English-speaking characters. Not that the last two films didn't have English-speaking characters but you get my drift. **THE WAILER 3** is definitely a departure, one might even say it's a re-imagining of the series.

Daniel (Josh DeLozier) and Alice (Maria Pallas of **NAZIS AT THE CENTER OF THE EARTH**) decide to break the silence with Alice's mother and drop by for an extended visit with the kids. Things haven't been quite the same for anybody after Alice's father died from a supposed swimming pool suicide. Despite the strained relationship between Daniel and his mother-in-law, he does his best to remain supportive of his wife's decision to patch things up. Just as things begin looking up for the family though, tragedy strikes and the old woman is found floating in the very same swimming pool her husband had died in.

Soon after, the family are set upon by strange, unknown forces that Daniel begins to suspect may have some connection with the swimming pool. When strangers confirm his suspicions that something is indeed going on at the house, he's determined to get his family out but the entity that resides within the waters of the pool has other plans for his wife and children.

I'll be honest: there's not much to this film but what there is, it works. What the film lacks in story and acting—it is low budget after all—it makes up in some pretty effective chills. The idea here is that La Llorona no longer trolls the river in which she killed her children, now she's become some kind of an elemental spirit that uses water as a means of transportation, and swimming pools as her portal. This also includes toilets, showers and sinks. Interesting. Normally I would be a bit pissy that they tried to change such a classic tale, in the process watering it down, but **THE WAILER 3**, as I said above, works and there's no denying that it looks nice doing it. In my opinion this film marks the start of a brand new, and probably profitable, franchise on Laguna's hands. Done right, we could see a half dozen more sequels with La Llorona making her way around the globe, just as popular Asian ghosts have done before her.

Gone are the juicy tidbits of nudity. Gone is the gruesome gore. **THE WAILER 3** attempts to class things up, giving the film a bit more of a thriller edge. Throw in a creepy-looking ghost, a small cast of characters that don't scream "victim" and the spark of a good idea and you've got yourself something worth watching on a lazy Sunday afternoon. Purchasing it is another thing altogether though. I just cannot recommend readers purchase this unless it's dirt cheap and they're willing to sacrifice shelf space. Like the first two, **THE WAILER 3** is fun to watch but just not good enough, in my opinion, to own. If Laguna ever decide to farm these films out for wider distribution, keep your fingers crossed that it's Echo Bridge, that way we get a 3-film set (all on one disc of course) for the cost of a McDonalds meal. Now that would be worth grabbing.

USA, 2012. DIRECTOR: JAVIER BARBERA
AVAILABLE FROM LAGUNA PRODUCTIONS

LA TÍA ALEJANDRA
(Aunt Alejandra)

Review by Brian Harris

After the death of a relative, the elderly Alejandra (Isabela Corona of **THE WITCH'S MIRROR**) goes to live with her nephew Rodolfo (Manuel Ojeda), his wife Lucia (Diana Bracho) and their children in their modest home in the city. Despite being strapped for cash and struggling to pay bills, the family take her in and do their best to make her comfortable. A wise decision on their part, as Aunt Alejandra has quite a nest egg stashed away for a rainy day and she seems to take quiet satisfaction from helping the family out by paying their bills. It doesn't take long though before the children and their lack of respect begins wearing heavily on the old woman.

When Alejandra falls down the stairs after slipping on a roller skate, a darkness soon settles over the family, especially between Alejandra and the absent-minded child that left the skate out. Not too long after the accident, while out skating the young boy attempts to use the stairs, still sporting the skates, and he slips and falls to his death. Even though the Aunt tries to keep up the family's spirits, the mood worsens and the eldest child—who blames Alejandra for the death—cracks under the pressure, tossing boiling water in her face, scalding the poor old woman.

What initially appeared to be a freak accident to one child becomes a terrifying pattern after an old record player in Aunt Alejandra's room starts a roaring house fire, killing the tea-throwing girl. Can Alejandra be a witch? Is she cursing her nephew's children and bringing them misfortune? Convinced his Aunt has something to do with the deaths of his children, he casts her out of the house during a downpour, leaving her there on the sidewalk, helpless. The kind-hearted Lucia brings her back in the next morning when she discovers Alejandra sleeping on the street. That day Rodolfo experiences horrible chest pains, collapses and dies from what appears to be drowning.

Now convinced, as her husband was, that Aunt Alejandra is the cause of all of their woes, Lucia tries to send her daughter away to relatives. She has a plan for the old woman. No witchcraft in the world can save her this time.

Upon my first viewing of **LA TÍA ALEJANDRA** I must admit to not being all that impressed, I found it to be a bit too subtle for my liking. Most of the violence is off-screen and director Arturo Ripstein attempts to keep things ambiguous for a while, opting to make the Aunt look eccentric but ultimately harmless. That doesn't last long. Is Alejandra really a witch? Thing is, she's obviously a witch, I mean the kind of coincidences that happen in this film are just too astronomically impossible to be anything but supernatural. Alejandra slips on a skate down the stairs, one of the children slips on a skate down the stairs. Okay, that could be possible. Alejandra is burned, one of the children dies in a fire. Yeah, that's stretching things. Alejandra is thrown in the rain to catch her death, her nephew Rodolfo dies coughing up water. Hmm...yeah... witch. Of course puppets that move on their own is also a good indication that something is amiss but I can see chalking that particular sequence up on a psychotic break from reality.

While it's still just as subtle as the first time I saw it, I actually felt Alejandra's menace rippling beneath the surface the second time around. Isabela Corona was a wonderful actress, she brought a surprising amount of intensity to the role. The way she coldly throws down on some black magic one minute and the next she's comforting the family as if the death that surrounds them is affecting her was definitely chilling. Diana Branco also turned in a commendable performance, bringing her inner conflict and emotional pain to life in a way so few actresses are capable of. You can see and feel her struggling with her love for her family and loyalty to the old woman after all the kindness she'd shown the family. Both of these actresses really made **LA TÍA ALEJANDRA** was it is and without them playing off one another it may not have worked so well.

Man, after I settled in to give this film another shot I was blown away by an unimaginably brutal finale rivaling anything one might see today and it just hadn't really registered with me the first time I saw it. Don't get me wrong, it was the same film but for some reason, the horror of the finale didn't really click. I won't give too much away but once I saw Alejandra's necklace, my mind immediately raced back to the significance of her dead birds, and the look on Lucia's face said it all. Stunning.

LA TÍA ALEJANDRA is undoubtedly a Mexican horror classic, one that should not be missed by fans of global cinema. Director Ripstein never lets up on the tension for one moment, there's no wonky comedic relief, no letting off of steam, the film drives headlong to its jaw-dropping destination

without taking any detours along the way. If you're a fan of Mexican horror cinema, you're going to need to track this down and own it, subs or not. If you're not all that accustomed to the ways of horror from South of the Border, I encourage you to check out **LA TÍA ALEJANDRA**. You're going to love it.

MEXICO, 1979.
DIRECTOR: ARTURO RIPSTEIN
AVAILABLE FROM VINA DISTRIBUTION

THE ABCS OF DEATH

Review by Steven Ronquillo

You can't look at **THE ABCs OF DEATH** like you would a normal horror film, or any other genre film for that matter, because this isn't a movie, it has more to do with the work Andy Warhol did in the Sixties than any Amicus-styled anthology. **THE ABCs OF DEATH** is a series of twenty-five 5 min vingettes. The rules were, directors would get $8,000 and a letter from the alphabet to base their short on, from there anything goes and we got what best can be described as a series of video art installations in the mode of early David Lynch. If this makes it sound pretentious, it isn't, it's balls-out fun and down and dirty disturbing at its best.

From "A for Apocalypse" to "Z for Zetsumetsu" there is something for everybody. From fart fetish porn, a gigantic middle finger to the U.S. and even a bit for the arachnophobic amongst us, this is truly a buffet unlike anything we've seen before. And like an art installment, seeing the reaction to those who have seen it is just as interesting and unique as the anthology itself. Whether you love or hate it, this as personal as it gets, which means there is no incorrect way to react to this experiment.

Since there were only two segments I really hated, I'll cover them first. "G for Gravity" is obtuse crap. When you rewind it twice and you still wonder "WHAT THE HELL JUST HAPPENED?!!" that's usually a sign of bad filmmaking. I wish I could

dissect it in more detail but that would mean I was able to grasp what happened and I didn't. And now for "M for Miscarriage"—if Ti West spent $5,000 on that lazy piece of shit, I will shave my head bald and paint it pink. I could reenact this trash with a bargain bin camcorder in under five minutes and not miss a godamn plot point!

Thankfully the good far outweighs the bad in this anthology. "H is for Hyrdo-Electric Diffusion" is a live-action Tex Avery cartoon set in WWII and it's just plain silly fun. "V is for Vagitus" is a jaw-dropping exercise in production money well spent. It would make a great standalone feature-length film. "X for XXL" is some soul-crushingly bleak stuff that really affected me in ways my jaded butt has rarely been affected. This one really got to me.

"Z for Zetsumetsu" is an insane "F-YOU" to the United States and its politics of corruption as well as the destruction of the Japanese culture. It is one of the most insane 5 minutes you will ever see and if you get what director Nishimura Yoshihiro is saying, it will either piss you off to no end or you'll laugh your ass of at it.

Now, before you start thinking this is a serious art film, the first end credit to scroll clears that up as it says "BASED ON A NIGHTMARE." The run time is 123 minutes, which means **THE ABCs OF DEATH** corresponds to the numbers 1, 2 & 3. Coincidence? This anthology is a fun, ballsy experiment and it's a miracle it works as good as it does. It's nice, for once, for us horror fans to have something like this rather than the usual crap that is being fed to us these days.

VARIOUS COUNTRIES, 2012.
DIRECTOR: VARIOUS
AVAILABLE FROM MAGNET RELEASING

S&M HUNTER
(Kinbaku · SM · 18-sai)

Review by Travis Goheen

Pink film machine Shiro Shimomoto, infamous director Shuji Kataoka, Japanese eye candy Pink actress Hiromi Saotome as well as Pink actor turned Director/Producer Yutaka Ikejima all return in the second installment in *The Roper from Hell* series.

For those reading this who may not know what a "Pink" film is, the quickest, most simplest but not quite so precise way of describing a Pink movie is a Japanese adult/softcore/grindhouse/arty-type movie but with far better production values. Not as good as the previous, much rougher Violent Pink & Roman Porno genres, but still much better than the typical grindhouse fare. These films were often produced on a very limited budget very quickly, rarely going over one week to film and were also around one hour in length. These films were then billed with 2 or 3 other films and shown in various theatres. A practice, unlike the grindhouse films in the West, which is still done today although not as abundantly.

In the confines of S&M club The Pleasure Dungeon, owner/dungeon master (Yutaka Ikejima) is introducing the house specials to a new client simply named Joe. After seeing the entire selections

visually, we learn that Joe is there to get his jollies by venting his anger and beating some bitches. Turns out Joe's boyfriend Jack has been kidnapped by the all-female and extremely horny gang The Bombers, and is being held captive as their lucky... er, I mean, tortured sex slave.

While this is all being disclosed, The Bombers are off in their lair using their "womanly" charms trying to convert Jack. We are then introduced to the S&M Hunter, the ultimate Sadist host for your S&M party and master of the infamous Kinbaku rope technique. We're not talking about some person here who can differentiate between a granny knot and macramé but someone who gets serious wood when he goes to the rope section at the local Home Depot. Not only is he is a master of this technique but he's quick, as in gunfighter quick. Before you can say Bob's your uncle he has woman hanging upside-down in crazy intricate spider web-type knots that Spider-Man could only dream about. It also serves as a warning to parents who have children that seem too keen on earning their knot-tying merit badge.

Much like the *Rapeman* films—being very heavily Hentai/Manga influenced—this movie also follows the theme where, even though the female culprits are assaulted in in one way or another, they were secretly wanting it and are left wanting more.

Once the female gang is taken care of, the gang's penis-hating leader Meg enters the scene (to those who haven't been watching the series, there is some serious old heat between the two). Since the leader is nothing like her silly little naïve schoolgirl lackeys, The Roper realizes he needs to bring his A-game, and is more than pleased to do so.

Which brings us to an amazing ending in which they try to one-up each other…I don't want to spoil it for you, but it involves a 200-ft. crane which truly needs to be seen to be believed, and actually caused a big hoopla when the film was released, and even moreso after, when actress Hiromi Saotome reenacted it live in front of a Train Station in Harajuku, Japan.

Just like the majority of Pink movies this film is only 1 hour long but yowza, what an hour it is! Right from the get-go this movie sucks you in and doesn't let up for the entire duration of the film.

The first 5 minutes of this film are hilarious and really dictate whether or not this film is for you. If you like the first 5 minutes you will absolutely love this movie, however if you're put off by the beginning of this film because of its content, imagery or super-silliness, this film is definitely not for you. Rather than playing out as a dark S&M perverse Nazi/Nunsploitation hardcore sex flick, this film goes in the complete opposite direction and that's where things get really light/silly and quite crazy.

The film itself is a parody of other films as well as Japanese society, which will be lost on much of its Western audience. Most notably this film is often commented on as taboo and very un-PC as it is abounding with homosexual, religious, sacred and Nazi imagery all wrapped up by a severe misogynistic theme which will offend some of the West's denser, mainstream audiences. However this is a clear example of the endless Japanese habit of borrowing from other societies and trying to blend it into something of their own—none of which should be taken at face value, but as tongue-in-cheek, because as you watch this you quickly learn it's all just there and is never really explained in any sense/level. Those looking for graphic, nasty, mean-spirited Nazi BDSM really need to go elsewhere as this film is extremely light, and—being a Pink film—is softcore with regards to sex; even on a softcore level this movie is very light. However, this is a very fun, highly entertaining and wacky film that will not only get repeated plays on my DVD player but gets me very excited about future DVD releases from Pink Eiga.

JAPAN, 1986. DIRECTOR: SHÛJI KATAOKA
AVAILABLE FROM PINK EIGA

QERIB IN THE LAND OF THE DJINN
(Qerib cinler diyarinda / Гариб в стране джиннов)

Review by Jared Auner

Qerib and his twin brother Sahib (Bakhtiar Khanizade, in a dual role) are virtuous, industrious young men, always ready to lend a hand to a

neighbor or lead the village children in a joyous song. One day while taking a deserved break from a hard day's labor, the brothers' bag of seed—food for the entire village—is stolen by a huge magical bird (an astonishingly amateurish creation seemingly stitched together from papier-mâché and twigs). They give chase, but are unable to catch up with the monstrous fowl. Frustrated and forlorn, Qerib is easy pickings for a mischievous being who shows up out of nowhere and persuades him to travel to the realm of the Djinn, a devilish race that dwells on another plane of existence.

After abandoning his home and family, he finds himself in the court of the Djinni king, who is besieged by enemies, possesses no arable land, and has traitors lurking among his inner circle. Qerib sets about righting these wrongs, much to the chagrin of the traitorous clique, who plot against him in secret. Qerib teaches the Djinn agriculture and some basic engineering and leads a brave military raid on a rival clan. But he faces constant attempts by the scheming courtiers to seduce or frighten him away from aiding the ruling monarch.

Eventually he remembers that his place is in the world of men and returns home by somehow compelling the Devil himself to sweep him up into the air and off to the land where he was born. There he finds the fields of his village set aflame, and again he compels his Satanic companion to do his bidding. Together they magically save the harvest from a fiery ruin and thwart the evil intent of his enemies. Qerib is reunited with his brother, his mother and his lady-love. And happily ever-after do they live...
Or something like that. Really, I'm not all that sure about that synopsis. The film is in Azerbaijani and my copy had no English subtitles. The plot is a wild flight of fancy that unfurls most illogically, like a dream or a fairy tale, which is big part of the charm. Making no sense is a value long held dear by fans of the more outré fringes of the cult movie realm, and this film doesn't make much sense.

I'm fairly certain the story told would have been more or less understandable to its intended audience. One might reasonably assume that the plot is based on some ancient folktale. The Djinn (or "genies") regularly figure in the mythologies of the Middle East and Central Asia, and the story has the structure of a morality tale, simple and sweet. But information on this film is very thin on the ground (the Internet, or anyone I know) so I cannot confirm that this is the case.

The movie itself is a riot of bad acting, dime-store special effects and children's theater-style set design. It gives all the signifiers of being a "bad film" and benefits from that perspective. Who cares what it's about? Who gives a damn about plot or characterization? Especially when there are huge, fire breathing papier-mâché pantomime dragons or caveman-looking genies that sprout horns from the tops of their heads (they look hauntingly like the savage witch doctors from the 1988 Indonesian trash classic **JUNGLE VIRGIN FORCE**).

There's a lot of magick (achieved by special effects that were old when talkies were the new thing in cinema), a handful of poorly-choreographed fight scenes, and a few belly-dancing scenes featuring sexy lady-Djinn. These scenes are especially fun, and owe an obvious debt to Bollywood musicals, which were popular with Azerbaijani audiences from the 1950s on. Bolly "mythologicals" would seem to be a primary genre influence, along with Soviet fairy tale films and Italian peplum. The music is exotic, the girls are pretty, and the costumes wild, making up most of the movies few true highlights. The movie is definitely not "good", but there's just enough goofy weirdness to keep one's attention throughout. It also helps that it's rather short too, barely longer than an hour. The cheapjack oddness doesn't overstay its welcome. Despite its cheapness, **QERIB IN THE LAND OF DJINN** is a pretty good-looking movie; director Alisattar Atakishiyev began his career as a cinematographer, and it shows. The mise-en-scène is well-composed, the camera movements are fluid—even graceful—and the frame is bursting with colors. Atakishiyev was an obviously talented artisan forced to work within severe budgetary limitations, a predicament in world cinema that most readers of this magazine will be well familiar with. Hardly any other information about him or

this film is available at this time, and reading this review might be the only time anyone you know ever even mentions the thing.

How this movie fits into the wider scheme of Azerbaijani cinema difficult to determine. But a casual look at a list of films made in this former Soviet republic reveals a large amount of comedies, melodramas and patriotic war films. It might be safe to say fantasy films like **QERIB** were not all that common, making this film—meager as it is—even more rare and special. It's not great, but I'm very glad I was able to see it.

USSR (Azerbaijan), 1977.
DIRECTOR: ALISATTAR ATAKISHIYEV

MAYA

Review by Brian Harris

While most horror fans tend to focus only on '60s, '70s & '80s work of Italian filmmakers like Dario Argento, Lucio Fulci and the Bavas, Italian horror cinema hadn't really given up the ghost until the early 90s. The last gasp of Italian horror cinema wasn't as memorable as **SUSPIRIA** (1977), **DEMONS** (1985) or **THE BEYOND** (1981), but some of the films released during that time have gone on to achieve a cult status of sorts based solely on their obscurity and lack of fan acknowledgment. Films like **SPIDER LABYRINTH** (1988), **SPECTERS** (1987), **WITCHERY** (1988), **GHOSTHOUSE** (1988) and **MADNESS** (1980) all have a respectable following but receive very little positive press by mainstream horror periodicals and websites. To be fair, there's definitely a good reason for that—some of the later entries take a kitchen sink approach to filmmaking. It's almost as if the filmmakers felt like everything of worth that could have been done was, so why not throw caution to the wind. If you've ever seen **SPIDER LABYRINTH**, you know exactly what I'm talking about.

Marcello Avallone's **MAYA** is another one of those "What the hell is this about again?" Italian horror films that gets all kinds of props from cult cinema fans for being atmospheric and violent, reminiscent of Fulci's **THE BEYOND**. It is...and isn't.

An American professor living in a small Mexican village researching a particular period of Mayan history is viciously murdered at the site of an old temple. His daughter—recently arrived in town to look into his passing—teams up with a womanizing American ex-pat to uncover the truth behind a series of murders connected to her father and a mysterious research partner. Is somebody emulating sacrificial kills from the Mayan era or is something more supernatural afoot?
MAYA has oodles of atmosphere, a few surprisingly brutal murder sequences and some delightful nude scenes but the story is a bit muddled in some places, making it occasionally hard to follow. It takes a few deaths before the killer's motive becomes clear; foreign invaders (ex-pats & tourists) are being targeted to satisfy an ancient curse. Interesting. Anyhow, yeah, the cinematography was tight, locations, sets and wardrobe looked great and the acting, while occasionally sketchy, was tolerable. There aren't

many characters in this film you'll find yourself connecting with, outside of the professor's daughter, but that kind of thing never stops some people from paying big bucks to own hard-to-find horror films. I think the one thing I took issue with was the illogical sub-plot that introduces the supernatural element into this film. Think 'séance' and you'll get my drift.

I can't say I hated **MAYA**—as a matter of fact, if it were available as an official release, I'd probably own the damn thing. Hell, I own **BLACK DEMONS** (1991) and **THE OGRE** (1986) so there's no accounting for taste when it comes to me! I know there are a few well-made bootlegs floating about out there so if you absolutely need to own this film, just keep in mind that, like most of the 'last gasp' Italian horror entries, it's fun to watch once but probably not worth owning unless you're a trash fan.

ITALY, 1989.
DIRECTOR: MARCELLO AVALLONE

BATH SALT ZOMBIES

Review by Dan Taylor

I miss the days of topical exploitation and horror cinema, when filmmakers would rip their storylines right from the headlines to offer up slightly (or more than slightly) fictionalized tales of the day's news events. Whether they were showing us the horrors of marijuana (**REEFER MADNESS**, 1936), teen pregnancy (**TEENAGE MOTHER**, 1967), cults (**GUAYANA: CULT OF THE DAMNED**, 1979) or savage dictators (**THE RISE AND FALL OF IDI AMIN**, 1981), trash filmmakers could often be counted upon to scare up some sort of cinematic boogieman that would make our own lives seem safe and tame by comparison.

Then again, after watching **BATH SALT ZOMBIES** maybe it's just a whole hell of a lot easier to rip-off the *Saw* and *Paranormal Activity* flicks.

Inspired by the recent wave of "bath salt"-related violent crimes and cannibalistic behavior, **BATH SALT ZOMBIES** feels like it wants to be this generation's answer to the aforementioned **REEFER MADNESS**. It even starts with a faux bath salts health class propaganda video, though I don't recall any of the 16mm flicks I saw in high school being peppered with profanity, face-eating and an appearance by Satan himself.

Once that's out of the way (and it's not half as funny as you'd hope a profane parody complete with Satanic cameo would be) the plot jumps to present day NYC where it appears about twenty people live. Ritchie (Brandon Salkil) and his bitchy, busty girlfriend Angel (Erin Ryan) are strung-out junkies in search of their next high, when Ritchie scores some new smokeable bath salts from Bubbles (Ethan Holey), a biz-savvy dealer willing to give away that first pack for free.

Little does Ritchie know that he'll not only be instantly hooked on the junk, but the military-grade designer drug will also turn him into a twitchy, super-strong monster with a proclivity for killing gals with big, natural boobs.

From there the film ping-pongs from Ritchie and his killing sprees to the DEA agent on his tail, to Bubbles and drug designer Sal (affably played by director Dustin Wayde Mills) complete with headache-inducing shaky-cam, comically grotesque makeup that gets more outrageous as the flick progresses and a couple flashes of not-quite-brilliance that made me wonder what could have been.

Made for less than the cost of a day's catering on **TWILIGHT** (2008), the micro-budget strains the production at the seams, highlighting both its pluses (a couple good performances, some inspired stylized mayhem) and minuses (a handful of bad performances, video-gamey CGI, flat script). Salkil makes a fine, twitchy junkie-monster and seems to be having a good time, especially during two over-the-top slaughter rampages that highlight the flick. Unfortunately, much of the flick's 70-minute running time is monopolized by Josh Eal's shouting DEA agent, who lays waste to drug cookers and doughnuts with equal aplomb.

With its mix of punk rock music (and filmmaking), face-ripping gore, "real" actors, junkie atmosphere and zero budget, **BATH SALT ZOMBIES** comes off like some bastard lovechild of the Cinema of Transgression and H.G. Lewis. Which is probably just enough of an endorsement for me to give Mills' **NIGHT OF THE TENTACLES** (also starring Salkil and Mills) a whirl.

USA, 2013. DIRECTOR: DUSTIN MILLS
AVAILABLE FROM AGGRONAUTIX

SPY AROUND THE WORLD
(Spie contro il mondo, a.k.a. KILLER'S CARNIVAL)

Review by Dan Taylor

When police track Wendt (Peter Vogel), a suspected woman-killer, to the home of Professor Alden (Richard Munch), it's up to the good doctor to keep the suspect occupied until he can formulate a plan to turn the tables. Naturally, the psychiatrist's plan includes showing the criminal the folly of his ways...by relating a trio of tales designed to illustrate that crime does not pay.

Yes, you've got that right, **SPY AROUND THE WORLD** (aka **KILLER'S CARNIVAL**) is an espionage anthology with each segment unspooling in a different exotic-ish locale (hence the title).
In the first segment (set in Vienna), a desperate woman seeks out suave man-of-mystery David Porter (Stewart Granger), a debonair detective who is the only one that can solve the murder of her journalist brother. With the help of his dutiful butler Karl (Walter Giller), Porter works his sources, runs afoul of a nefarious nightclub owner and trips up the killer just as he tries to eliminate

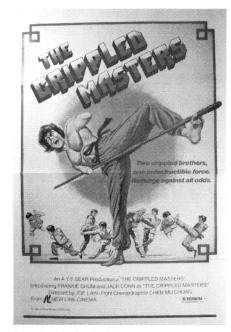

the detective. The lighthearted segment succeeds largely thanks to Granger and Giller, who have a fun crimefighter/sidekick dynamic that feels like they're two guys who have spent way too much time together. In fact, I was a bit disappointed when their segment ended—I could have taken a whole Porter and Karl flick.

If you think the first story sounds a tad lightweight, **SPY**'s Rome segment is downright comedic, complete with wacky sound effects, an identically-dressed gang of mismatched thugs, a Rosa Klebesque female villain, double agent Margaret Lee (natch) and '60s-era spy gags like a record pressed on pasta that our hero, Agent Brice (Pierre Brice), eats to destroy.

Your overall appreciation of **SPY AROUND THE WORLD** is likely to go as far as your willingness to dig this middle segment. Once I took a deep breath and remembered that by 1966 the tide of espionage cinema had turned from the rough-and-tumble **FROM RUSSIA WITH LOVE** (1963) to the jokier, gadget-filled world of **THUNDERBALL** (1965), I had a much better time with the flick.

The third—and perhaps best—segment features handsome, imposing Lex Barker (**THE TORTURE CHAMBER OF DR. SADISM**, 1967) as hard-drinking detective Glenn Cassidy. After uncovering a plot to assassinate the Brazilian president during Carnivale in Rio, Cassidy hightails it south of the border and impersonates the assassin. Klaus Kinski (replete with tiny moustache) turns up in a couple scenes as "Gomez", a sweaty Brazilian rebel.

(By the way, what is it with these guys? Kinski, of course, made headlines recently after his daughter Palo accused him of abusing her when she was an adolescent. While checking out details for this review I was surprised to learn that Barker, who died of a heart attack at the age of 54 while walking down a NYC street, was accused of similar horrors by Cheryl Crane, the daughter of third wife Lana Turner.)

Directed in workmanlike fashion by a quartet of directors, **SPY** is about as light and fluffy as '60s Eurospy cinema gets. It has all the trappings of the genre—exotic locations, colorful characters, double-crossing babes, convoluted denouements, a cast of familiar faces—delivered up in a series of bite-sized nuggets. Like a series of uninspired but pleasant sandwiches, I consumed **SPY** over three lunch breaks, and that may have been the best way to digest it. Certainly not required viewing, unless you're a Eurospy or Kinksi completist, but you won't hate yourself if you do end up downing it.

ITALY/FRANCE/AUSTRIA, 1966.
DIRECTORS: ALBERTO CARDONE, ROBERT LYNN, SHELDON REYNOLDS, LOUIS SOULANES

CRiPPLeD MaSTeRS

天殘地缺／*TIĀN CÁN DÌ QUĒ*

Review by Tim Merrill

If there's one thing to be said about HK cinema in its long and honored history is that it's always provided ample moments for equal opportunity beatings and brutality. From the young studious monk to the wizened, weathered sifu, everybody gets the chance to break off a foot and send someone home with a broken ass. But what if you don't have a foot to bust off—or arms or legs for that matter? When the sun sets at the end of the day, how will you be vindicated?

Leave it to the Shaw Brothers to help define a new disabled sub-genre in Chang Cheh's notorious film, **THE ONE ARMED SWORDSMAN** (*Dubei Dao*) in 1967, with Wang Yu. The 'Crip Fu' phenomenon would continue two years later with **THE RETURN OF THE ONE ARMED SWORDSMAN** in 1969, and Wang Yu's **ONE ARMED BOXER** (*Dubei Chuan Wang*) in 1972.

It must be noted that the Japanese were actually the first to make their mark in handicapped history with the, *Zatoichi* blind Samurai series that began in 1962 with director Kenji Masumi.

Throughout China in the 'Seventies, the cinematic "Dynasty of Disabilities" would roll on through countless swordsman and boxer spin-offs, but the Shaw Brothers were not yet finished.
In 1978, the studio released **THE CRIPPLED AVENGERS**, which would turn out to be their most successful film in the subgenre since the original swordsman. Now it was not only a lone hero learning to rise above his shortcomings, but an actual gang of crippled champions with payback in mind against their tormentors. While **THE CRIPPLED AVENGERS** proved to be successful for the Shaws, the genre proved to be deceptive. While the Hong Kong studios continued to make bank with the films up to that point, none of the actors who played the roles of the handicapped heroes were disabled at all. Sure, Danny Day-Lewis could get away with it in an art film like **MY LEFT FOOT** (1989), but when it comes to Asian exploitation cinema you can't go on duping the fans with scamboogery. Jimmy Wang Yu and Phillip Kwok could only pretend to hobble around for so long before fanatics demanded something that would truly deliver an arm and a leg, or lack thereof.

Finally in 1979 the crutches were thrown down, and the world's first truly disabled duo made their auspicious debut in Kei Law's **CRIPPLED MASTERS**. It is nothing short of astounding that the film was ever set to celluloid to begin with.

Director Kei Law made no bones about his intentions with the film, and took political correctness outside for a proper curb stomping. **CRIPPLED MASTERS** did the unbelievable and cast two leads who were actual survivors of birth defects as the twin maimed masters of martial arts mayhem. Once the disabled duo of Frankie 'The Chinese Chicken Wing' Shum and Jackie 'Air' Conn hit the screen, they soon demonstrated that if anyone is at a disadvantage in receiving a shit kicking, it's the rest of the world, and not them. While the acting is scant, and the directing is subpar, it's obviously Shum and Conn that steal the show with their jaw-dropping fight sequences.

The film begins in the palace of the evil Ling Chang Cao (Lee Chung Chien), who looks like a wacked-out Mark Dacascos from *Iron Chef*. The evil warlord sets out to punish Lee Ho (Frankie Shum) by forcing his lackey Tang (Jackie Conn) to hack off Lee Ho's arms. Soon the armless Lee Ho is pitched into the street like a sack of rotten rice, and is forced to struggle to survive with the help of a coffin maker. Before long, Lee Ho encounters the evil warlord's flunkies once again, and hauls ass to the countryside. In his escape, Lee Ho comes across a small village, and there trains himself to survive. Despite the bird-like wings that take the place of his arms, Lee Ho learns to carry jugs of water on a pole, water his garden, and fish with a bamboo pole held in his feet.

As Lee Ho struggles to survive, Tang (Jackie Conn) soon also finds himself on the receiving end of Ling Chang Cao's fury. In order to seal his fate, acid is poured upon his legs, and he soon drags himself into the forest, waiting to die. While fishing, Lee Ho comes across Tang, the man who took his arms, and begins to beat him like a Chinese rug. As Lee Ho sets out to seek vengeance on Tang, they are both surprised to encounter a wizened old master hidden in a water jug who promises to train them both to become the titular 'Crippled Masters'.

During the training montage, it is truly jaw-dropping to see Frankie Shum spin poles with his withered appendages, and fire bamboo shafts like missiles with his feet. Jackie Conn is no slouch either, pulling in his spindly legs and becoming the 'Human Cantonese Cannonball'. Due to his lack of lower extremities, Conn flows like water under chairs, between poles, and square into whoever gets in his way. When the paraplegic pair team up, they become the original Master Blaster as Conn sits on the shoulders of Shum—it's almost like a cinematic *Voltron* moment!

When it comes to Asian exploitation cinema, **CRIPPLED MASTERS** is rarely mentioned amongst the standard pantheon of titles, but it deserves its notoriety. This is a film that goes all the way out on a limb (I had to), and puts its proverbial money where its mouth is. Both Frankie Shum and Jackie Conn should be recognized and commended for their incredible physical feats of strength.

The film is a total gem of curiosity, and a total HK blender drink mixed with two shots of Browning's **FREAKS** (1932), and a jigger of **THE 36th CHAMBER OF SHAO LIN** (1978). While opinions will obviously be mixed in dealing with a film of this latitude, you can be guaranteed that you have never seen anything like this before, and it deserves a home in your collection.

TAIWAN, 1979. DIRECTOR: KEI LAW
AVAILABLE FROM TGG DIRECT

COMMAND PERFORMANCE

Review by Dan Taylor

Dolph Lundgren has been getting his share of ink lately thanks to roles in Stallone's *Expendables* flicks, not to mention John Hyams' fun reanimation of the long-thought-mothballed *Universal Soldier* series. But you'd be wise to keep your eyes peeled when walking through the local dollar store or steering around the bargain DVD bin at your local supermarket, because the Dolph-helmed **COMMAND PERFORMANCE** might be the best of the bunch.

Like the thousands of **DIE HARD**-inspired actioners that have come before it, **COMMAND**'s set-up is as simple as it gets: Joe (Lundgren) is the drummer for a Russian rock band on the brink of success, but things go horribly wrong when Soviet extremists take over a concert by Venus (Melissa Molinaro), an American pop sensation performing for the widowed Russian President (Hristo Shopov) and his adolescent daughters. Teaming up with the President's new head of security, Joe must employ the skills learned in his shadowy past to take out the bad guys and save the day.

Dismissed early in his career as a lunkhead beefcake, Lundgren has been a steady, reliable presence in the Action film marketplace over the years, which is more than I can say about some of his '80s action flick brethren. (Yeah, Big Steve, I'm looking at you.)

Despite a handful of well-known titles (**MASTERS OF THE UNIVERSE** [1987], **THE PUNISHER** [1989], **RED SCORPION** [1988], **SHOWDOWN IN LITTLE TOKYO** [1991]), the bulk of Dolph's work has been fodder for the Redboxes, Netflixes and IMPACT channels of the world. And—seemingly interchangeable names aside—Lundgren's flicks are almost always more reliable than, say, some of the more "expandable" '80s action stars. (Yes, Big Steve. Looking. Again.)

Plus, he seems less dickish than say Stallone, Snipes, Van Damme or Seagal.
COMMAND also illustrates that Dolph has been doing more than chasing skirts and scarfing donuts on all these sets over the years. The flick feels far bigger than its presence as a dollar-bin castoff would suggest; there are big concert and crowd scenes, at least one explosive action sequence that blew me off my couch, convincing location settings and the overall sense that the action really is taking place in the bowels of a huge arena, not two hallways and a janitor's closet like the excruciating Seagal-versus-vampires actioner **AGAINST THE DARK** (2009).

But the action—and the flick—is carried by Lundgren as Joe, the happy-go-lucky, pot-smoking, slightly mysterious drummer for CMF (which stands for Cheap Motherfucker in "honor" of their manager). The screenplay—credited to Lundgren and action stalwart Steve Latshaw—wisely avoids the easy out of having Joe be a member of some shadowy government force or cop whose wife and kids were blowed up real good by some filthy mobsters. Instead, he's a little bit darker than your usual "fish out of water" action hero, which fits both the character and Lundgren's laid back, muscle-bound persona.

In a world where direct-to-video sequels are all the rage I have to admit I'm a little disappointed there's not an entire series of Joe the Drummer flicks. I would totally "rock and load" every single one of them.

USA, 2009. DIRECTOR: DOLPH LUNDGREN
AVAILABLE FROM FIRST LOOK PICTURES

THE EVIL CLERGYMAN

Review by Dan Taylor

I used to be somewhat obsessed with all things Empire.

What can I say? When a studio releases what immediately becomes your favorite movie of all-time you become a fan—going to the theater to see everything they put out, immediately renting the flicks you loved or the ones that bypassed town in favor of a quickie theatrical release in NYC. It was a love affair.

The love affair with Empire flicks was frequently reignited when the big issues of Variety would hit the newsstands. Tied into industry events like Cannes or the American Film Market, the thick issues were a must-have, and I'd fritter away hours poring through the pages trying to glean whatever details I could about upcoming flicks from all the studios, but especially Empire (and the Go-Go Boys at Cannon).

I can still remember the full-page announcement ad for **PULSEPOUNDERS**, Empire's "upcoming" entry in the then-popular anthology genre. It seemed like a genius idea from the mind of Charles Band: three segments, each a sequel to or logical offshoot of one of the studio's biggest hits of 1985. There would be a sequel to **THE DUNGEONMASTER** (itself an anthology of sorts), a continuation of the heroic adventures of future cop Jack Deth from **TRANCERS**, and, most importantly (for me, at least) a return to H.P. Lovecraft territory with **THE EVIL CLERGYMAN**, complete with **RE-ANIMATOR** stars Jeffrey Combs, David Gale and the lovely Barbara Crampton.

And so we waited. And waited. And waited. Every now and then a **PULSEPOUNDRES** still

or nugget of news would trickle out, but that was about it. Releases like **FROM BEYOND** (1986), **DOLLS** (1987) and **ENEMY TERRITORY** (1987) kept me sated but it wasn't long before Empire's impressive average started to slide and **PULSEPOUNDERS** retreated into the dark recesses of my mind, emerging from the brain muck every now and then for me to ponder whatever happened to the flick.

Like most fans, I assumed that the end of Empire and Charles Band's subsequent move to Full Moon meant that **PULSEPOUNDERS** was lost forever, a myth to chat about on film boards and at hotel bars during conventions.

As it turns out, **PULSEPOUNDERS** *wasn't* swept away or left unfinished because Band was too busy making horrible vampire and puppet movies. As the producer/director explains in the featurette included on the long-awaited DVD release of **THE EVIL CLERGYMAN**, the original negative for the film was lost when one of the labs the studio used went out of business and it wasn't until 20+ years later—when a VHS work print was found—that wheels were set in motion for **PULSEPOUNDERS** to finally see the light of day.

Even if it is one segment at a time.

Besides Combs, Crampton and Gale, **CLERGYMAN** reunites us with composer Richard Band (who contributes a lush and romantically sinister new score), cinematographer Mac Ahlberg and scribe Dennis Paoli, who once again gets to indulge in the sexual side of Lovecraft with this atmospheric tale.

A young woman (Crampton) visits the castle room where she and her clergyman lover (Combs) consummated their illicit relationship—before he hanged himself. Left alone to gather her things, she soon finds herself being warned by a bishop (David Warner) that her lover was evil and simply wants to possess her soul. (And who can blame him?) It isn't long before the gropey clergyman returns, gets all handsy and is laying it on thick with lines like "your body is my religion". (Again, can you blame him?)

Pizza

Relying heavily on atmosphere, **THE EVIL CLERGYMAN** isn't a wild, occasionally gross ride like **RE-ANIMATOR** (1985) or **FROM BEYOND**. The 30-minute segment is—David Gale's rat suit by John Carl Beuchler aside—largely effects-free and more akin to the Lovecraft adaptations of *Night Gallery* or *Masters or Horror* with a dash of the atmosphere we'd later see in Stuart Gordon's 1995 **CASTLE FREAK** (an underrated Combs/Crampton outing).

Combs' snarky smirk is put to good use as the love'em-and-leave'em sinister minister who has left a trail of crazed and dead chicks in his wake. And nobody does "hot and kinda crazy" like Crampton, who shifts effortlessly from demure to sexy in no time.

Kudos to Full Moon for rescuing **PULSE-POUNDERS** from the trash heap and releasing it to the fans. Naturally, given the source material, the image quality isn't great but this is a rare opportunity to see a flick that was long thought to be lost forever.

The disc is currently a Full Moon exclusive and includes a featurette from the **CLERGYMAN** premiere earlier this year as well as 60-seconds of work-print footage from **TRANCERS 1.5** starring Tim Thomerson, Helen Hunt and Art LeFleur in a tale scripted by Danny Bilson and Paul DeMeo. Full Moon anticipates that disc being ready for October 2013.

USA, 1988. DIRECTOR: CHARLES BAND
AVAILABLE FROM FULL MOON PICTURES

PIZZA

Review by Chaitanya Reddy

The basic plot of **PIZZA** revolves around Michael (Vijay Sethupathi), who works as a pizza delivery boy and lives with his girlfriend Anu (Ramya Nambeeshan). Anu is an aspiring writer and has an obsession about ghosts and everything paranormal. Michael is shown to be both claustrophobic and very irritated with his girlfriend's obsession. Things start getting strange when Michael discovers that his boss' daughter may be possessed by an evil spirit. He experiences her being exorcised which causes him to panic, and he now suddenly believes in ghosts. The best sequence of the movie comes when Michael sets out for a pizza delivery to a house which turns out to be haunted.

PIZZA quickly switches genres from a bland comedy to an intense horror/suspense thriller which keeps the audience guessing. The film's ending supports all the strange goings on, making **PIZZA** nearly perfect, *and* the best thriller to come out of India in recent times.

Vijay Sethupathi excels in his role as Michael, taking the transformimng him a cowardly and vulnerable character to a courageous young man. He is able to show a wide variation of emotional states which are perfect for the character. Since most parts of the movie deal with Michael, the rest of the cast have only a little to offer, which works out well. Moving to the technical aspects of **PIZZA**, since most parts of the movie happen inside a haunted house, the music plays a major role, and Santhosh Narayanan provides a top-notch soundtrack that delivers eerily. Gopi Amarnath's cinematography is excellent in capturrng both the romantic and Haunting sequences. The screenplay is tight and adds to Debutante Karthik Subbaraj's excellent directorial skills.

PIZZA starts off well, nevertheless shifts into a familiar Tamil movie mode with romance and (subtle) humor for most of the first half, then it bounces back, furiously gripping the audiences 'til the last minute. The best thing about the movie is that despite having a simple plot it keeps one guessing the whole time. The haunted house sequences definitely make it a film worth watching. **PIZZA** is an absolute delight and will hopefully be the new wave of genre movies from India. My suggestion: order your "South-Indian" Pizza today.

INDIA, 2012. DIRECTOR: KARTHIK SUBBARAJ

NINJA SHADOW KILLERS: TIGER FORCE

Review by James Bickert

Director/Producer Tomas Tang is one of many pseudonyms used by cut-and-paste maestro Godfrey Ho. As the story goes, once Ho left brother-in-law Joseph Lai's company, IFD (which continued to distribute many of his films), he started his own production company by the name of Filmark. Ho would buy and sell the company to his alias Tomas Tang to avoid paying taxes in the many Asian countries he filmed in. After Tomas Tang (Ho) sold the company to Malaysian producer Ratno Timoer (who didn't know he had also sold the company to producer Wu Kuo-jen), Tomas Tang (Ho) conveniently died in a fire! After being investigated by police, Godfrey Ho kept making movies and Tomas Tang arose from the grave to make a dozen more.

NINJA SHADOW KILLERS: TIGER FORCE finds Godfrey Ho using the Tomas Tang credit and splicing newly-shot ninja footage into the Korean Women-in-Prison film **REVENGE IN THE TIGER CAGE** (1976). The new plot involves those pesky ninjas kidnapping women by disrupting picnics and boat outings with exploding ninja torpedoes. Once abducted, women are thrown into prison and eventually sold to the Middle East. A rich industrialist hires Jenny "the good ninja" to infiltrate the prison camp and save his daughter Sylvia from the clutches of the evil ninja warden. These ninja inserts are pretty fun, but Godfrey Ho has cut out the juicy bits from the **REVENGE IN THE TIGER CAGE** footage. It's a shame because the brutal pacing in the middle would surely benefit from some boobage. Who knows what Ho was thinking—he probably intended to put the exploitative footage into another film. He probably did already and I just haven't found it yet. My bad.

NINJA SHADOW KILLERS: TIGER FORCE is distributed by IFD so you know there's bound to be a WTF moment. Just when you're about to hit the eject button, that moment shows up in the last 15 minutes. When Jenny "the good ninja" must fight the dastardly warden ninja, they walk through

a wall which turns into footage from another film involving a wizard ninja, who can remove his head! All of a sudden rock'em sock'em wizard is fighting a sexy witch in a see-through top! The fight blows up in smoke and we are transported back to Godfrey Ho's footage. Slashed up, Jenny uses a magic rocket in a bazooka to even the odds. Looking like a smoking ship from the Japanese kids' show *Space Giants* (マグマ大使), this wooden object on a wire chases the ninja through a forest, up trees, around rocks and over cliffs for several Tex Avery minutes until he jumps through a window and blows up.

If you ever saw a strange ninja movie with cool box art in a video store back in the 80s, chances are it was a Godfrey Ho film. From **BLAZING NINJA** (1973) to **THUNDER NINJA KIDS: THE HUNT FOR THE DEVIL BOXER** (1991), he directed over 100 films with ninja in the title. What can I say? The man loves ninjas. Unfortunately this is one of Ho's least successful mushroom trips. Since Jenny can enter whichever film footage she pleases with a poof of smoke, it's a shame the obvious mismatched films were not incorporated as a science fiction element into the redubbed plot. "Can you transport out of my Ninja movie into a Women-in-Prison movie to save my daughter?" That would have been weird. I have the original **REVENGE IN THE TIGER CAGE**. Maybe with a little editing and a name change to Tomas Tang Jr., I could make this thing work. Hmmmm…

HONG KONG, 1986.
DIRECTOR: GODFREY HO

STRIKE OF THE TORTURED ANGELS

Review by James Bickert

I'm pretty sure all the anglicized credits on this Asso Asia Films teenage soap opera were invented by the Hong Kong-based distribution company to boost international sales. They were notorious for selling cheap, redubbed product in the West, and this film contains one of their strangest attempts to entice the English-speaking market—more on that later.
STRIKE OF THE TORTURED ANGELS is a convoluted mess that begins with feisty new fish Susan (billed as 'Susan Lee') thrown into a hardcore detention center where inmates haze the fresh meat until a rebellious mud fight breaks out. It doesn't take long before a love triangle/revenge story flashbacks into frame and we are forced to make a u-turn towards snoozeville.

Susan, along with a pet pig and two other inmates, escape so she can blackmail and kill the doctor who forced her sister to have an abortion (which resulted in suicide) and is currently bangin' her mother to further his career. Presumably to bolster international sales, a subplot involves one of the escapees named Julia ('Stella Jone') who has been diagnosed with TB, has troubles with her rock star boyfriend and is being hounded by the sympathetic prison doctor. Are you ready for this? The character is played by an Asian girl in blackface with a fake afro!

Before you send hate mail or get excited, I don't believe the production team had minstrel aspirations. The character is not played as a stereotype and one gets the impression the filmmakers believed they needed an actress from the Pam Grier mold for a commercial W.I.P. film. My guess is they couldn't find a black actress in Hong Kong that would work on such a low rent movie so they made their own. The makeup is pretty offensive but the freakish novelty wears off quickly. Thankfully, **STRIKE OF THE TORTURED ANGELS** only has one quick nude scene. These girls are very young and some of the scantily clad shots were making me uncomfortable. There are some pretty abrupt cuts around some suggestive scenes so there may be a more revealing print in some foreign markets with seedier child labor laws. I won't be searching for it. The version I watched is available on the Grindhouse Experience box set transferred from a crappy VHS print, complete with Danish subtitles.

HONG KONG, 1982.
DIRECTOR: ROY ROSENBERG
AVAILABLE FROM VIDEOASIA

VIRGIN APOCALYPSE

Review by James Bickert

If you want to put your mind through a wood chipper, IFD Films & Arts Limited is a one-stop shop. Joseph Lai inherited a studio with hundreds of unfinished and unreleased films sitting around collecting dust. Lai and his brother-in-law Godfrey Ho made a career of shooting new footage and inserting it into these reels. Often releasing one or two films a month over the past 30 years, there are so many director pseudonyms, made up cast names, shady dealings and alternate titles that I highly doubt anyone could produce an accurate filmography for IFD. Sometimes their cut-and-paste technique works and sometimes it doesn't. Rarely boring with plenty of aneurysm-inducing dialogue, these films often are comprised of the following formula: sex + violence + kung fu + numerous "What the Fuck?" moments = IFD.

If you love scraping the bottom of the celluloid barrel, digging deeper than Ted V. Mikels, Andy Milligan and Jess Franco, then grab a snorkel because there's a wealth of treasure to be brought up from Joseph Lai's briny deep. **VIRGIN APOCALYPSE** appears to be the merger of two films with some additional shorter scenes thrown in. The plot involves a detective investigating a gay photographer who sells women to a crime boss so he can throw them into a jungle prison/brothel. Three of the women stage a bloody riot which kills around 100 people. After their escape, they team up with the detective for a gang killing spree and eventually learn the crime boss is the detective's brother.

Sounds pretty simple right? Well, it took me two sober viewings to figure this thing out. Remember the WTF element I was talking about? It's in full effect. There are characters who walk in and never return, plot lines dropped, nude interpretive dance, discotheques, snake torture, whacking testicles with chopsticks, strip poker, a prostitute kicking

UK Video box art for VIRGIN APOCALYPSE

out a john because he's a lousy lay, firecrackers being tied to a penis, a guy hung upside down and drowned in a bathtub, foot fetishism, Asians with Australian accents, a hundred girl cat fight, two guys wrapped up like mummies fighting with a straight razor, a live pig decapitated and a hot n steamy lovemaking session interrupted by a zombie! You also get bad dubbing, actors walking out of frame and dialogue like, "You bitch! I'm no bitch, she's a dirty bitch and the bitch has it coming so shut up bitch." Every torture scene has to have three people laughing at the victim and all kung fu kicks sound identical. The work of IFD is a required taste. You'll know from the first frame if it's your cinematic smack or not. I love this garbage. If you don't like it, it's alright. I understand. For those of you who want to take the IFD plunge, **VIRGIN APOCALYPSE** is pretty good but I recommend starting with the 1982 films **WOLF DEVIL WOMAN** and **GOLDEN QUEEN'S COMMANDOS**. For those of you who watch with bongs next to your recliner, it's a must have.

HONG KONG, 1988. DIRECTOR: ANG SAAN

EVIL DEAD

Review by Steven Ronquillo

In 1980 a group of young filmmakers from Detroit went down to Morristown, Tennessee to make their first film, and that film was **THE EVIL DEAD** (1981)—the story of five college students who rent a cabin in the woods and run afoul of an ancient evil there. While never a financial hit, it was always a big seller and a cult hit on home video, and spawned two very-very-very lesser sequels. I didn't run into the original until it hit VHS, and it became one of my all-time favorite films.

So its 2013 and the original's director, Sam Raimi, is now a very successful director, with his two partners, Robert Tapert and Bruce Campbell,

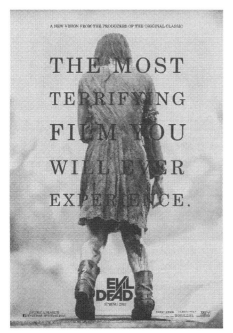

successful in their own ways, as well. When they announced plans to remake this movie, most fans were outraged and miffed like fans will be when someone messes with their nostalgia. But then the trailers and info came out, and we were intrigued. So now the question is asked: How is it, and is it as good as its predecessor? Well, as I go into this advance screening a month before the movie's release date, let us find out.

Five friends go to an isolated cabin in the woods to help out their friend who is trying to kick coke. So Mia (Jane Levy, in a balls-out creepy performance), her brother (Shiloh Fernandez) and three friends (Lou Taylor Pucci, Jessica Lucas, Elizabeth Blackmore) arrive to find out it was broken into and that something weird had happened there. Then the book is found…and the feces hits the oscillating cooling unit.

This is the **EVIL DEAD** follow up I wanted to see when I rented **EVIL DEAD II** back in the 80s! It's an amazingly brutal and gory film that, once it hits the ground running about 20 minutes in with the lesbianic tree rape scene, it doesn't let up. Mia is creepy as hell before- and post-Deadite transformation…when she starts doing the junkie twitch I just got a deep sense of fear in my gut and it paid off for me big-time, with me, a very jaded gorehound, almost losing it during one scene.

This is a gore film, no ifs, ands or buts. If you worship the campy crapfest that is **EVIL DEAD II** (1987) or **ARMY OF DARKNESS** (1992), this will be not your cup of tea, but if you loved the sick gory gem that was the original **EVIL DEAD**, you will eat this up and ask for more! The gore effects are all practical—no CGI here, Sir! And they are done by WETA Workshop in their first hardcore gore film since they redefined zombie splatter with **BRAINDEAD** (a.k.a. **DEAD-ALIVE**, 1992), and they paint the walls red, then use whatever gore they have left to make it rain in the final showdown between the last survivor and the abomination.

The only ones who won't love this are the flat-earthers who were predisposed to hate this with all their hearts and souls to begin with, but for me, the cynical movie reviewer left for 91 minutes and that kid who got freaked out at the original **EVIL DEAD** took over again…and boy, was he satisfied!

The direction by first-time director Fede Alvarez was very impressive and I hope he builds on this with more good work in the future. With a main cast of only five actors, this is a bare-bones movie and thank god they all do good work in it! So see this and enjoy it with a full audience if you can, if not, with friends on DVD, or however you watch movies at home!

USA, 2013. DIRECTOR: FEDE ALVAREZ

BLOOD BEAT

Review by Greg Goodsell

Sensitive New Age painter Cathy (Helen Benton) lives in rural Wisconsin in an isolated farmhouse. Her boyfriend is macho, bearded hunter Gary (Terry Brown), and as expected, the two clash on several issues. One of them is Cathy's adult son Ted (James Fitzgibbons) who arrives for the Christmas holidays with his new girlfriend Dolly (Dana Day) who gets all sorts of bad vibes from both Cathy and the farmhouse. Exploring one of the spare bedrooms, Dolly finds parts of a Japanese Samurai suit of armor under the floorboards. When she tells the others, the suit mysteriously disappears and they don't believe her. A hunting excursion ends in disappointment. The four drink and watch television around the Christmas tree. The time reaches the 45-minute mark in the 90-minute film and nothing has happened yet, and the viewer begins to worry, "Is this one of those shot-on-video things that they film-looked in post-production?" Not to fear—jars fly off shelves and every cheap optical they could cram into the space of a few minutes happens! Whoa!

Discounting a few fellow hunters in the aforementioned hunting scene, Blood Beat has a cast of four and quite a few minutes to kill just yet. What to do? Again, not to fear – a shambling, phantom Samurai kills a few drunks commiserating in the woods. Parts of the tiny cast are slowly picked off one be one until the ghostly Samurai warrior confronts Cathy! "It's you!" the warrior screams. The reason why a Japanese samurai warrior is stomping around a sparsely populated stretch of Wisconsin is revealed—but the sound recording was too muffled to make out. There are more cheap opticals, killings, etc., and a downbeat finale.

The ultra-obscure **BLOOD BEAT** shares an awful lot in common with Ulli Lommel's **THE BOOGEYMAN** (1980). Both films were shot in rural America with a European crew and both feature an unfamiliar, unsettled atmosphere. **BLOOD BEAT** director Fabrice A. Zaphiratos directed only one other film, in France, and the crew is littered with Gaelic names. A sharp perusal of the end credits turned up no familiar names associated with Bill Rebane, the only other notable regional filmmaker working in Wisconsin,

best known for such low-budget hokum as **THE GIANT SPIDER INVASION** (1975) and **THE ALPHA INCIDENT** (1978). This reviewer got a bootleg copy that bragged on the home-brewed liner notes that everyone who thought they had seen every Christmas-themed horror film probably missed this one. Natch, the DVD case features the old VHS cover graphic for **SILENT NIGHT, BLOODY NIGHT** (1972).

BLOOD BEAT does have an inexplicable atmosphere to its credit, with its isolated, nowhere setting and cast of most un-Hollywood actors. In particular, the brief topless shots featuring Dolly will have the horniest male yelling at the screen "Put it back on!" As such, **Blood Beat**, while not any good, will satisfy the obscure horror film addict looking for something

USA, 1982.
DIRECTOR: FABRICE A. ZAPHIRATOS
AVAILABLE FROM APPREHENSIVE FILMS

I WAS A MAN

Review by Greg Goodsell

With his powdered face, plucked eyebrows, pursed mouth with traces of lipstick and diffident manner, Ansa Kansas is a surefire chick magnet. All sorts of cute girls come barging into his crummy New York City apartment at all times of the day and night to play "Post Office." In a Finnish accent falling somewhere between Bela Lugosi and *The Muppet Show*'s Swedish Chef, Ansa sends them all away, "Noooo, plis koway!" A pretty blonde girl down the hall wants Ansa to be her first, as he is a worldly man who sails the seas as a cook with the merchant marine. "I am not a girl! I am a woman!"—she flashes her breasts to him. Ansa's female bar pickup strips down and nearly rubs herself in his face. Ansa looks askance and ill at ease. Don't get us wrong—Ansa wants what she has, but not exactly in the way that sounds…

I WAS A MAN belongs in the small distinct subgenre of transsexual exploitation. Other notable examples include Edward D. Wood Jr.'s **GLEN OR GLENDA?** (1953), **THE CHRISTINE JORGENSEN STORY** (1970), **I WANT WHAT I WANT** (1972), **DINAH EAST** (1970), Doris Wishman's **LET ME DIE A WOMAN** (1977), and **THE WOMAN INSIDE** (1981). While the outré subject matter was off-putting to mainstream audiences, these types of film reportedly did strong business in the rural American south. The docu-style **I WAS A MAN** is remarkable as it comes from the most prolific of all American nudie cutie filmmakers, Barry Mahon. Rest assured, all the flesh offered onscreen in this film is of nubile young women—there are no shock shots of sex change surgeries, et cetera. Put aside any fears of seeing wangs being whacked away, good people, as this title remains firmly ensconced in the world of Mahon's wonderfully feckless sex films!

Back to the (slight) story: Ansa finds solace in walking the Coney Island pier while dressed in drag. As a woman, Ansa is a real homely chick, a substitute school teacher. Tiring of living life as a male, Ansa goes to his doctor—a slimy white-coater—about his intentions to return to his native Finland to have the sex change to become a woman. "Yeah, whatever," says the doc (who also appears at the beginning of the film to offer a monologue on the rare medical condition known as "hermaphroditism.") Ansa hies it to Finland, and its Christmas time! Cue lots of grab shots of busy holiday shoppers in Helsinki. Ansa appears in a room that was probably shot anywhere, anyplace U.S.A. as a nurse injects him in the arm. Waking up the very next day, Ansa is a woman! (Gender reassignment surgery, as everyone knows, is a long, drawn-out affair, with years of psychiatric analysis, hormone therapy and role-playing. Overnight sex changes remain the province of the movies.)

Returning to New York City, Ansa begins his/her life as a woman. Squeezing herself into a frumpy dress, she begins to wash dishes in her rundown apartment when the landlady's son comes pestering her for rent. "You're Ansa? Get outta town!" he exclaims at first, then becomes more sympathetic when the transformed Ansa tells him she's a little flat this week following the trip to Finland and her operation. "Yeah, whatever," he says. He's gone for jut as a few seconds when his horny next-door neighbor comes knocking. Upon seeing Ansa's new look, she exclaims, "WOW! Did they chop everything off?" Yes, indeed.

All that's left is for Ansa to get up in front of a giggling nightclub audience to deliver a rambling monologue about the plight of being a "working girl." The story has no punch line, very much like the film itself.

I WAS A MAN may seem odd and alienating to the unprepared viewer, but anyone else who's swam through a Barry Mahon film knows what to expect: dark, harsh lighting and photography, muffled sound, knee-jerk sets and cue-card reading actors. The Something Weird DVD-R also throws in the trailer or this feature as well as a fine sampling of roughie previews!

USA, 1967.
DIRECTOR: BARRY MAHON

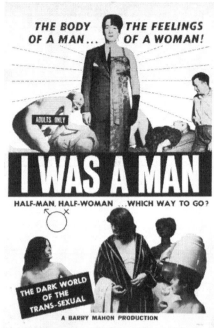

THE SEVEN DEADLY SYNTHS

by Aaron Dilloway

The Seven Deadly Synths is a collection of rare live video recordings of synth-punk bands filmed at NYC's "Harrah" nightclub in the early '80s.

After a somewhat confusing introduction by Scott Simon of Our Daughter's Wedding in which he talks about synthesizers, we get thrown into some excellent footage of primo-era Suicide running through "Ghost Rider". Martin Rev stands tough playing his minimal synth lines, as Alan Vega struts around half-growling heavily-echoed vocals, and at one point swinging the mic in front of the monitor speakers for a few flashes of controlled feedback. It cuts into a great interview with Alan Vega taking about seeing Iggy for the first time. "When he started to cut himself…I said, 'This makes sense to me.'"

From here Daniel Braun (Swans, Branca) talks of seeing Suicide and how they inspired him, then it segues into talk and footage of his dark no-wave/post-punk band Circus Mort—featuring a young Michael Gira of Swans on vocals. Great to see Gira's intense persona as a front man was already fully in place so early on. A few VHS glitches, but given the time of the recording and the fact that not many of these bands even got videotaped we are lucky to even be *seeing* this footage.

Up next are two live clips of minimal new wave from The Units. A bit dark, but again…we're lucky this even *exists*! However, this set of clips is somewhat marred in my eyes by distracting visuals recently added and definitely not "of the times". It takes away from the great vibe of the original footage.

Ah yes… the Minny Pops! I'd been waiting for this. Totally awkward and bizarre stage presence from all members. A couple standing as still as cardboard cutouts (the bassist RULES at this), while the guitarist calmly *and* spastically inserts off-beat stabs of clean hi-end guitar slashes. The plastic rimmed 4-eyed vocalist uncomfortably claps his hands and flails his arms around, kinda like Arto Lindsey doin' Ian Curtis's moves. These guys seem as uncomfortable with life as me, and I'm into that.

Xex is next. *Very* new wave…was really looking forward to see this stuff…though again, this has the unnecessary added visuals.

Our Daughter's Wedding…Definitely the most mainstream-sounding of all the acts on this collection. Mediocre synth-pop…Not my bag.

Next up we are dosed with a killer Sun Ra story and clip. Great story from the booker about having to deal with a late Arkestra, and the bar owner refusing to pay them…all while he's tripping balls on LSD he didn't know he took and has no idea what happening. This Sun Ra footage is cool…Monster masks!!!! Is that *June Tyson as Frankenstein*?! A great-but-straight jazz number from the Arkestra, though I was hoping for one of Ra's synth freakouts since this was a "synth" vid. But still a very cool view of the Arkestra.

Alright…back to some Suicide! The Four Horsemen. Great footage especially

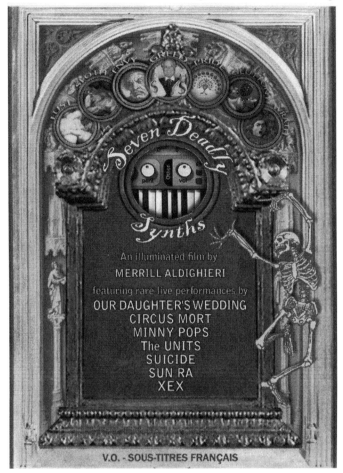

of Rev and his gear as the camera gets up real close…must be on stage. Also: full track this time, which is nice!

Despite my issues with the occasional added graphics, all-in-all a very exciting collection of some rare performances. A recommended grab for anyone into weirdo music and early post-punk.

US/FRANCE, 2013. DIRECTOR: MERRIL ALDIGHIERI
AVAILABLE FROM *artclips.free.fr*

MINNY POPS!

SUICIDE!

ALL I TOUCH, I CORRUPT:

An Appreciation of SIMON, KING OF THE WITCHES

by Ryan Carey

1. Busting The Fourth Wall

How many films well and truly grab you with their very first line? The moment Simon Sinistrari, incomparably brought to life on screen by the criminally under appreciated Andrew Prine, turns and looks right into the camera and says "My name is Simon. I live in a storm drain. When it rains, most people go in—but I go out," director Bruce Kessler's 1971 exploitation opus **SIMON, KING OF THE WITCHES** has you hooked. There's really not much you can do about it; maybe this guy really is a magician. His story begins and ends in massive, violent, torrential storms—and those are plenty exciting in and of themselves—but that 80-or-so-minutes in between book-ending monsoons, well, how many ways can you say "sublime"?

2. "Does the district attorney know that his daughter's dropping pills?"

Okay, none of it makes much sense. Simon's apparently been crashing in his concrete home beneath the obvious-stand-in-for-Los-Angeles that is "West Side" for some time, but he doesn't seem to know anybody. All that changes, however, when the cops decide to pick him up for vagrancy and he makes the acquaintance of fellow guest-of-the-establishment-against-his-will Turk (played with a mixture of impish glee and all-too-believable naïveté by George Paulsin), who's cooling his heels at County on a loitering charge. It's no secret how Turk makes his living—he tells Simon right off the bat—but, as with Kessler's previous effort, **THE GAY DECEIVERS** (1969), it's made clear from the outset that any homosexuality in this flick is engaged in by necessity, not choice. Damn, though, there sure are a lot of "poofters" to go around; take, for example, Hercules Van Zant, whose high-society parties Simon is introduced to by Turk. Or the hapless Stanley, an attendee at one of said soirees who Simon uses in his magickal working to energize the rod (snickering is most definitely permissible here) that he'll use to penetrate his mirror/portal and "take his rightful place among the Gods." Simon ropes him into his ritual because he discovers from an earlier failed attempt that his workings won't succeed if he has a partner who turns him on! Each gay guy in this flick is more over-the-top and, frankly, pathetic than the last, but hey—the movie's a product of its times, and even admitting that homosexuality existed was a bridge farther than most of its contemporaries were willing to travel. Portrayal with dignity would have to come later, I suppose.

Still, in some ways, **SIMON, KING OF THE WITCHES** was willing to buck societal preconceptions. Let's not forget that this was the height of Manson-era "hippies are evil" paranoia, and here not only is the obvious Charlie doppelganger portrayed sympathetically, he's even good enough to date the daughter of the D.A. (who he meets at one of Herclues' shindigs, naturally), while her old man is depicted as being an asshole for trying to keep them apart. Anti-authoritarianism has a definite friend in the King of the Witches.

3. "Don't touch me, I'm a religious object!"

It's said that this film's screenwriter, one Robert Phippeny, was some sort of occult initiate himself, and that he worked with several serious practitioners in the development stages of his story, but I don't buy it—and that's part part of the charm here, of course. Simon's tarot readings are like nothing I've ever witnessed, and he worships some strange combination of the old Greek gods and Left Hand Path-style, quasi-demonic forces. It's all about as "authentic" as Velveeta. Still, even Simon recognizes the hodge-podge nonsense of Wicca for what it is: his crashing of a local Wiccan coven's get-together, with Turk in tow as his chauffeur, is one of the film's more memorable sequences, and lays bare the secret of its ultimate success—simply put, nobody's taking this thing all that seriously. Simon's having fun exposing the priestess in charge for the fraud she is, Turk's trying to get a peek at the naked chick who serves as the group's living altar, and Kessler and Phippeny are probably off in the shadows snickering, wondering if anybody out there is stupid enough to take any of this at face value.

Gary Lachman's 2003 book *Turn Off Your Mind: The Mystic Sixties and the Dark Side of the Age of Aquarius*, an absorbing and well-researched examination of exactly what its title states, would have noted in detail all the contradictory messages, mixed pantheons, and outright hokum on display here, but for the non-academic among us, it's pretty fun to just sit back and enjoy the show. Remember the cardinal rule : if the people who made the film didn't take it, or themselves, too seriously, then there's damn sure no reason why we should, either.

4. "Magnetic—electric—charge—CHARGE!!"

It occurs to me that the photo above could be easily misinterpreted --- Simon's girlfriend, Linda (Brenda Scott) is actually holding a huge red ball in each of her outstretched hands, but they match the color of her dress so perfectly that you could be forgiven for taking a quick glance and thinking she's just got enormous boobs. Which brings up another of this movie's most endearing qualities, namely that appearances can be pretty deceiving here. We've already established that it's readily apparent that the people who made **SIMON, KING OF THE WITCHES** did so with their tongues planted firmly in their cheeks, but that doesn't mean they were out to deliver a shoddy piece of work. The costumes are first-rate. The sets all have a surprising air of authenticity. The performances—especially Prine's—are out of this world. And David L. Butler's cinematography is first-rate and endlessly inventive, especially when Simon passes through his mirror and has one of the most effectively-realized psychedelic "head-trip" experiences ever committed to celluloid. You don't have to set out to make great art to end up making great art—sometimes shit just happens.

5. "Please don't think I'm prejudiced, Rabbi --- I hope you'll be very happy here."

Those are the words spoken by Simon's landlord when he moves into his new pad (hey, a guy can't live in a storm drain forever) and draws a pentagram on the wall for mystical protection. And misunderstandings and fuck-ups play a

Sweet paperback movie tie-in.

6. Simon As Jesus?

It began with a storm, and ends with one, but this time the deluge is of Simon's creation. "The next few days are mine," Simon tells his pusher pals as he brings down the rain on West Side, and the pain on the heads of his foes. His girlfriend OD'ing doesn't do much to help his mood, either. And yet, just as he's taking righteous vengeance on those who would oppose his will, he's laid low by his own Judas Iscariot, who facilitates both his death and, it's strongly hinted, resurrection. Or ascendance. Or something. It's not Turk who deals the fatal blow—as a matter of fact, when Simon severs his bond with his youthful sidekick, it's a strangely emotionally resonant moment—but the betrayal stings just as harshly, if only for an instant, until the darkened lamp-post shown at the beginning of the film suddenly lights up out of nowhere and we come to realize that, hey, maybe Simon didn't miss his trip to the "other side" after all—he just needed to get there by means of a different, infinitely more painful, route.

There's no right or wrong way to achieve Godhood, I suppose—give Simon credit for eschewing, even if by accident, the easy road, and doing things his own way. Rather like the film that bears his name. Simon's a friend to dope pushers, hustlers, con artists, and petty thieves—when he finds himself stuck on our lowly mortal plane for the duration, the enemies of "his people" are sure to find themselves in for a very rough ride, indeed.

If you haven't yet, please—do yourself the favor and pick up Dark Sky's DVD release of this psycho-psychedelic gem. For a supposed "special edition," its selection of extras is pretty weak: there are interesting on-screen interviews with Prine and Kessler, the original theatrical trailer is included, and there's a selection of radio spots on hand, but geez, a commentary at the very least sure would have been nice. Still, the widescreen transfer looks great, and the remastered mono sound does the job nicely. This is everything I love about exploitation movies in one glorious hour-and-a-half potion. It's engaging, quirky, authentic in its lack of authenticity, sincere in its bracingly honest insincerity. These people didn't know squat about the occult, but they were game to give it a go, and the end result is pure magic.

•••

key role in the film's climactic third act. As far as fuck-ups go, none are bigger than the one Simon himself commits—he's been planning his whole life to take his place among the Gods. He's plotted the precise moment when his voyage to the "other side" absolutely must take place. Hell, for the entirety of the film's middle act it's pretty much all he talks about. And yet, he misses the preordained moment because he's listening to a couple of his small-time drug-dealer buddies bitching about the no-good, dirty narc who's been snitching out everyone in town to the cops.

Obviously, there's going to be hell to pay. You don't miss out on your one and only chance to become a God and just get over it and move on. Yet rather than blame himself, as you or I might do, Simon decides to take things out on the powers that be. He's got a vengeful side—watch what happens to the guy who writes him a bad check early on in the film—and this time, he's determined to exercise his wrath on, in his own words, "The mayor, the D.A., the whole system!!"

STEVE BISSETTE

is forever peddling all manner of his own comics (S.R. BISSETTE'S TYRANT®, SPIDERBABY COMIX, etc.), anthologies (TABOO), books (THE VERMONT MONSTER GUIDE, TEEN ANGELS & NEW MUTANTS, etc.), and new horror/monster prints (TYRANT® IN SLUMBERLAND, ALPHABET OF ZOMBIES, etc.) via his online shop. Visit his store at srbissette.com/store/

and happy horror hunting!

Back issues of WENG'S CHOP are available from Amazon.com or contact the fine folks at Kronos Productions for international sales:
kronoscope@oberlin.net

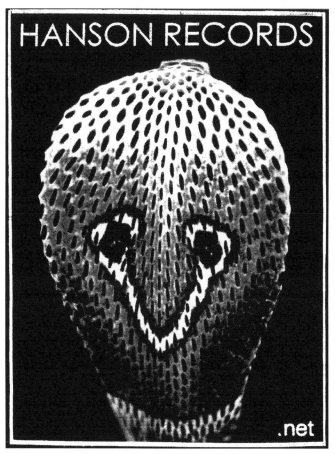

by Danae Dunning

Cult Cinema Under the Gun
Reevaluating the Classics & More

THE REINCARNATION OF ISABEL
(*Riti, magie nere e segrete orge nel trecento...*)
This is the part where I tell you about the plot. Problem is, I'm confused myself. I think it has to do with an executed vampiric witch named Isabel who is worshiped by dudes in red long johns who get really excited when a soon-to-be-married heiress Laureen (Rita Calderoni) moves into the castle where they hold their basement rites. And she happens to look just like, you-know who.

Meanwhile, a strange man and his servant (who looks like Donald Pleasance's ugly brother) lurk about the place looking sinister; we have vampires in Dracula capes wandering around the village putting the bite on nubile young Euro-babes and the trippiest engagement party ever. The back story, if there is one, consists of jarring flashbacks intercut between activities at said party. Are you still with me? Well, neither am I.

The acting, if you can call it that, consists of: histrionics, looking bored, hypnotized and/or confused, sinister and writhing in ecstasy. Or maybe they were writhing in agony because their careers are now in the toilet. The description on Netflix mentioned torture. There was torture alright, inflicted upon yours truly by this cinematic mess.

The whole "vampiric witch being reincarnated in a descendant" has been done before and much better in Mario Bava's **BLACK SUNDAY** (*La maschera del demonio*, 1960). Spend your hard earned bucks on that one instead.

ITALY, 1973. DIRECTOR: RENATO POLSELLI
AVAILABLE FROM IMAGE ENTERTAINMENT

THE CURIOUS DR. HUMPP
(*La venganza del sexo*)
A mad scientist (is there any other kind in these movies?) named Dr. Zoid (Aldo Barbero) sends his big-headed robot minions to kidnap people in various states of fornication, keeping them doped up on aphrodisiacs in order to harness their sexual energy for his immortality potion, all while bickering with his mentor, who is reduced to a talking brain (I am not making this up). However an intrepid (and horny) reporter (Richardo Bauleo) is about to, ahem, "screw' things up for the dastardly duo.

Okay, folks, this is the movie that humped my brain and gave it an STD. No antibiotics can cure me from what I have just experienced. This trippy dippy Argentinian flick, directed (and I use that term loosely) by Emilio Vieyra, has got to be seen to be believed. The aforementioned robots are ridiculous, the captives wander around like zombies when they aren't getting their "fix," and the dialogue is so groan-inducing it has been sampled by Rob Zombie ("Use my body to keep you alive. Oh, let me give you all the sex you need, oh please"). The brain is hilarious as it contracts and expands while speaking. And did I mention that the reporter and the head detective (Hector Biuchet) look like they're still in high school?

I know, I know…you want me to skip to the sex. There were pornographic inserts that were added post-production, and after being bombarded by them before the credits, I wasn't aroused, but in need of a painkiller. And this being the '60s, I was really wanting to take a bush mower to some of the ladies.

This may not sound like a favorable review of **THE CURIOUS DR. HUMPP**, but it kind of is. This crazy concoction is something I would highly recommend for all connoisseurs of Weird. Seeing as I fall into that category, I will probably watch it again. With my adult beverage of choice, this time.

ARGENTINA, 1969.
DIRECTOR: EMILIO VIEYRA
AVAILABLE FROM SOMETHING WEIRD VIDEO

SUKIYAKI WESTERN DJANGO
Two warring clans, The Heike Reds and The Genji Whites (a take-off on the historic Wars of the Roses), descend upon a small town where East meets West and battle it out over treasure that's supposed to be hidden there. Into the mix wanders a lone gunman (Hideaki Ito), a kinder, gentler version of Clint Eastwood's Man With No Name, who bonds with the remaining townspeople to help them settle the score.

Really folks, that's it. This is a Takashi Miike film. I have learned that, with the exception of **AUDITION** (1991), it is best to just throw common sense out the window and enjoy the ride when it comes to him, and even then, it's hard for me to finish some of his stuff. And this is Miike-lite. No sex, no gore (just cartoony blood spray.), no F-bombs, and no fetuses. A Miike film for the whole family [ducks]. Yes, those of you who are only familiar with his horror and violent Yakuza movies will discover the man is a jack of all trades, having done children's fare and drama as well.

While we do have the novelty of having people in traditional Japanese garb firing Gatlin guns and six-shooters and poking fun at Asian stereotypes, it

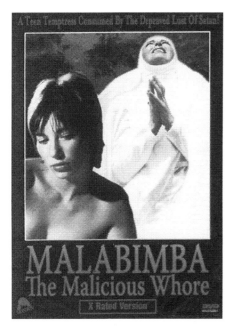

gets kind of repetitive after awhile. And the sheriff with the split personality becomes grating at times. However, the actors don't take any of this seriously, and seem to be really enjoying themselves. And for Quentin Tarantino fans, the director makes a couple of cameos.

How does **SUKIYAKI WESTERN DJANGO** compare to its inspiration, **DJANGO**? There really is no comparison. Django was a morally ambiguous protagonist with an agenda. His saving of a hooker from a group of rebels almost seems like an afterthought and helping the town seemed a means to an end. The hero of **SUKIYAKI WESTERNS DJANGO** was a good man who stumbled into a bad situation; his kind nature wouldn't let him abandon the people. Not to mention that **SUKIYAKI WESTERN DJANGO** was fun while **DJANGO** took itself very seriously.

All in all, not a bad time-killer, and it shows that the usually intense Miike knows how to let loose and have fun.

JAPAN, 2007. DIRECTOR: TAKASHI MIIKE
AVAILABLE FROM FIRST LOOK PICTURES

MALABIMBA; THE MALICIOUS WHORE

Andrea Karoli (Enzo Fishichella), patriarch of a wealthy Italian family, holds a séance, hoping to contact his recently departed wife Daniela, but ends up conjuring the much darker spirit of an ancestor, Lucretzia, who died a violent and suspicious death. Lucretzia wastes no time in taking control of Karoli's teenaged daughter Bimba, played by Katell Lannec (who in the hell names their kid Bimba?), and causing all sorts of mayhem in the household.

Yes, folks, *the* Andrea Bianchi: the one who a year later gave us **BURIAL GROUND: NIGHT OF TERROR** (1981). As bad as that one is, it has it's charm. So much charm that I actually bought it. Which is way more than I can say for its predecessor. I tell you, that Lucretzia was one horny broad! Immediately after possession, she makes Bimba do crazy things like masturbate with stuffed animals, French-kissing, humping her own reflection (again, I am not making this up), and flashing the guests at a cocktail party. When a concerned Andrea consults the family doctor, he assures him that this is a normal part of puberty. (Gee, I don't remember flashing my parents' friends at that age. I'm pretty sure that my friends didn't flash theirs either.) Possession is signified by the accompaniment of wind, a Theremin score, and Darth Vader-style breathing. And there are way too many sex scenes. I know that may sound like a horrible thing to say, but this is a case where less should be more. It slows the story down. Or maybe that is the story, I 'm not sure.

ITALY, 1979. DIRECTOR: ANDREA BIANCHI
AVAILABLE FROM SEVERIN FILMS

LADY TERMINATOR
(*Pembalasan ratu pantai selatan*)

The infamous South Sea Queen has a voracious sexual appetite that 99 husbands have not been able to satisfy. Instead of filing for divorce, though, their penises are devoured by an eel-like creature that resides in her vagina. (Don't blame me folks, I didn't write the script.) Husband #100 is the one lucky S.O.B who manages to capture the muncher before his own equipment is history. Before she vanishes into the sea, the Queen vows that, in one hundred years, she will take revenge on his ancestor (Claudia Angelique Rademaker). Exactly that much time later, anthropology student Tania Wilson (Barbara Anne Constable) goes diving in search of the Queen's sunken castle and ends up with more than she bargained for, becoming the host for the spirit and voracious eel of The South Sea Queen.

Fair warning: I am about to trash a beloved cult classic. Had they stuck with the basic plot I mentioned above, it might have been a better movie. I certainly was throwing out my best "MST2K" zingers. But alas, it was not to be. It isn't long before it morphs from a killer vag movie to an Indonesian **TERMINATOR** rip-off as Tania dons leather and an AK-47 and begins a bloody, yet laughable, killing spree in search of her target. We even get the famous, "Come with me if you want to live" line delivered by the handsome, yet bland, hero (Christopher J. Hart). Rademaker's character Erica is annoying, but I don't blame her, or anyone else in this mess. I blame whoever did the atrocious dubbing. We even have one mulleted character trying his best to channel Jeff Spicoli, Sean Penn's stoned surfer dude from **FAST TIMES AT RIDGEMONT HIGH** (1982), and failing miserably.

If you're looking to get into exploitation cinema, trust me, this is *not* the place to start.

PHILIPPINES, 1989.
DIRECTOR: H. TJUT DJALIL
AVAILABLE FROM MONDO MACABRO

DISCIPLE OF DEATH

Poor Julia just can't catch a break. She's madly in love with farmer Ralph, but her father, the Squire, just doesn't think he's good enough for his baby, even though Ralph owns his own land. So they meet in secret, in such romantic locals as...the lo-

cal graveyard. One night our two lovebirds decide to pledge their eternal love by pricking each other's fingers and mingling the blood—which is all fine and dandy, until a drop Julia's virgin red stuff falls onto the grave of a suicide (I hate it when that happens). The occupant of said grave (known only as The Stranger in the credits.) cuts a bloody path through the nearby village, making young virgins his undead slaves (through an elaborate heart-ripping ritual whose purpose I'm still trying to figure out), with the intent of making Julia his undead bride. With the help of the local parson and a Jewish mystic, Ralph sets out to rescue his lady love.

67

I have to give **DISCIPLE OF DEATH** some credit. It really tries to be a Hammer film. The production values are up to Hammer standards and there are a few creepy moments, but let's face it, Mike Raven is no Christopher Lee. He gives it a good shot, though. He's nicely restrained up until the first satanic ritual, and then he really starts to ham it up, probably because he was bored and trying to liven things up. And he's not the only one. Everyone involved chewed so much scenery that I would be surprised if there was any left by the time the movie wrapped. My favorite character has to be the Jewish Mystic; he was the perfect archetype of the doddering old fool and had the best lines. "Trinity, schminity! This is none of your Christian schmitters, this is kosher Yiddish Magic!"

UK, 1972. DIRECTOR: TOM PARKINSON
AVAILABLE FROM RETROMEDIA

BLOOD FREAK

Every time I think I've seen it all, something comes along that absolutely confounds me. Here it is: A hippie/Christian/vampire/mutant turkey monster movie (not only am I not making this up; I am stone cold sober)—the cult classic **BLOOD FREAK**.

Hershel is a biker, Vietnam vet, and all-around nice guy drifting across the country. He comes across cute hippie Christian chick Angel having car trouble; she shows her gratitude by letting him crash at her place and getting him a job at her pastor's turkey farm. Trouble brews when Angel's druggie sister get her hooks in Hershel and gets him addicted to pot. Things get even worse when he volunteers to be a guinea pig for the farm's scientific experiments. The lab assistants feed him a turkey laced with pot and god knows what. Poor Hershel turns into a turkey-headed monster who craves the blood of addicts. A desperate Anne, having fallen madly in love with the dude and feeling responsible for his plight, turns to Angel for help.

Can Hershel be saved? Will Anne clean up and turn her life over to God? Will everyone in this movie become vegetarians? Will you even care?

This has to be one of the most ridiculous movies I have ever seen—and I've seen a lot of ridiculous movies. There are endless scenes of people wandering around looking lost (probably because they couldn't make sense of the script.) The kill scenes are unintentionally hilarious with poor Hershel desperately scooping blood into his beak and a scream track that keeps skipping. Bad acting and dialog abounds, and the film's monster has to be seen to be believed! I kept alternating between yawning and laughing hysterically, especially when the then chain-smoking narrator, who spouts the most inane dialog since Bela Lugosi in Ed Wood's **GLEN OR GLENDA** (1953), erupts into a coughing fit towards the end! I was, however, appalled by a brutal and totally unnecessary turkey beheading scene.

So, if you have time, and a few brain cells to kill, trip out with **BLOOD FREAK**!

USA, 1972.
DIRECTOR: BRAD F. GINTER & STEVE HAWKES
AVAILABLE FROM SOMETHING WEIRD VIDEO

BLOOD GNOME

A rash of baffling murders plagues the local BDSM (bondage/domination/sadomasochism) community. When crime photographer Daniel (Vincent Bilancio, who also produced), still recovering from the murder of his wife, is called to the scene, he notices that in spite of the vicious bites all over the bodies, there's very little blood. Even more troubling is when he temporarily mans the video camera, which was rigged by the perv operator with x-ray vision to see through women's clothes, he can actually see little creatures feeding on the remains. Of course no one believes him. Things get weirder when he receives phone calls and emails from someone only known as "Blood Gnome", wanting the footage back. Doubting his own sanity, he ignores them. That prompts them to visit him in his home, and when Daniel bites one of the nasty buggers in self-defense, he gains the ability to see them without the aid of the x-ray camera. Meanwhile Daniel is getting increasing attached to Divinity (Melissa Pursely), a friend of a couple of the victims, and in the BDSM scene herself. When he learns that someone close to Divinity is involved, he begins to fear for her life and his own.

I have been intrigued by **BLOOD GNOME** ever since I read the description on Netflix. But I was antsy. I love indie horror, but I've been burned a lot lately. However, I've been let down by mainstream cinema too, so I always like to give the underdog a chance. And man, I was *not* disappointed. I was impressed at how good the performances were, especially Vincent Bilancio and Melissa Pursely. Not only are they talents to watch for, but their characters are incredibly likable and I cared about what happened to them. And I have to give props to the blood gnomes themselves. Director Lechago does well by keeping in them in the shadows, but when they are shown, they make an impression. I still think I hear them scurrying and whispering under my

bed at times. Kudos to special effects man Todd Rex. The look of **BLOOD GNOME** reminds me of such Full Moon Productions as the *Subspecies* series, when the company was at its peak. The production values definitely don't reflect the low budget. And I am amazed to find out that it was shot in only 12 days!

I am unfamiliar with John Lechago's other work, (**BIO-SLIME**, **MAGUS**, **KILLJOY 3** & **KILLJOY GOES TO HELL**), but I'm looking forward to remedying that and checking out his future films.

The only thing I was not impressed with was Ri Walton's performance as Mistress Elandra. It alternated between bland and over the top, and her character's exact role in the shenanigans is not quite clear. And of course, there's the open ending, which I wasn't fond of, but it didn't do anything to detract from what I experienced before.

Please don't let the terms "BDSM" and "indie horror" turn you off. You'll be missing out on a real gem if you do.

USA, 2004. DIRECTOR: JOHN LECHAGO
AVAILABLE FROM SCREEN MEDIA

•••

IT HAD TO BE YU:
The Ronny Yu Romance-tastic Action-Packed Triple Feature
by Danae Dunning

THE BRIDE WITH WHITE HAIR
(*Bai fa mo nu zhuan*, 1993. D: Ronny Yu)
In medieval China, Cho Yi Huang (Leslie Cheung) is tired of his warrior ways when he is chosen to be the successor to the leader of the Wu-Tang Clan. It is during a village raid by an evil cult, led by demonic Siamese twins known collectively as Ji Wu Shang (Francis Ng & Elaine Lui), that he meets their most effective killer, Lian (Brigette Lin). Not only is Lian deadly with a sword, but she can use her hair to strangle and dismember her opponents. Cho falls for the beautiful and sad woman, who is also disillusioned with killing, and the two plot to run away together. But the male half of Ji Wu Shang has designs of his own on Lian, and won't let her go without a fight. When she is framed for a temple slaughter, Cho turns against her, causing her to become a white-haired wraith sworn to vengeance at all costs.

Wow! What can I say? This movie is breathtaking; from the gorgeous visuals, epic score by Richard Yeun, the talent and beauty of Cheung and Lin, to the fight choreography by Philip Kwok and the script by Kei To Lam. David Wu, and Yu (based on the novel by Yusheng Liang) creates characters that you actually care about and a story that will never leave you bored. Those of you who are *Xena: The Warrior Princess* fans will feel the influence on the series, not only in the character of Lian, but in the scene in which she is made to walk a gauntlet before being allowed to leave the cult. And yes, I'd be lying if I said that the romance wasn't a selling point for me. Being both a hopeless romantic and a genre fan, this type of film appeals to me way more than mainstream fare like **THE NOTEBOOK** (2004, D: Nick Cassavetes). In other words, the perfect date movie for me!

I would highly recommend this movie. Rent first if you're new to Asian martial arts fantasy cinema, but I have a strong feeling you'll want to own this. I'm surprised I don't.

THE BRIDE WITH WHITE HAIR 2
(*Bai fa mo nu zhuan 2*, 1994. D: David Wu)
For ten years, Cho has been waiting on the snowy peak of Mount Shin Fung for a special flower to bloom, one that will not only turn his beloved Lian's hair to back to black, but will soften her heart, which was hardened by his betrayal. Meanwhile, Lian has been busy destroying the Eight Clans and poisoning women against men. When Cho's nephew Kit (Sunny Chan) marries the beautiful Lyre (Yee Man Man), she is kidnapped by Amazonian warriors led by Lian and brainwashed into believing Kit abused her. Kit organizes a ragtag search party intent on not only rescuing Lyre, but finding his wayward uncle, the only man who can reach the bitter and evil Lian.

I did enjoy this, even the comic relief provided by Christy Chung as Moon, Kit's tomboy best friend who harbors a secret crush on him, but it seemed so out of place in this dark tale. My favorite scenes take place inside Lian's remote palace, where she not only indoctrinates young women into her man-hating cult, but goes through a string of male musicians whom she kills for getting one note wrong. David Wu takes over directing chores for Ronny Yu, but both share writing credits, so his influence is definitely felt, and the film still has the same stunning visuals as its predecessor, but the camp-side scenes with Kit and his buddies tend to slow things down a bit.

I would recommend this even if you're not a completist, because despite its flaws, it ties the story up neatly. Avoid the dubbed version if possible.

THE PHANTOM LOVER
(*Ye bang ge sheng*, 1995. D: Ronny Yu)
In 1936 China, a washed-up acting troupe rent a ramshackle theater, where the great actor Song Danping (Leslie Cheung) died in a mysterious fire ten years before. One of the actors in the troupe, Wei Ping (Lei Huang), encounters the disfigured, but very much alive Danping, who trains Wei to sing like him and recreate his most famous role in a musical retelling of Romeo and Juliet, a performance that not only brings success to the little troupe, but attracts the attention of Danping's long lost lover, Yun Yan (Chien-lien Wu), who, after the fire, was forced to marry the repulsive Zhao (Fong Pao), then beaten and abandoned for not being a virgin. The mad woman believes Wei to be Danping, and Danping begs him to keep up the ruse because he's ashamed of his burnt features. But Wei doesn't feel right about this. Will Danping find the courage to face his love and take revenge on the ones who ruined them both?

This is another one of my favorites; the acting, the story, the visuals, and the amazing music by David Wu (who co-wrote **THE BRIDE WITH THE WHITE HAIR** and directed and co-wrote **THE BRIDE WITH THE WHITE HAIR 2**), all come together to enchant the viewer. If you're expecting death-defying martial arts feats in this one, you'll be disappointed, because this is purely a love story through and through. It did a good job of melting my dark heart and is definitely on my list of date movies. Sadly, the great Leslie Cheung committed suicide in April of 2003, so it's always with a bit of melancholy that I view this.

Those of you who are only familiar with Ronny Yu from **BRIDE OF CHUCKY** and **FREDDY VS. JASON** must check out these early definitive films.

●●●

ONE ON ONE WITH A KINDLY CRYPTID:
INTERVIEW WITH STEPHEN 'THE DANCING YETI' TAKO

Conducted by Brian Harris

If you struck out in search of the elusive Yeti, would you know where to start looking? Perhaps in the uncharted wilds of Asia or the snow-covered mountains of the Himalayas? Well, I'm here to tell you that you'd be wrong on both counts—you can find the Yeti in the unlikeliest of places...doing the unlikeliest of things...he's on the dance floor...doing his thing...getting down. This, ladies and gentlemen, is no ordinary species of Yeti...this is THE DANCING YETI!

Brian Harris: *Thanks so much for taking the time out for this interview Stephen. Months and months ago a mutual friend showed me a YouTube video that blew my mind. As a cult cinema fan, I'm always looking for out-of-the-ordinary entertainment and this video was just amazingly fun. Talk to me about THE DANCING YETI and how the character and project came to be.*

Stephen Tako: I was in a short film in 2011 titled Abominable where I played the father yeti. It was really fun to do and on the second day of filming, I asked the crew to film me dancing in the costume to the song *Hungry Like the Wolf* just so I'd have a funny video.

The costume was given to me at the end, at my request, because I wanted to create a fun-loving character that loves to dance. Thought it would be fun and silly to make music videos.

The Dancing Yeti and I have some similarities. We are both unusually tall; both have a passion for dancing. And both have a history of being outcasts.

When you made your first DANCING YETI video, did you have more in mind? A series of YouTube videos, perhaps a low budget feature film?

Yes. I intended to make music videos with my own original music and put out two CDs. One was going to be for Christmas. I am still interested in doing this as well as dance videos to popular songs from top artists.

Also, I considered having a television show based on the Dancing Yeti teaching children to accept people of all ethnicities and each episode would feature a type of dance.

I've started to write a children's book based on this character and how it was that he moved to California.

Sadly, I only have two YouTube videos to date.

There is no doubt in my mind that a series of shorts featuring your character would be a hit with children and adults. Have you considered any other kinds of merchandise? The concept is really original and incredibly wacky; it would make a great bobble-head, action figure or even a one-shot comic.

Funny you should ask, because I envisioned The Dancing Yeti to be a cult classic once I had a string of successful clips online. So I actually have a bobble head for the character and they are numerically coded for collectors. I made 24 for my first order and only have two left. My buddy makes them local, so I can get them done pretty quick.

In addition to the bobble heads, we've also got T-shirts, mugs and boxers made. Once the character takes off more, I'll be getting magnets, pencils and all sorts of fun and wacky items. www.thedancingyeti.com shows the items currently available.

Were you aware when you first started THE DANCING YETI that there's actually a Bigfoot sub-genre in horror/exploitation/fantasy here in the 'States and around the world?

I grew up believing the stories of Bigfoot. Plus I have seen the character and/or likeness portrayed in movies. But I'll be frank, that I'm not aware of a lot more than the old blurry photos, **HARRY AND THE HENDERSONS** (1987) and maybe one or two more references.

Outside of a few child-friendly Bigfoot flicks here and in India, the creature seems to be generally looked upon as a scary creature. Were you worried that kids might not take to your character?

In my mind, The Dancing Yeti was never scary. So when my niece, Melissa Kronenberger provided me with the original sketches, I was not thrilled with the fierce look she gave as an option. But when I showed the pictures to some kids, many boys tended to like the scarier look over the happy smiling Yeti. Most girls and moms liked the smiling Yeti better. Adults seemed more concerned with the scariness of Yeti than did any of the children.

For a while I considered catering to young preschool children with The Dancing Yeti and realized my big hit music video had a totally different feel and may hurt my preschool image. My follow-up video showed a more sensitive Yeti who was struggling with being different and misunderstood. He was tired of being thought of as a monster and questioned the reason for his own existence. I know, pretty deep, eh?

The direction I decided to take the character is really geared toward any kids that are faced with bullies. And also a creature to make adults laugh and want to dance. The Dancing Yeti is 'different' and he wants to identify with anyone else who feels they are different. And those people often are those who get picked on and bullied. If he has the confidence to be himself and get out and dance and enjoy life, then he is a great role model to help people overcome their fear of being special and unique.

What about the fierce Yeti? Well, he does not tolerate the act of bullying and puts on a fierce look to intimidate a bully and protects those that will dance with him.

It sounds like THE DANCING YETI can actually be quite a force for positivity, especially with young people facing the issues that they do today. A misunderstood Dancing Yeti in claymation could be classic. Have any animators contacted you about the property? Perhaps comic illustrators?

Word hasn't gotten out enough about The Dancing Yeti and what he stands for to fight bullying. The closest I am to having an animated show featuring Yeti is with the Artist Development Production Center in Los Angeles. I am collaborating with them on an anti-bullying campaign where I will be modeling some clothes and giving motivational speeches to particularly help men and boys. We are discussing ways to connect to some of these kids with The Dancing Yeti in an animated program. And then I can show up to their larger events in costume and pose for pictures.

Does THE DANCING YETI have any natural enemies?

Careless campers who start forest fires…and he's not fond of global warming threats…The Dancing Yeti doesn't like to label anyone as a bully, but he considers the act of bullying to be his worst enemy.

While Yeti is comfortable sharing the forest with Bigfoot, apparently the feeling is not mutual. I guess true Neanderthals just really struggle with the more advanced mythical creatures.

Outside of THE DANCING YETI, I know you're an actor and a writer—what are some of the projects on your plate right now?

The artist development group mentioned before is a cool project I'm just starting with and they are at *www.adpcigottalent.com* for more info. Additionally, I am working on an online service to help fathers and sons have better relationships.

Each Friday I am available, I will continue to co-host a relationship talk radio show from 2:30-3:30 at *www.latalklive.com* with my main host Julie Orlov.

I played one of the wicked witch's guards in the new movie **OZ: THE GREAT AND POWERFUL** (2013). I'm in five scenes in that movie.

I'll be doing more motivational speeches and book signings with my book *Motivated to Act*, encouraging people to follow their true life passions and dreams.

I'm waiting to hear if I'll be brought back to work on a new HBO series that starts this year.

Currently, I have two writing projects. One is a short film based on a murder mystery surrounding a class reunion. The other is a comedy web series based on my life as a mortgage lender.

NYLA International Film Festival and The Los Angeles Cinema Festival of Hollywood are both hosted by me.

And lastly, I am working on intensive monolog pieces for my acting reel as I am looking for an agent and a manager.

In what direction would you like to see the character of THE DANCING YETI evolve?

I'd love to see The Dancing Yeti be a mascot or licensed character of a company or organization that relates to people being free to express themselves without the fear of being picked on. He could appear in their commercial and print campaigns, much like Smoky the Bear does for forest fires. And I'd like to appear at functions for kids to take photos of us together and I can tell them how important it is to be themselves.

It would be cool to see the character be in an animated show as well as making cameo appearances in television and movies as a hero to the underdog…the one feeling helpless or different.

Since Yeti loves to dance, I also foresee many music videos. Some will be original music and some will be to songs already popular.

We really appreciate you taking the time out to do this interview Stephen, thanks a ton. One last question, has there been any other cryptid or mythological beasts you've been toying with creating or do you plan to remain with THE DANCING YETI?

So far the only other characters are actually related to Yeti. I have a children's book that I wrote where it explains how The Dancing Yeti got his name and the details of how and why his grandmother brought him to California. I do have plans of introducing the grandmother, one of his brother's, a potential wife and a son for the character.

It's been my pleasure discussing this character with you and I hope to make a positive difference in people's lives with my Yeti. We all feel 'different' at some point and Yeti is no exception. But he accepts who he is and likes himself and because of that, people who get to know him will grow to like him as well. He has the talent and passion of dancing and is not afraid to share his gifts with the world, so others will be encouraged to do the same with their gifts.

•••

*Thanks again to Stephen Tako for taking time out. To find out more about THE DANCING YETI, drop by the website at **www.thedancingyeti.com**! SEE YOU NEXT ISSUE FOLKS! - Brian*

SNAKES ALIVE!
INDIAN FANTASTIC CINEMA PART 4 - COBRA LADIES
by Tim Paxton

To understand the complexity of this genre of films full of human-snake entities, you must first have knowledge of what they are. My first exposure to the genre came in early 2001 when I bought the film **DEVI** *(1999). Prior to that, I wasn't aware of sexy Indian snake ladies. I grew up in the 1970s and our family occasionally went into Cleveland, Ohio for a rare night out. One restaurant which caught my mother's fancy was a Krishna establishment in Cleveland Heights. Besides offering delicious vegetarian food, the lobby of the place was packed with mythological comics full of blue gods, Ravaska demons, and cobras. Another early memory is Rudyard Kipling's "Rikki Tikki Tavi" which was required reading in the fourth grade. I liked the crafty character of Nag the cobra in the short story. I hated the mongoose. That bastard killed Nag! I had no idea that Indian cinema was full of cobras as well.*

A great many people with ophiophobia[1] may not want to hear this, but the snake has always been an important religious icon, and probably one of the earliest. Imagine a creature that's armless but can climb a tree, legless but can sprint as fast as a human, and one bite from some of them can kill you within minutes. That's a snake. And in India you have one of the deadliest in the world: the cobra. It's no wonder that they figure into the mythology of South Asian religion for thousands of years. They are both feared *and* respected.

The cobra is especially important to the Hindu religion, as it is associated with Shiva, possibly the most important male deity in their mythology. Shiva is often depicted with a protective cobra coiled around his neck. Vishnu is usually portrayed as reclining on the coiled body of *Adishesha* aka the Preeminent Serpent aka The *Sheshnaag*, a giant snake deity with multiple cobra heads. Cobras are also worshipped during the Hindu festival of *Nāg Panchamī*.

Reviews in this article will refer to various words and/or phraseology which may sound confusing at first (and believe me, it was) but after a while you'll get the hang of it. The word "*nāg*" or "*naag*", generally means snake, and is part of most of the official languages of India's 28 states[2]. Most of the time it is in reference to the cobra, which is one of four poisonous snakes in the country[3]. The type of cobra that makes its appearance in these films is usually the spectacled cobra with its hood fully extended. The word nag is interchangeable with that of its supernatural counterpart.

Nāg festivals have become popular over the past few years, with showings all over the globe. This phenomenon is due in part to the popularity of Bollywood through the ever-increasing Indian/Hindu diaspora, and that of world cinema festivals featuring female/Shakti-centric titles. The Nāg Genre in general has created niches which are exploited with abandon, and film festivals pop up around holidays such as *Nāg Panchamī* (last day of the Bengali month *Sravana*; July–August).

[1] *About a third of adult humans are ophidiophobic, making this the most commonly reported phobia. Recent studies have theorised that humans may have an innate reaction to snakes, which was vital for the survival of humankind as it allowed such dangerous threats to be identified immediately. ~ wikipedia.org/wiki/Ophidiophobia. I come from a family of snake handlers, and I routinely picked up garter snakes and so forth as a child.*

[2] *The genus name Naja comes from Indian languages ... deriving from the root of Naag (Hindi, Sanskrit, Oriya, Marathi), Naya (Sinhalese), Naagu Pamu (Telugu), Nāgara Haavu (Kannada), Naaga Pambu (Tamil) ... ~ en.wikipedia.org/wiki/Indian_cobra*

[3] *As a side note, the venom from the cobra is deadly, but not instantaneous. Unlike in the films where an unfortunate soul is bitten by a cobra and dies in minutes, cobra venom consists primarily of neurotoxins. These poisons causes convolutions leading to respiratory failure or cardiac arrest, with death in a few hours. Cinematic victims usually fall the ground and begin immediately foam at the mouth and sometimes turn blue. Not that accurate, but it makes for a fun show.*

The cinematic *Nāg* is related to the before-mentioned *Sheshnaag*, the seven-headed form of the cobra that is revered as being related to both Vishnu and Shiva (and, to some extent, other gods and goddesses, and even The Buddha). These beings, the *nāga* is male and the *nāgī* or *nāginī* is the female, are typically seen as the protectorates of the various temples of gods and goddesses associated with cobras. Many times they are put there to guard against thieves that want some treasure within the temple or, more importantly, the *Nāgmani*

I truly believe that one reason why the United States saw so few Indian films—outside of Art-House favorites like Satyajit Ray's **PARASH PATHAR** (1968) or **DEVI** (1960)—was primarily due to bigotry and prejudice. I guarantee that, had I seen some of Babubhai Mistri's mythological fantasy films or Nanabhai Bhatt's **SAMSON** (1966) as a child, I would have gone apeshit. Even if the U.S. editors had excised all of the musical numbers from the films they would have played just fine on Saturday afternoon TV. I wonder if the sight of multi-armed goddesses and nine-headed gods (not to mention that freaky elephant-headed one and the monkey with a club) may have caused an uproar with our God-fearing (and money-worshipping) brethren that ran the stations. I am at a loss as to why these fantastic films couldn't have been re-edited and dumbed/dubbed down? I grew up in Ohio in the 1960s and '70s, and like most kids at that time, I devoured weekends of TV movie shows hosted by the likes of Ghoulardi, The Ghoul, Sir Graves Ghastly, Super Host, and Hoolihan & Big Chuck.

I would have killed to have seen scenes of epic battles between gods and demons, strange snake creatures, and other mythological action.

The fact that "them Indians" worshipped animals like cows and snakes must've bothered some bigwigs in the industry. They pray to snakes, for God's sake! The fact is, most of the nagin films are devotional, and it's tough to separate the religion from the plot in these films. Major movies in the genre are productions full of gods, goddesses, acts of faith, swamis, yogis, Shaivites, Brahmans, and all sorts of magical folk medicine. Other than the odd slasher or mad killer film, in most of the supernatural films the horror elements cannot exist without the religious. There is no shame in being a devotee of any of the snake gods or goddesses mentioned in any of the films. It's a given.

When reading through the reviews in this article you must take into account all the religious symbolism and their importance in the films. Many of these films take place in and around temples associated with regional snake gods and the god Shiva, who wears a cobra around his neck. There are the classic hallmarks of these temples, which include sacred cork anthills called Karandi that also house cobras (see artwork to the right), numerous statues of snakes (see above left), and statues of the nine-headed hooded cobra Sheshnaag. This mythical cobra is often depicted in religious temples sheltering Shiva's lingam or the reclining body of the god Vishnu. The boy-god Krishna is often seen with the Sheshnaag, as well (see above photo from the 1919 film **KALIA MARDAN**).

Such wonders I missed as a kid. Pity ignorance kept these and other such treasures of World Cinema out of reach for us normal folks. Thank goodness for the Internet, is all that I can say. I for one welcome our new gods. I am not afraid to explore and grow.

or "snake pearl" a supernatural gem associated with cobras. This jewel can also be found atop a naga's head whether the creature is in cobra or human form. As with the romanization of many Indian words, it can be spelled *naagmani* or *nāgmani*. Many times these highly dramatized ceremonies occur on holidays such as the *Nāg Panchamī, Nāga Chaturthi* or *Nāga Puja*.

Many other Hindu gods feature snakes in their cosmic make-up, and their tales are often the basis for many plots in Indian Cinema. It is incredibly difficult to separate the two when you make a film about a cobra lady. In fact, I don't think I have seen one Indian nagin film which *doesn't* have elements of the supernatural, be it overt or sublime. Genre-wise, these snake films can be viewed as mythological, fantasy, or horror. Nevertheless, as with William Friedkin's **THE EXORCIST** (1972), the underlying fact is that they are essentially *devotional movies*. Yes, these are religious films, which may come as a surprise for a lot of Westerners who watch them.

When reading through the reviews you will encounter some definitions describing the nāga. The most numerous after nāga and nāgina will include *ichchadhari nāg*, which is a cobra that can assume the shape of a human at will. This is the most popular variant of the nāga and it is usually associated with the film **NAGIN** (1976) and its spawn. For a strictly religious race of cobra entities there is the *nagdevis,* which are big fans of Shiva and hang out in the holy realm of *Nāglok* or *Nāg Lok*, or *Naaglok*, depending on what school of romanization you adhere to[4]. Every so often you will run across other snake gods, goddesses, and demons mentioned such as *Nāgraj, Nāgadevata, Nāganeshwari, Manasa, Kethu,* and *Daakshayini*. I'm sure there are other deities mentioned in the films, and due to my specific lack of knowledge pertaining to all of the hundreds of Hindu gods, I know I'm missing out on names (lack of English subtitles for most of the films doesn't help much either). Confused yet? I've created a glossary for these Indian words and their meanings which can be found on page 93.

[4] **To accent or not to accent**; the accent you will see throughout this article on the word "nag" is used, for the most part, to indicate that the ā is a *long a*. The romanization for nag in Hindi typically uses one "a" as in nāg, and the Telugu, Tamil, or Kannada typically utilizes the "aa" spelling. But that isn't always the case. I switch between the two standards depending on the language source, accenting some instances of Nag as Nāg, etc. Nutty, I know.

Here's a good as time as any to give you the heads-up when it comes to the animal "actors" used in these films. Yes, there is animal abuse in practically any pre-2000 film containing live cobras. While some filmmakers respected the snakes and treated them with the proper religious piety, most didn't. You see scenes of cobras fighting and killing one another, cobras killing mongoose and vice-versa, as well as vultures ripping snakes apart. Snakes are strung with wires when required to move on cue or look cute playing drums and horns in mythological or devotional films. If you really think about it, these are not very pleasant sequences in otherwise wonderful productions.

Then there are portions within a film where actors, young and old, handle these deadly snakes. Babies pick them up and what looks like a cobra strike is eminent. The cobras you see on screen are "stunt snakes" who have had their fangs removed or their mouth sewn shut.

As frightening as this sounds, some directors have treated them better. Indian film critic Roshmila Bhattacharya wrote in 2001 that director Harmesh Malhotra poo-pooed claims of animal abuse during the filming of **NAGINA** and **NIGAHEN**, "Instead of sweltering in jungles or coiled in small baskets, they live in air-conditioned comfort," he claimed. "They are fed 4-5 eggs. And because one snake looks much like the other we rotated the shots between five snakes. No snake died on my sets."

This may be true for larger budget Bollywood films, but in the world of grade B or D films, snakes were often treated very badly. I don't enjoy watching those scenes, but accept them as how these films were made. Sometimes you can have the sweet without a whole hell of a lot of sour.

The same can't be said as to how women are treated in these films. Rape is often an unpleasant factor in some of the plots. I am really taken aback by some of the hostile family structure that was (and still is) prevalent in these films. I know that they are just *dramatic films*, but as recent headline-grabbing news has reported, women are not treated very well despite the overall religious belief in the Divine Mother (Shakti, Maa, etc.).

Bearing all of the above in mind, on with the reviews.

Pre-1950s

This is in no way the definitive article on the Indian cobra genre. What I have reviewed may only be *half* of the genre's films made during India's long and fruitful film industry. Perhaps the first was Dadasaheb Phalke's **KALIA MARDAN** (1919), a film about the young god-boy Krishna who triumphs over the venomous serpent king Kaliya Naag (and like most Indian mythological films they are constantly remade, as this tale was in 1935, 1954, 1965, 1979, 1989, etc.). Other earlier films that probably included cobra devis or demons include **KALA NAAG** (1923, 1934), **KALI NAGIN** (1925), **SOUL OF THE SNAKE** (1927), **NAAG PADMINI** (1928), **NĀGAN** (1934), **VISH KANYA** (1943), **NĀG PANCHAMĪ** (1948, 1953, 1972), and into the 1950s which is where I will begin this article.

A word about how the capsule reviews: to be honest, I really dislike short reviews. However, as this is an article that touches very lightly on the subject, not a book about nagin films (the book may come later), I settled for casual reviews that give the plot with notes or anecdotal information on the film's music, actors, or director. I have separated out a few films I feel are some of the more important ones in the history of the genre.

Everything has been listed by date rather than by title, except for those that I have separated for their importance or sheer coolness of production. The film titles used in this article come directly from their sources; that is, what was offered on the sleeve art of the VCD or DVD (or in a few cases as listed on YouTube). In a few rare cases I had to painstakingly copy the Hindi, Telugu, Kannada or whatever script by hand for interpretation. So what I may have is a transliterate title rather than a translated one.

Most of these titles are listed on various media websites as well, so you should be able to track them down if you ever want to buy your own copies. The date is usually accurate, but I do list a few films wherein that information is uncertain. The original language/origin is what is listed on the VCD or DVD, unless I have other data (some films I have are Hindi dubs of Telugu, or Tamil dubs of Bengali, etc.). I've only had one VCD that ever had English subtitles, and almost all of them have watermarks. Some VCDs even have ads scrolling at the bottom of the image (and one featured a very annoying and intrusive commercial for "hair oil" every fifteen minutes).

Hindi Horror comic featuring a story called "Ichadhari Naagin Aur Shaitan Nevlaa Ram Raheem" From the 1980s or 1990s.

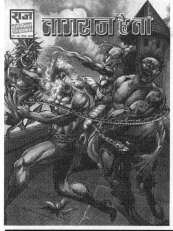

The cultural fascination of the snake—and cobra in general—is something that comes natural to the Hindu psychology. The fear and veneration of the serpent has always been represented in Indian art, be they sculpture (see page 74), film, or as seen above, comics. The superhero called Nāgaraj has been a popular icon of Indian comics since the late '80s when he was created by Sanjay Gupta. Nāgaraj's look has changed little in his 25 years in print.

The four comic covers above give you some kind of idea how his comic line evolved, in keeping with the aesthetics of the times. The covers are from the '80s at the upper left through the '90s on the right to the 2000s on the lower left to his present appearance (with snaky partner) from a recent comic cover.

The 1950s

The 1950s was a boom decade worldwide for Horror and Science Fiction films everywhere there was a thriving film industry. That is, except for India. Only a few movies were made that were full-blown horror films, even if they were of the subdued haunted mansion variety made popular by Kamal Amrohi's MAHAL ("Mansion") in 1949. The romantic idea of ghosts is one thing, but monsters are a wholly different matter. From doing research I come to understand monsters only appeared during the early part of Indian cinema on through the 1950s as part of mythologicals. These appearances were primarily as demons of one sort or another. Godzilla began his Japanese rampage in 1954 with Yotsuya in tow, Dracula and Frankenstein reemerged as British monarchs of a new bloody reign, Mexico served up some spicy monster romps, and the list goes on. But India, poor India, didn't join the party except for a few subtle ghost stories. The 1950s helped set the stage, the 1960s got the crowd going, and it wasn't until the 1970s that an honest-to-Shiva nagin horror film emerged.

In the meantime we have a few films that need to be mentioned; precursors to the vengeful nagin that was to follow.

NAGIN - "The Cobra"
(1954, D: Nandlal Jashwantlal, Hindi, DVD, subtitles)
NAGIN is a very famous film in India and not just for being a massive hit in the theatres as its soundtrack was immensely popular as well. It is a tale of two warring Nāgaland[5] tribes and the 'Romeo and Juliet' romance that occurs between two of the characters, Sanatan and Mala, from opposing tribes. A lovely film with exquisite cinematography and musical numbers. But what does this have to do with the supernatural nāgas? There are a few of the odd mythological references and a surreal segment at the end where a snake draws its poison out of a dying Mala. But that is not why the film has been singled out by movie critics as one of the most influential to the genre. You can toss aside the plot, the acting, and even the gorgeous cinematography just for one thing. That all-important element of this the film is its soundtrack.

In the film, Mala, the daughter of a warring Nāga tribe (played by the stunning Vyjayanthimala), is easily transfixed by the son of the rival chieftain whenever plays his snake charmer's horn (the horn is called a *been*). This odd-looking pipe weaves a funky harmonium-like sound that is hauntingly beautiful. Mala is always drawn to the sound and rocks as if she were a cobra caught in its magical musical vibes.

This weird melody was written by music director Hemant Kumar to be performed on the claviolin, a new experimental keyboard instrument, not unlike an early form of analog synthesizer. Its eerie sound was also utilized for an assortment of science fiction theme productions, as well as popular pop hits including "Telstar" by The Tornadoes in 1962, "Baby, You're a Rich Man" by The Beatles in 1967, and The White Stripes had it in their track "Icky Thump" (2007)[6].

The melody "Man dole mera, tan dole mere" from **NAGIN** (1954) became a staple for any self-respecting snake charmer and has been regurgitated for

[5] Yes, Nāgaland is a real part of India. See **Appendix A** for more details.
[6] Carlo Nardi, "The Cultural Economy Of Sound: Reinventing Technology In Indian Popular Cinema", The Journal on the Art of Record Production (JARP), Issue 5, Conference Papers, July, 2011.

Romantic poster art for **NAGIN** (1954)

decades in almost every nagin film since. For more on this matter check out page 97.

Another non-supernatural film of the 1950s that helped shape the genre is **NAGINA** (1951). Helmed by Ravindra Dave this mystery/thriller/horror film is primarily a haunted house effort with the element of crime tossed in for good measure. Seems like everyone is after the *nāgmani*, the magical gem that reportedly is formed on the noggin of a nagin. If one can possesses the gem then that person will be showered with riches and supernatural powers. In this film the *nāgmani* is in the form of a bejeweled ring worn by a mysterious woman. This motif of the special gem or jewel is central to many of the later films. As an interesting side note, **NAGINA** was the very first Hindi-language production to be issued an A certificate because of the film's Adult themes and the "frights and thrills" it could cause its audience.
Stars Bipin Gupta, Nutan, and Nasir Khan; music: Jaikishan Dayabhai Panka

NAAG PANCHAMI - "Festival of the Snakes"
(1953, D: Raman B. Desai , Hindi, VCD, no subtitles)
Beautifully shot mythological/devotional film about Shiva's spoiled brat of a daughter Mahadevi Mansa and her plan of torturing a devotee of her father into worshiping her as a legitimate goddess. Some fine cinematography and dance numbers, but not as accessible to a non-Hindu as the later 1972 color version by Babubhai Mistri (subtitles helped).
Stars: Nirupa Roy, Manhar Desai, Bipin Gupta, Durga Khote ; Music: Chitragupta

NAGULA CHAVITHI - "Festival of the Nag Devatas"
(1956, D: C H Narayan Moorthy, Telugu, VCD, no subtitles)
As with most of these early mythologicals, their main purpose was to deliver some sort of message of love and appreciation of the Hindu pantheon. In this tale, we find out just how the South Indian festival of Nagula Chavithi developed. Nagula Chavithi is a festival to worship *nāgadevatas*, who happen to be very important gods to expecting mothers (and women in general). The story is very similar to **NAAG PANCHAMI**, and as with that film, it is full of dense Hindu religious references.
Stars: Showkar Janaki, Jamuna, R Nagendra Rao, Nāgabhushanam and K Raghurammayya ; Music: Govardhan R, Sudharshan R

Contemporary package of Indian-made Nagin brand firecrackers with artwork similar to one of the posters for the film **NAGIN**.

The 1960s

As with the 1950s, nagin films of the 1960s didn't offer anything revolutionary in the way of plot development outside of your usual mythological run-ins. Directors Shantilal Soni and Nanabhai Bhatt were two men who did dabble in the more off-beat of India cinema. Soni was fascinated with mythological musicals and Bhatt delved into borderline science fiction and fantasy. Their films did spice up the nagin genre during this decade. The time for the sexy snaky siren was fast approaching.

NACHE NAGIN BAJE BEEN - "Dance of The Nagin With Music"
(1960, D: Tara Harish, Hindi, VCD, no subtitles)
There is nothing supernatural in this film, unless you count the actress Helen who is a dance goddess with killer moves. Her *item number* appearance alone is the only reason to sit through this wordy melodrama. An *item number* is a dance number created for a film to show off the dancing moves of a particular actor or actress. Helen is incredible as usual in this sequence. Title may refer to the first dance number of the film. In it a traditional snake charmer prances around with a *been* horn and some dancing *nāgadevatas* makes an appearance.
Stars: Kum Kum, Helen, Agha, K.N. Singh, and Sunder; Music: Chitragupta

NAAG DEVATA - "Snake Goddesss"
(1962, D: Shantilal Soni, Hindi, VCD, no subtitles)
Another classic mythological/devotional film by director Shantilal Soni, a man who loves fantasy cinema. It is really a pity that **NAAG DEVATA** and his other films have yet to make it to DVD with English subtitles.
Stars: Anjali Devi, Mahipal, Shashikala, B M Vyas, Leela Chitnis, Niranjan Sharma, and Anant Tiwari; Music: S N Tripathi

COBRA GIRL
(1963, D: Nanabhai Bhatt, Hindi, VCD, no subtitles)
Colossal Hindi starlet Ragini stars as "Cobra Girl", a very cute and perky princess who must risk her life to win back independence for her country, Naag Desh. Technicolor historical drama with some magic added to spice things up. Besides the feisty princess, the film also features an evil sorcerer, magic spells, battle sequences, and a fun soundtrack by S.N. Tripathi. Director Nanabhai Bhatt was responsible for over three dozen fantasy, devotional and mythological films, including Nāg-related title **NAAG RANI**, as well as weird cinema like **MR. X** (1957), its sequel **AADHI RAAT KE BAAD** (1960, loosely based on the H.G. Wells classic "The Invisible Man"), **SAMSON** (1964, a Dara Singh Indian "peplum" complete with giant lizard), **ROCKET GIRL** (1962), and **SON OF SINBAD** (1958—not to be confused with the 1955 American film of the same name directed by Ted Tetzlaff).
Stars: Ragini, Mahipal, Ramayan Tiwari, and Maruti Rao; Music: SN Tripathi

NAAG MOHINI - "Snake Goddesss"
(1963, D: Shantilal Soni, Hindi, VCD, No subtitles)
Famous mythological/period costume drama about a feisty Nagin princess who wants nothing to do with marrying the burly Nāga her father has chosen for her. Instead she sets her eyes upon a handsome young human prince. Loads of drama, supernatural hijinks, and some great musical numbers by Sardar Malik. Features Hindi superstar Vijaya Choudhury as the wandering nagin princess. Choudhury also starred in other supernatural-themed films such as **KHOONI KHAZANA** (1964), **BHOOTNATH** (1963) and another cobra lady film **NĀGA MANDIR** (1966).
Stars: Mahipal, Vijaya Choudhury, Rajan Haksar, Khurshid; Music: Sardar Malik

SUNEHRI NAGIN - "Golden Nagin"
(1963, D: Babubhai Mistri, Hindi, VCD, no subtitles)
This is director Bububhai Mistri's first hand at tackling the classical tale of bickering nagin sisters who fall in love with humans and all sorts of trouble occurs. Film stars the dancing sensation Helen, who happens to be one of my favorite Indian starlets, and in her first musical number of the film she tears up the dance floor doing an incredible cobra dance. Helena aside, this is a very entertaining devotional-theme Indian fantasy film full of magic, wizards, demons and other supernatural elements. Mistri was a famous special effects man and director of numerous fantasy and mythologicals from the 1940s until the 1990s when CG took over. It's a crime that **SUNEHERI NAGIN** and the rest of Mistri's delightful films aren't on DVD.
Stars: Mahipal, Helen, Sulochana, Anwar Hussain, Sapru, and Priti Bala; Music: Kalyanji Anadji

PAHADI NAGIN - "Mountain Nagin"
(1964, D: Azim; Hindi VCD No subtitles)
I've had this on back order from three different websites for over six months.

Sadly, looks as if this VCD is long out of print. There is precious little information on this film other than the usual: VCD sleeve art and minimal list of cast and crew.
Stars: Azad, Indira, B.M. Vyas, Dalpat, and Babu Raje; Music: Iqbal

NAAGA POOJE - "Prayers for the Snake"
(1965, D: Rajagopal, Kannada, VCD, no subtitles)
Devotional film wherein a young woman beseeches Nāga Devta to bless her with a child. Like most Indian fantasy films following this line of logic, it is then part-cobra, and reacts to snake charmers and their horns, etc. Enter a nagin who is jealous of the queen's half-god son and schemes on wrecking his life whenever possible. However her plans are screwed when the young boy grows up to be a handsome prince and the nagin falls in love with him. The prince spurns her advances for another women and, well, Hell hath no fury...blah, blah, blah. **NAAGA POOJE** stars Dr. Raajkumaar, an extremely popular actor and important figure in early Kannada cinema, who starred in over 200 films during his active years.
Stars: Raajashri, Dr Raajkumaar, Paapamma, Leelaavathi, and Shaantha; Music: T.G. Lingappa

The 1970s

You could say that the 1970s was the break-out decade for cobra films, with Raj Kumar Kohli's NAGIN becoming the second highest grossing film from 1976. NAGIN, with its horror elements, classic soundtrack and sexy lead actors, was responsible for creating a sub-genre all its own: the vengeance-seeking nāginī out for blood. But more about that when we get to it.

BALA BHARATAM - no translation available
(1972, D: Kamalakara Kameshwara Rao, Telugu, DVD, no subtitles)
This is a fine example of what constituted a nagin-based mythological without all the drama associated with the **NAGIN** (1976) horror. The film is based on the popular Hindu epic *The Mahābhārata*, which includes a few *nāgadevatha* in its

cast of characters. But that's all. No vengeful demon mourning her fallen mate. A very pleasant, family-oriented mythological about kings and gods during their childhood days. Sounds horrible, but the film is actually charming and has a fun traditional/pop-based soundtrack. Fun nāga note: **BALA BHARATAM** was the first "cobra" film to feature a very young seven-year-old Sridevi, who would later wow Indian audiences in her breakout film **NAGINA** in 1986.
Stars: Baby Sridevi[7], Satyanaryana, Anjali Devi, and S. V. Ranga Rao; Music: Saluri Rajeshwara Rao

NAAG MUNI - "Snake Saint"
(1972, D: Raza Mir, Urdu, YouTube, no subtitles)
A Pakistani nag film wherein a young scientist and his courageous crew travel to a remote area of the Himalayan foothills in search of rare snake venom. He meets and falls in love with a gorgeous tribal mountain woman. That doesn't go down well with the rest of her people. Nothing supernatural about this film other than weird cobra folklore (cobras drinking milk, sucking venom out of a victim's wound, etc.). Very pleasant Hammond organ-driven soundtrack and some great location work makes **NAAG MUNI** a film that begs for a proper DVD release (English subtitles would be great!). The film appears to be a remake of another Pakistani nāga film **NACHY NAGIN BAJY BEEN** ("The Mountain Snake Dance") from 1965, not to be confused with the Hindi film by Tara Harish from 1960 (I have very little data on that film other than random YouTube clips).
Stars: Swheed Murad, Rani, Sangeeta, and Masud Akhtar; Music: Nisar Bazmi

NAAG PANCHAMI - "Ceremony of Snakes"
(1972, D; Babubhai Mistry, Hindi, DVD, English Subtitles)
A film by Babubhai Mistry, Indian special effects master and director of many mythological and fantasy films—and this is his take on the tale of *Nāg Panchamī*. As with all of his productions, **NAAG PANCHAMI** is very

---

[7] Young actors and acctrees were typically billed as *Baby Whathaveyou*. Not all "Baby" actors ever made it big in film. In this case Baby Sridevi grew up to become one of the most successful and universally loved actresses of Indian cinema.

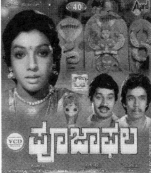

Soundtrack LP for **NAAG MUNI** and VCD for **POOJA PHALA**

colorful and very entertaining without getting preachy. Low-budget special effects, papier-mâché sets, crazy dance numbers and limited comedic bits help keep this tale of Shiva's spoiled daughter Mahadevi Mansa from wandering. Mansa presides over Naaglok, home of the nāginīs, and she's bored. She pays her father Shiva a visit, and also hangs with mother Parvati and her brothers Kartikeya (the god of war) and Ganesha (the elephant-headed god aka Remover of Obstacles). Mansa is pissed that everyone in her family is worshiped but her. She stomps and screams and throws a fit until Shiva instructs her that to be worshiped as a goddess by the humans she must first convert a very devout Shiva devotee to her cause. When this happens she will be accepted as a new goddess in the Hindu pantheon. As with the Old Testament Book of Job, Mansa tests the devotee's love of Shiva by destroying his family and causing all sorts of problems. Very entertaining.
Stars: Manher Desai, Vatsala Deshmukh, Sudarshan, and Uma Dutt; Music: Ravi

NAAGARAHAAVU - "The Cobra"
(1972, D: Puttanna Kanāgal, Kannada, DVD, English subtitles)
Famous socio-drama wherein the hot-headed lead is oft compared to a cobra, being a man who strikes first without considering his actions. One of the more important films to come out of the Kannada film industry in the early 1970s. I bought this thinking, wrongly, that there just might be some supernatural elements. Well worth checking out, but in no way a nag film other than by title. Powerhouse Kannada actress Aarathi, who plays a woman wronged by her family in this film, later appeared in the honest-to-god cobra flick **POOJA PHALA** (1974) before retiring from acting in the 1980s to become a director.
Stars: Vishnuvardhan, Aarathi, and K. S. Ashwath; Music: Vijaya Bhaskar

NAAG MERE SAATHI - "My Companion The Snake"
(1973, D: Shantilal Soni, Hindi, VCD, no subtitles)
The cute, crude animated title sequence is one of the fun parts of this devotional-period piece. Napoo, king of the naags and big fan of Shiva, answers the plea of Laxmi who's having problems producing a child for her husband the Prince. A baby is born and is under constant guard by a cobra (sent by the snake god) and soon grows up into a handsome young man. From director Shantilal Soni who made other cobra films (**NAAG DEVATA**, 1962; **NAAG MANDIR**, 1966; **NAGIN AUR SUHAGAN**, 1979) as well as one of India's earliest example of science fiction, **MR. X IN BOMBAY** (1962). In case you're wondering, **MR. X IN BOMBAY** is a thriller/Sci-fi/Fantasy/comedy, and it is as close to science fiction as early Hindi cinema comes, if you don't count the Telugu flying saucer epic **WAHAN KE LOG** (Flying Saucers over India) and moon-landing flick **CHAND PAR CHADAYEE** (Trip to the Moon), both from 1967.
Stars: Sujit Kumar, Sanjana, Mohan Choti, Dulari; Music: S.N. Tripathi

POOJA PHALA- "The Fruit of Righteous Prayers"
(1974, D: Dananjaya, Kannada, VCD, no subtitles)
Super silly but very fun film with sentient snakes, snake kung fu, a snake saving a woman from a burning building, and one of the weirdest cobra/nāga-inspired dance club routines ever. A young woman (Srinath) has a bond with cobras through her fervent worshiping at a local sacred anthill. Her family is none-too-pleased with her love of writhing serpents, and takes action. They unwisely burn the sacred cobra mound. A gang of criminals threaten the community, and a pair of nāgas show up to save the day. For some reason I keep thinking that the snakes in the film are called nāga phaal which is a very hot chili curry (yum).
Stars: Srinath, Aarathi, Arjunsarja, Mahalakshmi, and Dinesh; Music: Satyam

NĀGA KANYE - "The Cobra Girl Child"
(1975, D: S.V. Rajendra Singh Babu, Kannada, VCD, no subtitles)
Debut feature of popular filmmaker S.V. Rajendra Singh Babu, **NĀGA KANYE**

NAGIN
(1976, D: Rajkumar Kohli, Hindi, DVD, subtitles)

How influential and important this film may be is in contention, but I would like to point out that there wouldn't have been half as many of the *nagin* flicks produced if Rajkumar Kohli hadn't made **NAGIN**. Prior to **NAGIN** (not to be confused with the 1951 film of the same name), the overall genre was primarily devotional or mythological in nature, which isn't surprising when you consider the cultural significance of snakes. Kohli took the *nāgadevatha* and twisted it into a creature of hate and vengeance. In essence, **NAGIN** became one of the earliest and most successful Indian Horror films made prior to the rise of the House of Ramsay.

As Hindi movie scholar Amod Mehra puts it: "That was the age of innocence when an *ichadhari nagin* on a killing spree sent shivers up many spines." This was the mid-'70s when VHS tapes were just making their way into the stores in Mumbai, and precious few people could afford buying the tapes, let alone a pricey VCR.

The movie was a blockbuster by word-of-mouth, sending shockwaves slithering into the minds of producers and directors everywhere. **NAGIN** rip-offs started sprouting up overnight, reminiscent of the **HALLOWEEN** (1979, D: John Carpenter) or **ALIEN** (1980, D: Ridley Scott) clones that flooded the American theatres. The odd thing is that while **NAGIN** was a huge hit—as were a few other cobra films to follow—their overall box office draw was minimal. Horror still wasn't very popular as a genre mainstay as it has become today.

The plot of **NAGIN** will begin to sound very familiar the more you read deeper into this article. This is the film that set in motion the "vengeful *nagin*" sub-genre. A young man named Vijay (Sunil Dutt) saves the life of a male *nāga* (Jeetendra) and is invited to watch the *ichadhari nāg* and his mate perform their courtship dance. Vijay returns next day with a few disbelieving friends to watch the pair from hiding as the two snakes get down to business. During a particularly sexy dance number the female *naag* appears in human form (super sexy Reen Roy) while her male partner is in cobra form. Seeing what they believe is a snake about to bite the woman, one of the ignorant hunters shoots the male snake dead. Shit hits the fan when the *Nagin* cradles her dying lover and in his eyes she sees the images of all the men that were there that night. She knows what to do, and with hate in her otherwise kind soul, she sets off after the men.

Stars: Jeetendra, Sunil Dutt, Feroz Khan, Vinod Mehra, Rekha, and Reen Roy; Music: Laxmikant-Pyarel

The *nagin* tracks the men back to their city and proceeds to kill them one-by-one. The climax is a rather silly nail-biter wherein Vijay and his daughter are trapped on a rope strung between two buildings high above the streets. The *nagin* reverts to her snake form and slithers along the rope towards the humans. Luckily for them, she slips and falls to the road below only to be transfixed on a spiked gate. She passes away, but not all is in vain as we see her reunited with her late mate and they stroll off to (I assume) the peaceful land of Nāg Lok.

In case you want to have a **NAGIN** film fessssstival of your own, here's a short list of the best remakes and rip-offs: **NAGIN** (1976), **DEVATHALARA DEEVINCHANDI** (1977), **NEEYĀ** (1978), **NAAGINI** (1991), **JUNGLE KI NAGIN** (2003), and **POURNAMI NAAGAM** (2009). Break out some beer, chips or namak para, samosas, kachori, or whatever your favorite Indian snack may be. Get comfy on the sofa, but be ready to spend the weekend glued there because each of these films average 150 minutes.

is a fantasy film featuring an evil *tantrik* who turns the pretty daughter of a Brahman into a sexy nagin for evil magical purposes. He instructs her to make life miserable for a local royal family. Black magic, swordplay, spooky underground temples, fanged demons, a handsome prince, sexy ladies, and other fantastic elements make for a very entertaining film. A well-made period piece that's a throwback to the 1960s with its bizarre monsters and fine old-school musical soundtrack by the late Chellapilla Satyam, a prolific musical director of many Telugu and Kannada film.

As a sad side note, the only edition of NĀGA KANYE available is on a low quality VCD released by Shuthi Tracks Music. STM has some of the most obnoxious and intrusive watermarks ever to grace a VCD. There are times that you can't tell what's happening in the film because of the monstrously huge banner proclaiming that what you are watching is A SHUTHI TRACKS MUSIC PRODUCTION.
Stars: Vishnuvardhan, Rajashri, Bhavani, Rajanand, B V Radha; Music: Satyam

NAAG AUR NAGIN - "He Snake and She Snake"
(1976, D: Hassan Tariq, Urdu, YouTube, No subtitles)
A rarely-seen Pakistani nagin film which follows the traditional nagin tale of a snake charmer on the prowl for cobras. It is pretty much a by-the-book tale and is very mundane—that is, until the last ten minutes. In a wonderfully choreographed and handsomely photographed climax the snake charmer plays his *been* at a royal court to reveal that there is a pair of nāgas living among the humans. As the eerie melody of the been is piped, a voluptuous nāginī (the bodacious Kaveeta) dressed in a black skin-tight full body jumpsuit cavorts around the great hall in a breathtaking dance sequence. The film ends on a happy note as the pair of nāga revert to their animal forms and bite the snake charmer. The human perishes, writhing on the ground foaming at the mouth, as the snakes blissfully slither off into the sunset.
Stars: Waheed Murad, Rani, Shahid, Kaveeta; Music: Nisar Bazmi

BALA NĀGAMMA - "The Princess Bala Nāgamma"
(1976, D: P R Kaundinya, Kannada, YouTube, no subtitles)
Kannada remake of the classic 1942 Telugu film of the same name. The film has little to do with cobras other than the fact that a snake shows up from time to time to help folks out of assorted jams. Evil wizard Mayala Marathi kidnaps Bala Nāgamma, a young princess, and plans on making her his wife—by force if need be. Her family must rescue her. A fun magical mythological film that cries out for a good DVD release.
Stars: Dr. Rajkumar, Kalpana, Rajashri, Nāgaiah, Uday Kumar; Music: S. Rajeswara Rao

DEVATHALARA DEEVINCHANDI - "Prayers of the Snake Goddess"
(1977, D: Kommineni Seshagiri Rao, Telugu, DVD, no subtitles)
This is the very loose Telugu remake of **NAGIN** with elements of the 1966 film

THE NAKED PREY (starring and directed by Cornel Wilde—a film worth seeing if you can find it) added in for good measure. Whereas Kohli's **NAGIN** was a straight-ahead horror film that jumped into the supernatural within the first few minutes, director Komminenic (as he is better known) took his time to introduce the vengeful nagin. The plot entails a group of men discovering a Nāga Temple in the Nallamala jungle. There they destroy a Sheshnaag statue to uncover a treasure worth millions in jewels. To make matters worse they also interrupt a religious ritual of a local *nāgadevatha*-worshipping tribe, and attempt to kill the villagers' holy cobra. When that doesn't go too well and one of their gang is killed by the snake, they flee back to civilization with their loot. Unluckily for them they pick up a gorgeous hitchhiker (Jayamalini) who just happens to be the nagin in human form. What follows next is an assortment of attacks that leaves all but one of the transgressors dead. The major difference in this variation of the saga is that **DEVATHALARA DEEVINCHANDI** is clearly a devotional project. This is especially true as the person who saves the day is the wife of one of the men (who's an atheist). She is a very religious Shiva devotee. At the climax of the film the husband is dying from the nāginī's lethal bite. The wife she prays to Shiva for deliverance. She pleads to her god by performing a ritualized dance to save her husband. Shiva is apparently pleased and, since he is the supreme god of snakes, forces the nāginī back to the dying man to extract her poison from his body. The snake then bursts into holy flame. Clearly not the drawn-out high-wire dangling climax of **NAGIN** or the Tamil remake **NEEYĀ** (1979).

Director Kommineni Seshagiri Rao's film was a huge regional hit, but it didn't fare all that well outside of Andhra Pradesh, probably because it was shot in black and white (which was still fairly common for low-budget Telugu and Tamil films made in the 1970s). Too bad, as this was the best of the three films. Sure, **NAGIN** had the catchier musical numbers, but **DEVATHALARA DEEVINCHANDI**'s overall look was closer to home as a horror film...and, oddly enough, an Indian film that had a more satisfying Western horror film feel to it.

Incredibly, the voluptuous actress Jayamalini made over 500 films during her career in Telugu, Tamil, Malayalam, Kannada and Hindi movies. Most of these roles were as a dancer in an *item number* (a *filmi* sequence that doesn't necessarily have anything to do with the plot of the film). Jayamalini had a cameo as a belly dancer in the US/Hindi co-production **SHALIMAR/**

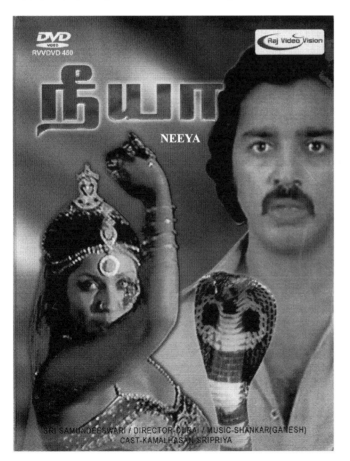
NEEYA

RAIDERS OF THE SACRED STONE (1977, D: Krishna Shah—the film also starred Sir Rex Harrison, John Saxon and Sylvia Miles). In **DEVATHALARA DEEVINCHANDI** Jayamalini totally takes the usual sexiness of a *nāgadevatha* and pumps it up a thousand-fold with some intense belly-button bared dance numbers. Great film, and one which took me ages to track down...mainly because the cover of the DVD made it look like a musical romance. Her follow-up film **JAGANMOHINI** was a huge hit as well. It's a very cool Telugu horror film with all sorts of South Indian folk elements in it.
Stars: Chandramohan, Giribabu, Jayamalini, Murali Mohan, and Prabha; Music: K. Chakravarthy

NEEYĀ - "The Snake Woman"
(1979, D: Durai, Tamil, DVD, no subtitles)
The Tamil language remake of the Hindi classic **NAGIN** (1976). The film shuns the flashier Bollywood look of the original and infuses itself with a South Asian flavor. The tale is the same; the music is pretty much the same (featuring yet another great score by Shankar-Ganesh who incorporate themes from the original Laxmikant-Pyarelali score). Famous Tamil actress Sripriya appears in the role of the nāginī made famous by Reen Roy. The opening dance track "Tere Sang Pyar" is the same as the '76 film, but as with the rest of the film, much of it is shot outside in a naturalistic setting rather than on a soundstage. In fact, all the musical numbers in this film are superior in their execution and, well, Sripriya makes for one hell of a sexy snake lady as she has some killer moves.

It's interesting to note that **NEEYĀ** is one of Sripriya's earliest roles, but it rarely shows up in her published filmographies. Granted, she made over 200 films, I still wonder if the cultural stigma of "horror" movies in India has anything to do with its being omitted.
Stars: Kamal Hassan, Sripriya, Latha, Ravichandran, Vijayakumar, and Srikanth; Music: Shankar-Ganesh

NAGIN AUR SUHGAN - "The Nāga and the Married Woman"
(1979, D: Shantilal Soni, Hindi, VCD, no subtitles)
One of four Nagin films made by director Shantilal Soni, and possibly his silliest. The gods in Naaglok decide they need to meddle in the religious lives of a family of humans. Two cobras are sent to earth to watch over the troubled family who has a young girl that can communicate with snakes. A devotional melodrama that includes scenes of live snakes "playing" instruments and a *nāgadevatha* rocking a baby in her hammock and singing her lullaby while in cobra form. A mildly diverting film at best. There is one weird scene where a cow runs to the assistance of a thirsty crying baby and dribbles milk from her udders into the child's mouth. For me, jaw-dropping scenes like that always save dull films like this.
Stars: Vijay Arora, Rita Bhaduri, Mahesh Bhatt, andiLaxmi Chhaya: Music: Usha Khanna

The 1980s

PUNNAMI NAGI - "Full Moon Cobra"
(1980, Raj Shekhar, Telugu, DVD, no subtitles)
One of the coolest South Indian horror films that has to do more with the concept of a "were-snake" than a nag. Naagulu is a young man that has been fed food poisoned with cobra venom since he was a boy by his father. Dad is a snake charmer and is building up his son's immunity to snake toxins. Sadly, something goes terribly wrong when Naagulu reaches sexual maturity. The "treatment" causes the young man to turn into a killer "werecobra" at the advent of every full moon. To his horror he soon realizes it is he who is murdering all the young women in his village. Unable to face the fact that he is slowly losing his humanity he throws himself from a cliff and ends the reign of terror.

PUNNAMI NAGI was one of actor Chiranjeevi's first roles, and his emotional skill at the inner realization and horror that Naagulu goes through is brilliant. This is a much-overlooked film, which really need to be released to a wider western audience with English subtitles.
Stars: Chiranjeevi, Madhavi, Rati Angnihotri and Narasimharaju; Music: K. Chakravarthy

GOLA NĀGAMMA - "Friend of the Serpent Goddess Nāga"
(1981, D: P. V. Raju, Telugu, YouTube, no subtitles)
Sequel to **BALA NĀGAMMA** wherein the evil wizard Mayala Marathi is accidentally revived by a "mad scientist" (you know he is a scientist because he has glasses and a goatee) who discovers the devil's old lair while

escaping a gang of angry Nāgaland tribesmen. The wizard is astonished at the development of mankind when he visits local bustling cities. As with the earlier film, there is nothing much to do with nāgas other than the occasional cobra. **BALA NĀGAMMA** is played more for laughs than thrills, and is in keeping with earlier mythological/modern mash-ups (The Hindi film **LOK PARLOK** is one of my favorites of this screwy genre). Pretty funny at times.
Stars: Satyanarayana, Narasimha Raju, Kavita, Sarathi, Jayamalini, Maada, Chalam, Gokina Ramarao, Indira, and Nāgabhushanam; Music: Chakravarthy

GARUDA REKHE - "Holy Retribution"
(1982, D: P.S.Prakash, Kannada, VCD, no subtitles)
One of the best post-**NAGIN** (1976) films to come out of the Kannada film industry in the 1980s, with great cinematography and a neatly-paced script with limited amounts of inane humor and some great cobra numbers by good-looking actors that can actually dance. A boatful of fishermen go out to sea and are caught in a horrible storm. Their boat capsizes and they are washed up on the shores of an unknown land inhabited by a savage Nāgaland tribe. Three of the men are initiated into the tribe and witness a pair of supernatural nāgas doing their mating dance. A plan is hatched to rob the tribesmen of a fabulous hoard of holy nāga treasure. The plan is hatched, the treasure is stolen, and they eventually make it back to their homeland rich beyond belief. Unfortunately for the thieves, the two nāgas track them down and are hell-bent on getting back the treasure. Features favorite nāga dance number "Aaa ravi jaarida, baa shashi moodida", as well as a rocking lounge instrumental soundtrack by Saryam.
Stars: Srinath, Madavi, Ambika, Vajramuni, and Dinesh; Music: Satyam

NAAG LOK - "Snake World"
(1982, D: Sassi Kumar, Telugu, YouTube, no subtitles)
Incredibly dull period piece/costume drama concerning murder and mayhem in a royal court. This is the third remake of the film (that I know of), and should not be confused with the similarly-named production from 2003 which is a different animal altogether. Somewhere in this mess a cobra, a nagin and even a demon pop up for just a few minutes. Low-budget melodrama with some sparse action scenes.
Stars: Prem Nazir, Jaya Bharati, Adoorbhast, Shankarnkadi, Ravi Kumar and Jagdee; Music: Shekhar Sharma

NAGIN AUR SUHGAN, one of those films where actual snakes are seen playing musical instruments. The animals where probably attached to the drums and horns in some crude fashion. Nowadays such scenes are only allowed if the cobras are computer generated effects.

SATI NAAG KANYA - "The Snake Woman"
(1983, D: Babubhai Mistri, Hindi, VCD, no subtitles)
A snake princess marries a prince of Lanka, which isn't all that great since it is about to be demolished as part of the mega-mythological tale of *The Ramayan*. Another magical devotional film from director Babubhai Mistri, with some very cool fantasy moments. **SATI NAAG KANYA** is the remake of an earlier 1956 classic of the same name by (yet again) Babubhai Mistri. Features the actor Hercules as a very chubby Lord Hanuman, the faithful monkey god. As expected there are magical moments of cheap special effects, funky musical numbers, Mistri's wry sense of humor and flair for the dramatic and very little to do with cobras.
Stars: Neera, Vikram Gokhale, Manher Desai, Jayshree Gadkar, and Anita Guha; Music: C. Arjun

SHIVA KANYE - "The Woman Devotee of Shiva"
(1984, D: Hunsur Krishnamurthy, Kannada, VCD, no subtitles)
Lush devotional film concerning Shiva and his daughter Manasa who is ceremonially worshipped on *Nāg Panchamī*—a festival of snake worship. Although Manasa is a snake goddess (one of many, but the chief one) **SHIVA KANYE** is less nagin and more mythos. Nevertheless, like the three previous **NAAG PACHAMI** films, watching **SHIVA KANYE** gives you an idea of the cultural importance between the folklore and veneration of cobras. One of the best of the mythological/devotional films (and director Hunsur Krishnamurthy liked to make them!) Too bad this has yet to have a DVD release with English subtitles. Not unlike a lot of Indian films, there was a Telugu version filmed simultaneously called **SHIVA KANYA** by the same director.
Stars: Madhavi, Rupadevi, Ramakrishna, and Rageev; Music: T.G.Lingappa

NAAGARA MAHIME - "The Miracle of the Nāga"
(1984, D: Kallesh, Kannada, VCD, no subtitles)
Devotional film about a rural village and a young boy born with scales like a snake (possibly a severe form of psoriasis). He is looked upon with scorn by everyone in his community and, after accidentally causing an injury to a young girl, he runs away to hang out in a Shiva/Nagdevi temple miles from his home. After charming a cobra with his horn to sit upon the temple's Shiva lingam, he is adopted by a local family. His is later cured of his skin affliction after a magical encounter with a cobra. Meanwhile back in his home town folks are being bitten left and right by angry snakes after the local sacred snake mound was destroyed. The prodigal son returns, snake flute in hand, to save the day and is reunited with his father and mother. No cobra humans, but plenty of sentient and magical snakes.
Stars: Sundar Krishna Urs, Sripriay, Dinesh, Jayamalini, and Musuri; Music: Ilayaraja

NAGIN AUR SAPERA - "Nagina and her Snake Charmer"
(1986, D: Bharathi Kannan, Kannada, VCD, no subtitles)
A gang of young men are goofing around the countryside when they encounter a young woman who is held against her will at a rich man's plantation. They

NAGINA
(1986, D: Harmesh Malhotra, Hindi, DVD, subtitles)

If there is one Indian film that features knock'em dead dance numbers, the ultimate in snaky sexiness, and some fine cinematography you *need* to experience, it's **NAGINA**. It is also important to note that after the mesmerizing soundtrack of the 1954 snake-charmer film **NAGIN**, Harmesh Malhorta's film contains the most influential and popular song to grace any fantasy film. More about that later.

Lovable numbskull Rajiv (Rishi Kapoor) comes from a very wealthy family. After returning from studies abroad, he settles into living in the family mansion with his mother. One day, while investigating a local temple ruin, he encounters a mysterious woman named Rajni (Sridevi). After a short courtship they get married and apparently live a happy life until a brooding snake charmer/Shiva devotee arrives on their doorstep. Bhaironnath (Amrish Puri) senses the presence of a *nagin* and confides with Rajiv's mother, telling her that Rajni is in reality a shape-shifting *nāga*. According to the holy man, she married her husband in a long-planned out case of vengeance, as Rajiv was responsible for the death of her snaky mate years earlier. But the holy man is not being up front with Rajiv's mother, as his real plan is to trap the *nagin* and force her to take him to where he will find the magical jewel known as the *nāgmani*.

What follows is a wonderful semi-devotional Fantasy film that helped set up one of the most popular themes in the genre, that of an innocent and loving *nagin* marrying a human and the menacing swami/baba/holy man/snake charmer who stalks her. The film's climax is the final number wherein Bollywood bad man Puri confronts the

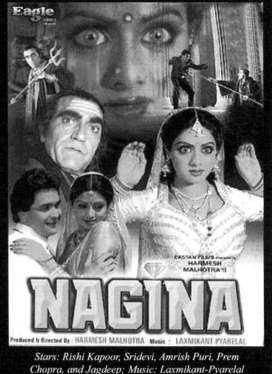

Stars: Rishi Kapoor, Sridevi, Amrish Puri, Prem Chopra, and Jagdeep; Music: Laxmikant-Pyarelal

gorgeous Sridevi (sporting bright blue "snake eye" contacts) and they have a musical showdown. It is this dance scene which is the key element that makes **NAGINA** so important. Never has a snake charmer wooed the *nāga* or *nagin* with the melody of the *been* in such a stylish and confrontational manner. Laxmikant-Pyarelal's "Main Teri Dushman" ("You are my Enemy") speaks volumes in its simplicity of verse as well as delivering the anthem that was to forever influence *nagin* soundtracks. The song also became a huge pop hit. Also, very few actresses could hope to match Sridevi when it comes to dancing (well, maybe Helen, as can be seen in the 1960 film **NACHE NAGIN BAJE BEEN**).

rescue her using their expertise as snake charmers. She falls for the hero of the film, a cocky man whose mother has some odd power over cobras.

Huge outdoor displays for the 1987 film **NAGIN AUR NAGINA**.

Flashback twenty-some years: could our young hero actually be the hybrid result of a Nag/Human romance? A difficult birth sends a father into a panic and he summons a sacred cobra from a nearby temple to save his wife and unborn son. Meanwhile, a gang of thieves sneak into the temple and steal the *nāgmani* jewel. The boy's father is blamed for the loss of the jewel and is executed. His mother is framed for the murder of a prominent member of the village and is sent to jail. Flash-forward: it's up to her son and his buddies the snakes to right a bunch of wrongs. The film goes from light and fluffy to dead serious very quickly; still, in all the scenes of brutal violence, we get at least one good Nagin dance routine. In the finale the boy is possessed by the spirit of his dead father and he brings all the remaining criminals responsible for all the tragedy in the film to justice.
Stars: Sharat Kumar, Dev Anand (not THAT Dev Anand, though), Suchitra Anandraj, Senthil, and K. Prabhakaran; Music: Deva

BELLI NĀGA - "In Nagaland"
(1986, D: N.S. Dhananjaya, Kannada, VCD, no subtitles)
Kids' film that follows the adventures of three bratty young rascals lost in the wilds of Karnataka with only a sentient snake and cow to help them survive. Not a great film, but much better than it sounds, and definitely an essential film to see if you want to see what passed as kiddie fare in 1980s India. One of the children, a young boy, is imbued with the spirit of *Nāgadevata*, and snakes just love him. Rocking soundtrack by the awesome Telugu/Kannada composer Satyam.
Stars: Tiger Prabhakar, Nalini, Ku. Nāgabhushan, B.K. Shankar, Master Vasanth, Dinesh; Music: Satyam

NACHY NAGIN - "The Dancing Snake"
(1987, D: Haider Chaudhry, Panjabi, YouTube, no subtitles)
A miserable Pakistani Nagin film; pretty bad. I would like my 150 minutes back, please.
Stars: Muzaffar Adeeb, Arif Dar, Nadira, Izhar Qazi, and Humayun Qureshi; Music: Manzoor Ashraf

NAGIN AUR NAGINA - "The Two Snakes"
(1987, D: P.S.Prakash, VCD/DVD, Hindi, no subtitles)
Another hard-to-locate film that was available on DVD and VCD, but is now out of print. Brought to you by the director of the excellent 1982 Nagin film **GARUDA REKHE**, which is why I would like to see **NAGIN AUR NAGINA** one of these days.
Stars: Ambika, Madhavi, Prabhakar, and Srinath, Music: Jeetu Tapan

NAGIN KE DO DUSHMAN - "Nagin and The Two Enemies"
(1988, D: N. Kumar, Hindi, VCD, no subtitles)
A criminal gang robs a Sheshnaag temple in broad daylight, stealing a precious *naagmani* jewel from the altar. In a daring escape they ditch their stolen goods before being caught by the police and sentenced to jail. The criminals break out of jail and terrorize a family that they believe has their loot. A cobra comes to the rescue. Okay, but nothing special.
Stars: Jayshree T, Asrani, Iftekhar; Music: Laxmi Kiran

DUI NAGIN - "Blessing of the Snake"
(1988, D: Deloyar Jahan Jhantu, Bangela, VCD no subtitles)
Highly theatrical low budget tale of nāgas vs. *tantrik* action. Fun flick full of stagy acting, inventively bad special effects, and some wild dance numbers. A happy family of *nāgdevtas* living inside a hollow tree encounter problems when a pesky snake charmer/yogi decides to cause them grief. The family—dad nāg and mom nagin with their tween son and two babies—flees their tree with the yogi in hot pursuit. In desperation the cobra couple asks some local villagers to look after their babies, however, they encounter a bad nag that is an associate of the *tantrik*. Flying snakes, black magic, a wild leopard girl, and other nuttiness make this one of the best fantasy films from India. It is almost, but not quite, as insane as Taiwanese fantastic cinema from the same decade.
Starring: Sakib Khan, Urmi, Maruf, Nasir Khan, Ahamed Sarif, Dipjal; Music: Anwar Jahan Nantu

NĀGA POURNAMI - "Moon Cobra"
(1989, D: Chola Raja, Telugu, YouTube, no subtitles)
Silly, overwrought melodrama about a young woman whose son is bitten by a poisonous snake. The boy is saved when a blind holy man infuses the dying lad with the life essence of a nāga. Sadly, the cobra expires, and when the boy grows up into a man he has to deal with the deceased snake's vengeful mate. **NĀGA POURNAMI** is a pretty sad production overall, full of tired set-pieces, bad martial arts and truly awful musical numbers by Sankar-Ganesh. The highlight comes early on in the film when we are introduced to the lively and loving pair of snakes who have ten minutes to themselves dancing and romancing before the holy man arrives on the scene.
Stars: Arj un, Radha, Kovai Sarla, and Radha Ravi; Music: Sankar Ganesh

NIGAHEN: NAGINA PART II - "The Snake Goddess Part 2"
(1989, D: Harmesh Malhotra, Hindi, DVD, subtitled)
In the 1986 film **NAGINA** we are first introduced to the writhing loveliness of Sridevi as the snake goddess acting alongside Rishi Kapoor, my least favorite Bollywood actor. In **NIGAHEN** we at least get someone who can act as her love interest. In this film, Rajni (Sridevi) is a snake woman who has married a human (Sunny Deol) and would like to live a normal life. Nevertheless, she is tracked by Bhairo Nnath, a religious man who is capable of controlling snakes. The holy man wants only one thing: the Cobra Jewel, with which he can become very powerful. Although a rehash of **NAGINA** in more ways than one, there are many effective scenes. One such predictable sequence pits Rajni against her tormentor and proceeds to perform "Khel Wohi Phir Aaj" in a lovely gold outfit.

Director Malhotra is again at the helm, steering the film into very familiar waters. I really wish he could have piloted the production into murkier depths with more horror elements, but he didn't follow that path and instead produced what he thought was something the Indian public wanted: a carbon copy of **NAGINA**. The film was very good for its genre, but it didn't fare too well at the box office.

Stars: Sridevi, Sunny Deol, Anupam Kher, AnjanaMumtaaz, Jagdeep, and Aroona Irani; Music: Laxmikant-Pyarelal

NACHE NAGIN - "The Dancing Nagin"
(198?, D: ?, Bangeladesh?, YouTube, no subtitles)
A village snake charmer has his mind set on capturing a couple of happy-go-lucky nāgas that want nothing more than to dance and worship the Sheshnaag. But as luck would have it, when the couple helps a young man who has been bitten by a snake, their supernatural actions are reported to the snake charmer who sets out after them. A fun low-budget effort with minimal effects work and a good, solid soundtrack. **NACHE NAGIN** features something rarely seen in any nagin film: a female snake charmer who uses her horn to lure out a male nag. The video source for this YouTube release comes from a battered and damaged and awkwardly film-chained VHS original. As of this publishing date I have yet to find any further information on this film, and have questions as to its actual name, date, director, language (could be Urdu), stars (other than the name Mahmud Koli), and musical director. Sad, really, as this is a very entertaining film.

NACHE NAGIN GALI GALI - "Street of the Dancing Nagin"
(1989, D: Mohanji Prasad, Hindi, VCD, no subtitles)
An evil *tantrik* will stop at nothing to obtain the precious *nāgmani* gem to cure him of curse-induced leprosy. A great deal of magic and mayhem occurs when two nāgas become involved. High drama, mistaken identity and chases happen as the nāgas transforms into little human children to escape the *tartaric*. Years pass and the two cobras decide it's high time that they resume their real forms and get on with their snaky lives—but the wizard has other plans for them. One of the better magical Nāga films not influenced by either **NAGIN** (1976) or **NAGINA** (1986)—which is a refreshing change of pace.
Stars: Meenakshi Sheshadri, Nitesh Bhardwaj, Sheerm Lagoo, and Sadashiv Sadashiv; Music: Kalyanji Anandji

NAAG NAGIN - "The Snake God"
(1989, D: Ramkumar Bohra, Hindi, VCD, no subtitles)
Weird-o **NAGIN** rip-off film from the producer of the totally screwy 1969 production **THE THIEF OF BAGHDAD**. A game warden (villainous Raza Murad) witnesses the mating dance of two nāga, and plans on snatching the female Ichchadhari Nagin Chandni (the ravishing Mandakini). Our nāgmani-hungry warden hires a thuggish snake charmer for protection after he kills the male nāga, and the female gets the okay from Shiva to take vengeance. So, technically, Nagin Chandni is a good character in this flick. One by one the warden's buddies get bitten and die. A problem occurs when the nagin falls

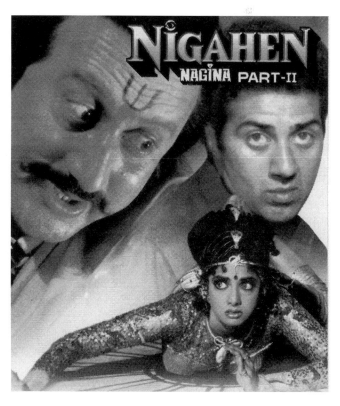

in love with the warden's son (Rajiv Kapoor). There's the ever popular motif of a snake vs. snake dance-off where the loser is struck by Mandakini and dies. The final battle sequence between the snake charmer and nagin include Kapoor's character getting tied up in a temple and being savagely beaten. What's suprising is that Laxmikant-Pyarelal's soundtrack is so very mediocre. It is made even worse by the use of a cheesy and incredibly annoying Fairlight CMI synth for the sound of the *been* horn, rather than the clavioline keyboard made popular with the film **NAGIN** (1954).
Stars: Rajiv Kapoor, Mandakini, and Raza Murad; Music: Laxmikant-Pyarelal

The 1990s

NĀGASTRAM/NAAGLAXMI - "The Snake Woman"
(1990, D: Krishna, Telugu, DVD, no subtitles)
Directed by and starring self-proclaimed Superstar Krishna, who has made over 350 movies in his long career in the Telugu film industry (as well as being one of the favorite actors in director K.R.S. Das's filmography). Krishna plays a local game warden who saves a fleeing nagin (the famous Telugu actress Vijayashanti) from a dive-bombing vulture (the sworn enemy of all cobras—them and mongooses). There is much dancing and merrymaking to be had as Krishna woos the cobra girl in defiance of her stogy old father and his family, who frown on their affair. They plan to be wed, but on that auspicious day someone observes the woman turning into a snake and killing a gang of rapists. Things go from bad to worse when a wily demon-worshipping yogi is asked by Krishna's family to ferret out the nagin out in a no-holds-barred throw-down between good and evil. As expected from a Superstar Krishna production (he wrote, edited and directed), there are some entertaining and totally frenetic fight scenes and classic weirdness, such as a cobra bottle-feeding a baby, traditional black magic, flying snakes, and funky special effects. Not to be missed.
Stars: Superstar Krishna, Vijayshanti, Sathyanarayan, Kota Srinivas Rao, and Annapoorna; Music: Chakravarthy

TUM MERE HO - "You Are Mine"
(1990, D: Tahir Hussain, Hindi, DVD, subtitled)
While not as important as other nagin-based films, this tale of snaky vengeance is a very entertaining film. A young father is cursed by a nagin when he accidentally kills her little snaky kids. She assumes cobra form and sneaks into his family's bedroom at night and bites his young son, who convulses and appears to die. A sad family sets his body adrift in a river, but he is rescued by a good snake charmer/*tantrik* who cures the boy of the snake venom. The wizard raises the boy as his own son, calling him Shiva, and teaching him all sorts of magical rituals as well as a command over snakes. When the boy grows into a man, he meets and falls in love with Paro (Juhi Chawla), from a nearby village. A very convoluted plot ensues wherein the nagin, who originally wanted Shiva dead, learns of his existence and vows to destroy his life and those he loves.

On an interesting note, this film was expected to be a blockbuster at the box office upon its initial release. The producers banked on the popularity of snaky films along with the exploits of superstar actor Aamir Khan and actress Juhi Chawla. It bombed, although the soundtrack did very well. Director Tahir Hussain was better known for his popular family films until he made **TUM MERE HO** which pretty much buried his career. As a sexy sidenote: actress and former Miss India Kalpana Iyer plays the nagin. She also starred in a guilty pleasure of mine, the insane 1982 film **DISCO DANCER**. That film was made by director Babbar Subhash, who brought the world the testosterone-fueled vehicle for Hemant Birje called **THE ADVENTURES OF TARZAN** (1985).
Stars: Aamir Khan, Juhi Chawla, Ajit Vachani, and Sudhir Pandey; Music: Anand & Milind Chitragupth

ARANYADALLI ABHIMANYU - No translation available
(1991, D: Bhargava; VCD, no subtitles)
A police officer/game warden becomes involved with a lovely Nagin who masquerades as his girlfriend for nightly flings. Local poachers set out to get him and his snaky lady friend by hiring a yogi to kill her. Film includes distasteful scenes of live cobras battling to the death. This is not uncommon as live animals are usually cheaper than special effects in Indian productions. In a weirdly cool segment, the nagin hears the rooster's crow and attempts to transforms back into her snake…in front of the warden's *real* girlfriend. But something goes embarrassingly wrong and she is left lying on the bathroom floor, a large snake body with a human head. This sequence is very odd because as far as I know, *ichchadhari nāgin* are not nocturnal, nor do they react to a rooster crowing (which is very Western Horror in origin). Our game warden discovers that he is the reincarnation of the female nagin's long-dead mate. Another low-budget Kannada film with various post-**NAGINA** elements.
Stars: Ambarish, Ramesh Bhat, Tennis Krishna, Taara, Devaraj, Jaggesh; Music : Lakxmikant Pyarelal

NAAG MANI - "The Holy Snake Jewel"
(1991, D: V Menon, Hindi, DVD, subtitles)
The god Shiva grants a boon to a devoted cobra: the precious *naagmani*, a magical jewel. Unfortunately the stone is lost and is in the clutches of the evil *tartaric* Trikaal (Kiran Kumar). A nāga appears to a holy man in the form of a snake to ask for help, but the creature is mortally struck down by the fearful human. Before succumbing to the wounds, the nāga informs the priest of the *tartaric* and the stolen *nāgmani*. The priest sends his son (Sumet Saigal) to carry out the mission, and in the meantime the young man falls in love with Nagina, Trikaal's daughter (1988 Miss India winner Shikha Swaroop). While beautifully shot and full of musical numbers sure to get your foot tapping, the film gets bogged down with way too much mushy love stuff…but then again, this wouldn't be an Indian fantasy film if there weren't such scenes. Two nāgas show up just in time to save the film, and the last 30 minutes is definitely worth watching. The final battle between Trikaal and the nāgas include a band of cobras who play musical instruments while the magical battle commences. Yes, *real live* snakes strapped to traditional Indian drums and horns. It was a decade before India's Ministry Of Social Justice And Empowerment enforced the "Performing Animals (Registration) Rules" when this kind of animal abuse would be tempered and CG cobras would flood the cinema.[8]

Director V. Menon was also responsible for a 1989 nagin film **TUE NAGIN MAIN SAPERA** which I have yet to find. Prior to **NAAG MANI** Mernon directed the 1990 "A"-certificate sexy/action film **JUNGLE LOVE – A TARZAN MOVIE**, an entertaining (and unofficial) Apeman film.
Stars: Sumeet Saigal Shikha Swaroop Kiran Kumar Aruna Irani Gulshan Kumar; Music: Annu Malik

SHESHNAAG

(1990, D: K. R. Reddy, Hindi, DVD, subtitled)

SHESHNAAG isn't a great film, but it does have all the elements of a very entertaining one. K.R. Reddy approached this on the level of a comedy, or at least a film that wanted very much to be a parody. It doesn't work all that well, what with all of the comedic interludes, Rishi Kapoor's "idiot brother" act, and the occasional mugging for the camera. However, by the brutal end of the film SHESHNAAG turns out rather satisfying.

The film opens with the evil snake hunter Aghoori (Danny Denzongpa) hunting is after two *nāgas*, Pritam (Jeetendra) and Banu (Madhavi). On every lunar eclipse the two *nāgas* perform a sacred dance at an ancient underground Shiva temple and unlock a treasure trove that holds immense wealth. Aghoori believes they also hold the key to immortality. He and his minions track the snaky couple to a nearby village where they are hiding. Our story then shifts to the turbulent lives of a kindly sister, Champa (Rekha), and her simple animal-loving brother, Bhola (Kapoor). Champa is married to a real asshole who "loses" her in a gambling bet to a gang of rapists. To save her honor, Champa throws herself off a cliff and into the sea, where she perishes. Shortly thereafter the female *ichchadhari nagin* shape-shifts into Champa, and her mate takes the form of the household's new servant. Bhola is oblivious to the entire ruse as he spends his free time playing with animals. The *nāgas* watch over Bhola while hiding out from the wizard. Eventually Aghoori sniffs out the snakes, and there is a final violent confrontation at an old underground Shiva temple wherein our sorcerer discovers—much to his chagrin—that he is not all that immortal.

SHESHNAAG is no classic, but is one of the more accessible films of the genre. The addition of Bollywood powerhouse stars Rishi Kapo and Danny Denzongpa to the roster of sexy heavyhitters Jeetendra (who played the male *nāga* in Kohli's NAGIN) and Rekha (who had just come off a string of successful thrillers including the bizarre facial-surgery themed Khoon Bhari Maang from 1988) can't hide the fact that the story is yet another rehashing of earlier *nagin* tales. The *filmi* sequences are pretty good, especially the confrontation between Aghoori and Pritam, wherein the *nagina* is all decked out in a form-fitting gold-scaled outfit. The final temple battle stands out, as I don't mind seeing Kapoor getting beaten bloody and senseless.

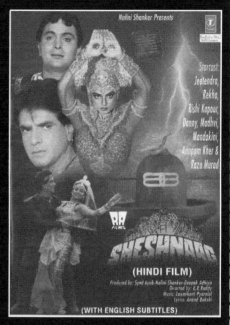

Stars: Rishi Kapoor, Jeetendra, Rekha, and Danny Denzongpa; Music: Laxmikant-Pyarelal.

NAAGINI - "The Snake Woman"
(1991, D: Sripriya, Kannada, VCD, no subtitles)
More or less a sequel to Kohli's NAGIN, wherein the spirit of the dead cobra lady hunts down and kills various humans whose parents killed her in the past. The nāgin senses something oddly familiar about one young man; she is drawn to him, and he to her. There's a haunted painting, good vs. bad cobra battles, funky stage show numbers, demonic possession, snake charmers, and a weirdly satisfying ending wherein we discover that the young man is none other than the nāginī's reincarnated mate. The film ends when they finally hook up and make out. In the throes of passion both of them revert to cobra form and slither off to a nearby sacred termite mound together. Sweet. Ain't love grand!
Stars: Shankarnag, Geetha, Devarj, Radhika, Ananthanag, Rajani; Music: Shankar-Ganesh (with tracks by Laxmikant-Pyarelal)

SHIVA NĀGA - "The Snake of Shiva"
(1991, D: K.S.R. Das; Kannada, VCD, no subtitles)
When an evil yogi attempts to snatch sacred cobras from a snake mound, he is stopped by a woman and her child. Her baby is killed by the yogi, but because the mother defended the mound, the local nāga goddess impregnates her and a girl child is born. Years pass and the child grows into a young woman who falls in love with a young man who just happens to be a reincarnated cobra. But as with all Indian dramas, there are problems with his family. VCD sleeve promised snaky fun with sexy dance numbers and an evil yogi, however all we really got was a load of bad comedy about poop fetishes and only a smidgen of supernatural thrills. One of director K.S.R. Das' least-effective films (and one of his last), although the actual Ichchhadhari mating dance toward the end and the confrontation between the yogi and the creatures is entertaining. A variant of NAGINA and SHESHNAAG. Opening theme is a wonky Indian rip-off of "Funky Town" by Lipps, Inc.
Stars: Malashri, Arjun Sarja, Muma Chandru, Doddanna; Music: Rajan-Nagendra

NĀGA KANYA / AMMA NĀGAMMA - "The Snake Woman"
(1992, D: Chola Rajan, Tamil, YouTube, no subtitles)
Strangely compelling account of a young woman, a nagin (Nirosha), who falls in love with a crooner (Suresh) at a local community college. Her initial sexy snakiness also attracts the attention of campus goons who stalk and rape women. She is a good Shiva-worshipping nagin though, in town to help people, and it is soon revealed that the object of her infatuation is actually the reincarnation of her long-dead nāga mate. After the criminals knife her object of affection she goes on a snaky rampage. She seduces then kills the men one by one. A snake charmer/swami is hired to save the gang from her attacks, but to no avail, as she is able to shoot laser beams from her eyes, and even invades a secure home

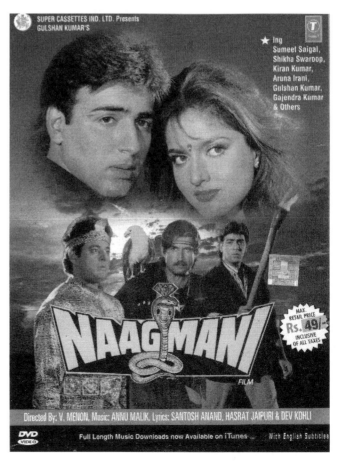

85

by possessing a television set. By the end of the film the supernatural lovers are once again reunited and get married—in snake form. Well-produced little epic for a Grade-C thriller with decent acting from most everyone involved. On the bizarre-o-meter, the seriousness of the film is constantly interrupted by odd passages of actual live snakes used for scene of celebratory musical numbers that take place in *Nāg Lok*. The actual animals are taped or otherwise secured to the instruments so they can "play" drums and horns.
Stars: Suresh, Nirosha; Music: unknown

NAAG PANCHAMI - "The Festival of The Snake"
(1992, D. Vijay Bhaskar, Oriya, YouTube, no subtitles)
Oriya Cinema isn't very large, but it did produce a few devotional/thriller productions including this nagin film that has little to do with the traditional tale of "Naag Panchami" and more to do with the *ritual* associated with *Nāg Panchamī*. A gang of criminals is being stalked by a nagin due to past transgressions. Years ago they had kidnapped a young woman and her baby daughter, murdering the woman so that her husband could inherit the family fortune. The thugs bury her corpse under a sacred cobra mound outside a temple to Lord Subramanya (another name for a local snake god). Not a smart move since she had a gift with animals verging on the holy (she had a sentient elephant as a pet). Her abandoned child is discovered by the goddess Durga and raised by a monkey with assistance from a monk associated with Shiva Ji. Years later the child, named Nagina, shows up at her father's home and soon folks begin to die. Everyone should have known the kid was supernatural from the moment she spoke, as her voice has that echoing quality Asian audiences instantly associate with ghost, demons, and gods. A priest is brought in during the final half an hour of the film and that's when things really begin to roll. Clocking in at 164 minutes, **NAAG PANCHAMI** is one of the longest Nagin films that I know of.
Stars: Uttam Mohanty, Prasanjeet, Rutupurna Ghosh, Debashree Roy; Music: ?

NAGIN AUR LOOTERE - "The Girl and the Cobra"
(1992, D: Mohan T. Gehani, Hindi, VCD, no subtitles)
I cannot for the life of me get my hands on this film. **NAGIN AUR LOOTERE** is not available on YouTube, and every time I try to order the VCD it mysteriously sells out. However, I do have the LP, and the soundtrack by Anand-Laxman is very good. For all intents and purposes, **NAGIN AUR LOOTERE** sounds like fun. The plot is that of the traditional barren mother

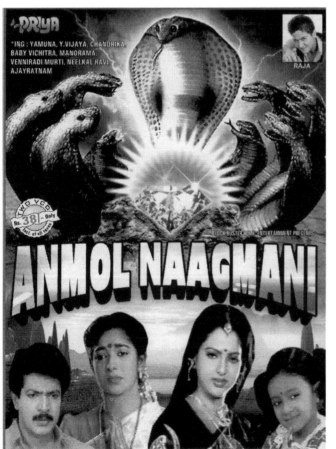

who prays to *Naagraj* the snake god and has a very special baby, this time around, a son they name Nagesh. Nagesh falls in love with a pious woman of the town, but unbeknownst to him he was promised to Rajni, to whom he was married in a previous nāgan life. Apparently, there is lots of court room drama and shape-shifting antics in this film.
Stars: Neelima Azim, Goga Kapoor, Shakti Kapoor, and Anupam Kher; Music: Anand-Laxman

NĀGA VALLI / NĀGA KANYA - "The Snake Woman"
(1992, D: OM Sai Prakash, Tamil, DVD, no subtitles)
A father begs the local Shiva-based snake deity Rjanāga to help his wife who is having a difficult delivery. The boon is granted and she gives birth to a baby girl—one which has a strange connection with snakes. Great sexy stuff by actresses Ooha and the late Silk Smitha. Not a bad film, full of some great musical passages and featuring Rami Reddy as a menacing snake charmer/yogi facing off against nāginī-possessed Ooha in a wonderfully filmed devotional battle. From director Om Sai Prakash who also made one of the best nagin films with **NAAG SHAKTI/NĀGA DEVATHAI** (2000) and one of the least successful with **SHRI NĀGA SHAKTI** (released in 2010).
Stars: Ooha (Sivaranjani), S. Smitha, Prakash Raj, Ranganath, Rami Reddy, and Y. Vijaya; Music: Vandemathram Srinivas

DAAKSHAYINI - "The Goddess Daakshayini"
(1993, D: Ram Narayan, Kannada, VCD, no subtitles)
A very pregnant woman collapses outside of a Sheshnaag temple and gives birth to a very auspicious baby at the foot of a sacred anthill/cobra nest. Years later her child—now an obnoxious loud mouthed little seven year old girl—discovers that she's imbued with divine powers after a visit to a temple dedicated to the goddess Daakshayini. There she encounters a nagin who informs the child of her divinity. **DAAKSHAYINI** is a fairly dull tale of criminals and religious devotion, but there are a few interesting sequences wherein supernatural elements come into play. Actress Baby Syamili runs around flicking her tongue like a cobra and delivering religious knowledge with obnoxious abandon. She is attacked by a condor (another arch-enemy of snakes), has a sentient dog as a protector, kills criminals with her cobra venom powers (not sure how this works, she stares at someone then they fall to the grown foaming at the mouth), and is pestered by a snake charmer hired by a criminal gang. Not horrible, but not all that great either. Final dance number where the little star dances with a temple full of belly-dancing nāginī is pretty weird. The title of the film, **DAAKSHAYINI**, refers to the goddess Sati who is an aspect of Devi, and first consort of Shiva.
Stars: Baby Syamili, Srinath, Vinay Aprasad, Shruthi, and Zsuneel; Music: Shankar-Ganesh

NĀGA JYOTI - "The Shining Cobra"
(1994, D: Ramnarayan, Oriya, VCD, no subtitles)
A young girl has always had some connection with cobras. She plays with and shares her toys and milk with the snakes of a local sacred anthill mound. As she grows into a precocious tween she develops psychic powers and is chosen by a local female nāginī as her special human. A scientist (and we know that because he wears glasses and has a goatee—sure sign that he is a scholar of some sort) uses his sophisticated nāga-hunter computer and mechanical gadgets to track down the same cobra lady. He wants to capture the nāginī and use her powers to fuel his nefarious studies. In a final showdown between religion and science, our cobra lady is captured by the scientist and subjected to the vicious attacks of robotic vultures. Luckily, our *devi* is able to fashion a holy *lingam* (male symbol of Shiva) and *yoni* (female symbol of the Goddess Shakti) out of sand. She prays to Shiva for help and turns the awful avian automatons on the scientist who is then killed. Features a wonderful soundtrack by Prafulla Kar.

Director Ramnarayan (sometimes credited as Ram Narayan) has made over 120 films in many languages. His nagin-related films include **DAAKSHAYINI** (1993), **NAG DEVTA** (this has yet to be confirmed, 1994), **NAAG LOK** (2003), devotional ones like **RAJA KALI AMMAN** (2006), and most recently the incredibly bizarre demon-possession/cyborg/kid film **KUTTI PISASU** (2010). If you warp reality a tad bit you could say that Jennifer Lynch's film **HISSS** (2010) is a very loose remake of **NAAG JYOTI**. Seriously, I think it is.

NAAG JYOTI is also a fine example of how different video companies repackage the very same film. A Hindi-dubbed version of **NĀGA JYOTI** was released in 2007 on VCD as **ANMOL NAAGMANI** listing a different cast and crew on the sleeve art. Of course, I bought this twice. Who wouldn't?
Stars: Uttam Mohanty, Satabdi Roy, Anushree Das; Music: Prafulla Kar

NĀGAMANDALA

"The Snake Mandala Magic"
(1997, D: T.S. Nāgabharana, Kannada, DVD, no subtitles)

Based on a famous stage play by Girish Karnad, this is the story of a young bride who, bored with her husband's lackluster lovemaking, decides to rev up his libido with a love potion. She mixes the drug with milk for him to drink, but accidentally spills the concoction on a sacred anthill/cobra mound. A *nāga* drinks up the drug and falls in love with the young woman, visiting her nightly in the form of her husband. All good things must come to an end, and when her spouse discovers the affair, all hell breaks loose. An excellent film that needs subtitles and has been gaining a wider audience due a recent revival of the stage play. NĀGA MANDALA is considered one of the more important films to come out of the Kannda film in the 1990s.

While doing research for this article, mining the Internet for any information available on this genre, NĀGA MANDALA frequently popped up. However, Google results were not for the film, but rather the stage play. Thanks in part to the Indian/South Asian diaspora in other countries, many of the classic plays by Girish Karnad and Rabindranath Tagore have become popular again.

Stars: Prakash Rai, Vijayalakshmi, Mandya Ramesh and B. Jayashri; Music: C. Aswath and Srihari L. Khoday.

NAGINER PROTISHODH - "To Fight of The Cobra"
(1994, D: K. Sankar, Bengali, VCD, no subtitles)
Fun low-budget production wherein a nagin protects a young girl. Silly, but engaging film featuring cobras, ghosts, and floating skeletons. Another lost classic that needs to be released on DVD with subtitles.
Cast: Sreedhar, Shovana, Korai Sarala, SM Chandram, KR Bijaya; Music: KV Mahadevan

NAG DEVTA - "The Snake Goddess"
(1994, D: Ramanarayan, Marathi, VCD, no subtitles)
Horrible film about a little girl who is possessed by a pesky nagin out to ruin everyone's lives. Features a really annoying little child actress as the giggling cobra-possessed girl. Nightmarishly bad. Features the staples of all bad nagin films: a funny monkey and sentient dog. Ugh. The only redeeming sequence in this feature is when Lord Hanuman the Hindi monkey god shows up upon request of the film's simian star. This chubby low-budget variant of the god pops in, blesses the little girl, then vanishes.

Director Ramanarayan may or may not be the same individual that made the superior **Nāga JYOTI** (1994) or **NAAG LOK** (2003). I wouldn't be surprised if he was. Sometimes the data available on these film are be very conflicting. Whatever the case, **NAG DEVTA** is a horrible film.
Stars: Ramesh Bhatkar, Rekha Rao, Meenakshi and Lalitesh; Music:?

NAG DEVTA/COBRA - "The Snake Goddess"
(1994, D: Masud Butt, Pakistani, unknown, no subtitles)
No additional information on this film. Information on it is rather sketchy. It could very well be a remake of the previously reviewed film of the same title. But let's hope not.
Stars: Afzaal, Mustafa Qureshi, Reema; Music: ?

NAGIN KANYA - "The Snake Woman"
(1995, D: Swapan Saha, Bengali, VCD, no subtitles).
An anxious father prays to Shiva to save his expecting wife from a troubled childbirth. His boon is met and when he gets the news of his daughter's birth he rushes from the temple and accidentally bumps into a meditating swami. The annoyed holy man curses the excited father who drops dead at the site of his newborn. Years later the child, Pooja, is chasing a human-faced cobra and gets lost in the forest. A man from a local tribe of cobra charmers discovers the child and takes her to his people. There Pooja encounters the cobra again and befriends it. She grows up worshipping the cobra and becomes a much-desired performer with the snake charmers and catches the eye of a handsome young man called Vijay. It's the typical tale of rich boy falling for peasant girl and all the baggage that comes with loving outside of your caste (not to mention there's that whole thing with the cobra-goddess). This is an early film for the now-popular (and gorgeous) Bengali and Hindi actress Rituparna Sengupta who shakes her booty and sizzles in this colorful low budget supernatural drama.
Stars: Chiranjeet, Rituparna Sengupta, Koushik Bannerjee, Anuradha Ray, Anushree Das, Dulal Lahiri, Lily Chakravarty; Music: Anupam Dutta

MANI NAGESWARI - "The Power of the Cobra"
(1995, D: Bijay Bhaskar, Oriya, YouTube, no subtitles)
Snaky melodrama intermingled with murder and mayhem when a small town is terrorized by a madman killing young women. The good-looking killer targets a woman blessed as a child by the cobra aspect of Shiva. This is when the film really begins to pick up steam. Besides being tormented by her step-sisters, she is murdered by the psycho. Her spirit returns as a nagin-like entity to torment her hateful family and seek solace in the destruction of her murderer. Pretty dull for the most part, but there are brilliant moments of devotional horror, not to mention the wide-eyed beauty of Bengali actress Rachana Banerjee in an early role (not normally on her filmography). Pity the soundtrack and musical numbers are horrible.
Stars: Rachana Banerjee, Debu Bose, Siddhant Mahapatra, and Runu Parija; Music: Akhaya Mohanty

HASINA AUR NAGINA - "The Bandit and The Snake"
(1996, D: Gautam Bhatta, Hindi, VCD, no subtitles)
Mildly entertaining crossover/mash-up where the Daaku (bandit) genre bumps uglies with Nagin. Two orphaned girls are found by the riverside by two good samaritans. One is adopted into the local bandit gang, and the other by a clan of snake charmers. One sister grows up to be a bad-ass and gorgeous criminal, and the other an equally-attractive nag dancer who communes with cobras. When our bandit queen is wooed by a male nāg (he presents her with a *nāgmani* jewel), snaky fun kicks in and the sisters are reunited—but not before lots of drama ensues.
Stars: Sadashiv Amrapurkar, Jagdeep, Kiran Kumar, and Ekta Sohini; Music: Dilip Sameer Sen

PRATIRODH - "The Opposition"
(1997, D: Srinibas Chakraborty, Bengali, VCD, no subtitles)
A low-budget Bengali film that is a loose remake of **TUM HERE HO** (1990). A big-city police officer is called to a rural village to investigate a murder. The suspect is a young woman who he knew when he was a child. He had believed that she had died of a snake bite received after tormenting some cobras at the local sacred snake mound; however, she didn't die, but was raised by a poor family who had discovered her unconscious body floating down a river. Somehow in all this mess there is a subplot of drug trafficking, prostitution

DEVI

(1999, D: Kodi Ramakrishna, Telugu, DVD, subtitles & dubbed)

You always remember your first love, as it is usually an experience that is burned into your psyche forever. It's like a meth high, or so I've heard. That is what the film **DEVI** became for me after I first saw it. The tagline "A SPECIAL EFFECTS FILM" caught my attention. **DEVI** delivered on that regards, and gave my libido a good workout when the actress Prema strutted on the scene as the titular snake entity. **DEVI** is, without a doubt, the film to see if you want to fully experience a *nagin* film. Lucky for you, it has been released in the USA as **GODDESS** (which is what **DEVI** means anyway), and is available on DVD as well as through Netflix!

The plot is nothing too terribly original, but its execution is rather fun to watch. In an opening sequence not unlike Steven Spielburg's kiddie classic **E.T. THE EXTRA-TERRESTRIAL** (1982), a group of *nag kanya* disembark from a weird spaceship to gather around and worship a holy *lingum*. After a clever dance routine, all the snakes are taken back up into the ship except for one…Devi, who must've been off in the bushes peeing or something. The ship vanishes up into the clouds and Devi is left in the human realm to fend for herself. In the meantime, a young woman (Vanitha) who is a Naag-Shiva devotee, is constantly harassed by her no-good family members. Devi assumes the lovely form of a young woman (Prema) and comes to her aid (she might as well, because the nag has no idea when Spaceship Shiva will return).

If guarding her ward against her conniving family isn't work enough for the snake, an evil wizard invokes the power of the dark arts in order to destroy Devi. The wizard joins forces with the young woman's family and together they plot the destruction of both the goddess and her devotee. There are numerous exciting close calls leading up to an exciting climax where the wizard, now imbued with demonic powers, has all but destroyed everything good in Devi's life. Time for the Good vs. Evil showdown: Devi dances a devotional whirl wind and a gigantic multi-headed cobra known as the *Sheshnaag* appears to gobble up the wizard.

The ending shouldn't be too much of surprise, as director Kodi Ramakrishna was responsible for the wild production **AMMORU** (1995). That film is the coolest goddess vengeance movie ever. The man has a love for special effects and his films are really good-looking, to boot. Sure, he uses extensive CG effects, but for the most part their integration into the final product works for me. Ramakrishna's other devotional thrillers **DEVI PUTRUDU** (2000), **DILER/ANJI** (2004)—and especially his latest, **ARUNDHATI** (2009)—are all worth seeing if you can find them.

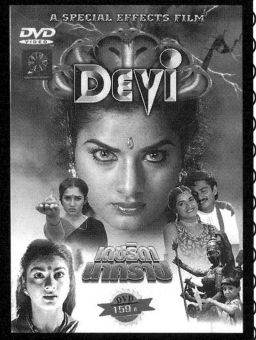

Stars: Prema, Vanitha, Abu Salim, and Bhanuchander; Music: Devi Sri Prasad

As a side note, the actress Prema has appeared in many Devotional, *Nagin*, and Horror films, as well as the usual number of dreadful comedies and soapy melodramas that seem to be an essential for any Indian actress wanting to advance her career.

---

rings, and baby snatching. A very talky film with a few interesting supernatural moments and traditional musical numbers in and around temples.
Stars: Tapas Pal, Satabdi Roy, Sumitra Mukherjee, Anup Kumar, Biplab Chatterjee, Chinmoy Roy, Gyanesh Mukherjee, Nirmal Kumar; Music: Pradip Hardeb

NAG NĀGINĪ - "The Female Snake"
(1998, D: Swapan Saha, Bengali, VCD, no subtitles)
Low-budget but colorful costume drama about a snake charmer on the hunt for cobras who discovers an orphaned little girl and adopts her into his family. Little does he realize she's a supernatural creature…yes, a nagin. She grows up in his family keeping an eye on him and his charmer ways. Things get complicated when a male nāg catches her scent and there is love in the air. We later learn that he is an 'Icchadhari Saap' known as *Seshnaag* who is in love with his *Seshnaagini*, from whom he had been separated during childhood. Of course humans can't help but stick their noses into the courtship of the cobras and all heck breaks loose. One of the coolest "hip" soundtracks of any Bengali nagin movie. Stars sizzling hot Bengali actress Sreelekha Mitra as the nagin.
Stars: Rituparna Sengupta, Abhishek Chatterjee, Sreelekha Mitra, Biplab Chatterjee, Kaushik Banerjee, Dulal Lahiri, Anamika Saha, Gita Karmakar; Music: Ashok Bhadra

The 2000s & Beyond

BISHE VORA NAGIN - No translation available
(2000, D: Delowara Jahan Jhantu, Bengali, VCD, No subtitles)
A mean ol' snake charmer is out to capture as many of the magical nag and nagins as he can get. In the meantime, he creates problems for a happy family of shape-shifting cobras that live inside an old temple. Similar to **DUI NAGIN** (1988) in its tale of family separation and reunification, love, and the battle of good versus evil. A bit talky and staged, but fun nevertheless.
Stars: unknown; Music: Anwar Jahan Nantu

NAAG-RANI - "The Snake Child"
(2000, D: Ramnarayan, Telugu, VCD/DVD, no subtitles)
"Family" comedy-drama about a "wonder snake, a wonder dog, and a wonder child" and their misadventures involving the loves and lives of a small rural village. Pretty horrible stuff. Even the best scene in the movie involving "cobra kung fu" can't save **NAAG-RANI** from the shit pile.
Stars: Arjun Ambika, A Wonder Snake, A Wonder Dog, and A Wonder Child; Music: Shankar Ganesh

AMMA NĀGAMMA - "Mother Snake Goddess"
(2001, D: C.H. Balaji Singh Babu; Kannada, VCD, no subtitles)
Another remake of Rajkumar Kohli's **NAGIN**; the well-worn tale of a group of men who kill the mate of a Nagin, and the vengeance that ensues. ZZZzzzzzzz....
Stars: Damini, Kumar Govind, Charanraj; Music: Gopi Krishna

NAGULAMMA - "The City of the Snake"
(2000, D: K.S.R. Das, Telugu, YouTube, no subtitles)
Last film by famed Telugu director K.S.R. Das, the genius behind the craziness of **MOSAGALLAKU MOSAGADU** (1971) and **PISTOWALI** (1972). This is also his second nagin-based film, and one of his best-looking to boot. **NAGULAMMA** isn't as nutty as his earlier films, and the violence is dialed down a bit, although there are some fun scenes of "kung fu". Not the most exciting cobra film, but the last fifteen minutes are worth checking out. The film's snaky nagin runs afoul of a dedicated snake charmer in a very colorful psychedelic-tinged snaky devotional dance off. One of the better uses of computer generated effects for any Indian film made during this decade.
Stars: Pruthvi, Maheshwari, Arun Pandian, and Ramya Krishna; Music: Dina

NAAG YONI - "The Snake & Her Boyfriend"
(2000, D: S.D.N. Azhar; Hindi, VCD, no subtitles)
More of an Indian **ANIMAL HOUSE** than a horror film; when college pranksters dress as fellow female coeds so they can shower with the ladies (fully clothed, of course). After an hour of this college nonsense, the film begins to cook when the college party king runs over a male cobra with his jeep. The

creature's mate vows vengeance. Dreadfully dull film.
Stars: Usha Bachchani, Shradha Sharma, Sikander, and Ahmed Kahn; Music: Ram Shankar

JAANI DUSHMAN EK ANOKHI KAHANI - "The Arch Rival"
(2002, D: RajKumar Kohli, Hindi, DVD, subtitled)
This film was a major disappointment for fans of nagin films worldwide. The shock was that this movie was from the director of the original **NAGIN** (1976) and the Hindi "werewolf" film **JAANI DUSHMAN** (1979). The story is weak (two nagdevtas are separated due to a curse, but are reunited in the 21st Century), the computer-generated creature effects are atrocious, and the musical numbers and overall soundtrack just don't work. Horrible. The only redeeming feature of this embarrassment is the magnificent Amrish Puri making an all-too-brief late career appearance as the holy man Sadhu.
Stars: Munish Kohli, Sunil Shetty, Sunny Doel, Sharad Kpoor, and Manisha Kopirala; Music: Anand Raaj Anand

NAAG LOK - "The Snake World"
(2003, D: Ramanarayanan; , DVD, English subtitles)
High-tech nagin goddess film crossover directly influenced by the popularity of Durga goddess film **AMMORU** (1995), no doubt because Ramya Krishan, the lead cobra actress in this film, appeared as the Durga-associated goddess Ammoru in that film. A mother and her child visit a sacred Nāga temple, where they are attacked by a drunk and some of his friends. The mother is murdered, leaving her orphaned child to be nursed by the goddess Nageswari Amman, and brought up by a local clan of snake charmers. Years later the young girl is murdered by four drunken thugs and she is buried outside of the same temple. She comes back from the dead as a vengeful nagin, marrying one of the thugs. From that point onward she begins to torment and torture her husband and his friends. Computer-generated special effects run rampant throughout the film: hundreds of snakes attack a village, a giant statue chases a man and stomps him into the ground, and all sorts of cheap CG wackiness.
Stars: Ramya Krishnan, Karan, Prithvi, and Vivek; Music: S.A. Raj Kumar

JUNGLE KI NAGIN - "The Snake of The Jungle"
(2003, D: Ramesh Lakhiani, DVD with subtitles)
This low-budget crapfest stars Kanti Shah regulars Amit Panchori, Anil Nagrath, Reena Kapoor, Tina Joshi, and Vinod Tripathi, but despite its obvious

limitations **JUNGLE KI NAGIN** is very entertaining (whereas a similarly-budgeted film **NAAG YONI** isn't), and it doesn't hurt that this was released on a DVD with English subtitles. A nagin possesses the body of a young woman with the intention of causing the woman and her boyfriend harm. Of course, this was because of the usual transgression involving the death of the creature's mate. Stupid but fun... and a hell of a lot better than Kohli's **JAANI DUSHMAN EK ANOKHI KAHANI** (2002).

Director Ramesh Lakhiani has made other Grade-C horror and action trash including **KHOPDI: THE SKULL** (1999), **Kabrastan** (2000), **DAKU RANI** (2000) and **ZINDAGI AUR MAUT** (2002).
Stars: Amit Panchori, Anil Nagrath, Reena Kapoor, Tina Joshi, and Vinod Tripathi; Music: Naeem Shrahan

NAAGESHWARI - "All Hail The Snake Goddess"
(2003, D: Alahari, Telugu, DVD, no subtitles)
Released on DVD as both **JAI MAA NAAGESHWARI** and **JAI MAA NAAGDEVI**. A young devout woman is having a miserable time conceiving a child with her husband, and begs Naageshwari (Prema), the local cobra goddess, for a child. While pregnant with child she and her husband are murdered by an

NAAGSHAKTI
(NAAG SHAKTI/NĀGA DEVATHAI - "The Snake Goddess"
(2000, D: Om Sai Prakash, Kannada, DVD, subtitles)
NAAGSHAKTI could have been the ultimate Nagin film featuring two amazing actresses, Prema (of **DEVI**, 1999 fame) and Soundrya (of **AMMORU**), had the production on this devotional thriller not been so...um...weird. Director Om Sai Prakash returns to familiar territory in this loose remake of his 1992 film **NĀGA VALLI/NĀGA KANYA**. What I find odd about this film—other than the very stagy representation of Nāg Lok, which resembles some hi-tech high school play—is that Om Sai Prakash had the chance to work with Soundrya and Prema. Both women had previously starred in two special effects blockbusters by Kodi Ramakrishna, **AMMORU** and **DEVI**, and Prakash tries his damnedest to make them as spectacular as Ramakrishna's. He doesn't quite pull it off. **NAAGSHAKTI** resembles a papier-mâché Mythological from the 1960s with loads of cheap trick photography and CG effects. As bad as that may sound, the film does have some truly bizarre images and sequences. Again, I'm not trash-talking Prakash, as I really enjoy his films.

A farmer kills a *nāga* that he witnesses drinking from one of his cow's udders. Too bad for him, as Shiva and the rest of the *nāgadevathas* proceed to torment the man and his family, turning all his wealth and food into holy cobra mounds. The horrified man begs for forgiveness and burns the corpse of the cobra he killed on a ritual funeral pyre. Satisfied with his devout action, the gods return his wealth and also bless his wife with a baby. The child grows up to become a gorgeous woman named Nāgalakshm (Prema) who is given the ability to communicate with snakes and all of those other benefits that come with being baptized by the gods. An equally-pretty *angina* (Soundrya) is assigned to watch over her. Life is sweet and everyone is happy (there are even swinging parties in Nāg Lok accompanied by live cobras—via cheap effects—playing drums and so forth).

But of course there has to be some family jealousy in the plot, and here is where the film really gets good. There are were-cobras and special effects galore. Enter a trash-talking wizard in form-fitting red tights...and his pet vulture. When goddess Durga makes an appearance we have the setting for a proper supernatural/devotional throwdown. It's no surprise when the film's finale is reminiscent of both **DEVI** and **AMMORU**.

Stars: Soundrya, Prema. Saikumar and Charulatha; Music: Hamsalekha

WARNING: there are scenes of serious animal abuse throughout this film.

demon that was summoned by an evil *tantrik* her family had hired. She dies, but gives birth to a baby girl who is then rescued by Naageshwari who raises the child as her own. Years later the young girl, now a tween, is returned to her evil family (for reasons I can't fathom, subtitles would have helped here). She is greeted with surprise by all, but is accepted into the family. However, she is tormented by members of her family jealous of her popularity and her powers over snakes. It gets so bad that she is actually beaten to death by her relatives and buried in a shallow grave. She is then resurrected by Naagshwari only to be returned to the family, who then tries to burn her alive. When that doesn't get rid of the girl they turn again to the *tantrik*. In a final outlandish devotional battle it's the wizard with his demons against the young girl aided by the ghost of her mother and Naagshwari. In the end the bad man is crushed to death by a giant snake. Pretty nutty stuff. I loved it, especially the totally over-the-top underground temple lair of the evil wizard with fright-wig-wearing demon henchmen, cheap cut-out of a Kali statue, and other trappings of a brahamian gone wrong. Very loose remake of the 1995 Oriya language film **MANI NAGESWARI**.
Stars: Prema, Baba Dipika, Mani Chandra, Chakravarthy, and Prasad; Music: Sai Laxman, Nagesh, and Ravindra

ZAKHMI NAAGIN - "The Wounded Nagin"
(2004, D: Suresh Jain, Hindi, VCD, no subtitles)
Super sexy tale of a group of photographers out on a photo shoot at an old hotel. On the way to their job they run over the mate of a female nagin with their jeep. The distraught cobra goes after the murderers and kills them one by one. Low-budget thriller with loads of fun Certificate A material. Covered extensively in Weng's Chop #1.
Stars: Tanveer, Bhavana, Saazid, Kanchan, Raj and Yasmeen ; Music: Syed Ahmed

SWETHANAGU/SWETHA NĀGARA - "The Pure Snake Woman"
(2004, D: Sanjeeva, Telugu, VCD, no subtitles)
Film stars the late Soundarya as a young research student who travels into the wilds of Nāgaland looking for new material for study. There she encounters a Nāga tribe, whom she befriends. She chronicles various aspects of their traditional life, and eventually becomes involved with the supernatural. **SWETHA NĀGARA** is probably the first of the modern Nāga films to treat the subject somewhat seriously. That is, there are moments of magical

Actress Prema holds the record for the most appearances in Naag Devi films. Seen here in a promo still from **DEVI ABHAYAM** (2005)

manifestations, but nothing overtly silly. Soundarya was one of the few classy actresses other than Prema who seemed to love to star in fantasy films as well as in "serious" dramas and comedies. If you're into this type of cinema, may I suggest finding her breakout film, which is the excellent Durga devotional horror film **AMMORU** (1995).
Stars: Abbas, Sarath Babu, Brahmanandam, and Soundarya; Music:Koti

NAAGMANI - "The Gorgeous Snake"
(2004, D: Kishan Shah, Hindi, VCD/DVD, no subtitles)
Micro-budget variant of the familiar Nagin-drama wherein a man falls in love with a cobra girl whom he meets while visiting a local temple. He and the nagin marry, but his family calls him out on the deal by hiring a snake charmer to get rid of her. A fairly blatant rip-off of **NAGINA** (1986) which includes a straightforward cover of the classic song "Main Teri Dushman", made famous in the before-mentioned film. Sadly, Monica Tripathi is no Shridevi. One of director Kishan Shah's least static productions, involving some nicely staged musical numbers and action sequences (which is really not saying much).
Stars: Vinod Tripathi, Monica Tripathi, Viswajeet Soni, Deepak Rajput, Neha, and Nisha; music: Praveen Kunwar Bablia

PYAASI NAGIN - "The Thirsty Cobra"
(2004, D: Kishan Shah, Hindi, VCD/DVD, no subtitles)
One could almost see this as a sequel to Kishan Shah's **NAAGMANI**, as the film opens with Vinod Tripathi saving a male nag from from cobra hunters. Tripathi is unfazed that the young man can turn into a cobra, and that a female nagin pops up out of nowhere. He witnesses the two supernatural creatures do the cobra courtship dance to a boombox playing the main theme from **NAGIN** (1976). It's such a weird scene. As it turns out, **PYAASI NAGIN** is a cheap carbon-copy of **NAGIN**, which isn't all that unusual since Kishan and his brother Kanti (or cousin; I have yet to figure this out) have enjoyed "duplicating" famous films like **SHOLAY** and **JAANI DUSHMAN**.
Stars: Satnam Kaur, Kashish Khurana, Karishma, Riya, Anil Nagrath, Jr., Amitabh Bachchan (!), Ali Kahn, Pooja, and Vinod Tripath; Music: Sawan Kumar Sawan

DEVI ABHAYAM - "The Snake Goddess"
(2005, D: Vijaya Sarathy, Telugu, YouTube, no subtitles)
A Shiva devotee and his daughter Laxmi rescue a snake from certain death when they interrupt a cobra-vs.-mongoose show on the city streets. The cobra returns to the Shiva temple and calls forth a nagin to dance with. Two naags show up and begin a ceremonial devotional dance for the Lingum. An evil snake charmer, who is after the fabled *nāgmani* jewel, witnesses the dance, and with the use of his horn attempts to snag the nagins. He is stopped by the young girl and storms out of the temple. Decades later the very same girl is now a grown woman, and the female nagin, Nāgamma, returns to watch over her when her father falls on hard times. Of course, the nasty snake charmer shows up to try and trap the cobras once again. Stars Prema in yet another role of a nagin out to do good (see **DEVI**, 1999 and **NAAGESHWARI**, 2003).

Nāginī (Prema) and her husband (Prabhakar) are nāgadevathas in human form. Nāginī's husband has the diamond that the sorcerer is looking for. A surprisingly effective and very colurful nagin film full of wonder, with good use of limited CG effects and some fine musical numbers, a subtle instrumental score, and lovely location shoots. One of the best post-2000 snake lady films despite some very long segments of drama and those horrible comedic bits.

The actress Prema apparently has a love for the devotional aspect of the films she stars in. Her most recent film to date is a 2011 ghost film called **SHISHIRA**. In that film she as a lonely *bhoot* (ghost) looking for redemption.
Stars: Prema, Manthra, Prabhakar, Narra Venkateshwara Rao, Ranganath, and Raasi; Music: Srileka

ICHCHHADHARI NAAG NAGIN - "The Guardian Cobras"
(2006, D:B L V P Parsad, Telugu, VCD, no subtitles)
This movie offers up lots of ugly animal abuse, plus some incredibly cheap special effects that give this film an oddly surreal look. The producers, A. R. Arts, typically load their productions up with badly-choreographed dance numbers and poor cinematography, which is why I was pleasantly surprised as to the film's lovely location shoots and color *filmi* sequences. It's a pity that the source for this VCD looks as if it is from an awful distorted Hindi dub of the film. As with **SHESHNAAG**, we have two horny "Ichchhadhari" that guard the sacred cobra mani jewel at a local shrine who become involved with a newly-married couple. The male snake is killed when criminals break into the temple to steal the jewel, and all hell breaks loose (as is to be expected). Features one of the scummiest holy men ever to appear in one of these films.
Star: Arul Pandian, Ranjeetha, Rami Reddy; Music: S. Vandematram Srinivas

SHAPMOCHAN - "To Be Free From The Curse"
(2007, D: Hira Chowdhury, Bengali VCD; no subtitles)
The story is of a young man who becomes involved with a female nagin who then falls in love with him. As with **NAGINA** (1986) and **NAAG NAGIN** (1989), there is a final showdown between the nāg and the *sadhubaba* hired by the young man's family to get rid of the pesky cobra goddess. Actress Meghna Halder stands out as the gorgeous Nagin. The CG effects work is pretty subtle for an Indian devotional film.
Stars: Jishu Sengupta,, Subhashish Mukherjee, Hara Patnaik, Dulal Lahiri; Music: Babul Bose

NINDU POURANAMI - "The Full Moon"
(2007, D: Thota Krishna, Telugu, YouTube, no subtitles)
Annoyingly hip tale of the "fun times" in The Kasturi Bhai Women's Hostel and the possibility that one of the young girls there is a cobra. There is a police investigation into criminal activities at the hostel…and some mysterious murders of young men. Utterly dull film that picks up steam when a swami is brought in to find the supernatural cause of the deaths, and the nagin is exposed during the final two minutes of the film. ZZZzzzzzzz....
Stars: Rajendra Babu, and Payal; Music: Koti

POURNAMI NAAGAM aka
PUNNAMI NAGU / NAGIN KA INTEQAAM-
"Full Moon of the Snake"
(2009, D: A. Kodandarami Reddy, Telugu, DVD, subtitled)
The film opens in Nāglok wherein two *nāgadevatas* want to perform a ritualistic dance for their god Shiva in order to save the human race from a worldwide catastrophe ("because without the humans, who will there be to worship us?"). However, a gang of snake skin poachers is planning to kill this same pair of nagin and steal the magical *nāgmani* jewel. A mouthy witch called Mayadevi Bhairavi assists the criminals in killing the male of the mated pair, which, according to the well-worn plot line we all know and love, leaves the female open for revenge. The nagin possesses the body of a dying woman and from then on its two hours of long and unexciting nonsense.

There is just too much razzle-dazzle in the cheap digital effects department which isn't helped at all by uninspired "arty" cinematography and a really shitty soundtrack. The highlight of this thriller is the sexy snakiness of actress Mumait Khan as Naagraaj, who manages to keep most of her scenes fairly interesting (although she really can't act a lick). In past films Kahn is typically brought into a film for her looks and dancing skills, both of which are properly utilized. Sexiness aside, I must admit I did like the insane character of the witch Mayadevi Bhairavi, played with scene-chewing and reckless abandon by Nalini, who is better known for her comedic roles. Nevertheless, this film (of which I bought three because it has been marketed under three separate titles) is a pretty sad affair from a once-hot director who worked with the likes of Sridevi. **POURNAMI NAAGAM** (its official Telugu title) was written in part by Yaar Kannan, who made the interesting but flawed Indian SF film **YUGA** in 2006.

To make matters worse, this film can be confused with the 1982 film **DAUGHTER OF THE JUNGLE** by Italian director Umberto Lenzi. Lenzi's jungle thriller was re-dubbed into Hindi in the late 90s and released on DVD/VCD as **NAGIN KA INTEQAAM**. Go figure. However, if any of you are interested in this film, I would suggest buying the Moserbaer edition (see photo on this page) as it includes a bonus DVD of Kohli's **NAGIN** (1976). A pretty good two-fer, if you ask me.
Stars: Mumait Khan, Rajeev Kanakala, Aditya Om, Suhasini, Vinod Kumar; Music: S A Rajkumar

SHRI NĀGA SHAKTI - "Holy Snake Goddess"
(2010, D: Om Sai Prakash, Kannada, YouTube, no subtitles)
Obscure Kannada language Nagin film which is an old fashioned tale of a protective nāginī. No new ground broken with this film. Appears to be a much older film that may not have seen the light of day until 2010. **SHRI NĀGA SHAKTI** has a decent soundtrack by Sri Ganesh with some nice snaky moments by Sangeetha. From the director of **NAAG SHAKTI** (2000)
Stars: Ramkumar, Shruti, Shashikumar, Baby Kruthi, Abhijit, and Ramesh Bhat; Music: Sri Ganesh

NĀGAVALLI - The main female character from the film; a hot peppery spice
(2010, D: P. Vasu, Telugu, DVD, English subtitles)
An uninspired horror/thriller/comedy involving a cursed painting of a long-dead madwoman. The ghost of the woman inhabits the daughter of a rich man and also appears as a giant killer cobra. When things get deadly, the family calls upon a wiseass superstar yogi who has to battle with the monster snake as well as the young woman's serious attitude. A fun film if you ignore the fact that it sucks and you go along for the ride. The most interesting thing is its pedigree: It is a remake of the Kannada movie **APTHARAKSHAKA** and

MAIN NAGIN TU NAGINA

a sequel to the 2005 Tamil film **CHANDRAMUKHI**, also directed by Vasu, which was dubbed and released in Telugu, which *itself* is a remake of the 1993 Malayalam film **MANICHITRATHAZHU**. (Thank you Wikipedia!).

The best parts of this supernatural thriller are various fight sequences between our hero and an evil wizard, and the climatic face-off between the female ghost and the wizard. The sub-par CG effects actually enhance these scenes, giving them an unreal appeal. Too bad the rest if the film was total junk.
Stars: Venkatesh Daggubati, Anushka Shetty, Richa Gangopadhyay, and Kamalinee Mukherjee: Music: Guru Kiran

NAAG DEVTA GOGAJI PEER – "Devotion of the Saintly Snake"
(2011, D: , Rajasthani, YouTube, no subtitles)
Horrible shot-on-HD-video devotional crapola that is lacking in style and depth of any sort. Follows the popular "please god, bless my baby" routine where a mother enters a temple and pesters a god for a special boon. The resulting child is blessed with supernatural powers. Pretty dull.
Star and music information unavailable

MAIN NAGIN TU NAGINA -"I am Your Nāga You Are My Nagina"
(2011, D: Rajkumar R. Pandey, Bhojpuri, YouTube, no subtitles)
Extra-silly but very entertaining film full of horrible pop music. A snake charmer falls in love with a nāginī who pleads to Shiva to make her human so she can marry him. There are a few nāga dance numbers with delightfully skimpy outfits, but the plot meanders a great deal for about two hours until we enter he magical realm of the nāgs. It's good-versus-bad cobra action for the remainder of the film. The pinnacle sequence is a pretty fun final nagin dance off.
Stars: Manoj Pandey, Pakkhi Hedge, Sapna Singh, and Awadhesh Mishra; Music: Madhukar Anand

NANJUPURAM - "Village of Snakes"
(2011, D: Charles, Tamil, DVD, no subtitles)
Semi-devotional/horror film which opens with a snake attack on a young man who was disrespectful to a local nag/Shiva holy site. After the young man urinates he is attacked by a snake that proceeds to pluck his eyes out and eats them. The film begins on a promising note, but peters out quickly, turning into a socio-drama about a young devotee of Shiva and his forbidden love for a woman with moments of magical realism. Another case of misleading DVD sleeve art.
Stars: Raaghav, Monika, Naren, and Priya; Music: Raaghav

AFTER THOUGHT

That's it for film. This is in no way a compete filmography concerning Nagin Cinema. Before going to press I had discovered additional possible leads to still more titles. Most of these were obscure Telugu or Tamil devotional films from the 1940s, '50s and '60s. There are even mainstream films that use cobra lore as throw away plot elements or odd *filmi* sections as filler. I doubt I will ever have a complete catalogue of Indian Nagin-related films, but what you have read is a pretty good start.

There have been a few television shows as well. Zee TV, a Hindi language satellite television channel owned by Zee Entertainment Enterprises based in Mumbai, had *Naaginn - Waadon Ki Agniparikshaa*. This TV show ran for 219 episodes from 2007 to 2009. It told a tale of a female Ichchadhari nagin with some very familiar plot elements found in almost every movie I've mentioned here. I've sat through about twenty episodes (found on YouTube) and enjoyed what I saw: a cheap series from Ramsay clan members Tulsi and Shyam. No subtitles, sorry.

•••

Interested in Indian film? YouTube as a lot to offer. Want to own your own? Amazon..com has some of the more popular titles such as **DEVI, NAGIN**, and **NAGINA** as well as oddball ones like **JUNGLE KI NAGIN**. If you're feeling adventurous here are suggestions for the best companies on the be to buy DVDS and VCDs: **induna.com; webmallindia.com; myindiashopping.com; bhavanidvd.com;** and **kannadastore.com**. You can rent some of the titles in this article from **njmtv.com** (which is a US company out of New Jersey).

A Serpent's Guide To Nagin Appendix A
The Idiom of The Nāgas
A Brief Glossary of Words You Will Find In This Article

The Key Players

Nāg, Naag, Nāga - is the human-snake deity, or class of creatures or entities that are divine or demonic in origin. One of the earliest records of there being snaky humans comes from the epic Sanskrit story *The Mahābhārata* from the 4th Century BCE. In my article, these words are used when referring to the male of the species. (also written as nāgá, but not used as such in this article).

Nāgin, Nagin, Nāgī, Nāgmani, Nāginī - The female of the species. Usually the most interesting of the pair. In some films she is the nice and helpful *nāgadevata* to her human devotees, while in others she is the vengeful *ichchadhari nāgin* out to destroy the humans who killed her mate. When in human form she is often portrayed as a saucy vixen wearing traditional dress, which resembles a belly-dancer's outfit, or a skin-tight silk body sock with loads of gold jewelry and a cobra-shapes tiara. The word *nāgin* can be spelled with our without the accent (I haven't figured that one out yet).

Nāgadevatas - The holy variety of the *naga*. Typically, these are the snaky folk that inhabit Naglok and are best of friends with gods like Shiva and his daughter. *Nāg* means snake, and *devata* means god or deity. Put them together and you have *nāgadevata*. By the time the 1990s roll around, *nāgadevata* had lost some of its religious connotation in films and they are now interchangeable with *ichchadhari nāgin* or *ichchadhari nāginī*.

Ichchadhari nāg - A shape-shifting *nāgā* or *nāgin* from Indian folklore. Usually used in the negative sense in horror or fantasy films. For example, when someone gasps, "That was a ichchadhari nāgin!" it would be akin to a westerner remarking "That was a werewolf!" An *Ichchadhari Naga* is often seen wearing the *nāgmani*—the magical snake jewel that is often at the center of a lot of these films.

Swami, Yogi, Baba, Brahman, Tantrik - These are the holy men of the Hindu religion. Although they may be of different orders depending on their choice of god or goddess, they are usually called upon to get rid of a pesky *ichchadhari nāgin*. Some of these holy men are straight-up priests or monks or ecclesiastics, while others are part-time snake charmers. In any event, their presence usually means troubling times are ahead for any *ichchadhari nāgin*. Swami, Yogi and Baba are pretty much interchangeable as being "learned men" or an ascetic of a religious order. Brahmans are a little harder to pin down, but usually are hardcore followers of the Vedic branch of Hinduism; most but not all in the films reviewed are associated with Shiva. Tantriks are another guise of holy men altogether. In these films, they usually dabble in the dark arts and are often seen worshiping the violent and wild aspects of the goddesses Kali or Durga (or some other angry deity). The close analogy of this misunderstood branch of the Vedic tradition would be the West's misunderstanding of what is now commonly called Wicca.

Gods, Goddesses & Religion

Ammoru - A goddess variant of Durga, but for most of this article it is in reference to the 1995 Telugu devotional horror film **AMMORU** about a young Durga devotee terrorized by an evil *tantrik*.

Durga & Kali & Shiva - Two of the most important of the Hindu goddesses—and are branches off of the ancient pre-Vedic female power referred to as Devi or Shakti—and most often their fierce aspects are the focus of *tantrik* worship. Durga and Kali also figure into some of the films as positive elements, and sometimes though other regional snake goddesses such as *Naagshwari* (*Naganeshwari Maa*), *Manasa*, and *Daakshayini*. Male snake gods appear in the form of *Ketú*, *Nagraj*, and hundreds of other aspects of Shiva, the most popular male deity of the Hindu pantheon and someone who wears the eternal cobra Vasuki around his neck. Shiva is the master of all snakes, and the *Sheshnaag* (see below) is almost always seen in conjunction with Shiva's lingam in temples dedicated to that supreme god. There is more that can be written about the connection between Shiva, snakes and Nagas, but I don't have the space to go into what would be a very complicated discussion.

Nāglok - *Nāglok, Naaglok Naag Lok* or *Nāgaloka*, is the sacred underground world of snake folk. As per the Hindu *Puranas* (religious text) there are seven worlds below the earth; the Nāglok is the last one and it is the abode of *devas* (demi gods). Sunlight does not reach the Nāgaloka, but it is illuminated with light emitting from a giant *nagmani* atop a large Sheshnaag statue and the fangs of all the *nāgadevata* that dwell there. *Nāglok* is most often seen in Mythologicals, but it does make a rare appearance in strait-ahead Horror or Fantasy films. Naaglok is the home of the snake god Vasuki, and Shiva is sometimes seen hanging out there.

Sheshnaag - Multi-headed snake that is usually seen in conjunction with Shiva or Vishnu. In the films you will see huge seven- or nine-headed statues of the *Sheshnaag*.

Miscellanous

Nāgaland - A state in the far north-eastern part of India that has been badly represented in Indian cinema for decades as a backwards land full of as savage and primal people. In reality, the chief religion of the Nagaland tribes' people is Christianity (Baptist, to be more precise), to which they converted *en masse* in the late 1800s. They often show up in films as primitive, superstitious clowns or drunks, the butts of jokes, and people not to be trusted. Nice.

Naganeshwari Maa, Snake Goddess

Shiva and his Nag Snake Vasuki.

Vishnu chilling with Brahma and Lakshmi with the protective Sheshnaag over his head.

Nagin Appendix B
"THE HORROR!"
BRIEF SURVEY OF SNAKY FILMS FROM OTHER PARTS OF THE WORLD

Crappy frame grab from 忠臣蔵 / *Chushingura*

After months of research I have come to the startling conclusion that the most popular animal represented in film other than Man is the snake. This may come as a shock to some dog- or horse- (or cat- for that matter) lovers in the film community. Nevertheless, there are the facts: the snake is both feared and revered the world over. It figures into almost every culture where the reptile can live. It is a favorite foil of villains, is the cause for instant death, and often seen as evil. The creature evokes an instant reaction from most anyone who sees it featured in a movie poster, which is, for the most part: "Eeeeeww!"

Maybe I'm off-base here, but I must say that the snake (or snaky abilities) or the mere name "snake" can lead to box office gold. Of course, a lot of the appeal or disgust has to do with what part of the world you come from. Without getting too far into the social/anthropological aspect of Snaky Cinema, I'll just mention a handful of examples. These films are by no means the end-all when it comes to snakes. To narrow the genre down further, I will be looking at a few of the "human-snake" hybrid films which, like their Indian cousins, feature anthropomorphic serpent beings. You would think that by doing just that I would only have a handful of titles. No such luck.

Snakes have always been part of Magical cinema, and one of the earliest examples of their existence that I know of comes from a Japanese samurai epic. Makino Shozu's tale 忠臣蔵/*Chushingura* is a silent film that had conflicting dates of 1910-1917. Be that as it may, it is about supernatural ninjas and brave samurai. In one of the surviving sequences from the production, one of the ninjas magically transforms into a giant snake (and another into a giant toad). The very act of transformation gives this ninja the distinction of being one of the earliest cinematic forms of Snaky Folks.

Snakes never really figured into early Western film as religious or downright cool creatures unless you count "The Snake" which appears in numerous early Christian cinema offerings. I'm sure there may have been early *Maciste* films from Italy that feature monstrous serpents, or maybe some crazy films from Germany or France. But what I am looking for are the hybrids…even if just hinted at in highly-entertaining exploitative movie posters. So, without further exposition, here's a very truncated (and randomly chosen) hisssssstory (sorry, couldn't resist) of Snaky Films the World Over (*sans* India for obvious reasons):

Almost all snake movies have some basis in a myth or legend. One of the most popular tales—and thus, most-filmed (outside of India's *nāgadevathas* of course)—is China's 白蛇傳/"The Legend of White Snake". Already a very ancient oral myth to begin with, the tale was first recorded in print during the Ming Dynasty (1368-1644). The story was originally a horror story—that of a scholar who learns his wife is actually a shape-shifting snake demon. But over the centuries it has evolved into a tale of longing and love. And it is still one of the most popular myths in Chinese lore. Not unlike the popular tale of The Monkey King, there have been numerous films, TV shows, cartoons, books, comics, and operas about 白蛇傳.

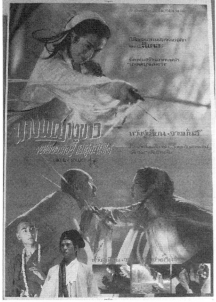

Tsui Hark's 青蛇 / GREEN SNAKE

As for the film versions of this story, I do have a couple of favorites. First up is the Japan/Hong Kong co-production 白夫人の妖恋/*Byaku fujin no yoren*/"The Legend of the White Serpent" from director Shirō Toyoda. Toyoda, known more for his "women films" handles this tale with some flair not usually seen in an early '50s Japanese Fantasy film. A wonderfully-crafted tale which Toho Studios sank a boatload of cash into the production, going as far as far as to making it in color. This was a hard film to track down, but I managed to find it on a Chinese movie streaming site. Director Toyoda is also known for his creepy horror film about a haunted painting called 地獄変/*Jigoku-hen*/"Portrait of Hell" (1969).

There have been other films since, and even a few cartoons that have dealt with the legend—some faithful, but many not so much. Taiwanese director Sun Yang's 1977 soap-operish 白蛇大鬧天宮/"Snake Woman's Marriage" and the Shaw Brothers' fantasy 蛇王子/**THE SNAKE PRINCE** (1976, D: Zhen Luo) are two good example of taking the snake demon theme in different directions. But it was Hong Kong director Tsui Hark who forever altered the legend (if not HK cinema) with his overtly sexual and incredibly beautiful 1993 film 青蛇/**GREEN SNAKE**. Stars Joey Wong (be still my beating heart) as White Snake and Maggie Cheung as Green Snake. The two demon-snakes long to be human and interact with mankind in the forms of gorgeous women. It is pretty innocent, but a strong-headed Buddhist monk doesn't see it that way and he is dead set in destroying the snaky pair. A fun, infectious, and visually mind-blowing adaptation of the Lilian Lee novel (itself an adaptation of the legend).

The moody and dark low-budget Chinese horror film 妖魅謎蹤/**PHANTOM OF SNAKE** is another take on the Legend of White Snake. It could also be seen as a variation of Lee's novel, as a female snake demon called White Snake flees to the seedy underworld of Hong Kong's bars and sex shops to escape her abusive lover, Black Snake, and his other female partner, Green Snake. The film features some wonderfully creepy moments and, despite its lack of budget, does function well as a postmodern take on the classic.

蛇王子 / THE SNAKE PRINCE

CG effects weighed heavily into the 2011 Siu-Tung Ching project starring Jet Li and Shengyi Huang,

白蛇傳說/**THE SORCERER AND THE WHITE SNAKE**. No new ground was broken with this film, but it does look mighty good. For serious artiness, you may want to catch the 2012 short, **LEGEND OF LADY WHITE SNAKE**. This 10-minute short is based on a poem by Neil Gaiman and directed by fashion photographer Indrani, who is, yes, Mumbai-born.

There have been a few Chinese TV shows concerning Madame White Snake. HK bombshell Cecilia Yip starred in the 1993 serial that is considered the best TV adaptation: 新白娘子传奇/"*New Legend of Madame White Snake*". There few at least two additional stabs at the legend for television: in 2001 with 白蛇新传/"*Legend of the Snake Spirits*", and in 2006 with 白蛇传/"*Madam White Snake*". Yep, a very popular cultural tale indeed!

As for European hybrids, there is little to offer in our mythology that has been successfully translated into film or television. The tired (and wholly inaccurate) serpent in the Garden of Eden has never been made a cinematic creature all its own—rather, the poor critter has been a stand-in for "The Devil" or "Satan". The few movies that referenced snaky humans almost always referenced "exotic" origins for their monsters. None of these Western "nāgas" were in any way very intelligent.

The classic Fantasy film **THE 7TH VOYAGE SINBAD** (1957, D: Nathan Juran) borrows from a supposed Arabian source to feature a poor woman who is magically transformed into a four-armed, half-human/half-snake hybrid by the evil magician Sokurah. This creature was only on screen for a short time, brought to life by the skills of animator Ray Harryhausen, to perform a lovely slithering dance to an excellent track by Bernard Herrmann.

One of the earliest and most fascinating of these films is the shoddy low-budget British horror film called **THE SNAKE WOMAN**. The film was made in 1961 by director Sidney J. Furie—who also handled the Welsh zombie/mad scientist opus **DR. BLOOD'S COFFIN**—who then went on to become slightly more famous with **THE IPCRESS FILE** (1965), **LADY SINGS THE BLUES** (1975), and **THE ENTITY** (1982). He's still active today, although most of his newer films have been direct-to-video productions. Whatever the case, **THE SNAKE WOMAN** is the film of his I currently find the most fascinating. It's not that it is all that well-made, but there are elements within it that are pretty intriguing:

Sometime in the 1890s an oddball scientists administers snake venom to his troubled wife, even knowing that she is pregnant with their unborn child. Unfortunately the effects of the venom cause an unnatural birth of a young girl who is cold to the touch and never blinks her eyes. It seems that for years to follow, folks are dropping like flies from deadly king cobra venom. A cobra in England? Yes! A snaky hybrid is running amok, able to change from a young woman into a cobra at the drop of a hat. Luckily, Scotland Yard sends in one of their best men who knows a thing or two about cobras. At the exciting climax of this bizarre tale, he draws the cobra out into the open by playing snake charmer with a *been*! The cobra "hears" the music and sticks its head up out of some bushes only to be shot dead, whereupon it falls to the ground and changes back into the girl. A fairly tight 66 minutes of no-frills UK cinema.

I don't mind that the effects are nonexistent (gorgeous woman standing in front of you, quick cut to cobra slithering on the ground, and presto-change-o, you have a shape-shifting entity); I've sat though almost 100 Indian films featuring the same sort of "thrills". What I find the most fascinating about this British film is that it plays fairly close to what was going to be the staple of Indian *nagin* films from 1976 onward. I wonder: did **THE SNAKE WOMAN** ever play in India? So far, no research has ever proven that to be a fact.

The film's heavy-handed screenplay was penned by the late Orville H. Hampton, who was no stranger to weird cinema. Hampton also authored **LOST CONTINENT** (1951), **THE ALLIGATOR PEOPLE**, and two personal favorites, **THE FOUR SKULLS OF JONATHAN DRAKE** and **THE ATOMIC SUBMARINE** (both 1959). Hampton would later pen many episodes of popular US TV shows like *Flipper, Lassie, Hawaii Five-O, Fantasy Island*, and numerous Saturday morning cartoon shows.

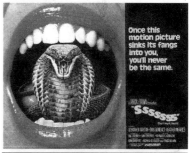

Hammer Studios offered up an unusual monster with John Gilling's 1966 film **THE REPTILE**, adding a new monster to the studio's rogues gallery. It's the 1890s again (England…again), and it seems that yet another doctor has a strange daughter that is a snake creature. Apparently the girl is the result of a curse and can transform from a pretty young lady into a human snake-headed monster. She transforms into a hideous reptile monster every winter as the result of contact with a tribe of "snake people" from the wilds of Borneo. The film's unique monster may be the one reason why this film is rarely remembered among all the *Frankensteins, Draculas*, and *Mummies*. Nevertheless, **THE REPTILE** is worth checking out.

Bernard Kowalski's 1973 film **SSSSSSS** (seven Ss is the official number, by the way) takes the mad scientist and his cobra creation to the next level. A young college student in need of cash is hired by a kindly-though-crazy scientist as a lab assistant. Unbeknownst to the kid, the mad scientist plans on creating a race of reptile human hybrids that will survive after an atomic war…and the young man is his next test subject. What follows is a well-crafted and low-budget Science Fiction thriller with a fun script and some nice special effects. By the end of the film we get to see the student transform into a half-cobra/half-human mutant and then finally into a full-fledged snake before being torn to shreds by the traditional arch-enemy, The Mongoose.

The snake monster was created by the late John Chambers, who pioneered monkey make-up for the *Planet of the Apes* film series (1968-1973), Spock's pointy ears and other prosthetics for the original **STAR TREK** series (1966), and **BLADE RUNNER** (1982, although uncredited). SSSSSS works on most levels as a low-budget monster movie. That's familiar territory for Kowalski, as he was responsible for two of the best cheap SF films from the early days of the '50s indie craze. You can thank him for the creepy and cool **NIGHT OF THE BLOOD BEAST** (1958) and the dark and dank **ATTACK OF THE GIANT LEECHES** (1959).

How many of you have seen Ken Russell's 1988 film **THE LAIR OF THE WHITE WORM**? In that fun film we have sexy Amanda Donohoe as Lady Sylvia Marsh, an English/Roman pagan snake goddess (sort of

Recent Indian VCD **AMERICAN NAGIN**, the Hindi dubbed version of Ken Russel's **LAIR OF THE WHITE WORM** (1988).

like the Nāga, but more of a demigod or demon) with a rather nasty habit of biting folks and either turning them into snake monsters or offering them up to her god as a meal. There is a segment in the film where she is coaxed out of her lair by using a record of old Indian snake charmer's music. Being very British and very hip, I'm sure that Russell had seen **NAGIN** (1976), **NAGINA** (1986) or was himself somewhat familiar with the Hindu cobra ladies. For that one sequence, Lady Sylvia Marsh is decked out in a tight-fitting black outfit not unlike those worn by actresses in the Indian films. **LAIR OF THE WHITE WORM** was banned in India upon its initial release—probably due to its rampant nudity and the occasional psychedelic anti-Christian imagery (The Indian government is very touchy about films that may insult a religious minority). Funny thing is: there is now a VCD (from 2006) of it under the silly title **AMERICAN NAGIN** which is no doubt heavily-edited for content. But I can't confirm this as I've yet to find it available to purchase on the Web.

There have been a few actual Indian genre co-productions in the past that attempted to mix both cultures. It's not a new thing. The failed Hammer Studios production *Kali Devil Bride of Dracula* was rumored to be a follow-up to Roy Ward Baker's 1974 Hong Kong co-production **LEGEND OF THE 7 GOLDEN VAMPIRES**, but failed to get any interest (the poster looked pretty cool). Jennifer Chambers Lynch's 2010 film **HISSS** has been the most successful to date (that I liked). Lynch, who wrote the film as well, also made the 1993 film **BOXING HELENA** and is the daughter of director David Lynch. I was not surprised that she picked the *nagin* genre to experiment with.

HISSS varies *slightly* from the traditional tales of The Snake Charmer vs. the *ichchadhari nāgin*. A scientist takes the place of the Snake Charmer/*tantrik* and hunts for a pair of *nāga* when learns that he has brain cancer. The scientist plans on using the supernatural powers of the snake gods to cure him of his disease and make him immortal. Of course, nothing goes as planned and everything ends horribly for all involved.

The film looks good except for the GC effects, which were okay at best. I was hoping for something more along the lines of the Indonesian horror film **PETUALANGAN CINTA NYI BLORONG/THE HUNGRY SNAKE WOMAN** (1986, D: Sisworo Gautama Putra). In that film you have a very cool half-woman/half-snake creature which worked despite being a low-budget effect. For **HISSS**, I would have loved to have seen the *Nagin* (actress Mallika Sherawat) in a practical effects costume. Nevertheless, Lynch does a good job translating some of the phantasmagorical elements of the *ichchadhari nāgin* to the English-speaking world. Gripes aside, **HISSS** is worth seeing.

Serpentine shape-shifters and their brood have also popped up in popular African cinema as well. Any true connoisseur of World Cinema should at least watch a half dozen or so of Nigerian or Ghana popular cinema. Both countries experienced a similar collapse of their traditional film industries, and by the 1980s relied more on video production rather than actual film to produce movies. Instead of cinema theatres projecting celluloid, most "movie houses" in Nigeria or Ghana are tents or dance halls (or just about any place an adventurous soul can set up a VCR and a large TV). The films themselves—if you can call them that—are shot-on-video, no-budget yackfests with little or no time given to special effects other than limited CG. However, when supernatural elements make an appearance—which they often do—it's usually with unbridled exuberances. Greasepaint demons dance around, there are flying heads, laser beams zap from the eyes, sorcery, evil smashing balls of holy Jesus blast monsters, possession by good and evil spirits, and women turn into snaky demonesses.

If you live near an African community I almost guarantee that you will find bootleg DVDs of these shot-on-video classics in the any grocery or gift store. If not there, they are readily-available to watch on YouTube or one of a dozen or more Nigerian film fan sites on the Web. Emeka Hill Umeasor's *The Snake Girl* series (Parts 1, 2, 3 & 4) were filmed sometime in the late 1990s, and all feature a young woman who is also a deadly snake demon. She is able to shape-shift from human form to that of a cobra, and then back again. Most of these films are less than an hour in length, and their plots aren't the most cohesive, but that's not the reason that they're made. Like **THE SNAKE WOMAN** from 1961, they are here to entertain, rational plotting be damned.

As I close out this mini-article, I'm sure that folks in the know may ask: Hey, what about those snaked haired monsters from Indonesia, Cambodia, Thailand and The Philippines? I'm saving those for a later article. Most of these Medusa lookalikes are based off an ancient Cambodian legend about a snake demon that makes love to a beautiful woman. She becomes pregnant and the resulting child (boy or girl) becomes entangled in the lives of the humans around it. This tale has been filmed at least seven times that I know of. Three of the best are listed below just in case you want to check them out for yourself:

PUOS KENG KANG/*The Snake Man* (1970, D: Tea Lim Koun, Cambodia, Film, subtitles)
Neang Sak Pus/**THE SNAKE GIRL** (1973, D: Tea Lim Koun, Cambodia, VCD, subtitles)
SNAKER (2001, D: Fai Sam Ang, Cambodia/Thai, DVD, subtitles)

Last-minute honorable mention must be made to a trio of little-known Japanese "Snake lady" films. These movies really have very little to do with any kind of unearthly serpent transformations, but are so darned weird that you should check them out. They are:

白蛇小町/*Hakuja Komachi*
("White Snake Girl", D: Mitsuo Hirotsu, 1958),
青蛇風呂/*Ao Hebi Buo*
("Blue Snake Bath", D: Mitsuo Hirotsu, 1959),
執念の蛇/*Shounen No Hebi*
("Vindictive Snake", D: Kenju Misumi, 1958).

PUOS KENG KANG

These and other snaky films will probably be covered, eventually, in a future issue of Weng's Chop.
Promise. Cross my heart.

NĀG NĀG NĀG!
SNAKY SOUNDTRACKS & MORE

Nagin Appendix C

As important as characters are in most any Indian film, one of the biggest selling points is almost always its soundtrack. A great many Indians love music in their films, and I must admit I was skeptical to the odd scene of song and dance interrupting a horror film. Nevertheless, as lover of both classical and pop music, I quickly fell under the spell of the alternate narrative of *filmi*. Despite what most people may believe, many—but not all—Indian films are *filmi* productions. That is, no matter the genre, the songs presented can be imaginative non-narrative fluff, or carry the weight of the film's plot. There have been instances when a film flopped horribly at the box office only to have one of its songs become a huge (usually regional) hit. This is true for *Nagin* films, both in the Devotional and Horror sub-genres.

Without a doubt, one of the most influential songs to ever emerge from any *filmi* production came from a cobra film.

Charming a snake with a flute or horn has been an integral aspect in India since early times. It is a popular way of street entertainment—possibly going back as far as 4,000 years to the Hindu mythological tale of Krishna and the Snake Demon Kaliya. In this story of the young god's life, Krishna confronts and does battle with a wicked multi-headed *nāga* that inhabits a lake. He defeats the creature and dances on its hoods playing his flute. Cobras are also associated with Shiva, Vishnu, and an odd assortment of other gods.

The haunting melody played by the son of the *Nāga* tribe chief from **NAGIN** (1954) has become a staple for over fifty years and is often confused with a traditional snake charmer's tune. And the fact that composer Hemant Kumar's "Man dole mera tan dole" is often played on the streets by traditional snake charmers helped cement that melody into the minds of Indians and the nagin music.

The horn that is most associated with the snake charmer is an odd, gourd-shaped instrument called a *been* (or *bin, beene, beens, pungis*). As most everyone knows, a snake has very poor hearing, and doesn't react to the sound emanated from the *been*, but rather the rhythmic swaying of the person playing the instrument. But it does make for a good show…and who's to say that a *nāgadevi* wouldn't react to the charm of the *been*? Indeed, in **NAGIN** the Nāgaland she-warrior Mala hears her forlorn lover Sanathan playing the *been* during cobra hunting season, and along with the snakes, she too dances to the tune of 'Man dole mera tan dole'.

Brothers Kalyanji and Anandji Virji Shah, more popularly known as the soundtrack duo **Kalyanji Anandji** scored over 400 films including the classic action flick **DON** (1978).

As for the mega-popular melody "Man dole mera tan dole" and its influence on Indian culture as a whole, it is interesting to note that the sound created for the film **NAGIN** did not come from the traditional instrument, but rather an early form of synthesizer-keyboard called a Clavioline. Like the *been*, it delivers an unwavering drone, sounding much like a bagpipe; unlike the *been*, which takes some skill with circular breathing, the Clavioline could be mastered and played rather easily, thus making it the go-to instrument for composing unearthly melodies. Early on in his career, musician Kalyanji Virji Shah was the master of the Clavioline, and was responsible for its use which was used for the famous music of Hemant Kumar.

When writing about **NAGIN** and other uses of music in Indian cinema, Italian author, sociologist and musicologist Carlo Nardi wrote, "As a matter of fact, the connection between the Clavioline and such themes as space exploration and sci-fi can be found in other recordings, including Van Phillips' soundtrack for the successful science-fiction radio programme 'Journey Into Space' (1953-58, interestingly, this show was also translated into Hindi), Sun Ra's 'Cosmic Tones for Mental Therapy' (1967, recorded in 1963), and 'The Heliocentric Worlds Of Sun Ra, Volume Two' (1966), the Louis and Bebe Barron score for the film **FORBIDDEN PLANET** (1956), and Joe Meek's concept album 'I Hear a New World. An Outer Space Music Fantasy' (1960)."

The melody of "Man dole mera tan dole" became a standard for nagin films all throughout the 1960s and into the 1970s. Various renditions on the song's phrasing become increasingly poppy and by the time that **NAGIN** (1976) introduced us to the vengeful she-*Ichchhadhari nāga*, the world was ready for yet another super-hit track. This time around the *nagin* love song "Tere Sang Pyar Main Nahi Todna" was destined to *almost* one-up the 1954 hit. Various riffs of this track appeared in a few snaky films, but as

97

lovely as it is as a song, "Tere Sang Pyar Main Nahi Todna" just didn't have the staying power of the Hemant Kumar original.

In 1985, **NAGINA** delivered a one-two punch with the incredible "Main Teri Dushman", which was outstanding for both the classic poppiness of the Laxmikant-Pyarelal score and the intensity that actress Sridevi put into her dance moves. Few *nagin* films ever matched this single classic scene where in the ill-tempered snake charmer *tantrik* (played to perfection by the late Amrish Puri) confronts our lovely Nagina. With his *been* at the ready, the *tantrik* whips up a magical time-honored melody that borrows heavily from the Kumar song, but is still able to deliver as a standard all its own.

The unearthly sound and lovely drone of "Man dole mera tan dole" is even heard in field recording as late as 2008. I've collected a few LPs and CDs of such recordings, and my favorite can found on a Hanson Records release called "The Sounds of the Snake Charmer" by The Nath Family, as recorded by Aaron Dilloway. Track one of this amazing recording weaves the Bollywood theme in, around and through more traditional melodies. However intoxicating the music is, the entire show sounds like it's something not to be missed if you ever get the chance...

Aaron describes the experience: "For the first half of 2005, I lived with my wife Erika in Kirtipur, Nepal. ...I was roaming the streets and villages of the Kathmandu Valley in search of sounds and music. While kickin' round the tourist district of Thamel picking up cassettes, I met a family of Snake Charmers from Haryana, India. An old man probably in his 70s or 80s, his 2 grandsons, and one of the grandson's sons. They asked if I wanted to see a show...I said Hell YES!! They gave me a show...a KILLER show...we're talkin' 3 fuckin' king cobras dancing at once, while a giant boa chilled at the side and few other random li'l snake dudes are wigglin' around here and there. ...I spent about 3-4 days a week for the next 2 months, recording their music and their snake shows on mini-disc and videotape. I drank a lot of *chiyaa* with them, smoked a lot of cigarettes and *bidis*. They taught me how to make reeds out of bamboo, and I traded them some clothes for a snake charming horn. They call them *Beens*; they are also known as *Pungis*. These guys were the best. At the end of April they left Kathmandu, heading to Pokhara, after that it was time for them to head back home with their earnings... These tracks were recorded in an alley. There is the occasional rumble of a car passing by, and the low murmur of the locals checkin' out the white kid with the fancy gadget hangin' with the snake dudes." HN 132CD, $12 from **hansonrecords.net**; **thenevaributchers.blogspot.com**; Hanson Records, MPO Box 73, Oberlin, OH 44074 USA.

The sound of the snake charmer's horn is an old one, and has been utilized and sampled in a good many popular dance recordings. The coolest track that I've heard that uses an actual horn rather than a sampled field recording is "Snake Charmer" by British-born Panjabi MC, a London-based recording artist whose inventive and unique sound comes from the South Asian experience. I was lucky enough to catch him for a quick interview.

"I've grown up to the sound of many traditional Indian instruments. The *beene* is one of them. It is used by a variety of musicians and one of them is the snake charmer or *nagin*. He plays it to the snake, hypnotizing him and making him dance. (If you want to see what it looks like check my website. Or watch the snake charmer video).

When I was in India I heard a street snake charmer outside a studio kitchen. We called him & the snake into the studio. I thought that if the guy can make a snake dance then he will reach into the inner snake of everyone on any dance floor. We recorded him. It became an anthem."

This single can be bought from iTunes, and the video can be seen on YouTube as well as Panjabi MC's official website **pmcrecords.com**.

Ol' Skool vinyl from 1986.

~ Tim Paxton & others

THE BOOKSHELF

DARK STARS RISING:
CONVERSATIONS FROM THE OUTER REALMS
by Shade Rupe

Reviewing books has never much been my forte but occasionally a work comes along that has me so excited it's hard not to share my enthusiasm with others. Such is the case with Shade Rupe's *Dark Stars Rising: Conversations from the Outer Realms*. It's a book unlike anything I have in my collection as it features candid, in-depth interviews with personalities very few would consider for a mainstream publication. While most would jump at the chance to sit down with Spielberg, De Palma or Sting, journalist Shade Rupe looks to the "outer realms" of art, seeking the inside stories behind true innovators and visionaries. Ranging from underground filmmaking and (true) alternative music to bloody performance art and subversive comic illustration, Rupe never insults readers with sophomoric questions designed to titillate the rag sheet crowd—instead he gets to the heart and soul of each interview subject, peeling back the layers to reveal their innermost thoughts and feelings on a variety of topics. As a fan of many of the people interviewed in this book, I can state emphatically that I have no desire to know which diet this one is on or what pop band that one is listening to now. If you're like me, you're going to want to read, re-read and re-re-read this book over and over again. I've only had my copy for a short time now and it's already scuffed, bent, slightly torn and stained (with coffee, you fucking pigs!). Good books go wherever you do.

Packed with 27 incredibly fascinating interviews with beloved, and often larger-than-life, cult personalities like Divine (**PINK FLAMINGOS**), Tura Satana (**FASTER, PUSSYCAT! KILL! KILL!**), Richard Stanley (**DUST DEVIL** and **HARDWARE**), Udo Kier ("Andy Warhol's" **FLESH FOR FRANKENSTEIN**), James VanBebber (**THE MANSON FAMILY**), Gaspar Noe (**IRREVERSIBLE**), Bill Lustig (of Blue Underground), *Dark Stars Rising: Conversations from the Outer Realms* is on the cutting-edge of the Cult/Subversive/Transgressive (Cinema/Music/Art) movement. It's a shame Rupe himself wasn't interviewed for his own book as I would love to of read about some of his more outrageous experiences—in the world of cinema, especially. Surely the sheer insanity of this book is enough to qualify him worthy of his own interview!

Dark Stars Rising: Conversations from the Outer Realms is a must-own book; it's off the fucking wall! Shade Rupe has done a fantastic job of giving us the "inside look" so many journalistic efforts promise but so few provide. This is how good books are done right and the best thing about the author is, he's "One of us! One of us! Gooble-gobble, gooble-gobble!" ~ **Brian Harris**

FORGOTTEN HORRORS
TO THE NTH DEGREE:
DISPATCHES FROM A COLLAPSING GENRE
by Michael H. Price and John Wooley

The new essential book from two authors who have to be the hardest working film historians around. Michael H. Price and John Wooley, has been in the business of chronicling film since the 1970s, and both have authored over 20 books in that field as well as covering comics, music, and hidden history. The Forgotten Horrors series has other books in the series, with *The Nth Degree* being the latest edition chock-full of dense text and wonderfully rare illustrations. The book isn't your typical list of films covering the '60s through the '80s—instead, *Nth Degree* reads as if it's a film 'zine from the '90s; each film or subject is treated as an essay rather than a capsule review. Every entry is a gem, so it's hard to pick out highlights but here goes: David F. Friedman Box Office Spectacular 1963-65, The films of Larry Buchanan, a Leo Fong retrospective, lengthy reviews of **MARS NEEDS WOMEN** (1966), **THE WITCHMAKER** (1969), **WEREWOLVES ON WHEELS** (1971), **BLOOD FREAK** (1972), **THE MANITOU** (1977), **WITHOUT WARNING** (1980), etc. The capper to the book is a mighty excerpt from Stephen R. Bissette's work-in-progress *The Green Mountain Cinema DVD & Video Companion*, covering "Vermonsters", films made around his home state of Vermont.

$30, 303 pages, paperback, available from *amazon.com*; for more information visit *forgottenhorrors. blogspot.com*, *johnwooley.com*, *srbissette.com*, and the Forgotten Horrors Podcast Facebook page.

TRUTH OR DARE: A CRITICAL MADNESS
Screenplay, Storyboards & Press Kit
By Tim Ritter
Createspace 2013

The film **TRUTH OR DARE: A CRITICAL MADNESS** (1986) is one of my favorite homebrew horrors of the '80s, and to be honest I had *no* idea that the creator was so young at the time it was made (or that one of The Backstreet Boys played the killer in a flashback!)—so when Tim Ritter released *Truth or Dare: A Critical Madness - the Screenplay, Storyboards & (AND????) Press Kit*, I had to hit BUY IT NOW and get that sucker expressed to my door.

For those that don't know, **TRUTH OR DARE: A CRITICAL MADNESS** is the charming story of a man done wrong that falls prey to his own twisted psyche that goads him into games of Truth Or Dare. Along the way a little-leaguer gets decapitated and lots of other hijinks ensue—many of which are memorable for being particularly gung-ho on the gore. It's pretty amazing that someone that was 17 could put all this together not just on paper, but go on to make a film that most certainly has made more profit than most big films could ever hope for. Hell, SRS Cinema just put the film back out on VHS! So, a chance to read the screenplay is certainly interesting, and it holds up surprisingly well. It's interesting to see where imagination on paper gets pulled back once actual effects get involved (read the description of that aforementioned baseball playing kid!), but the match of intensity and idea translated amazingly well on very few resources.

But the screenplay is just the start; while I would have definitely enjoyed reading more about the making of the film, the challenges of getting the entire thing financed and certainly the marketing of the movie (I still have that old VHS release!), what we do get is very interesting. The storyboards are fun to look at and again add to how impressed I am with young Tim Ritter's clarity in getting the movie made. Between these images and the surprisingly large amount of dialogue for a cheap gore flick made by teenagers that actually holds up when reading it now, I'm not surprised the director has been able to keep making small films for the market that wants them. Also, it's cool to see that the copper mask sequences from the storyboards look like a Quiet Riot cover being animated into a splatsterpiece with big maces smacking orderlies in the head!

Finally, the real meat for the VHS collector gets THWOKKED hard with the axe of nostalgia as we get a look at the promotional materials sent around to sell the VHS cassette to the market directly. ToD was definitely one of the early DTV flicks, and it took some selling I'm sure—especially being done on such a small scale. I worked in video stores from the mid-'80s until the early '00s and it was a wild time for DIY productions to get seen on a level that was never possible before. After a few sell sheets featuring different sized ads for the film (with that cool minimal title and bloody razorblade graphic), there are some behind-the-scenes makeup shots. Then the entire price of admission is cashed in as you read the pitch sheets, behind the scenes make up shots and extensive gore splattered storyboards. Notices about the cast and their qualifications are interesting, as well as some of the credentials of the team producing the film. Some of the claims are really great in that they do exactly what they should to the video buyer of 1986—go bold or go home. According to these notes there would be *seven* special effects *never* attempted in the film industry! Also funny is that Ritter is listed as being 25 (he wasn't) and that he wrote for *Creepy*. And let's not forget that he was born on Friday, October 13th! It's the exact kind of horror legend I would buy into (at only $49.99 retail, which was an interesting strategy at the time—you could sell 2 for 1 pretty much) ...and I did!

This is a fun read for fans of the film, the series (which I'm glad to say is getting new life in previously unavailable director's edits on VHS as you read this via SRS) and low budget horror as well. Sign me up for more of these and I'd *definitely* love to see a full blast book using the old documentary title, **BLINDED BY THE BLOOD**, by Tim Ritter any day. The stories he could share would be fun to read and certainly inspirational to not just the gorehounds of tomorrow, but the fans of VHS and splatterday afternoon mayhem. Go Copperface and pick up a copy today. I DARE YOU TO READ THIS BOOK!!!!
Available through *amazon.com*. ~ *David Zuzelo*

MAD...MA VIE!
by Jean-Pierre Putters

What can I say? This book has a whole lot of cool stuff in it. Jean-Pierre Putters has been in the business since the 1970s and the early chapter dealing with early French 'zines is priceless. This book is about the life and times of Jean-Pierre Putters, his publications and projects. From what I gather, it is also a decent chronicling of French horror and SF film fandom. Here's a little bit from the book's press release (which I've re-written somewhat):

"Jean-Pierre Putters became interested in fantasy and science-fiction at a very early age. After writing for several fanzines in the early '70s, Putters began publishing *Mad Movies* magazine in 1972. In 1979 he opened his movie shop, Movie 2000, in Paris. In 1982 *Mad Movies* moved from being a fanzine and turned professional in order to cover a wider spectrum of the genre including the films that were huge at the box office. In 1984, Putters created the *Festival du Super 8 & 16mm* allowing young directors to get some exposure. In 1985, Putter created the magazine *Impact* which concentrated on the Action, Thriller, and Adventure genres. After a long time as editor and publisher Putters joins his friend and longtime *Mad Movies* reader Fabrice Lambot and they create Metaluna film productions in 2005. Putters' book *Mad...Ma Vie!* chronicles all this and more."

Mad...Ma Vie! is a mighty 225 pages, illustrated (most in full color), paperback. Contact: Jean-Pierre Putters, 458 rue Lherminot, 77550 Moissy Cramarel, France, or order the book through *amazon.com*.
Check out the Metaluna Facebook page for more details: *www.facebook.com/metalunacinocknroll*.

AENIGMA! #1
Nigel Maskell, editor

32-page, digest-size throwback to the daze of DIY Xerox 'zines. Which is fine by me. Nigel concentrates on the EuroScene with reviews of Luigi Batzella's **THE BEAST IN HEAT** (1977), Lucio Fulci's **ZOMBIE FLESH EATERS** (1979) and Ruggero Deodato's **CANNIBAL HOLOCAUST** (1980). Not just mere reviews but chronicles of the editor's exposure and absorption of these films, it is an example of what 'zines were like in the days before blogs clogged the Internet.

Issue #1 is available for 2 quid (UK) but with postage that is 3 quid UK, 4 quid EU and 5 to the rest of the world—it's priced in Pounds so that will vary with the exchange rate. Currently the easiest way to get info/order is via *www.facebook.com/Aenigmafanzine*. If you didn't live through the 'zine scene of the '80s & '90s then this is the closest you'll get in doing so.

METALUNA #1
Jean-Pierre Putters, editor

Slick, oversized (for US standards) French movie zine from Jean-Pierre Putters, former editor of *Mad Movies*. MM was one of the longest-running French film 'zines, and for those who would like to know more about it, checkout the book review for Putter's *Mad...Ma Vie!* The premier issue follows in the footsteps of Putter's other publication in that it is chock-full of reviews, articles and interviews—all in French, of course. The 'zine covers a lot of ground with information on Riccardo Freda, Raymond Chow, Kirk Hammett, Rob Zombie (an interview), Priez Porno (films), and much more.

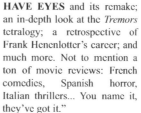

From some the crazies that bought you the French film magazines *Mad Movies* and *Impact*, so you know you're in for a visual treat. In French (no subtitles).

For ordering information, check out their Facebook site: *www.facebook.com/metalunacinocknroll*.

As luck would have it, just as this issue of WC is going to press, issue two of *Metaluna* has been released with an interview with director John Carpenter as the headline.

MEDUSA Magazine #24
Didier Lefevre, Editor

From their recent press release:
"After a seven year hiatus, Medusa has returned to the newsstands in January 2012 with issue 23. A year later, issue 24 came out, proving once and for all that Didier Lefevre got his second wind as an editor. Coming in at a healthy 150 pages, Medusa #24 is chock-full of fun. There's a very detailed article about Tobe Hooper's years under contract with the Cannon Group, aptly titled "A Pact with the Devil"; side by side reviews of **THE HILLS HAVE EYES** and its remake; an in-depth look at the *Tremors* tetralogy; a retrospective of Frank Henenlotter's career; and much more. Not to mention a ton of movie reviews: French comedies, Spanish horror, Italian thrillers... You name it, they've got it."

Medusa is the work of true enthusiasts. Love of cinema oozes from its pages and boy is it contagious! It will send you running to your favorite video store, streaming service, or online auction site in a desperate attempt to find the movies you just read about. Whether you want to reminisce about 80's horror or discover entire genres you never suspected even existed, Medusa #24 is a must read.

The price for the USA is $15 (including postal charges). It's possible to buy it with PayPal to: ornelladidier@yahoo.fr. For more information, check out the Medusa blog at *medusafanzine.blogspot.fr*.

MONSTER PIE #1
by Stephen R. Bissette and Denis St. John

SEE: The MOST Gruesome Wrap Around Cover EVER!
SEE: The Bride as you've NEVER seen her before!
SEE: A Zombie CUDDLE with a Kitty!

MONSTER PIE is a near-perfect Xerox 'zine that is dedicated to a subject very dear to my own heart: the veneration of monsters. The zine is a 40-page digest size full of funky, funny and downright incredible monstrous illustrations by Stephen R. Bissette and Denis St. John. B&W and colour.

But that's not all—there's an article on the 1978 indie-produced monster flick **SLITHIS**, a fun *Popular Mechanics* reprint (from 1941!) about Ray Harryhausen—one of the greatest stop-film animators in all monsterdom, a full color *Herculoids* centerpiece, loads of sexy monster maidens, and much, more more!

Pen and ink, wash, water colour, and I'm sure loads of blood and sweat.

Worth every penny. Issue #2 is in the works and will be released soon!

All this and *much* more when you read *Monster Pie* #1, available now from Spider Baby Grafix & Publications at: *http://srbissette.com/store/* or through Denis St. John's Etsy store: *www.etsy.com/shop/denisstjohn*.

You just need to keep telling yourself: it's only a fanzine... it's only a fanzine... it's only a fanzine... it's only a fanzine... it's only a fanzine...

OOP - OUT OF PRINT
Zines and Books from the Bygone Days of Yesteryear

Technically speaking, anything OOP is hard to find by any means other than searching high and low in book shops or on the Internet. Not all OOP books and magazines are horrendously expensive. Some, like the French fanzine Eurocine *goes for a lot of money, while Baxter Phillips'* Cut: The Unseen Cinema *can be found for under $10 on a variety of online websites; suggested sites include* half.com, abebooks.com, bibliopolis.com, *and, of course, Ebay. Unless you're a completest or collector, the true value is not what you pay for the book, but what's in it.*

CINEMA CULTE EUROPEEN, VOLUME 1 : EUROCINE

It took some times for French fandom to realize they had their own B-movie material to discover. The French film company Eurociné mostly dazzled in horror, zombies, crime movies, exotic adventures, and eroticism (starting with educational film). They also co-produced a lot of Spanish and Italian exploitation movies, or imported films in which they would include new sequences. Stepping in Eurociné land is like walking through a maze where some gems are lost and some are of the cheapest movies ever done, where the good is mixed with much-less-watchable materials.

This is why a bunch of fan publishers started working on a fully detailed filmography of Eurociné productions with complete credits and video releases available at the times. Thanks to the help of film historians Jean-Claude Michel and Bertil Lundgren, the base for this one-shot fanzine was solidly and seriously anchored.

With the opportunity to meet directors Jess Franco and Alain Payet, actors Olivier Mathot, Monica Swinn and Michel Charrel, the team had the most documented testimonies ever collected on the oldest low budget film company still existing. A screening of two Eurociné movies at the French Cinematheque also brought the opportunity of a public debate with Daniel Lesoeur (actual owner and head of Eurociné), which provided the opportunity to record the facts from the horse's mouth. The baby was born: a 200-page complete detailed history of the firm. The first printing with a color cover culled from the French flyer for **REVENGE IN THE HOUSE OF USHER** and its half-size booklet *Eurociné Blues* supplement rapidly sold out. A second printing with a different cover followed with the cover culled from the French poster art for **PIGALLE, CROSSWAY OF ILLUSIONS**.

14 years later, this complete study and analysis of the most mysterious film company is out of print and is still sought after. It is available on Ebay... for a price. ~ ***Lucas Balbo***

CUT: THE UNSEEN CINEMA
Baxter Phillips, Bounty Books, 1975

The recent passing of Spanish director Jesus Franco has sent me for a loop. Not that his death surprised me. The man was old; nevertheless, in his passing I realized how much his films and their very existence influenced me in my early adult life. The essence of erotica has always been around me as I grew up, and while I've never obsessed about the subject, I now recollect that books like Baxter Philllips' *Cut: The Unseen Cinema* were always present in my head. Bounty Books published a series of film books on what would now be called "Trash Cinema"—a term I detest and would rather dub "Genre Cinema", as I rarely found many of these films trash.

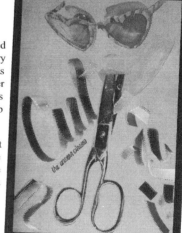

Cut was definitely the most eye-opening of Bounty's line, with copious amounts of "boobs, butt and bush" as a childhood friend once exclaimed when he flipped through the book (nonplussed, he returned to his stack of Penthouse and Hustler magazines and left me to my gawking at the image of Indian maidens bathing from W. Merle Connell's 1960 nudie **NOT TONIGHT, HARRY**). I was thirteen years old at the time and *Cut* was my porn.

The text covers erotica from the early days of pre-code Hollywood and foreign film up through what was then the most recent shocking display of the flesh and monster-sex that included Walerian Borowczyk's **IMMORAL TALES** (1974). Baxter lays down a fairly decent account of film and censorship, and as a kid it was my first time I ever read about the subject. It's a breezy read (as are all of the Bounty line) and I ate it up, and have ever since been a staunch supporter of anti-censorship in the arts.

Text aside (sorry Mr. Phillips), it was the sheer amount of naughty images that took me to the darkside. *Cut* was my what-to-see book at the time. I borrowed an 8mm print of Benjamin Christensen's **HÄXAN: WITCHCRAFT THROUGH THE AGES** (1922) to see the monstrous devil *and* the naked lady on the Satanic alter. I fantasized about seeing early Sophia Loren topless and nearly died when Jean Negulesco's 1957 **BOY ON A DOLPHIN** played on late night TV with her braless wet-shirt scene intact. I was totally stoked at the images films by José Mojica Marins, Jean Rollin, Ken Russell (**THE DEVILS**, of course), Wakamatsu Koji, and especially that two page spread featurng Brando and Stephanie Beecham from **THE NIGHTCOMERS** (1971) and **THE LAST TANGO IN PARIS** (1972). My god...SEX!

Cut: The Unseen Cinema is way out of print, but I found a hardback copy for $5 on *half.com* (a subsidiary of Ebay). All the books from Bounty's line are fairly inexpensive and are worth buying for your collection. I have most of them as paperbacks from the 1970s. Choice titles include *Kung Fu: Cinema of Vengeance* (Verina Glaessner), *Movie Fantastic: Beyond the Dream Machine* (David Annan), *Robot: The Mechanical Monster* (David Annan), *Savage Cinema* (Rick Trader Witcombe) and *The Seal of Dracula* (Barrie Pattison)—the book that first introduced me to Jess Franco's sexy vampires. ~ ***Tim Paxton***

Weng's Chop Literary Classics presents a Kronos Productions archives reprint special.
MONSTER! INTERNATIONAL #2 and the "Mexi-Monster Meltdown" article by PANICOS editor Steve Fentone.
A rare look back at a fanzine from 1992. From the blissful days before the avalanche of blogs buried the land.

MEXI-MONSTER MELT-DOWN

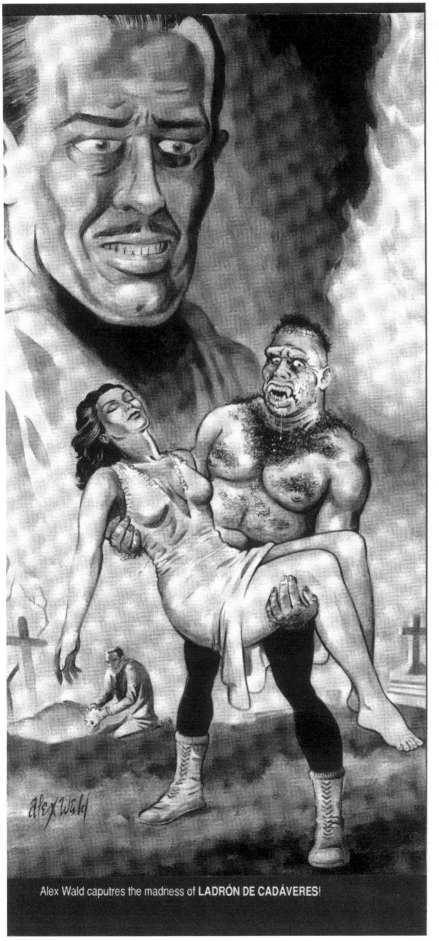

Alex Wald caputres the madness of **LADRÓN DE CADÁVERES**!

BY STEVE FENTONE

Mexican B-films, but especially Mexi-monster movies (hereinafter referred to as "MMM") seem to be generally held in low esteem, and are often outright reviled by even those select few who might otherwise be exponents of the loweliest-of-low in diverse international cinecrap. Whereas ethnic works from Italy, Spain, France, Hong Kong and nowadays even Brazil (eg: the long-elusive output of mad movie maestro Jose Mojica Marins) seem to be gobbled up voraciously by an increasing number of loyal enthusiasts, many still seem ignorant of —or perhaps simply indifferent to?— the wealth of obscure delights waiting to be unearthed down Mexico way, especially in the horror, and more specifically, monster genre.

"Mexploitation" films are often largely dismissed as cheap and puerile rehashings of established U.S. movie cliches. Mexican monster movies in particular are guilty of this, but simultaneously exhibit their own unmistakable cultural characteristics, as defined and singular as Japan's giant rubber monster mashes or Europe's Gothic horror pieces. Undoubtedly Meximonster films, like most of the country's other popular domestic genres, extensively borrow from (some might say plagiarize) the Hollywood "Golden Age" of the thirties to the fifties (earlier more independent Mexican horror entries include **EL FANTASMA DEL CONVENTO** / tr: THE GHOST OF THE CONVENT, D: Fernando de Fuentes; and **EL BAÚL MACABRO** / tr: THE MACABRE TRUNK, D: Miguel Zacarias, 1936). Plots of the US-derivative MMM almost invariably incorporate tried-and-worn-out pulp archetypes, though are invested with a personal signature care of the distinct Mexican style.

As with most formulaic film types, overly serious "academic study" of MMM is pretty much a redundant consideration. These films tend to exist in an alternate dimension of their own creation, making stodgy, realist critical analyses (accent on the anal, *woof-woof*) kind of pointless. MMM (especially those that also contain masked wrestlers, or *enmascarados*) are best ingested on their own terms, minus too many unfair preconceptions or lofty expectations. Chances are if you come in excessively biased against them, you're not gonna change your prejudices by watching. Erase your mind. Keep your brain a blank slate, and simply permit their infectious atmosphere to have its way with you... In regard to some of the more oddball MMM, forget merely suspending your pathetic *gringo* disbelief — try *abandoning* it entirely!

Jack Taylor, an American-born actor usually based in Spain, spent some time in Mexico during the mid/late 1950s doing westerns and an episode of *SHEENA, REINA DE LA SELVA/ SHEENA, QUEEN OF THE JUNGLE* (1956). Billed pseudonymously as *"Grek Martin"*, he filled supporting roles in two notable MMM sagas, the NOSTRADAMUS vampire serial, as well as the first three adventures of that masked monster-wrestler, "Neutron, The Atomic Superman". I recently collaborated on a career-spanning interview with *señor* Taylor, which encompassed his little-known early Mexican tenure. On the topic of the nation's apparent fascination with fantasy, monsters and legends, Taylor remarked:"Mexico is really a fantastic country. I mean, it's a fantasy land. There's fantasy built into the genes of the people; into the minds. People will tell you the most amazing stories with a straight face".

Taylor went on to recount a tale concerning an ugly little mythical creature spoken of by superstitious *paisanos*. If you could manage to capture this imaginary (?) animal and not be alarmed by its fearsome appearance, when you took it home and fed it warm milk it would shake its body in contentment and emit a shower of gold coins in gratitude."I had a lady swear to me that her mother had one!" Taylor concluded his story.

As this little tale might illustrate, Mexico is a country steeped in folklore. Her cultural superstitions, as elsewhere, often take the form of tall tales encompassing fantastic mythical entities. For instance, another supernatural creature indigenous to rural Mexican legend is *la Llorona* (tr: "The Wailing Woman"). Closely aligned with Gaelic/Celtic legends of howling female spirits called banshees, *la Llorona* was a similarly forlorn she-ghost whose moaning cries of grief were said to portend doom to those that heard them. She found her way to Mexican screens upon numerous occasions, firstly in **LA LLORONA** / tr: THE CRYING WOMAN (D: Ramon Peon, 1933; remade by René Cardona in 1959). The 1933 version was followed by **LA HERENCIA DE LA LLORONA**/tr: THE LEGACY OF THE CRYING WOMAN (D: Mauricio Magdaleno, 1946), **EL GRITO DE LA MUERTE/THE LIVING COFFIN** (D: Fernando Mendéz, 1958), **LA MALDICIÓN DE LA LLORONA/THE CURSE OF THE CRYING WOMAN** (D: Rafael Baledón, 1961) and **SANTO Y MANTEQUILLA NÁPOLES EN LA VENGANZA DE LA LLORONA**/tr: SANTO AND MANTEQUILLA NAPOLES IN THE REVENGE OF THE CRYING WOMAN (D: Miguel M. Delgado, 1973).

Origin of such tales seems hardly surprising coming from a country wherein low-paid "common man" *luchadores* (wrestlers) are frequently elevated to the esteemed status of folk superheroes. This by an adoring public that seemingly remains oblivious to the dividing line that usually severs fantasy from reality. Such obsessive hero worship and blurring of the boundary between the real and unreal seems to serve as relevant social catharsis for the country's downtrodden *paisano* masses. A seeming unconditional acceptance of fantasy is also a given in the escapist cinema of many cultures (Hong Kong's mystical brand of monsters'n'magic most readily springs to mind). Mexico is no exception. Monsters and fantasy play an important role in her popular culture, so it is only natural that the country's pop film industry adopted them with notable relish.

Because this article shall try to limit itself strictly to bonafide MONSTER titles, I have decided to gather analogous films into block categories. For instance, werewolves, vampires, zombies..you get the gist. Crossovers from category to category are inevitable in such intermingled and co-dependent sub-genres, but I have tried not to be too repetitive. The intent of this overview is not *necessarily* to pinpoint *every* MMM ever made, but simply to briefly touch upon some of the best, most interesting, worst and/or wackiest examples.

LUCHADORES CONTRA MONSTRUOS
MASKED MAULERS vs. MEXI-MONSTERS

When one first thinks of MMM, invariably that indigenous variety incorporating masked luchadores should spring to mind like El Santo swan-diving onto your skull from over the top rope. Colourful and eccentric costumed superheroes coming to grips with monstrous foes are certainly not a unique phenomenon. Witness for example Japan's ULTRAMAN, not to mention a slew of obscure Turkish SUPERMAN imitators. Undoubtedly Mexico's quirky, earthy ethnic style is most in evidence within its monster films; and especially those including masked wrestlers. Many people disregard these often delightful and unpretentious films as outright worthless garbage; and, from a purely aesthetic standpoint they're possibly right. But who reading *MONSTER INTERNATIONAL* cares about purely aesthetic standpoints?

Even pioneering fan-oriented publications like the late Calvin Beck's inspirational *CASTLE OF FRANKENSTEIN* routinely cast aspersions on often very worthwhile Mexican efforts. *C.O.F.* dismissed the non-wrestling horror film **LA INVASIÓN DE LOS VAMPIROS/ INVASION OF THE VAMPIRES** as 'trite' and 'routine', but at least 'fessed-up to its 'nice atmosphere'. Basic atmosphere is sometimes the sole available commodity in films that often defy the soundest tenets of sense, science and scenario. As far as the luchador flicks are concerned though, just bear in mind the following golden rule: seeing a film with a masked wrestler may be desirable, but seeing one with a masked wrestler and a monster is damned essential!

The seminal monster-wrestling effort came with Fernando Mendez's amazing **LADRÓN DE CADÁVERES** (1956; variously translated over the years to everything from THE BODY SNATCHER to THIEF OF CORPSES). The film did not star or feature El Santo, contrary to some reports and published evidence (he may well have been edited in on re-issue, but this is neither the time nor place to launch that debate). **LADRÓN** established a great roster of durable *luchador contra monstruo* cliches. Key elements of its plot (ie: a misguided surgeon conducting experiments to turn top athletes into supersubhuman monsters) resurfaced in at least two René Cardona films: **LAS LUCHADORAS CONTRA EL MEDICO ASESINO/DOCTOR OF DOOM** (1962), as well as that film's remake, **LA HORRIPILANTE BESTIA HUMANA/ NIGHT OF THE BLOODY APES** (1968). Refracted trace elements can be found even in Cardona's **LAS LUCHADORAS CONTRA EL ROBOT ASESINO/THE WRESTLING WOMEN VS. THE KILLER ROBOT** (1968).

While Santo didn't really come into his own as a film personality until 1958 (his debut efforts being a pair of extremely sub-par Mex/Cuban crime "thrillers" starring Joaquin Cordero), **LADRÓN DE CADÁVERES** helped further cement its star Wolf Ruvinskis' reputation as one of wrestling cinema's most frequent fixtures. He possessed the mettle combined with the muscle demanded of comicbook heroes. Wolf's *lucha libre* film experience dated back to the early '50s, but he also essayed a part made famous by Marlon Brando — that of Stanley Kowalski — in a homegrown Mex theatrical version of "A Streetcar Named Desire"; perhaps as far removed from Meximonsterdom as you can get. Ruvinskis got firmly back on track by portraying black-masked, sinewy super *hombre* "Neutrón" in a series of five films. A so-called sixth adventure bandied about for decades in numerous reference guides as "NEUTRÓN TRAPS THE INVISIBLE KILLERS" is in actuality an unrelated, retitled Cardona film from 1964 called **EL ASESINO INVISIBLE** /tr: THE INVISIBLE KILLER.

Ruvinskis Neutron's first trilogy of filmic adventures was **NEUTRÓN, EL ENMASCARADO NEGRO/ NEUTRÓN AND THE BLACK MASK, NEUTRÓN CONTRA EL DR. CARONTE/ NEUTRÓN VS. THE AMAZING DR. CARONTE.** and **LOS AUTOMATAS DE LA MUERTE/ NEUTRÓN AGAINST THE DEATH ROBOTS** (D: Federico Curiel, 1959-60). These pitted Neutrón against the mad Dr. Caronte (played by white-masked *"Beto el Boticario"* aka Roberto Ramírez). Caronte concocted, amongst other things, "Death Robot" monsters — lumbering, lumpyfaced henchthings clad in baggy boiler suits — in his megalomaniacal bid to rule the world by perfecting a devastating neutron bomb. Neutrón (the hero, not the bomb) puts a stop to it all by the final reel of Chapter Three with the assistance of Jack Taylor "Grek Martin" as the brainy and dependable Professor Thomas.

Neutrón was just one among many identity-incognito superheroes who periodically tussled with monsters. Usually though when you consider the term "masked wrestling monster films", the name of El Santo should strike an archetypal chord. If not, you'd best begin questioning whether you truly deserve your Monster International subscription, *muchacho*.

To lesser degrees — in terms of output, not always necessarily quality— El Demonio Azul or "Blue Demon" (aka Alejandro Cruz), Mil Máscaras or "Thousand Masks" (aka Aaron Rodríguez) and other *enmascarados* fought with monsters on film. Perhaps last and least in overall movie output and quality of finished product was Huracán or "Hurricane" Ramírez (aka David Silva). Ramírez's main claims to fame seem to be his former offscreen pro-wrestling career (now perpetuated by his successor, H.R. Jr.), along with the fact that he was an *amigo* of Santo's (Ramírez even acted as an enmasked pallbearer at the Silver-Masked One's funeral). Huracán's cinematic escapades were far less auspicious. Of his half-dozen or so motley filmic forays, only **LA VENGANZA DE HURACÁN RAMÍREZ**/tr: THE VENGEANCE OF HURRICANE RAMÍREZ (D: Josélito Rodríguez, 1967) featured anything that might charitably be classified as a "monster": namely, a poverty-stricken Jekyll/Hyde beastman created by an insane Darwinist's animal serum experimentation coupled with some of the worst time-lapse/ double-exposure photography ever. Lately, Huracán's filmic career is kept alive (barely) by Huracán Jr., who headlined the unbelievably abominable shot-on-video "production", **HURACÁN CONTRA LOS TERRORISTAS**/tr:HURRICANE VS. THE TERRORISTS (D: Juan Rodríguez, 1989). This contained no real monsters, though a rotten-faced zombie shows up in a brief nightmare sequence. This one token monsterrific reference sums up the extent of Hurricane's filmic legacy.

On the other hand, El Santo's movie monster-wrestling career was as prolific and prestigious as Ramirez's was paltry and pathetic. Santo, El Enmascarado de Plata grappled valiantly with most of the customary monster species, from vampires (a LOT of those) to mummies to aliens to werewolves to assorted whatsits mutated from various established pulp origins. A few of his better films were even honoured with limited international distribution, but Santo himself was often renamed for foreign markets: in the US/UK, he became known variously as "The Saint" (the literal translation of his Spanish handle) or "Samson". In Italy, he became "Argos"; in Germany, "*Superheld*/tr: Superhero"; in France, he was actually christened "Superman"! Santo's finest cinematic period was without question the early 1960s. Such densely-ambient megaclassics as **SANTO CONTRA LAS MUJERES VAMPIRO/SAMSON AND THE VAMPIRE WOMEN** (1961) and **SANTO EN EL MUSEO DE CERA/SAMSON IN THE WAX MUSEUM** (1963) remain prime Santonian choices. The former toplined a sexy sect of top-heavy vampirettes in sleazy eyeliner, as well as at least one werewolf; while the latter contained most of the classic monster repertoire, including an inanimate Frankenstein monster job very similar to the copyrighted Karloff/Jack Pierce conception.

Santo (Rodolfo Guzmán Huerta was beneath the mask in both real and reel-life) starred in numerous other inconsistently awesome or awful adventures. Of over fifty films in all, less than half contain monsters of sorts. Most of the titles are self explanatory: **SANTO CONTRA LOS ZOMBIES/ INVASION OF THE ZOMBIES** (D: Benito Alazraki, 1961), **SANTO CONTRA EL ESPECTRO DEL ESTRANGULADOR**/tr: SANTO VS. THE GHOST OF THE STRANGLER (D: René Cardona, 1963), **SANTO VS. LA INVASIÓN DE LOS MARCIANÓS**/tr: SANTO VS. THE MARTIAN INVASION (D: Alfredo B. Crevenna, 1966), **SANTO Y BLUE DEMON CONTRA LOS MONSTRUOS**/tr: SANTO AND BLUE DEMON VS. THE MONSTERS (D: Gilberto Martínez Solares, 1969), **SANTO CONTRA LA HIJA DE FRANKENSTEIN**/tr: SANTO VS. FRANKENSTEIN'S DAUGHTER (D: Miguel M. Delgado, 1971), **SANTO Y BLUE DEMON CONTRA EL DR. FRANKENSTEIN**/tr: SANTO AND BLUE DEMON VS. DR. FRANKENSTEIN (D: Miguel M. Delgado, 1973), etc.

As well as monsters, Santo polished off such stalwart B-grade criminal elements as gangsters, counterfeiters and even Nazis (the biggest monsters of all?). He made a handful more cheap films in the early-'80s, including his penultimate duo, **EL PUÑO DE LA MUERTE**/tr: THE FIST OF DEATH and **LA FURIA DE LOS KARATECAS** /tr: THE FURY OF THE KARATE-KILLERS (two very similiar movies both directed by Alfredo B. Crevenna, 1981). Despite nominal promise of martial arts mayhem, they do fit our rigorous Meximonster criteria. However, any tertiary critters present —namely a few ratty-looking "wolfman" types— are eclipsed by the monstrous two-headed gargantua of sex kitten Grace Renat's *pechos* (that means tits). El Santo retired from the screen shortly thereafter (how could he compete with *señorita* Renat's impressive acting talents?); he died of a heart attack in 1984, and the world's been a mess ever since.

THE BRAINIAC
IN A CLASS BY ITSELF!

In addition to the unique brand of wrestling films, MMM also encompass a substantial number of "straight" monster films in both contemporary and period settings. One of the true wonders of non-wrestling Meximonster cinema, **EL BARÓN DEL TERROR**/tr: THE BARON OF TERROR (D: Chano Urueta, 1961) will sound much more familiar under its famous K. Gordon Murray release title, **THE BRAINIAC**. Murray's several-dozen strong "Spookies" package that was sold strictly to US tv in English-dubbed state during the '60s boasted many of the finest MMM. However, it is **THE BRAINIAC** which remains one of the strangest and most wonderful acquisitions ever Mexported. Among the frequently incestuous Meximonster lineage, it succeeds in standing alone as a totally unique concept, its pedigreed roots completely untainted by the mongrel genes of the main family tree. The basic plotline about an accused warlock burned at the stake and returning centuries later to exact revenge on his condemning inquisitors may well have been assimilated from Italian Mario Bava's **LA MASCHERA DEL DEMONIO/BLACK SUNDAY** (1960). There similarities end. Woven into **THE BRAINIAC**'s otherwise stock storyline is a pointy-snouted, throbbing-headed monstrosity -*señor* BRAINIAC himself— with a penchant for slurping out assigned vendetta victims' brains using his elongated forked tongue. **THE BRAINIAC** has no equivalent in the multi-nuanced Mexploitation spectrum, yet it somehow ideally personifies the MMM mythus. It is *the* prototypical example by which all others may be measured. And the absolute optimum place to start if you're of a mind to cultivate an appetite for either Mexican monster films — or human brains.

LOS VAMPIROS & LAS VAMPIRAS
MALE AND FEMALE BLOODSCUKERS, ETC.

As in many worldwide horror film markets, vampires were probably the most prolific and steadily employed monsters within all of Mexcinema. Beginning with Carlos Villarias' variation on Lugosi in the Spanish language cut of **DRACULA** (1931), the better Mexican vampire films —primarily the monochromatic ones— were among the most ambient and picturesque in all MMM.

Standouts in the undead sub-genre are Fernando Mendez's (he of **LADRÓN DE CADÁVERES** acclaim) frequently eloquent **EL VAMPIRO/THE VAMPIRE** and its debatably superior sequel, **EL ATAÚD DEL VAMPIRO/THE VAMPIRE'S COFFIN** (both 1957). This strikingly photographed duo attains a plateau of elegant, elegiac quality seldom reached in even the much-lauded Hammer hickey sagas. The first Mendez film is a more traditional rural Gothic romance with fangs; the second transplants its continuous plotline to an urban locale. It offers some incredibly-atmospheric light and shadow *chiaroscuro* camera compositions worthy of the finest in German Expressionism and American *noir*. A major sub-plot

Ad mat from SANTO VS. THE GHOST OF THE STRANGLER.

unfolds in a wax museum/torture chamber no doubt influenced by André De Toth's 1953 **HOUSE OF WAX** (wax museums figure prominently in a large number of Mexi-horrors, including Rafael Baledón's virtual **HOUSE OF WAX** remake, **MUSEO DEL HORROR**/tr: MUSEUM OF HORROR, 1964, and Jaime Salvador's **LA SEÑORA MUERTE**/tr: LADY DEATH, 1967). Stepping into **EL VAMPIRO**'s shoes and the Meximonster hall of infamy was instant star Germán Robles ("Edward Tucker" in some foreign releases, for instance the German print of **COFFIN**, known as **DER SARG DES VAMPIRO**). Robles played the charismatic Count Lavud/Duval with aristocratic detachment, pale hair and inch-long eyeteeth. The portrait of Robles in character as the Count is — along with El Santo's familiar enmasked visage— perhaps the most instantly recognizable image in all Mexploitation.

Ironically, Mexico's greatest vampiric thespian also made a name for himself as a stage actor playing Biblical characters in passion plays like **PROCESO A JESUS**/tr: TRIAL OF JESUS (1959). This theatrical production was staged specially for the Archbishop of Mexico (it also featured Robles' Spanishized American colleague from the NOSTRADAMUS serial, Jack Taylor). However, it is for Robles' commanding portrayals of undead bloodsucking aristos in films like the **EL VAMPIRO** duet, his spoof cameo in **EL CASTILLO DE LOS MONSTRUOS**/tr: THE CASTLE OF THE MONSTERS, his Nostradamus characterization, and even the Argentinian-made **EL VAMPIRO AECHECHA**/tr: THE VAMPIRE STRIKES/**THE LURKING VAMPIRE**, 1959) that have made him one of Mexploitation's most easily identifiable faces. He is the Mexican Chris Lee, or perhaps more accurately a Mexican precursor to Italian glampire, Walter Brandi. Robles was hereinafter to be almost exclusively associated with cultured vampiric roles.

Germán Robles belatedly returned to the bloodsucker genre for **LOS VAMPIROS DE COYOACÁN**/tr: THE VAMPIRES OF COYOACÁN (D: Arturo Martínez, 1973). Surprisingly, he did not fill the expected lead vampire's cape, and was a heroic character for a change. **COYOACÁN** is a loose companion-piece to same director Martinez's much-inferior **LAS MOMIAS DE SAN ÁNGEL**/tr: THE MUMMIES OF SAN ÁNGEL (also 1973), in that it stars multi-masked luchador Mil Máscaras (ably assisted by tag-partner Superzán - *not* a typo). **COYOACÁN** is routine vampirized shenanigans, but bolstered by some eerie ambience, a handful of nasty killer dwarves (what other kind *are* there?), and a remarkably well-accomplished man-into-werebat transmogrification. But, truth be told, Robles was rather wasted in this film.

A less familiar Mexploitation face many might be hard-pressed to attach a name to belongs to one Yerye Beirute, who was Robles' brutish 'assistant' in **THE VAMPIRE'S COFFIN**. Beirute also appeared in a vampire comedy called **ECHENME AL VAMPIRO**/tr: BRING ME THE VAMPIRE (D: Alfredo B. Crevenna, 1961), as well as many non-vampire horror/monster pictures. He usually portrayed second-string scuzzball henchmen or criminal degenerates in the healthy number of MMM he appeared in. These encompassed some of the very BEST '50s efforts (**LADRÓN DE CADÁVERES**), some of the '60s *worst* (Boris Karloff's **LA CÁMARA DEL TERROR/THE FEAR CHAMBER**, 1968), as well as one of the '70s wackiest (René Cardona's bizarre **EL INCREÍBLE PROFESOR ZÓVEK**/tr: THE INCREDIBLE PROFESSOR ZÓVEK, 1971). Beirute never played a monster *per se*. The striking fact alone that he was a homelier facial hybrid of Karloff and Spanish

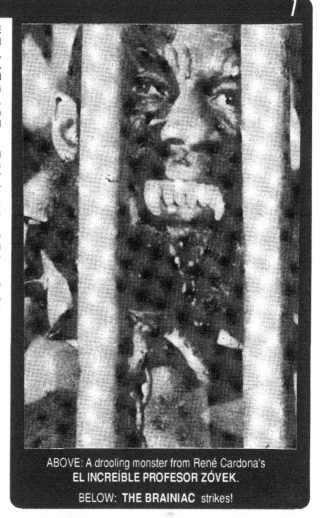

ABOVE: A drooling monster from René Cardona's **EL INCREÍBLE PROFESOR ZÓVEK**.
BELOW: **THE BRAINIAC** strikes!

sleazemeister Howard Vernon assures him of at least a passing nod here! Yerye's stint opposite Robles in **THE VAMPIRE'S COFFIN** is perhaps his most unctuous, reptilian role.

As a consequence of Germán Robles' popularity from the **VAMPIRO** duo (almost simultaneous to the rise of Hammer Films' DRACULA cycle), a plethora of mood-thick vampire melodramas resulted. **EL MUNDO DE LOS VAMPIROS/ THE WORLD OF THE VAMPIRES** (D: Alfonso Corona Blake, 1960) emerges as one of the campiest and most deliriously choreographed. Its Roblesian vampire lord, skull-bedecked supernatural pipe organ, bustaceous Hispanic vamp-vixens and solemn procession of pug-ugly minions converging on their Satanic Majesty's underground crypt-cavern exemplify the peculiar slant of supreme Mexican *camp*.

Further *primo* examples of the distinct Mexican vampire style can be seen in another complementary twosome, Miguel Morayta's arcanely saturated **LA INVASIÓN DE LOS VAMPIROS/ THE INVASION OF THE VAMPIRES** (1961) and its sequel, **EL VAMPIRO SANGRIENTO/ THE BLOODY VAMPIRE** (1962, **EL CONDE FRANKENHAUSEN**/tr: COUNT FRANKENHAUSEN). For these, a mild but detectably kinky S/M tone and Carlos Agosti as evil Count Frankenhausen dominated. Agosti was another seemingly eternal Meximonster fixture, his *curriculum vitae* numbering such films as **DR. SATÁN Y LA MAGIA NEGRA**/tr: DR. SATAN VS. BLACK MAGIC (D: Rogelio A. González Jr., 1967) and **THE WRESTLING WOMEN VS. THE KILLER ROBOT** (D: René Cardona, 1968).

In **INVASION OF THE VAMPIRES** and **THE BLOODY VAMPIRE**, director Morayta competently combined a funereal black carriage pulled by slow-motion horses, a deliciously audacious, stiff-winged bat-cum-hang glider with furry Bugs Bunny ears, and oodles of dry-ice fog. If you took a knife, you could feasibly slice hunks of atmosphere off these two films like *cheese*. They even somehow had room left for stiff-legged resuscitated *vampiro*-zombies that predated and neatly foreshadowed Romero's **NIGHT OF THE LIVING DEAD** by more than a half-decade.

Seductive predatory vamp-vixens have of course been a main facet of most international bloodsucker industries, and Mexico's was certainly no exception. Vampire seductresses with almondine eyes and melon breasts also figure prominently (ahem) in a small sub-genre of Meximonster cinema. They most notably appeared in above-mentioned **SANTO CONTRA LAS MUJERES VAMPIRO** (D: Alfonso Corona Blake, 1961), headed up by sultry Cult Queen Lorena Velázquez and her vampirized beefcake-boys. Lorena reprised her role in Jose Diaz Morales' **ATACAN LAS BRUJAS** /tr: THE WITCHES ATTACK (1964), a Santo opus involving alleged ghostly bitchwitches that was basically a verbatim but uncredited remake of **MUJERES VAMPIRO**. Senorita Velázquez acted in numerous B-film genres. She is most remembered for her horror movies, and especially ones in which she teamed up with voluptuous she-cat Elizabeth Campbell as a female wrestling tag-team (ie: **LAS LUCHADORAS CONTRA EL MEDICO ASESINO** and **LAS LUCHADORAS CONTRA LA MOMIA**, both D: René Cardona, 1962/64).

As far as flitting vampire ballerinas in skintight body stockings and serrated-edge Batgirl capes go, **LAS VAMPIRAS**/tr: THE VAMPIRE GIRLS (D: Federico Curiel, 1968) simply couldn't be surpassed. Toss in Mil Máscaras again as the husky hero, John Carradine as a decrepit caged vampire, and some wobbly cardboard bats on strings, and this film's combination just can't be beat. Curiel struck again with **SANTO EN LA VENGANZA DE LAS MUJERES VAMPIRO**/tr: SANTO IN THE VENGEANCE OF THE VAMPIRE WOMEN (1970), another wrestler outing with murderous blood-drinking Meximinxes.

Voracious vampirettes made yet another appearance in René Cardona's **SANTO EN EL TESORO DE DRÁCULA**/tr: SANTO IN DRACULA'S TREASURE (1967). An alternate version designated for release to certain more permissive "adults only" markets (including the Continent) was retitled **EL VAMPIRO Y EL SEXO**, literally "THE VAMPIRE AND SEX"! This sexed-up edit contained a bevy of stacked *señoritas* whose topless feminine pulchritude was more explicitly exposed than in the "straight" version. Knowing a lucrative trend when he latched onto its bra-straps, famed Mex producer-director-writer-actor Cardona released tittified editions of three subsequent non-vampire monster-wrestling films. These were: **LA HORRIPILANTE BESTIA HUMANA/NIGHT OF THE BLOODY APES, LAS LUCHADORAS CONTRA EL ROBOT ASESINO/THE WRESTLING WOMEN VS. THE KILLER ROBOT** and **SANTO CONTRA LOS JINETES DEL TERROR**/tr: SANTO VS. THE TERROR RIDERS. These three were renamed **HORROR Y SEXO**/HORROR AND SEX, **EL ASESINO LOCO Y EL SEXO**/THE MAD KILLER AND SEX and **Y LEPROSOS Y EL SEXO**/THE LEPERS AND SEX respectively (bonafide gun-toting lepers were ostensible "monsters" of the final title, a strange wrestling/western hybrid).

Also from the horror horse-opera stable trotted a nominal vampire picture, Juan J. Ortega's elusive **LOS MURCIÉLAGOS**/tr: THE BATS (1964), which saw its 1965 release in Mother Country Spain as **LOS VAMPIROS DEL OESTE**/tr: THE VAMPIRES OF THE WEST. This was a mock monster-western whose villainous protagonists wore the disguise of supernatural vampires. Still more spurious (literal and figurative) vampires showed up in **CHANOC VS. EL TIGRE Y EL VAMPIRO**/tr: CHANOC VS. THE TIGER AND THE VAMPIRE (1971) and **CHANOC Y EL HIJO DEL SANTO CONTRA LOS VAMPIROS**/tr: CHANOC AND THE SON OF SANTO VS. THE VAMPIRES (D: Rafael Peréz Grovas, 1981). Chanoc (usually played by beefy Gregorio Casals, a veteran of several Santo films) was a popular Mexicomix creation who found his way into a short-lived series of poverty row "action adventures". Monster content was most minimal, although in **CHANOC VS. LOS DEVOURADORES DE HOMBRES**/tr: CHANOC VS. THE MANEATERS (aka **CHANOC EN LAS GARRAS DE LAS FIERAS**/tr: CHANOC IN THE WILD BEASTS' CLAWS, D: Gilberto Martínez Solares, 1971) our hero was seen to battle *the* fakest, most flaccid inflatable-vinyl "giant octopus" of all time! While on the topic of lamentably phoney monsters, along with vampires and octopi, it should be mentioned that a bogus "gillman" played a fishy red herring in Rafael Baledón's **EL PANTANO DE LAS ANIMAS/THE SWAMP OF THE LOST MONSTER**

Rare Spanish release ad mat for the Mexican horror-westetrn, LOS MURCIÉLAGOS.

(1956; US release 1965). This was another mutant western, employing a SCOOBY-DOO plot structure that ends with its piscean prowler being unveiled as a hoax engineered by a greedy villain.

At least there was an honest-to-goodness vampire in **EL IMPERIO DE DRÁCULA**/tr: THE EMPIRE OF DRACULA (D: Federico Curiel, 1966), a nicely-made colour film with many intentional similarities to Hammer's **DRACULA, PRINCE OF DARKNESS** (1965), which was something of a box-office success in Mexico. A decade or so later, the prolific Alfredo B. Crevenna's similarly-titled **LA DINASTÍA DRÁCULA**/tr: THE DRACULA DYNASTY (1978) helped contribute to/capitalize on the late-'70s resurgence of post-Hammer vampire romances. **DINASTÍA** sure as hell beats John Badham's **DRACULA** hands down, and it's dense, intoxicant mood is not surprising in light of the other vampire mood-pieces discussed hereabouts. What *is* surprising is the fact that former US teen heart-throb Fabiano "Fabian" Forte fills the role of a descendent of Count Dracula — and, it's *not* a comedy!

LOS ZOMBIES
WALKING CORPSES & HUMAN AUTOMATONS

A prototypical example of a "zombie" from the Golden Era of MMM is the disfigured reanimated lunatic (Antonio Raxel) who claws frantically from his shallow grave amidst a thunderstorm in the pseudo-cerebral **MISTERIOS DE ULTRATUMBA/ BLACK PIT OF DR. M** (D: Fernando Mendéz, 1958). The "rebirth" of this walking dead man prefigures the clawing, uprooting corpses in such better-known *gringo* productions as **PLAGUE OF THE ZOMBIES** (1966), **COUNT YORGA, VAMPIRE** (1971), and **RETURN OF THE LIVING DEAD** (1985).

Science ostensibly aligned with voodoo brought the radio-controlled human robots of **SANTO CONTRA LOS ZOMBIES/INVASION OF THE ZOMBIES** (1961) to "life". Still another symbiotic collaboration between the occult/alchemical sciences and the technological endowed unnatural mobil-

U.S. ad-mat for **MISTERIOS DE ULTRATUMBA**

ity to the heavily eye-shadowed automaton slaves of **EL DR. SATÁN**/tr: DR. SATAN (D: Miguel Morayta, 1966) and their swish mini-skirted zombie sisters in the sequel, **DR. SATÁN Y LA MAGIA NEGRA**/tr: DR. SATAN VS. BLACK MAGIC (D: Rogelio A. González Jr., 1967). Both films also featured cameos by a translucent-winged demoniac Satan; latter also highlighted the machinations of a sinister halfbreed Oriental/Occidental vampire-sorceror (Japanese/Mexican character actor Noé Murayama), just in case zombies and the Devil Himself didn't suffice.

As for the "traditional" utilization of the zombie, **SANTO CONTRA LA MAGIA NEGRA**/tr: SANTO VS. BLACK MAGIC (D: Alfredo B. Crevenna, 1972) is perhaps the most faithful to the superficial pulp cliches assigned to voodoo by Hollywood.

As well as actually being lensed on location in Haiti, **MAGIA NEGRA** contains lengthy peeks into authentic voodoo ceremonies, and numerous black guys stiff-legging around the island wearing realistic special effects makeup (ie: corn flour). At one point, these "evil zombies" are warded off by Santo when he brandishes a cruciform *tire-iron* of all things in their direction!

An earlier quite customary manufactured walking dead occurred in **LA MUERTE VIVIENTE/ISLE OF THE SNAKE PEOPLE** (D: Juan Ibáñez and Jack Hill, 1968). As is by now very well documented, the film is one of the much-reviled four-pack that an ailing Boris Karloff appeared in during the lattermost stage of his career. The other films were **LA CÁMARA DEL TERROR/THE FEAR CHAMBER**, which featured a prehistoric rock monster, **LA INVASIÓN SINIESTRA/THE INCREDIBLE INVASION**, and **SERENATA MACABRA/HOUSE OF EVIL** (all directed by Ibáñez and Hill, 1968). Actually, **LA NUERTE VIVIENTE**/tr: THE LIVING DEATH is probably the best of the motley bunch, boasting some thick, eerie mood, as well as zombies against a pronounced necro-erotic undertow. Much of the latter ingredient is provided by luscious actress/dancer Yolanda *"Tongolele"* Montes in her sparsley-clad capacity as an evil juju princess, complete with mandatory phallic pet boa constrictor. *Hubba-hubba...*

The closest I've yet seen a Mexploitation zombie entry come to resembling Romero's **NIGHT OF THE LIVING DEAD** (besides the foreshadowings found in **INVASION OF THE VAMPIRES**) would have to be **BLUE DEMON Y ZÓVEK EN LA INVASIÓN DE LOS MUERTOS**/tr: BLUE DEMON AND ZÓVEK IN THE INVASION OF THE DEAD (D: René Cardona, 1972). Therein a mysterious globular meteorite impregnated by cosmic rays settles in the Mexican badlands. Its radiation causes revivification of a horde of shambling undead extras. These massed zombies proceed to chase Blue, effeminate escape-artiste Prof. Zóvek and delectable blonde heroine Christa Linder around an isolated desert. Why the same radioactive meteor apparently also causes two other dudes to devolve into vampire/werewolf-fanged growling beastmen is anybody's guess. Just for variety's sake...?

The obvious Americanisms of **INVASIÓN DE LOS MUERTOS** were diluted by enough Mexcentricity to keep my incredulous attention. On the other hand, one of the most modern Meximonster films I've seen to date, Rúben Galindo Jr's zombified **CEMENTERIO DEL TERROR**/tr: CEMETERY OF TERROR (1985) is a pretty sorry juxtaposition of blatant yankee-wank components. **FRIDAY THE 13TH** and **RETURN OF THE LIVING DEAD** are equally plagiarized in a sloppy mock-US script that mimics both films with its copycat living dead teen-slasher and climactic zombie party. **CEMENTERIO** offers ample testimony that the contemporary Mexican horror picture is a stumbling, undead shadow of its former self, and should perhaps be mercifully and conclusively laid to rest.

LAS MOMIAS

THE CRUSTIER, DUSTIER WALKING DEAD

Another popular monster species within MMM is *la momia*. With its above reanimated cousins the vampire and the zombie (the Frankenstein monster makes only sporadic appearances), it is one of the more commonplace Meximonstrous antagonists. Mexico's built-in morbid cultural fascination with Death and the Afterlife no doubt helps explain the motion picture prominence of these resuscitated corpses. Evidence of the Mexican people's collective infatuation with the mechanics of Death is provided by such extinct native societies as the Aztecs, Toltecs and Mayans, who were known to embalm important personages and entomb them for

JOAQUIN CORDERO y ALMA DELIA FUENTES en **"EL DOCTOR SATAN"**

all Eternity inside huge, multi-tiered stone pyramids. Parallels with the more familiar ancient Egyptian tradition are quite obvious. But, whereas Hollywood and elsewhere took to the idea of mummified Egyptian pharaohs or high priests returning from the grave for revenge or romance, the uniquely Mexican species of *momia* has maintained a considerably more subdued profile.

Probably the highest visibility Mexi-mummy character is *Popoca*, the aptly-named "Aztec Mummy". Popoca initially gained prominence in a three-film series directed by Rafael Portillo: **LA MOMIA AZTECA, LA MALDICIÓN DE LA MOMIA AZTECA** and **EL ROBOT HUMANO** (all 1957). All three films were re-dubbed/recycled to various degrees for US release as **THE CURSE OF THE AZTEC MUMMY, ATTACK OF THE MAYAN MUMMY** and **THE ROBOT VS. THE AZTEC MUMMY**. Incidentally, the human robot, Popoca's clanking opponent in the final instalment, was subsequently re-used (à la **FORBIDDEN PLANET**'s "Robby") for appearances in both **CAPERUCITA Y PULGARCITO CONTRA LOS MONSTRUOS/LITTLE RED RIDING HOOD AND THE MONSTERS** and **LA NAVE DE LOS MONSTRUOS**/tr: THE SHIP OF THE MONSTERS (both 1960).

The scruffy Aztec mummy meanwhile rose again to face voluptuous grappling *chicas* Lorena Velázquez and Elizabeth Campbell in René Cardona's **THE WRESTLING WOMEN VS. THE AZTEC MUMMY**, and even put in a belated comeback cameo alongside Velázquez and chaperon Johnny Legend in the Mexi-wrestling film episode of Jonathan Ross' Brit tv series, *SON OF THE INCREDIBLY STRANGE FILM SHOW* (1989). Similar crusty mummy-zombies arose for **MISTERIOS DE LA MAGIA NEGRA**/tr: MYSTERIES OF BLACK MAGIC (D: Miguel M. Delgado, 1957) and **SANTO EN LA VENGANZA DE LA MOMIA**/tr: SANTO IN THE MUMMY'S REVENGE (D: René Cardona, 1970).

Mexico's other indigenous mummy species made its welcome motion picture debut in 1970 for Federico Curiel's **LAS MOMIAS DE GUANAJUATO**/tr: THE MUMMIES OF GUANAJUATO. Among the real-life Mexican town of Guanajuato's top tourist attractions are its museum exhibits of "real-life" mummies. These withered cadavers -atrophied and stiffened by *rigor mortis* into grotesque simulacrums of living human postures— are preserved after interment by some mysterious and apparently random process of natural mummification, possibly via some remarkable chemical reaction of the soil. The embalmed corpses are donated by loved ones to be dug up when the time is "ripe" for display among the desiccated ranks of other Mummies of Guanajuato.

LAS MOMIAS DE GUANAJUATO: the film showcased wrestling mega-stars Blue Demon and Mil Máscaras (with El Santo contributing a bit part), plus a horde of motile mummies rampaging through authentic hometown locations. The film spawned a pair of sequels, **EL ROBO DE LAS MOMIAS DE GUANAJUATO**/tr: THE THEFT OF THE MUMMIES OF GUANAJUATO and **EL CASTILLO DE LAS MOMIAS DE GUANAJUATO**/tr: THE CASTLE OF THE MUMMIES OF GUANAJUATO (both D: Tito Novaro, 1972). Such emulations no doubt occurred on account of the originating series entry being the highest-grossing monster-wrestling flick to date. Seeing as these films simply aren't produced anymore (bar recent "art film" homages like José Buil's incredible **LA LEYENDA DE UNA MASCARA**/tr: THE LEGEND OF A MASK, 1990), it looks as if **LAS MOMIAS DE GUANAJUATO** shall retain its enviable title.

Due to **MOMIAS** #1's success, it inevitably had its imitators and pretenders. Alfredo Zacarías' **CAPULINA CONTRA LAS MOMIAS**/tr: CAPULINA VS. THE MUMMIES (aka **EL TERROR DE GUANAJUATO** or **CAPULINA ENTRE LAS MOMIAS**/tr: CAPULINA AMONGST THE MUMMIES, 1972) was a parodic screwball mum-com that headlined its title pudgy comedian (aka Gaspar Henaine). Zacarías later cameo'd the genuine Guanajuato museum mummies in his "possessed hand" film, **MACABRO: LA MANO DEL DIABLO**/ aka **DEMONOID** (980).

LAS MOMIAS DE SAN ÁNGEL/tr: THE MUMMIES OF SAN ÁNGEL (D: Arturo Martínez, 1973) was a poor man's emulation of the first **GUANAJUATO**'s formula. The real-life town of San Ángel boasts its own more modest collection of "mummies". As with similar victims of Mt. Vesuvius' eruption in ancient Pompeii, several San Ángel priests and nuns were ossified centuries ago by a flash-flood of volcanic lava. This historical fact seems to be the basic source idea fancified and elaborated upon by **LAS MOMIAS DE SAN ÁNGEL**'s scriptwriters, who took many liberties with the truth. Granted, it had some positive points in returning star Mil Máscaras, heroine Lorena Velázquez and a goodly contingent of mummies. But it never attains the manic, tacky gusto and surreal brilliance of its inspiration source.

Mouldy mummies (of the more traditional, bandage-bound Hollywood kind) walked in numerous films, like **EL CASTILLO DE LOS MONSTRUOS**/tr: THE CASTLE OF THE MONSTERS (D: Julian Soler, 1957), **SANTO Y BLUE DEMON CONTRA LOS MONSTRUOS**/tr: SANTO AND BLUE DEMON VS. THE MONSTERS (D: Gilberto Martínez Solares, 1969) and **LA MANSIÓN DE LAS SIETE MOMIAS**/tr: THE HOUSE OF THE SEVEN MUMMIES (D: Rafael Lanuza, 1975). In the mid-to-late-'70s, mummies (led by pro wrestler/part-time actor Tinieblas "Darkness" in skintight linen wrappings) battled a bullwhip-cracking Zorro impersonator (Mex-action star Juan Miranda) in Ángel Rodríguez's **EL LÁTIGO CONTRA LAS MOMIAS ASESINAS**/tr: THE WHIP VS. THE MURDERING MUMMIES. A plot-thread connection to the first **GUANAJUATO** film is apparent in that the title monsters are able to appear or vanish instantaneously and so doubly confound their stunned victims. Unfortunately, the mummies in this film are far too tightly-wound and immaculate in appearance, and provoke pangs of nostalgia for the sloppier dress sense of old Popoca of yore.

In more recent times, the Meximummy — like most of his late, lamented monster compadres — seems to have been permanently laid to rest thanks to a now-negligible domestic film industry.

LOS HOMBRES LOBOS & LAS LOBAS
Werewolves and She-Wolves

Attack of Los Lobos! from (top) **SANTO CONTRA LAS LOBAS** and (above) **EL HOMBRE Y EL MONSTRUO**.

Lycanthropy and shapeshifting (including the related Jekyll/Hyde syndrome) were once mainstays of the Meximonster industry. Though most films with a pronounced lycanthropic theme were heavily influenced by Lon Chaney Jr's Lawrence Stewart Talbot persona first popularized by Universal's **THE WOLFMAN** (1941), Chaney did not really have a comparable counterpart in Mexico. Things came full circle of sorts when Lon ventured south of the border to appear in a (non-speaking) lycanthrope role for the Germán *Tin Tan* Valdes comedy, **LA CASA DEL TERROR**/tr: THE HOUSE OF TERROR (D: Gilberto Martínez Solares, 1959). As is by now common knowledge, a butchered, English-dubbed and nigh-unwatchable version with additional US-shot footage was released in 1965 by notorious hack gringo Jerry *"I display nothing but utter contempt for the cinematic medium"* Warren. Known as **FACE OF THE SCREAMING WEREWOLF**, it may easily join Warren's other fancifully-titled import Mex/US graft-jobs, **ATTACK OF THE MAYAN MUMMY, CREATURE OF THE WALKING DEAD** and **CURSE OF THE STONE HAND** as one of the cruddiest repackaging non-attempts *ever*.

Thankfully, Warren didn't get to inflict his disastrous anti-Midas touch on **EL HOMBRE Y EL MONSTRUO/ THE MAN AND THE MONSTER** (D: Rafael Baledón, 1957), starring suave Mexican horror hero/producer Abel Salazar in his pre-**BRAINIAC** days. **HOMBRE** owed as much to Robert L. Stevenson as to Larry S. Talbot, with its tale of a haunted pianist (Enrique Rambal) reverting to a Mr. Hyde-like werewolf beastie when a certain composition is played on his keyboard. Stirred in to make this somber tale even more so is a dark Faustian sub-plot about a soul sold in furtherance of a glorious musical career, and also murder. The serious mood is not undone even by comical makeup (the fully transformed monster boasts a prominent schnozz with the general dimensions of a proboscis monkey's!). Director (and actor) Baledón rose from helming faceless US-emulative matinee westerns and the like to briefly become one of Mexico's finest purveyors of monster/horror/fantasy fare in the later '50s to mid-'60s period. Now in his early seventies, Baledón currently acts in daytime Spanish-language soap operas!

The other notable Baledónian werewolf entry was **LA LOBA**/tr: THE SHE-WOLF (1964), which co-starred Joaquin Cordero and an inordinate amount of graphic splatter for the period (perhaps the antithesis of Baledón's whimsical *Tin Tan* comedy-musical from the same year, **LOS FANTASMAS BURLONES**/tr. THE GHOST JOKERS). **LA LOBA** details the exploits of a ferocious, white-furred wolf *señorita* (Kitty de Hoyos), and again was slightly marred by occasionally laughable monster makeup (ie: "werewolf feet" that look more like fuzzy slippers!). All-in-all though, a worthy effort.

Other wolf-chicks bared their talons and wore scimpy fur bikinis in the unrelated **SANTO CONTRA LAS LOBAS**/tr: SANTO VS. THE SHE-WOLVES (D: Jaime Jiménez Pons & Rúben Galindo, 1972). **LAS LOBAS DEL RING**/tr: THE SHE-WOLVES OF THE RING (D: René Cardona, 1964) were figurative rather than literal (a fierce but fully human all-girl wrestling team — part of the Wrestling Women series).

While (wolf)woman roared, male lycanthropes appeared in the likes of **SANTO Y BLUE DEMON CONTRA DRÁCULA Y EL HOMBRE LOBO**/tr: SANTO AND BLUE DEMON VS. DRACULA AND THE WOLFMAN (D: Miguel M. Delgado, 1972), **EL HOMBRE Y LA BESTIA**/tr. THE MAN AND THE BEAST (1972 — a version of Dr. Jekyll and Mr. Hyde) and **PEPITO Y CHABELO VS. LOS MONSTRUOS**/tr: PEPITO AND CHABELO VS. THE MONSTERS (1972). Wolfmen also had supporting parts in b/w fare like **SANTO EN EL MUSEO DE CERA/ SAMSON IN THE WAX MUSEUM** (D: Alfonso Corona Blake, 1963) and **EL DEMONIO AZUL**/tr: BLUE DEMON (D: Chano Urueta, 1964).

As for the latterday lycanthropy scene (what there is of it), the best we can do is **CAZADOR DE DEMONIOS/DEMON HUNTER** (D: Gilberto de Anda, 1985). Although the monster is not actually called a werewolf in the film (which has been English-dubbed and released to N. American tv/video, a rarity in modern-day Mexploitation), the plot essentially follows the typical wolfman blueprint. It depicts the murderous rampage of a liberated demon from Indian lore: but you might as well classify the sporadically glimpsed lupine/ursine monster as a werewolf. **DEMON HUNTER** is far from remarkable, but it is a rare competent milestone in the now pitifully barren Meximonster landscape.

LOS MONSTRUOS PREHISTORICOS, ETC.

DINOSAURS, BATMEN, & EVEN A YETI

No doubt because the nation does not possess atomic technology, Mexico's '50s monsterthons never reflected the same paranoid nuclear concerns of US-made s.f. films from the period. The closest Mexico really came to a bonafide titanic-monster-on-the-rampage flick was **THE BLACK SCORPION** (1957), a Hollywood production lensed south of the border. Of course, the US/Mex coproduction, **EL MONSTRUO DE LA MONTAÑA HUECA/ BEAST OF HOLLOW MOUNTAIN** (aka **LA BESTIA DE LA MONTAÑA/**

Ad mat from the rarley-seen film THE VOLCANO MONSTER.

*The starry-eyed bat-monster carries off Ana Luisa in Alfredo B. Crevenna's **AVENTURA AL CENTRO DE LA TIERRA**.*

(aka **EL FANTASMA DE LAS GRUTAS**/tr: THE GHOST OF THE CAVES and **EL FANTASMA DE LAS NIEVES**/tr: THE GHOST OF THE SNOW, D: Jaime Salvador, 1962). The monster here was a towering and impressive-looking (at least according to stills) white cottonpuffball apeman. I hope to live long enough to see either or both of these incredibly obscure films *(editor's note: in fact, the second movie, although a sequel to the first one, does not feature a real monster, but a human impostor as the snowman)*.

Both starred commonplace Mexploitation face Joaquín Cordero, whose roles were divided fairly evenly between heavies and heroes. Cordero can be seen in both **DR. SATÁN** films, as well as others covered by this article. His latest MMM appearance to date is in **PESADILLA SANGRIENTA**/tr: BLOODY NIGHTMARE (D: Pedro Galindo III, 1990). This is a cheap monster-thriller; a loose sequel to the demonic dolly film, **VACACIONES DE TERROR**/tr: TERROR VACATION (D: René Cardona III, 1988). **PESADILLA** also concerns a possessed girl's doll, which transforms into a toothy demon and boasts of mostly **GHOULIES**-level spfx and pronounced Americanization, but it is nice to see Cordero still at it. He appears remarkably well-preserved, almost physically unchanged since his halcyon days as the disfigured wax sculptor in Baledón's moody **MUSEO DEL HORROR** (1964). Cordero often bears a striking resemblance to a younger Cameron Mitchell, which seems highly appropriate considering his longevity in the Mexploitation movie industry.

LOS MONSTRUOS CÓMICOS
GOOFS AND SPOOFS

A standard "straight" Meximonster film can often yield its quota of off-the-wall moments. When a Meximonster film decides to lampoon itself or the genre, prepare for even more zany and unpredictable results! Perhaps an apex within the spoof sub-genre was reached in **AUTOPSIA DE UN FANTASMA**/tr: AUTOPSY OF A GHOST (D: Ismael Rodríguez, 1967). Teaming up Basil Rathbone, John Carradine and Cameron Mitchell, the film is probably the craziest and most anarchic in structure, with its living skeleton,

tr: THE BEAST OF THE MOUNTAIN, D: Edward Nassour & Ismael Rodríguez, 1954/56) showcased some passable Willis O'Brien-designed allosaur dinomation. But, this was mainly your routine oat opera, enlivened in its final minutes by a spot of diverting dinosaur action.

Speaking of dinosaurs, **LA EDAD DE PIEDRA**/tr: THE STONE AGE (D: René Cardona, 1962) was a comedy starring popular *paisano* funnymen *Capulina* and *Viruta*. It contained some prehistoric beastie footage that later saw recycling along with additional stock shots from **ONE MILLION B.C.** (US, 1940) and **UNKNOWN ISLAND** (US, 1947) in order to pad out the running time of **AVENTURA AL CENTRO DE LA TIERRA**/tr: ADVENTURE AT THE CENTRE OF THE EARTH (D: Alfredo B. Crevenna, 1964). Essentially a loose remake of **JOURNEY TO THE CENTER OF THE EARTH** (US, 1959), the Mex version — in addition to being mercifully much shorter — actually emerges as a substantially more entertaining film. This in spite of a lack of the Technicolor and CinemaScope of its forerunner. Of course, it also lacked insufferable smeghead Pat Boone, which helps explain everything. Location work done in real Mexican volcanic caverns, a cyclopean primeval lizard monster, as well as a bipedal bat-humanoid with amorous aims on comely heroine Ana Luisa Peluffo are only three reasons why **AVENTURA** remains one of my perennial faves in all-out Meximonstermania.

Borrowed stock footage from **ONE MILLION B.C.** also resurfaced in **LA ISLA DE LOS DINOSAURIOS/ THE ISLAND OF THE DINOSAURS** (D: Rafael Portillo, 1966). This was a Mex/US coproduction with Hal Roach Studios (originators of the 1940 **ONE MILLION B.C.**), which meant they actually had permission to re-edit the older footage. **ISLAND** was shot in glorious b/w, just so it could more conveniently accomodate said loaned stock. The film is roughly *seventy per cent* (!!) vintage footage mixed with crudely matched newly-shot scenes. These insert 1966 Mex principals Armando Silvestre and Alma Delia Fuentes into 1940 action, wearing lookalike costumes (and ridiculously outdated hairstyles) to better 'match up' with original US stars Victor Mature and Carole Landis. It's surprising on account of the effort expenditure required to pull off this less-than-flawless 'illusion' that the Mex distribs didn't just merely redub and reissue Roach's original film instead.

What's ironic is this hashed-together hackjob of sampled footage and neanderthals-in-love was basically a quickie cash-in on the then-current Raquel Welch/Hammer hit, **ONE MILLION YEARS B.C.** — which in turn was a remake of the very film from which **ISLAND** derived its pasted-in footage! Jerry Warren, eat your heart out... Fair's fair, I suppose. Jerry-builder Warren bastardized several perfectly adequate Meximonster films for US consumption (and immediate nauseous regurgitation), including **ISLAND** director Rafael Portillo's own earlier Aztec Mummy trio. So, I guess Rafael tasted sweet revenge, and us *gringo* bastards got a taste of our own medicine.

In addition to dinosaurs and batmen, in the same period Mexico went a-hunting down the well-trod Abominable Snowman trail. This resulted in **EL MONSTRUO DE LAS VOLCANES**/tr: THE VOLCANO MONSTER (aka **EL HOMBRE DE LAS NIEVES**/tr: THE SNOWMAN, D: Jaime Salvador, 1962) and **EL TERRIBLE GIGANTE DE LAS NIEVES**/tr: THE TERRIBLE SNOW GIANT

feminine android and various ghostly goings-on. Epitomizing **AUTOPSIA**'s infectious dementia, its kooky credit sequence is populated by assorted witches, spectres and goblins rendered as frantic marionettes. These are accompanied by a theme instrumental that's a frenetic Tex-Mex approximation of Sam the Sham, with improvised vocal twitterings possibly provided by the Chipmunks on *peyote!*

Another favourite, **LOCURA DE TERROR**/tr: TERROR MADNESS (D: Julian Soler, 1960) is a spoofish *Tin Tan* opus that includes lumpy-faced henchmen — allegedly zombies? — and a duo of mad scientists working in cahoots who, when they're not churning out creepy-looking monsters, enjoy melting people (literally!) into puddles of goop using their electrical machinery. Before his death in 1973, Tin Tan (real name Germán Valdés, brother to other Mexicomics Ramon and Manuel *Loco* Valdés) made probably more horror-based comedies than any other filmic comic, Mexican or otherwise. His screwy repertoire includes **EL FANTASMA DE LA OPERETA**/tr: THE PHANTOM OF THE OPERETTA (D: Fernando Cortés, 1959), wherein he encountered a spectral, disfigured killer, and the above-mentioned **LA CASA DEL TERROR** (1959). Tin Tan concluded his formerly illustrious career (his domestic fame rivalled that of Mario Cantinflas Moreno himself) sidekicking for the muscle-bound prettyboy title hero in **EL INCREÍBLE PROFESOR ZÓVEK**, and fighting a feeble blow-up cephalopod in the abysmal **CHANOC VS. LOS DEVOURADORES DE HOMBRES**/tr: CHANOC VS. THE MANEATERS (D: Gilberto Martínez Solares, 1971).

Clavillazo Antonio Espino, another popular clown (he co-starred with Tin Tan in **LOS FANTASMAS BURLONES**/tr: THE GHOST JOKERS, D: Rafael Baledón, 1964), also frequently graced spoofs, some even containing monsters. **EL CASTILLO DE LOS MONSTRUOS**/tr: THE CASTLE OF THE MONSTERS (D: Julian Soler, 1957) is undoubtedly his most-monstered film: a mummy, a wolfman (sort of), a rubberized gillman ("*Bestia de la Laguna Seca*/tr: Beast from the Dried-Up Lagoon"!), a bolt-necked Frankensteinian creature (called "*Frentestein*"), as well as a vampire called "*El Murciélago*/tr: The Bat" (**EL VAMPIRO**'s Germán Robles doing an in-joke bit part) all receive ample screentime. **CASTILLO** is primarily a copycat of the Abbott and Costello formula pioneered in **MEET FRANKENSTEIN**.

Another *Clavillazo* film took a lot of pointers from **A/C GO TO MARS**. Clavillazo took one small step for Mankind and a giant step for stupidity in the consummately *odd* extraterrestrial excursion, **EL CONQUISTADOR DE LA LUNA**/tr: THE CONQUEROR OF THE MOON (D. Rogelio A. González, 1960). Here, the zoot-suited comedian met Martian monsters transplanted onto Earth's satellite (his rocketship arrives there via a large amount of transplanted stock footage from **DESTINATION MOON**). The Moonmen themselves are rather standard reptilian humanoids, albeit with multiple arms, but the Great Martian Brain is something *else* entirely! It squats in a huge aquarium, fountaining gouts of frothy brain-jizm from its cerebrum; attended by drooling giant eyeballs on stalks that bring to mind the Penisauri with their winking foreskins in **FLESH GORDON** as they wave suggestively over helpless love interest Ana Luisa Peluffo. **CONQUISTADOR**'s one *weird* viewing experience, and could only have originated in Mexico, *muchachos!*

Also directed by Rogelio González was **LA NAVE DE LOS MONSTRUOS**, which explored more subliminal s.f. fetish territory. As well as Amazonian alienettes Lorena Velázquez and Ana Berthe Lepe decked out in revealing tinfoil Futurist fashions, this goofball film could boast of several strangely-conceived BEMs and the re-used tincanman suit from **THE ROBOT VS. THE AZTEC MUMMY**. An eye-catching blend of alluring space dominatrixes, latex monsters, laughs and musical numbers (the latter two departments covered by singing fool Lalo *Piporro* González), the film is a must-see of veteran Mexican chintzkitsch.

Further related comedies are **PEPITO Y CHABELO VS. LOS MONSTRUOS** (1973), which included the gamut of mandatory beasties: vampire, mummy and gill-creature inclusive. Long-running Mex funnyman Gaspar Capulina Henaine, as well as starring with El Santo and facing killer doppelganger robots in **SANTO CONTRA CAPULINA** (1968), in addition made bids in the Meximonster stakes with **CAPULINA CONTRA LAS MOMIAS** and **CAPULINA CONTRA LOS MONSTRUOS** (both 1973).

Along even zanier lines were Mexico's juvenile-oriented "fairytale" adventures. Without doubt the fullest and most prototypical in this colourful sub-genre is **LITTLE RED RIDING HOOD AND THE MONSTERS**. This was the only real monster-ous entry in an otherwise cutesy and innocuous four-film saga. **MONSTRUOS** dealt with youthful fairytale heroes Little Red aka Caperucita and Tom Thumb aka *Pulgarcito* (played by child stars Maria Gracia and Cesareo Quezadas) combating the sinister Witch Queen aka *Reina Bruja* (Ofelia Guilmain). This sorceress is a live-action dead-ringer for the wicked witch of Disney's **SNOW WHITE AND THE SEVEN DWARFS**. The green-faced witchqueen (who radiates an implicit erotic/dominatrix charisma that was probably lost on kiddie audiences) commands an extensive army of Heinz 57 monsters. These include the omnipresent aristocratic bloodsucker ("*El Señor Vampiro*/tr: Lord Vampire"; played by Mex supporting player Quintin Bulnes), a Frankenstein monster lookalike, even an incendiary midget dragon, as well as sundry less readily-identifiable denizens. The film is crammed to the rafters with so many outrageous and colourful characters — including José Elias Moreno as the burly *El Ogro*/The Ogre and Tin Tan's bro Loco Valdés as *El Lobo Feroz*/The Big Bad Wolf — that cataloguing them all here would be pointless.

Nowadays, the MMM comedy scene is dominated by the likes of **MATENME PORQUE ME MUERO** (D: Abraham Cherem, 1990). This admittedly atmospheric film mostly only provides a forum for the doofus muggings of its amiable star comic duo, Pedro *Chatanuga* Weber and Raul *Choforo* Padilla. It's essentially a haunted house spook spoof containing two seductive ghostesses. These horny succubus spirits turn into vengeful rotten-faced ghoulgirls for the last five minutes of the picture (zombie makeup fx fittingly courtesy of "Necropia"). Though the monster stuff herein is a long time in coming and rationed sparingly, it is played sufficiently creepy and straight; including some actual graphic *splatter*. This seems to bode favourably — however infinitesimally — for the future of what's up for rent at your neighbourhood video *cantina*.

There seem to be more monsters gradually creeping back into the castrated Mex movie scene, what with **MATENME PORQUE ME MUERO**, **PESADILLA SANGRIENTA**/tr: BLOODY NIGHTMARE and **AL FILO DEL TERROR**/tr: AT THE EDGE OF TERROR (1990). This lattermost title concerns the demoniacal activities of killer midget clowns. While seemingly inspired by **MUNECOS INFERNALES/CURSE OF THE DOLL PEOPLE** (D:Benito Alazraki, 1961) by way of Charles Band/Full Moon's **PUPPETMASTER** series and **KILLER KLOWNS FROM OUTER SPACE**, **AL FILO DEL TERROR** marks a welcome return to the MMM directorial fold for erstwhile Mexploitationeer Alfredo B. Crevenna (he of the great-fun **AVENTURA AL CENTRO DE LA TIERRA**). With René Cardona dead, René Cardona Jr. seemingly stuck in a sexcom/action rut, and Rafael Baledón consigned in semi-retirement to acting in boobtube soap operas, perhaps it will be left to old-timer Crevenna to carry the torch in a welcome '90s renaissance of Meximonster movies. We can all only hope. El Santo's eternal Silver Mask will crack a smile from beyond the grave, and He'll be *ready* for 'em...

¡Bienvenida, monstruos!

Weng's Chop Literary Classics presents a Kronos Productions archives reprint special.
VIDEO VOICE #9 and the "Michael J. Weldon Interview" conducted by Kronos Productions editor David Todarello.
A rare look back at a fanzine from 1988. From the blissful days before the avalanche of blogs poisoned the land.

THE AMAZING PSYCHOTRONIC MAN

INTERVIEW BY DAVID TODARELLO

Cleveland isn't as bad a place as most popular entertainers would claim it to be. Yea, the city went bankrupt years ago and had to live that down. However, a lot of innovative people came out of the city's coagulated brew of international soup. The musical groups PERE UBU, (along with Akron's TIN HUEY, DEVO and the CRAMPS), THE DAZZ BAND, and (ick) THE MICHAEL STANLEY BAND, are but a few of the bands that thrived and were ultimately exported worldwide. Then there is Michael Weldon, someone who my brother met a few times while living in Columbus, but I never had the chance to meet. This guy is crazy about what he labels "psychotronic" films. His book, THE PSYCHOTRONIC ENCYCLOPEDIA, is a fun one to read and have by the tv when some of those off-the-wall late night films come rolling on the tube at odd hours of the early morning (sadly, this staple of the U.S. TV addict is fast becoming extinct, thanks to cable and late night/early morning game shows, etc.). So, without further hesitation, here is Dave's interview with Mr. Weldon, conducted around 6PMish one day in my bedroom with some antiquated phone-recording equipment....

VIDEO*VOICE: Micheal, this is Dave from VIDEO*VOICE.
Michael Weldon: Oh yea, hi! Hold on a second...

°°PAUSE°°

MW: We're about to eat dinner, but we have about twenty minutes if that's long enough...
VV: Yes, sure! First of all we wanted to ask you about growing up in Cleveland. When you were younger did you check out a lot of the local TV horror hosts like Ghoulardi or Superhost? Do you find that they influenced what you do now?
MW: Ghoulardi was my idol. He was my role model, my idol...I even had a fan club for him.
VV: Really! (laughs)
MW: Oh yea, really! I'm not kidding, I'm not kidding at all! He's a major influence on everything I've done. When I was growing up in Cleveland I never missed Ghoulardi. When he started out, this was when I was in elementary school, first he was on Friday night and Saturday afternoon and then at the height of his popularity he was Friday night, Saturday afternoon, and for a half an hour every week day, so he was on A LOT! I really loved everything that he did. He got me, along with FAMOUS MONSTERS OF FILMLAND magazine, more interested in horror movies than anything else. Where are you from?
VV: Well, I live in Oberlin now but I was born in Bay Village.
MW: Bay Village—ok, then you could've seen some of them.
VV: Sure and we also remember the Ghoul, which was much later, and Superhost.
MW: Yea, well Superhost I never really got into. The Ghoul I liked even though he was admittedly an imitation of Ghoulardi. I interviewed both of them for FANGORIA magazine (they did a series on Horror Hosts); this was about four or five years ago. I had a good time interviewing Ernie Anderson and Ron Sweed. Stop me if I go one about this too long...
VV: No, no, no -- please continue.

MW: Okay, well a couple of weeks after the article came out in FANGORIA, someone at the David Letterman show saw the magazine, and because I wrote all about how he has become the spokesman for ABC, they had him on as a guest. I'm kinda proud of the fact that my article led to him being a guest on David Letterman (I have it on tape). A year later I went to Los Angeles and HOLLYWOOD for the first time and was staying with a former Clevelander who was a movie PR person and it just happened to be the week that he was helping to organize a party for all the ex-Clevelanders in the HOLLYWOOD area. This party was particularly in honor of a columnist for the Plain Dealer (*Cleveland's only newspaper - Dave*) named MARY MARY. Ernie Anderson was there and I got invited along with a high school friend. I had been on stage with Ernie Anderson as a kid when he did live shows -- but I actually got to hang out and talk with him at this party. He had seen my article and really liked it. Ernie was very friendly, very nice, and proceeded to get quite drunk. He became the center of attention and began telling old Cleveland media stories, y'know about BARNABY and Dorthy Fuldheim and stuff...it was really great! TIM CONWAY was there, he used to be his comedy partner, and other minor TV people. It was really fun for me! Someone just told me something, I haven't found out if this is true or not, that there's a person in Akron right now who revived the Ghoulardi character and Ron Sweed's trying to stop him.
VV: Well, Ron's been doing the GHOUL character at local rock concerts...
MW: He can't get on TV anymore, right?
VV: No, no...the only thing we had come close to that recently is a show called FRANK & DRAC, but they were pulled off the air.
MW: I didn't know about them. I don't...I can't say that I enjoy any of the horror hosts that are on TV now. Ghoulardi was just very important to me and just because of the association I watched the Hooligan and Big Chuck show. That was Ghoulardi's show that they took over. I imagine Big Chuck is still on?

6

VV: He's *still* on!

MW: That's really incredible. He's broken some kind of record, I'm sure!

VV: Let's talk about the Cleveland rock scene in the late 70s. You were in the MIRRORS, right? (legendary Cleveland band with one single to their name, SHIRLEY b/w SHE SMILED WILD - Hearthan Records #105, 1977).

MW: At that time I was working at a record store called The Drome and Crocus, as he was was called then (now you know him as DAVID THOMAS lead voice for PERE UBU), was working there and running Hearthen Records out of the store. He liked the MIRRORS, we used to play on bills with ROCKETS FROM THE TOMBS (David Thomas' pre-UBU gig led by CREEM rock-crit Peter Laugher (RIP) - Dave), so he decided to put out the single. Later on I helped get out the ELECTRIC EELS single on Rough Trade Records (CYCLOTRON b/w AGITATED --Rough Trade #008). Earlier this year I was trying to negotiate the release of an ELECTRIC EELS album along with Paul Marotta. The album is all ready, all old material, the cover is ready, the liner notes are ready, and everything has been touched up in the studio and then something fell through with the people who were going to put it out. I don't know the status is with it now but I think it's really good and it should come out.

VV: Are you planning a second volume of your book, THE PSYCHOTRONIC ENCYCLOPEDIA OF FILM or have you had enough?

MW: No, no! I actually have the groundwork for doing an entirely different second edition with maybe three thousand more reviews. Since the book has come out I've discovered a lot of things I wish would've been in there. People tell me about things they wish would've been in there...

VV: Like **PINK FLAMINGOS**?

MW: Basically, I didn't deal with John Waters or Russ Meyer movies and I should've because they certainly need to be covered. If you look at the number of horror movies or general psychotronic movies that have been released during the eighties there is a phenomenal number of them.

VV: Oh Yes! Was it difficult getting the first book published?

MW: It was only easy because I got New York media attention for the original Psychotronic weekly newsletter. Publishers have people who look for things they might want to publish as I had publishers approach me. I didn't have to do the typical knock-your-head-against-the-wall-trying-to-be-published routine.

VV: That's great! Are you under contact to do a second book?

MW: At this point I'm about to go to another publisher even though Ballantine is keeping the PSYCHONTRONIC book in print, and it's selling better than ever; which I'm very happy about! A second book is going to be published by someone else, I'm just not sure who yet.

VV: How did you start working for HIGH TIMES? We just recently discovered you column there.

MW: Well, what happened was two years ago they asked me if I wanted to write for them, and I had friends who had worked for them before who told me, "Don't do it! There's nothing good about the magazine, they're disorganized, they don't pay...." I just told 'em, "thanks but no thanks!" In the meantime they hired a friend of mine to write a movie review column. His name is Jim and I like what he does; he does a good job, but they originally wanted me to do that. Eventually they got some new people working on the staff there and they called me again, asked me if I wanted to write a column about anything I wanted. They created a new section called the Media Scene and it's in the back of the magazine.

For about a year that went really well--they were excited about I, thought it was helping their sale, got some good response. Finally they had more about movies, books, and music instead of just pot info. which is very boring to me and I never bought that magazine...

VV: Yea, well that's why we never discovered your stuff. We never looked at it.

MW: I had fun writing for them, but lately the publisher is starting to threaten to take away the section because he convinced that people only buy it for pot stuff (*a real Al Einstein, this guy - - Dave*). So the future of my writing in High Times is very much in question.

VV: That stinks! Okay--How did you get involved with the people at RE:SEARCH? You're credited with special thanks in INCREDIBLY STRANGE FILMS (RE:SEARCH #10). Do you know Jim Morton?

MW: Yea, that goes back to when Jim Morton did TRASHOLA and we used to correspond through the mail. The first time I went to San Francisco I stayed with him. He showed me some amazing rare video tapes and took me to some great San Francisco trashy movie theatres. We went up to the RE:SEARCH offices where I met Andrea Juno & Vale. The INCREDIBLY STRANGE FILMS book was Jim Morton's project (along with Boyd Rice) originally, and I know he wasn't happy with the results because they took away a lot of what he wrote and reworked it. A lot of people really liked the way it turned out and I do too, it just wasn't exactly what they originally planned, or at least what JIM planned. It was very successful for them and it turned a lot of people onto a lot of new alleyways of weird movies which is really nice!

7

VV: *Let's talk about some films now. Are there any recent films that you think qualify for classic status or anything you've been really excited about?*

MW: Oh yea! Every year there are movies that excite me, and movies I like.

VV: *What did you think of BRAIN DAMAGE?*

MW: I like **BRAIN DAMAGE** a lot but it's not as good as Henenlotter's first movie. It just wasn't as exciting but it's good and certainly deserves to be seen by more people. I was, in a way, more amazed, although I can't 100% recommend it, by a movie called **STREET TRASH** which was made by a guy who's kinda Frank's protegee, Jim Munro. They've been friends for years. When I met Jimmy he was a high school student and he actually did an imitation PSYCHOTRONIC TV GUIDE after I stopped PSYCHOTRONIC. It said right on it "This is like Psychotronic." I thought **STREET TRASH** was a really strong movie. There were some things that maybe he shouldn't have put in there, but I thought it was pretty amazing. I also saw a movie that hasn't been released yet at a screening just the other night called **LAIR OF THE WHITE WORM**—the new Ken Russle movie. I was really knocked out by that and I always expect to have really mixed feelings about Ken Russle movies or even not like them at all. I like **WHITE OF THE EYE** a lot; I hear that's doing well on video. There are a lot of movies I've liked since the book came out. There have been some acknowledged horror classics like **THE EVIL DEAD, RETURN OF THE LIVING DEAD, HELLRAISER**...

VV: *The problem is that there are no theatres that show some of the smaller films. The STANDARD in Cleveland is the only place to see some of these hidden gems.*

MW: I used to see sex movies there.

VV: *Well, it's still there and it still plays new horror and genre films every week.* **BRAIN DAMAGE** *(here we go again -- Dave) played there, and only there, for only one week.*

MW: Great! That's the perfect place to see it! I'm so happy there's one theatre left in downtown Cleveland. Those theatres are disappearing everywhere. Here's another film not too many people know about. It's called **SHOCK! SHOCK! SHOCK!** It's out now and it's only one hour long and in black and white. I don't generally like horror spoofs or comedies, so many of them are terrible, but this is great! Another one that didn't get much attention, I didn't even think I wanted to see it, is **THE OFFSPRING**. The title was changed but that's how it was released. It's a horror anthology that's surprisingly good--uneven, but there's some good stuff in it. Here's one I liked that everyone else hated: **CRIMEWAVE**...

VV: *We love CRIMEWAVE! Big Fans!*

MW: I thought **CRIMEWAVE** was great, and I loved **MIXED BLOOD**, the Paul Morrissey movie. That one really died! I finally saw **THE STEPFATHER**, and thought that was great. I'm finally getting to see some movies!

VV: *Thanks to videotape!*

MW: I saw **SPIDER BABY** after the book came out and I loved it!

VV: *That's a mind-blowing movie!*

MW: Okay...if we're gonna talk much longer we're going to have to do Part 2 because dinner is about ready to eat. Maybe ten minutes...(pause)....make that five.

VV: *Okay, five minutes, here we go... How do you feel about being the grandfather of all the exploitation and horror fanzines that are creeping up everywhere these days?*

MW: I think I'd be more comfortable with Uncle, but Uncle Bob already did that. No, I'm happy about it and I'm proud of it and I'd like to see more books out in the future. I'm putting together plans to do a PSYCHOTRONIC Video Magazine (*WOW! -- Dave*). I'm doing it on my own and I think I can get some good distribution through some video chains and Tower Video stores wants to carry it. It's just a matter of getting some ad money to put it out. I'm gonna start working on that soon.

VV: *Are there any fanzines that you think are particularly good?*

MW: Well, I'd love to see yours, by the way. Just briefly: I just got one I hadn't seen before called SHOCK REVIEW. The early issues are really crude, but it's gone up and I like it. I thought ECCO was pretty amazing. I like some stuff in SUBHUMAN. There's a local one called BLOOD TIMES that no one seems to know about that I like a lot. TEMPLE OF SCHLOCK I like okay. VIDEO DRIVE INN (*from Columbus, Ohio -- Dave*) I liked a lot. I've got every issue of GORE GAZETTE which still amazingly comes out. I like SLIMETIME. I like EXPLOITATION RETROSPECTIVE. That about covers it. I've tried to at least sample all of them lately because for a couple of years I was out of touch with this whole fanzine scene.

VV: *We'll wrap it up now with this final question: If you had to pick one movie as your all time favorite what would it be?*

MW: Ah....Well, if we keep it in the Psychotronic category, there's a lot movies I like that I wouldn't put in there. **ISLAND OF THE LOST SOULS**. Okay -- the food is ready!

VV: *Mr. Weldon, thank you for your time!*

MW: I'm glad you did call, and I always like to talk to people who know who Ghoulardi is and people that appreciate him.

VV: *Thank you, and enjoy your dinner.*

--------------------the end--------------------

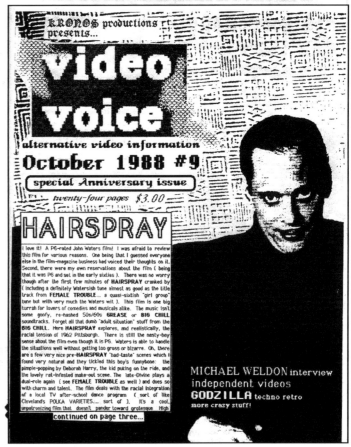

Interview copyright 1988 David Todarello & Kronos Productions

Weng's Chop B-Movie Krisword Puzzle, #1 by Kris Gilpin.

Since I was a kid (& have always been a huge film buff) I've searched for film-based crossword puzzles and have never understood why there have been so relatively few of them ever made, with millions of film lovers all over the world—so a few years ago I simply started to construct my own at www.tinyurl.com/3seq3cc, on the great, huge crossword site, BestCrosswords.Com. I have 135+ puzzles on there so far; please try more of my old ones—do the film-trivia clues first & enjoy, Thanks so much to Tim for getting my by-line back into a 'zine after decades. Please let us know if you enjoy it!

Across

1. If Dane Cook had starred in **MAMA**.
5. Relinquished.
10. VHS alternative.
14. Uneven 2004, 3-storied film about love & sex, from Soderbergh, Antonioni, etc.
15. Adult insect.
16. Fred Ward's name in **TREMORS**.
17. Sam Neill watched a bloody creature screw his wife in this trippy, 1981 horror drama.
19. The bleak **OPEN WATER** was shot in one.
20. Eskimo boat.
21. 1960 Ed Wood "thriller" about porn-actress murders, **THE** ____ (see 58 Down).
23. **PATRICK** was about one, who killed via telekinesis from his hospital bed.
26. **THE EXORCIST** ____ some moviegoers into the lobby in 1973.
27. The **RE-ANIMATOR** used it to make dead tissue live again.
29. "Amscray!"
33. 1954's ____! starred giant, man-eating ants.
37. The Who's "Dr. Jimmy": "...He only comes out when I drink my ___."
38. A young man horribly blinded horses in one, from **EQUUS** (play & film).
39. Georgetown athlete.
40. A gorilla with a deep sea-diving helmet starred in 1953's wonderfully shitty ____ **MONSTER**.
42. Vomit elicits loving affection?!
43. Though I still like Romero, his zombie films ____ be better early on.
45. Gorgeous Ms. de la Reguera, who was in **COWBOYS & ALIENS**.
46. A young falcon taken from the nest for training.
47. The late Michael O'Donoghue wanted to make a film about a boy who enters his dead horse into one.
48. 1995 drama about a gay serial killer.
50. Zappa's hilarious "Lonesome Cowboy Burt" ends with, "____, you hot little bitch!"
52. Bill, stocky character actor who was in many Larry Buchanan epics (& **CLOSE ENCOUNTERS**!).
57. Some snowbound folk have ____ down in Florida.
61. "____ apathy, our studio has passed on producing Uwe Boll's next project."
62. The poster for Larry Cohen's **IT'S ALIVE** showed a little claw hanging out of one.
63. Have any Mondo Movies featured these unfortunates who stuck their necks out?
66. Like Rondo (**HOUSE OF HORRORS**) Hatton's screen persona.
67. Like Lugosi…or Danielle Harris.
68. Most PG-13 horrorshows suck? "____!"
69. Eye drop.
70. Horror fans always hope for some in their movies.
71. Like Dusty Hoffman & James Marsden in **STRAW DOGS** (in the first half of the films, that is!)

Down

1. A lotta gore will always ____ a horror film.
2. John Waters's hilarious **POLYESTER** offered ____s on a card with the movie.
3. "I ____ that **THE CREEPING TERROR** was a turd, but funny." "As a film professor, you just figured that out?!"
4. Very, as in some film music.
5. U.S.S.R. successor.
6. What these are: M, M, M, M, M.
7. Where (horror) actors speak at a con.
8. Charlie Sheen & Madonna suffer badly from this.
9. "Death, Be Not Proud" poet.
10. Monte (**TWO-LANE BLACKTOP**) Hellman's first flick was 1959's ____ **FROM HAUNTED** ____.
11. Troma Films is located on this coast.
12. Pretty Jenny Seagrove was a nanny who was a wicked druid ____ priestess (!) in **THE GUARDIAN**.
13. Banned apple spray.
18. Many a B-movie character actor barely ____ out a living.
22. Psychotherapist Oli. Reed ran the Somafree ____. in David Cronenberg's **THE BROOD**.
24. A noun heard a lot in **TO KILL A MOCKINGBIRD**.
25. Michelle Yeoh & Maggie Cheung were 2 stars of 1993's Hong Kong action fantasy, **THE HEROIC** ____.
28. Open, in a way.
30. What the aliens in **THEY LIVE** told us to do.
31. Spiced stew of meat & veggies.
32. Russ Meyer's first skin feature was 1959's **THE IMMORAL MR.** ____.
33. Paris Hilton's **HOUSE OF WAX** landed with one, grossing $8 million under its budget.
34. Pia Zadora got raped by Ray Liotta with one in the shit flick, **THE LONELY LADY**.
35. Ogler, like a teen watching a B-skin flick.
36. Neville Brand got blown up by Chuck Conners while masturbating in B.I. Gordon's 1973, great **THE** ____ ____.
38. Cheech & Chong: "Yeah, my dog ate my ____, man. Had it on the table, and the little motherfucker ate it, man."
41. I love me a cone at the movies, with choco mint chip ice cream ____.
44. Torture has become a ____ of horror film.
48. Rip off.
49. A large African antelope, the male of which has large corkscrewlike horns.
51. Buddhist who has attained Nirvana (not Steven Seagal).
53. Like Gage in **PET SEMATARY** & Damien in the original **OMEN**.
54. A part of MGM.
55. Audiences ____ Larry Cohen's ho-hum **THE STUFF**? Not quite.
56. Bad body bumps, baby.
57. **28 WEEKS LATER**'s Robert Carlyle is one.
58. (The last word of 21 Across).
59. Ms. S., pretty star of **MIMIC**.
60. A lotta tech-gibberish tried to pass as this in old Sci-Fi B-movies.
64. (Pre-Matrix.)
65. Multiple 60-minute batches (abbr.)

Answer key on page 61 -- NO CHEATING!

Made in the USA
Charleston, SC
05 March 2014